Economic Development as a Learning Process

Variation Across Sectoral Systems

Edited by

Franco Malerba

Professor of Applied Economics and Director, KITeS Bocconi University, Italy

Richard R. Nelson

Columbia University, USA

Edward Elgar

Cheltenham, UK • Northampton, MA, USA

Published by
Edward Elgar Publishing Limited
The Lypiatts
15 Lansdown Road
Cheltenham
Glos GL50 2JA
UK

Edward Elgar Publishing, Inc.
William Pratt House
9 Dewey Court
Northampton
Massachusetts 01060
USA

A catalogue record for this book
is available from the British Library

Library of Congress Control Number: 2011939355

ISBN 978 0 85793 788 9 (cased)

Typeset by Servis Filmsetting Ltd, Stockport, Cheshire
Printed and bound by MPG Books Group, UK

Contents

List of contributors   vi

1 Introduction   1
   Franco Malerba and Richard R. Nelson

2 Explaining divergent stories of catch-up in the
   telecommunication equipment industry in Brazil, China, India
   and Korea   21
   Keun Lee, Sunil Mani and Qing Mu

3 The global computer software sector   72
   Jorge Niosi, Suma Athreye and Ted Tschang

4 Explaining variations in semiconductor catch-up strategies in
   China, Korea, Malaysia and Taiwan   113
   Rajah Rasiah, Xin-Xin Kong, Yeo Lin and Jaeyong Song

5 Catching up in the pharmaceutical sector: lessons from case
   studies of India and Brazil   157
   Shyama V. Ramani and Samira Guennif

6 The agro-food sector in catching-up countries: a comparative
   study of four cases   194
   *Shulin Gu, John O. Adeoti, Ana Célia Castro, Jeffrey Orozco
   and Rafael Díaz*

7 Conclusions   281
   Franco Malerba and Richard R. Nelson

Index   293

Contributors

John O. Adeoti, Economic and Technology Development Department, Nigerian Institute of Social and Economic Research (NISER), Ibadan, Nigeria

Suma Athreye, Brunel Business School, Brunel University, UK

Ana Célia Castro, The Centre for Law and Economic Sciences, Federal University of Rio de Janeiro – CCJE/UFRJ, Rio de Janeiro, Brazil

Rafael Díaz, Centro Internacional de Política Económica para el Desarrollo Sostenible, Universidad Nacional, Costa Rica

Shulin Gu, Institute of Policy and Management, Chinese Academy of Sciences, and School of Management, Zhejiang University, China

Samira Guennif, CEPN, Université Paris 13, France

Xin-Xin Kong, Chinese Academy of Science and Technology for Development (CASTED), China

Keun Lee, Seoul National University, Seoul, Korea

Yeo Lin, Zhejiang University, China

Franco Malerba, KITeS, Bocconi University, Milan, Italy

Sunil Mani, Centre for Development Studies, Trivandrum, Kerala, India

Qing Mu, Shanghai University of Economics and Finance, Shanghai, China

Richard R. Nelson, Columbia University, New York, USA

Jorge Niosi, Department of Management and Technology, School of Management Science, UQAM, Montreal, Canada

Jeffrey Orozco, Centro Internacional de Política Económica para el Desarrollo Sostenible, Universidad Nacional, Costa Rica

Shyama V. Ramani, UNU-MERIT, Maastricht & Ecole Polytechnique, Paris, France

Rajah Rasiah, University of Malaya, Malaysia

Jaeyong Song, Seoul National University, Seoul, Korea

Ted Tschang, Singapore Management University, Singapore

1. Introduction

Franco Malerba and Richard R. Nelson

1.1 INTRODUCTION

This book examines the processes of technological and organizational learning in five different economic sectors: telecommunications, pharmaceuticals, software, semiconductor and agro-food, in several different developing countries: China, India, Brazil, Korea, Taiwan and others. The chapters presented here are part of a larger programme of studies – the Catch-up Program – concerned with the examination of a range of variables affecting the ability of countries behind the technological and economic frontiers to 'catch up' with the leaders, in particular the roles of indigenous and multinational firms, and of non-firm actors like universities and public labs, how IPR regimes affect catch-up, the government policies that are effective in supporting catch-up, and other important variables.

The five sectors examined in this book represent a wide range of cases according to various classifications. They include a science-based sector: pharmaceuticals; two sectors where product design and engineering are important for competitiveness: semiconductors and telecommunications; a service sector of a specialized supplier type: software; and a traditional sector: agro-food.

The evolution of these sectors has been examined in a variety of different countries, ranging from those that started their catching up quite early (such as Korea and Taiwan), to those which are now becoming major protagonists of economic development (such as China and India). These countries differ very much in terms of size of domestic market: in some of these countries (such as China, India and Brazil) the size of the domestic market has been a major target for firms, while in others the internal market is small and exports have played a major role.

In several cases the sectors examined in this book have been major drivers of the economic growth of a country. This is the case for pharmaceuticals, semiconductors and telecommunications in the developing countries where these sectors have taken hold. These sectors have been

1

development drivers in several senses: the relatively high-income employment that they generated, the amount of capital investments required, and the knowledge spillovers that have affected other sectors. Some of these sectors have vertical linkages with other sectors within a country: think of telecommunications and software, agriculture and the food industry, semiconductors and machine tools and computers.

Other books on industrial economic development have either focused on a specific industry in a specific country (see for example Amsden and Chu, 2003; Breznitz, 2005) or, when they have examined different sectors, they have considered each of them in a different country (Chandra, 2006; Malerba and Mani, 2009). This book takes a different perspective: it analyses the evolution of several industries, each of them examined in several countries.

The reason for this orientation is that we want to examine the differences, as well as the similarities, of what is required for catching up in different economic sectors. The nature of the technologies used differs significantly across economic sectors, as do the nature of the customers, and the kind of competition indigenous firms face, and hence the needed skills and appropriate forms of firm organization and management. Industries differ significantly in the extent to which they need to draw on universities for the skills and knowledge they need in order to be competitive, and in the kinds of government policies needed to support them. Countries differ in the extent to which they can provide the broad background conditions for the development of different industries. Because of these differences, we believe that analysis of the processes involved in economic development requires a detailed and fine-grained analysis of the interplay between sectoral factors and country-level factors.

Before entering into the core of this book, we need to briefly discuss what we mean by the term 'catch-up'. The term has been used in macroeconomics in analyses of the extent to which the growth of income per capita of different countries significantly behind the frontier at the start of the time period enabled them to 'catch-up' with the leading countries in that dimension by the end of the period. However, in characterizing the development of particular economic sectors, as we have noted, we believe it is important that the description and analysis be relatively fine grained, which calls for a somewhat more flexible and qualitative conception of catching up. Once one looks at sectoral economic development in detail, one can recognize that each country does things in a somewhat different way. Product mixes differ. Industrial structures vary. Often the markets served vary.

However, if interpreted broadly, the concept of catching up still seems a useful one for thinking about economic development at a sectoral level. In all of the sectors considered in this book, much of the learning of firms in developing countries involved learning about what firms at the frontier were doing. And the higher performance of firms at the frontier provided both a model and an aspiration for efforts of firms behind the frontier to improve their performance.

This introductory chapter is organized as follows. In section 1.2 we discuss the basic orientation of the broad 'Catch-up Program'. In section 1.3 we argue for the importance of analysis at a sectoral level, because there are significant differences across economic sectors in the variables and mechanisms involved in catch-up. It introduces the notion of sectoral systems and identifies the main sectoral variables used in the following analysis. In section 1.4 we introduce the five sectors and lay the ground for the following analysis.

1.2 ECONOMIC DEVELOPMENT, CATCH-UP AND INNOVATION SYSTEMS

In the following pages we briefly review the basic analytical orientation of the Catch-up program (see Nelson et al., 2005 for a more in-depth discussion). Economic development involves deliberate efforts to catch up, in the sense that economic and technological practice in leading nations is almost always used as a model. Catch-up, however, does not mean cloning. What actually is achieved invariably diverges in certain ways from practice in the countries serving as the model.

In part this divergence reflects the fact that exact copying is almost impossible, and attempts to replicate at best get viably close. In part it reflects modifications required to tailor practice to local circumstances. The organizational, managerial and institutional aspects of productive practices are often the most difficult to replicate, and the most in need of adaptation to indigenous conditions, norms and values. So, each developing country does things in a different way, as a result of an indigenous process of learning.

The development process involves innovation in a sense of Schumpeter, as a break from traditional ways of doing things. In the process of catch-up the practices being brought in are certainly not new to the world, but they are new to the country, and bringing them in involves considerable risk, and requires a lot of trial and error in learning to be effective.

The learning of new capabilities by firms is of central importance in almost all economic sectors. In catching up many different kinds of capabilities need to be acquired. These capabilities involve a lot more than what engineers generally mean when they talk about technology. While important aspects of these activities are indeed structured or embodied in machinery or other physical artefacts they also involve modes of organizing coordinating and managing activities. These latter capabilities are often much more difficult to develop than the required engineering know-how. Thus various capabilities are needed for catch-up: capabilities to access complementary assets, absorptive capabilities, and innovation capabilities. All these capabilities are required in order to adopt, adapt and modify technologies developed elsewhere, introduce modifications and incremental innovations and eventually generate totally new products and processes.

But firms do not act alone. They are linked, upstream, to their customers, and downstream to their suppliers. More generally, they must be understood to be operating in the context of innovation systems that include other kinds of economic actors that are involved in supporting and orienting economic activity and innovation: primary and secondary education, universities, the public research system, and government programmes (Nelson, 2006). The structures of the financial system and of labour markets are also pivotal.

In the present era, the education system is of vital importance. Over the last century all the countries that have been successful in catching up have had a system of primary and secondary education that endowed a large fraction of the young population with the basic skills needed to operate in a modern economy, and also provided high-level training for a sufficient group of scientists and engineers to enable foreign technologies to be absorbed. The fact that today so much of technology is science based means that a country's system of advanced training in science, technology and the other bodies of knowledge needed to master modern ways of doing things is quite important. And research at universities and public laboratories has increasingly played a central role. Public sector research has long been an important element of catch-up in certain fields. This is certainly so in agriculture and medicine, where developing countries often could not simply copy technology and practice in countries at the frontier, but needed to develop technologies suited to their own conditions because soil, climate conditions and the prevalent diseases tend to be different.

In addition, active government policies have supported the catch-up process, involving various forms of protection and direct and indirect subsidy (as the cases of Japan, and of Korea and Taiwan illustrate). In many countries, however, these policies engendered not successful catch-up but a protected, inefficient home industry.

1.3   SECTORAL SYSTEMS AND CATCH-UP

This book is based on the belief that the concept of a sectoral innovation system is a useful one for illuminating the catch-up process in different economic sectors (see Malerba, 2002, 2004). While analyses of sectoral innovation systems and national innovation systems (see Freeman, 1987; Nelson, 1993; Lundvall, 1993) share a perspective that economic change is evolutionary, and that multiple actors are involved, the national innovation system concept is more aggregative and is particularly oriented to broad national characteristics. In contrast, the sectoral innovation system concept, while recognizing broad factors that influence development across a wide range of industries, is particularly concerned with highlighting characteristics of the environment within which development proceeds that are sectoral specific. The relevant sectoral system may involve some aspects that are national, but also others that are regional, and still others that are transnational. That is the perspective taken in this book.

Both the national and the sectoral innovation systems concept is associated with an evolutionary theory of economic change. Evolutionary theory places a key emphasis on dynamics, innovation processes and economic transformation (Nelson and Winter, 1982). Learning and capabilities are key elements in the change of the economic system. Boundedly rational agents act, learn and search in uncertain and changing environments. Agents know how to do different things in different ways. Thus learning, capabilities and behaviour entail agents' heterogeneity in experience and organization. Their different capabilities affect their persistent differential performance. A central place in the evolutionary approach is occupied by the processes of variety creation (in technologies, products, firms and organizations), replication including imitation (that engenders both continuity and a collective element to the process of economic development), and selection (that reduces variety in the economic system and discourages the inefficient or ineffective utilization of resources) (Nelson, 1995; Dosi, 1997; Metcalfe, 1998). For evolutionary theory the environment and conditions – such as the sectoral context – in which agents operate and which affect agents' cognition and behaviour may drastically differ.

Drawing from this perspective, a *sectoral system* framework focuses on the nature, structure, organization and dynamics of innovation and production in sectors. One can identify the following elements: (a) actors; (b) knowledge base; (c) institutions.

1.3.1 Actors

Firms
Much of the writing on industrial development as an evolutionary process is focused on business firms and the determinants of the evolution of their capabilities. Kim (1997) has identified different stages of capability development, from duplicative imitation to creative imitation to innovation.

Amsden and Chu (2003) have examined the combination of production engineering and design by large-scale enterprises in electronics in Taiwan. Lee (2005) has discussed the passage from the creation of absorptive capabilities to the development of complementary assets (complementary to those of firms in advanced countries). Lee and Lim (2001) have focused on different trajectories of catching up, from path-following to stage-skipping, to path-creating. Mathews (2002) and Lee (2005) have discussed different steps that firms have followed in the process, from OEM to ODM to OBM for Taiwan, and from OEM to OBM for Korea. The process sometimes goes from learning from FDI as an initial channel, to licensing, to indigenous R&D (for example, Amsden and Chu, 2003 for electronics). This last process, as Lee (2005) has pointed out, has to be supported in various ways: production and R&D consortia and joint ventures, scouting and foreign alliances and support from government research institutes. In this book we claim that firms' specific learning processes, competences and organizations, as well as beliefs, expectations and goals, are highly affected by the specific sectoral system in which they are embedded. In addition to firms active in a sector, other actors are relevant for innovation and production, but their importance, role and effects may greatly differ across sectors. They are:

Upstream suppliers of components and systems   Suppliers may have different types of relationships with the innovating, producing or selling firms. In a dynamic and innovative setting, suppliers greatly affect and continuously redefine the boundaries of a sectoral system.

Users, customers and consumers (both national and international)   In a sectoral system view, demand is not seen as an aggregate set of similar buyers or of atomistic undifferentiated customers, but as composed of heterogeneous agents who interact in various ways with producers. Demand may be largely local or national, or international. Transactions may involve close interaction between providers and customers, or may proceed through impersonal market arrangements. The principal customers may be firms or households. Particularly if they are firms, they may be highly sophisticated and demanding of quality, or they may be less so.

Universities and public laboratories   In several sectors, universities play a key role in basic research, applied research, and human capital formation and this has proven crucial for economic development (Mazzoleni and Nelson, 2006). In addition, in some sectors (such as biotechnology and software), universities are also a source of start-ups and even innovation.

Financial organizations Finance plays a major role in supporting innovation, technology diffusion and production and does that with a variety
of different organizations – from banks, to the stock market, to internal
finance. In some sectoral systems, such as software or biotechnology-
pharmaceuticals, new actors such as venture capital companies have
emerged over time, but these financial organizations have played a
different role according to the stage of the industry life-cycle.

Government Government and public policies play a major role in sectoral systems. In catch-up, they have often targeted specific sectors using
a variety of tools and instruments. Think for example of semiconductors
and computer hardware in Japan (Odagiri and Goto, 1993), Korea (Kim,
1997; Lee and Lim, 2001) and Taiwan (Mathews, 2002; Amsden and Chu,
2003; Hobday, 1995) and aircraft in Brazil (Dahlman and Frischtak, 1993;
Viotti, 2002).

Networks of agents

Within any sectoral system, firms and non-firm organizations are connected in various ways through market and non-market relationships. The
evolutionary approach and the innovation systems literature have paid a
lot of attention to the wide range of formal and informal cooperation and
interaction among firms. According to this perspective, in uncertain and
changing environments networks emerge not because agents are similar,
but because they are different. Thus, networks integrate complementarities
in knowledge, capabilities and specialization (see Lundvall, 1993; Edquist,
1997). Relationships between firms and non-firm organizations (such as
universities and public research centres) have been a source of innovation
and change in several sectoral systems, such as pharmaceuticals and biotechnology, information technology, and telecommunications. The types
and structures of relationships and networks differ greatly from sectoral
system to sectoral system, as a consequence of the features of the knowledge base, the relevant learning processes, the basic technologies, the characteristics of demand, the key links, and the dynamic complementarities.

In the catching-up process, domestic firms benefit from being part of
various types of networks. In some cases, vertical networks with suppliers
have provided new inputs and shared relevant information for production and innovation, leading to capability development. Suppliers can be
a major source of knowledge and innovation, because they can be char
acterized by high innovativeness, specific technological knowledge, and
dynamic capabilities (Von Hippel, 1988; Lundvall, 1993). In some industries close interaction with sophisticated and demanding users has been an
important vehicle for firm learning.

Networks vary in their geographical and substantive scope. In some cases local networks have been important for the catching-up process. For example, industrial districts, as in the case of Taiwan, have played a role in the development of the Taiwanese electronic industry. At the regional and local level, the presence of local networks allows intense formal and informal interaction, knowledge sharing, and intense division of labour. Such networks may involve horizontal collaborative agreements regarding production or R&D among domestic firms or between domestic firms and foreign firms. In this way, complementary knowledge and capabilities may be shared. Participation in the global value chain is another way to catch up. Here the participation in the network involve specialization in specific stages of production (Gereffi et al., 2005; Ernst, 2002), and it is particularly relevant in the electronics industry. Often global value chains are coordinated by some key (multinational) firms. A final way to catch up through networks is subcontracting. In a dynamic view of capability formation, subcontracting is considered one of the earlier forms of learning and catching up (Lee, 2005).

1.3.2   The Knowledge Base

Different sectors are characterized by different knowledge bases. Knowledge plays a central role in innovation and affects the types of learning and capabilities of firms. Knowledge can be highly idiosyncratic at the firm level, and where it is it does not diffuse automatically and freely among firms. In other cases, knowledge may be relatively easy to transfer or acquire. The evolutionary literature has proposed that sectors and technologies differ greatly in terms of the knowledge base and learning processes related to innovation. Firms need several different kinds of knowledge in order to operate effectively. One knowledge domain involves the specific scientific and technological fields at the base of innovative activities in a sector (Dosi, 1988; Nelson and Rosenberg, 1993). Other kinds of required knowledge relate to the nature of applications, and user needs. The sources of technological knowledge and opportunities markedly differ among sectors. As Freeman (1982), Nelson and Winter (1982) and Rosenberg (1982), among others, have shown, in some sectors research carried out in universities or public laboratories is a major source of new technological opportunities. In other sectors, while the knowledge contained in public science may play an essential background role, R&D carried out by firms in the industry directed to the design of new products and production processes is the driver of technological opportunities. In yet other sectors new types of equipment and instrumentation created by firms outside the industry may facilitate innovation by firms in the industry. In a dynamic way, the focus on knowledge and technological domain places at the centre of the analysis the issue of sectoral boundaries, which are usually not fixed, but change over time.

1.3.3 Institutions

Agents' cognition, actions and interactions are shaped by institutions, which include laws, standards, norms, common routines and habits, established practices, and so on. And institutions may range from those that bind or impose enforcements on agents to those that are created by the interaction among agents (such as standardized contracts); from more binding to less binding; from formal to informal (such as patent laws or specific regulations vs. traditions and conventions). While some institutions are national (such as the patent system), others are specific to sectors (such as sectoral labour markets or financial institutions). National institutions can also have different effects on different sectors. This is so for the patent system and IPR more generally. Often the characteristics of national institutions favour sectors that fit better the specificities of the national institutions. In certain cases particular sectoral systems become predominant in a country because the existing institutions of that country provide an environment more suitable for certain types of sectors than others. However, sometimes the direction of causality goes the opposite way, from the sectoral to the national level. In fact, it may occur that the institutions of a sector, which are extremely important for a country in terms of employment, competitiveness, or strategic relevance, end up emerging as national, thus becoming relevant for other sectors. But in the process of becoming national, they may change some of their original distinctive features.

One final general remark: catch-up is inherently a dynamic process. Because the various actors, knowledge and institutions are more or less closely connected, it follows that their change over time often results in sector-specific co-evolutionary processes, as Nelson (1994) and Metcalfe (1998) have discussed in a broad way. During the evolution of a sectoral system, change may occur in the technological and learning regimes and in the patterns of innovations. Often an industrial structure characterized by new firms and high turbulence may over time become oligopolistic with a more cumulative rate of technological change. Moreover, the knowledge base of innovative activities may change in different ways, such as the evolution towards a dominant design or as a consequence of a drastic change. In the first case, a growth of industrial concentration and the rise of large dominant firms may take place (Utterback, 1994). In the second case, new types of competencies may be required for innovation, with major industrial turbulence, entry of new firms and turnover in industrial leadership (Tushman and Anderson, 1986; Henderson and Clark, 1990). Finally, changes in demand, users and applications represent another major modification in the context in which firms operate and may favour the entry of new firms rather than the success of established ones (Christensen and Rosenbloom, 1995).

1.4   THE SECTORS EXAMINED IN THIS BOOK

This book examines five sectors: pharmaceuticals, semiconductors, telecommunications, agro-food and software. Here we briefly introduce the main features of the sectors (for a deeper discussion of some of these sectors, and of their evolution in the United States and Europe, see Mowery and Nelson, 1999 and Malerba, 2004).

1.4.1   Pharmaceuticals

In the early stages (1850–1945), the industry was related to chemicals. However, little formal R&D was carried out by pharmaceutical firms. The following period (1945 to early 1980s) was characterized by the introduction of large-scale deliberate screening of natural and chemically derived compounds to try to discover substances that might make useful pharmaceuticals. This required formal R&D. The advent of molecular biology in the 1980s led to a new learning regime based on molecular genetics and rDNA technology. In general, pharmaceutical products fall under one of three categories: drugs, vaccines and diagnostics. The commoditization of diagnostics is a recent phenomenon of the post-biotechnology period, as earlier all testing for detection of medical conditions was performed by trained personnel in clinical testing laboratories. The manufacturing of modern drugs and vaccines involves three main steps: the production or the acquisition of the 'active pharmaceutical ingredients'; the combination and process of active pharmaceutical ingredients into the 'bulk drug'; and the 'formulation' of the bulk drug in the form of a tablet, capsule, syrup, injection, plaster, and so on. The manufacturing capabilities associated with the three steps decrease in terms of technological complexity. Therefore, to catch up, developing country firms would start by developing manufacturing capabilities in 'formulations', acquiring the inputs from national and international markets. The next step would be to develop manufacturing capabilities in 'bulk drugs', buying the active pharmaceutical ingredients from the market, and the last step would be to establish 'active pharmaceutical ingredients' production units. In the pharmaceutical sectoral system, a wide variety of science and engineering fields play important roles in renewing the search space. The different industrial actors – large firms, small firms and new biotech firms – who generally do different things are connected through networks. In this sector, a very rich set of non-firm organizations and institutions greatly affect innovation, ranging from universities to public and private research organizations, the financial system and venture capital, the legal system and IPR. Demand channelled through agencies, physicians and the health system, and institutions such as regulation play a significant role in the diffusion of new drugs. Nowadays no individual firm can hope to gain control of more than a subset of the search space. The innovativeness and competitiveness of even the largest pharmaceutical firms depend on strong scientific capabilities and on the ability to interact, on one side, with science and scientific institutions (in order to explore such a complex space) and, on the other, with specialized innovative firms (in order to develop new products).

1.4.2 Telecommunications

In telecommunications, the knowledge base has been quite diversified because the sectoral system encompasses fixed communications, mobile phones, the Internet and other services. All these product groups present different features, but they are related in various ways technologically. In most developing countries, in recent years, mobile communications have overshadowed fixed line technology. This broad sectoral system has recently been affected by processes of convergence between information and communication technologies and between ICT and broadcasting-audio-visual technologies. Until the advent of the Internet, the telecom service industry did not experience major technological and market discontinuities. With the Internet and its open network architecture, modular components and distributed intelligence, both the knowledge base and the types of actors and competences have changed significantly. The process of convergence has generated the entry of several new actors coming from various previously separated industries, each one emphasizing different sets of competencies. Specialized competencies and specific knowledge have increasingly become a key asset for firms' survival and growth. Even more important in the new telecom environment is the combination of existing and new competencies – software programming, network management, content provision – which traditionally belonged to different companies. Networks among a variety of actors (not only firms, but also standard-setting organizations and research organizations) are relevant. Demand plays a key role in innovation, not just in terms of

user–producer interaction, but also in terms of emerging service characteristics. Regulation, liberalization/privatization and standards have
played a key role in the organization and performance of the sector, in the
behaviour of incumbents and in the transformation of the structure of the
industry. Given the complexity of its technology and the consequent huge
investments required, the equipment part of the industry has in the past
been dominated by a handful of MNCs based in the developed world. But
the arrival of mobile technology has allowed enterprises from the developing world to enter this otherwise oligopolistic industry based in the North.
The distribution segment, on the contrary, traditionally was nationally
owned, very often by a public telephone and telegraph (PTT) provider.
But with the liberalization and deregulation that has taken place in most
countries, the distribution of telecom services has now been privatized
and very often thrown open to private sector competition. The natural
monopoly status enjoyed by the PTTs has been eroded. In most developing countries one could find only one part of the industry, namely the distribution segment, while the manufacturing segment is largely based in the
developed world with most countries relying on imports of this equipment.

1.4.3   Computer Software and Services

The computer software industry is a global sector with multiple product
and service niches. It is composed of software publishing, computer
systems design and services, and data processing services. Also telephone
call centres may be related to software. The software sectoral system has
a quite differentiated knowledge base, with extended complementarities.
Knowledge refers both to the control of the operations of the computer
system, providing the platform for the different functionalities, and to the
software employing these functionalities. The boundaries between operating systems and application software are becoming blurred, because of the
dynamics of the inward and outward integration of software functions,
outward (from system-level software to the user interface) and inward
(from software designers to the definition of system resources). A very
important distinction in the software industry is between mass-produced
package software sold on impersonal markets, and software which is
customized to particular uses and users, in terms of situated software,
middleware software and fully custom software. These types of software
require different types of knowledge and learning processes, and may have
different intellectual property regimes. Mass-produced package software
is characterized by the search for generic solutions, experience as a major
input for innovation, and a key role of process innovation. Custom, situated and embedded software, on the other hand, have knowledge related to

specific contexts, specialized purposes and specific applications, and often require close user–producer interactions. Recently, the changing knowledge base of software development and the blurring boundaries between operation systems and application software have created an evolving division of labour among generic 'platform' developers, specialized software vendors and users, and a further tension between horizontal integration and specialization. The historical key role of computer producers has largely been displaced by a division of labour between software and hardware 'platform' producers, governed by the needs of the other as well as by the aim to preserve market positions. For mass-produced software sold on the open market, IPR play a major role in strengthening appropriability, but have been greatly affected by the emerging open source movement. In addition, standards play a major role. Networks of users also play an increasingly important function, particularly in applications and in open source software. In sum, software has a highly differentiated knowledge base in which the context of application and user–producer interaction, global and local networks and high mobility of skilled human capital often play a key role. This has created several different and distinctive product groups.

1.4.4 Semiconductors

The semiconductor industry is characterized by a variety of actors doing different things, ranging from merchant semiconductor manufacturers, to silicon foundries, vertically integrated producers, and fabless[1] and design firms. The types of actors have been quite different from period to period and from country to country during the evolution of the industry. New entrants and specialized producers were quite relevant in the United States, with entrants particularly high either early on in the history of the industry or during phases of technological discontinuities. Large, vertically integrated producers were more common in Japan and Europe. In semiconductors, other main actors have played a major role. The military was one of the major factors responsible for the growth of the American industry, compared to that in Europe and Japan, because it supported the entry of new firms and provided competent firms with a large and innovative demand. During the 1970s in Japan, MITI was a major factor in allowing the Japanese industry, composed of large producers, to close the gap with American producers in some product ranges (such as memory devices). Although the processes of manufacturing semiconductor chips vary in sophistication – from simple transistors that replaced cathode ray tubes in the transfusion of pictures in televisions to sophisticated microprocessors that power supercomputers – the design and fabrication of chips remains high technology. Hence, catch-up attempts in fabrication have required lumpy investments in large physical plants, machinery and equipment, human capital, and its requisite matching demand. Scale economies have not fallen despite continued miniaturization and the decomposition of semiconductor manufacturing vertically into chip design, chip fabrication, assembly and test. Even in Taiwan scale requirements have driven up firm size. Recently, a change in the knowledge base of the industry which has allowed design modularity and has separated design from production, has lead to the entry of new types of actors, fabless firms, which are small firms focused on the design of components. As a consequence, countries that have advanced human capital and limited financial investment, may focus on only one part of the research and production process and enter the industry with small fabless firms.

1.4.5   Agro-food

The agro-food sector constitutes a crucial part of developing economies. Nearly half of the population of developing countries live in rural areas (the World Bank, 2008) and are mainly involved in agriculture. In this book, the case studies of four crops in different countries have been examined in order to shed light on the different dynamics of the sector growth and to explore the implications for development strategy.

A first crop examined is cassava in Nigeria. Cassava is Africa's second most important food staple, after maize, in terms of calories consumed, and it is widely acknowledged as a crop that holds great promise for addressing the challenges of food security and poverty reduction. Nigeria is currently the largest producer of cassava in the world. Most farmers in the main cassava belts of the south-eastern, south-western and central zones of Nigeria grow cassava. A second crop is vegetables in China. The emergence of a large and nationwide system for vegetable production, distribution and technological change, is a phenomenon that has been appearing in China along with rapid economic growth in the past twenty or so years. Earlier the sector was much smaller, weak in R&D and extension services, poor in variety provision, and developed primarily for farmer self-sufficiency. Demand factors, technological progress, and development of market institutions have all been major driving forces for the growth of the vegetable sector. A third crop is coffee in Costa Rica. Today, coffee is one of the most popular beverages worldwide, and one of the most traded commodities. Due to the limited areas suitable for coffee plantation which locate mainly in the South, and high income elasticity of coffee consumption, the coffee value chain is international. The coffee value chain embraces cultivation, milling, roasting, distribution and consumption. The two main cultivated species of the coffee plant are Arabica coffee and Robusta coffee. The former is considered higher quality than the latter. However, Robusta is less susceptible to disease and can be cultivated where Arabica will not thrive. Costa Rica cultivates Arabica. Also central America, eastern Africa and Arabia are Arabica cultivating areas. Western and central Africa, south-east Asia, and, to some extent, Brazil cultivate Robusta. The fourth crop is soybeans in Brazil. Soybeans are the primary ingredient in many processed foods: dairy product substitutes, soybean oil, tofu, veggie burgers, soynut butter and soy crisps, among others. The relevance of the soybean agro-industrial complex to the Brazilian economy rests on the fact that this sector is related to many processed foods and to a number of markets, the most important of which is the production and export of raw beans to the emerging international consumers in recent decades. Also important are the production of soybean oil and its by-products, and the production of animal feed. All these relate to agro-industrial meat chains.

1.5 THE MAIN QUESTIONS ADDRESSED

This book addresses several crucial questions related to catching up in different sectoral systems:

1. A first set of questions concerns the commonalities that are present in the process of catching up across different sectors.
   - Is it possible to identify some basic factors that are common to the five sectors examined?
   - Which is the most important factor across all sectors?
   - Does government policy play an active role in catching up?
2. A second set of questions deals with the specific sectoral differences.
   - Are there differences across sectors in the factors that affect the catching up of countries?
   - Is the industry structure conducive to catching up differences across sectors?
   - Are there other differences related to sectoral systems, such as demand, universities and institutions?
3. A third set of questions is related to country differences.
   - In a sector, are there differences across countries in terms of institutions and government policies?
   - And are these differences similar across different sectors?

- Do these national differences also affect the specialization of countries in specific sectors?

4. A final set of questions refer to the usefulness of the concept of sectoral innovation systems to organize the discussion about industry differences and catching up.

  - Is a sectoral system view able to identify the key variables that are responsible for innovation and catching up by a country in a sector?
  - Is a sectoral system view able to identify the main differences across sectors in those variables?
  - Does a sectoral system view point to the need to focus also on a meso dimension, such as sectors, as a relevant unit of analysis for catching up (in addition to a micro dimension, such as firms, and a macro dimension, such as countries)?

1.6   THE STRUCTURE OF THE BOOK

After this introductory chapter, five long chapters compose the main part of the book. Each chapter examines one sector and it is written by several authors. Then a concluding chapter discusses the main lessons emerging from the book.

We have deliberately chosen a methodology of having one single integrated 'sectoral' chapter written by authors from different countries rather than having different chapters, each examining the sector in a specific country. While this second route would have been easier in terms of coordination and delivery of individual papers, we are convinced that a multiple author 'sectoral' chapter provides a much better comparative and integrated view of the process of catching up in a sector in several countries. In this way, in fact, the main factors of development can be identified in a comparative perspective, and similarities and differences in the national experiences can be highlighted.

Undoubtedly, this effort has proved quite lengthy, research intensive and highly interactive because of the difficulty of having researchers from different countries and views working together in a coordinated way. Several meetings shaped the emergence of this book in order to discuss the various drafts, in New York, twice in Milan, in Maastricht and in Mexico City. But the meetings were indeed an exciting and enriching learning experience for all participants. And we are convinced that the effort was absolutely worthwhile and has proven very successful scientifically.

NOTE

1. Fabless firms are companies that design and sell devices and that outsource the fabrication to specialized manufacturers (foundries).

BIBLIOGRAPHY

Abramovitz, M. (1986), 'Catching-up, forging and falling behind', *The Journal of Economic History*, **46**(2), 385–406.

Amsden, A. and W. Chu (2003), *Beyond Late Development: Taiwan Late Development*, Cambridge: MIT Press.

Arora, A. and A. Gambardella (2005), *From Underdogs to Tiger: the Rise and Growth of the Software Industry in Brazil, China, India, Ireland and Israel*, Oxford: Oxford University Press.

Arthur, B. (1988), 'Competing technologies, increasing returns and lock-ins by historical events', *Economic Journal*, **99**(394), 116–31.

Athreye, S. (2005), 'The Indian software industry and its evolving service capability', *Industrial and Corporate Change*, **14**(3), 393–418.

Bell, M. and K. Pavitt (1993), 'Technological accumulation and industrial growth: contrasts between developed and developing countries', *Industrial and Corporate Change*, **2**, 157–201.

Bernardes, A. and E. Albuquerque (2003), 'Cross-over, thresholds and interactions between science and technology: lessons for less-developed countries', *Research Policy*, **32**(5), 865–85.

Breznitz, D. (2005), *Innovation and the State*, Cambridge: MIT.

Chandra, V. (2006), *Technology, Adaptation and Exports: How Some Developing Countries got it Right*, Washington, DC: The World Bank.

Christensen, C.M. and R.S. Rosenbloom (1995), 'Explaining the attacker's advantage: technological paradigms, organizational dynamics, and the value network', *Research Policy*, **24**(2), 233–57.

Cohen, W. and D. Levinthal (1989), 'Innovation and learning: the two faces of R&D', *Economic Journal*, **99**(397), 569–96.

Commander, S. (2005), *The Software Industry in Emerging Markets: Origins and Dynamics*, Cheltenham, UK and Northampton, MA, USA: Edward Elgar.

Cowan, R. (1990), 'Nuclear power reactors: a study of technological lock-in', *Journal of Economic History*, **50**(3), 541–66.

Dahlman, C. and C. Frischtak (1993), 'National systems supporting technical advance in industry: the Brazilian experience', in R. Nelson (ed.), *National Innovation Systems: A Comparative Analysis*, New York: Oxford University Press, pp. 414–50.

Dahmen, E. (1989), 'Development blocks in industrial economics', in B. Carlsson (ed.), *Industrial Dynamics: Technological, Organizational, and Structural Changes in Industries and Firms*, Boston, MA: Kluwer Academic Press.

Dosi, G. (1988), 'Sources, procedures and microeconomic effects of innovation', *Journal of Economic Literature*, **26**(3), 1120–71.

Dosi, G. (1997), 'Opportunities, incentives and the collective patterns of technological change', *The Economic Journal*, **107**(444), 1530–47.

Edquist, C. (1997), *Systems of Innovation: Technologies, Institutions and Organisations*, London: Frances Pinter.

Ernst, D. (2002), 'Global production networks and the changing geography of innovation systems: implications for developing countries', *Economics of Innovation and New Technology*, **11**(6), 497–523.

Fagerberg, J. and M. Godinho (2004), 'Innovation and catch-up', in J. Fagerberg, D. Mowery and R. Nelson (eds), *Handbook of Innovation*, Oxford: Oxford University Press, pp. 514–43.

Fagerberg, J. and M. Srholec (2006), 'The role of capabilities in development: why some countries develop (while others stay poor)', University of Oslo, working paper.

Fransmann, M. (2006), *Global Broadband Battles: Why the US and Europe Lag Behind While Asia Leads*, Stanford, CA: Stanford University Press.

Freeman, C. (1982), *The Economics of Industrial Innovation*, London: F. Pinter.

Freeman, C. (1987), *Technology Policy and Economic Performance: Lessons from Japan*, London: F. Pinter.

Gereffi, G., J. Humphrey and T. Sturgeon (2005), 'The governance of global value chains', *Review of International Political Economy*, **12**(1), 78–100.

Gerschenkron, A. (1962), *Economic Backwardness in Historical Perspective*, Cambridge, MA: Harvard University Press.

Gu, S., J. Adeoti, A. Castro, J. Orozco and B. Sinh (2007), 'The agro-food sector system', Draft, Catch-up Project.

Hayami, Y. and V. Ruttan (1985), *Agricultural Development: an International Perspective*, Baltimore, MD: Johns Hopkins University Press.

Henderson, R.M. and K.B. Clark (1990), 'Architectural innovation: the reconfiguration of existing product technologies and the failure of established firms', *Administrative Science Quarterly*, **3**, 9–30.

Hobday, M. (1995), *Innovation in East Asia: the Challenge to Japan*, Aldershot, UK and Brookfield, VT, USA: Edward Elgar.

Hyun, Y., Y. Wang and M. Laplane (2007), 'The automobile industry in Brazil, China and Korea', draft, Catch-up Project.

Johnson, C. (1982), *MITI and the Japanese Miracle*, Stanford, CA: Stanford University Press.

Katz, J. (2005), 'Market-oriented structural reforms and domestic technological capabilities: lessons from the Latin American experience', working paper.

Kim, L. (1997), *Imitation to Innovation: the Dynamics of Korea's Technological Learning*, Boston, MA: Harvard Business School Press.

Kim, L. (1999), *Learning and Innovation in Economics Development*, Cheltenham, UK and Northampton, MA, USA: Edward Elgar.

Kim, L. and R. Nelson (2000), *Technology, Learning and Innovation: Experiences of Newly Industrialized Economies*, New York: Cambridge University Press.

Lall, S. (2001), *Competitiveness Technology and Skills*, Cheltenham, UK and Northampton, MA, USA: Edward Elgar.

Lee, K. (2005), 'Making a technological catch-up: barriers and opportunities', *Asian Journal of Technology Innovation*, **13**(2), 97–131.

Lee, K. and C. Lim (2001), 'Technological regimes, catching-up and leapfrogging: the findings from Korean industries', *Research Policy*, **30**(3), 459–83.

Lee, K., S. Mani and Q. Mu (2007), 'Explaining variations in the telecommunication equipment industry in Brazil, China, India and Korea', draft, Catch-up Project.

Lundvall, B.-Å. (1993), *National Systems of Innovation: Towards a Theory of Innovation and Interactive Learning*, London: Frances Pinter.

Lundvall, B.-Å. and B. Johnson (1994), 'The learning economy', *Journal of Industry Studies*, **1**(2), 23–42.

Malerba, F. (2002), 'Sectoral systems of innovation and production', *Research Policy*, **31**(2), 247–64.

Malerba, F. (2004), *Sectoral Systems of Innovation: Concepts, Issues and Analyses of Six Major Sectors in Europe*, Cambridge: Cambridge University Press.

Malerba, F. and S. Mani (2009), *Sectoral Systems of Innovation and Production in Developing Countries*, Cheltenham, UK and Northampton, MA, USA: Edward Elgar.

Malerba, F. and L. Orsenigo (2000), 'Knowledge, innovative activities and industry evolution', *Industrial and Corporate Change*, **9**(2), 289–314.

Mani, S. (2004), 'Coping with globalization: an analysis of innovation capability in Brazilian telecommunication equipment industry', UNU-Intech WP 2004–3.

Mani, S. (2007), *Innovation Capability in Developing Countries: A Study of the Telecommunication Industry*, Cheltenham, UK and Northampton, MA, USA: Edward Elgar.

Mani, S. and A. Bartzokas (2002), 'Institutional support for investments in new technologies: the role of venture capital institutions in developing countries', Intech Discussion papers no. 2002–4.

Mathews, J.A. (2002), 'Competitive advantage of the late comer firms: a resources based account of industrial catch up strategies', *Asia Pacific Journal of Management*, **19**(4), 467–88.

Mazzoleni, R. and R. Nelson (2006), 'The roles of research at universities and public labs in economic catch-up', LEM Working Paper Series.

Metcalfe, S. (1998), *Evolutionary Economics and Creative Destruction*, London: Routledge.

Morrison, A., C. Pietrobelli and R. Rabellotti (2006), 'Global value chains and technological capabilities: a framework to study industrial innovation in developing countries', Working paper.

Mowery, D. and R. Nelson (1999), *The Sources of Industrial Leadership*, Cambridge: Cambridge University Press.

Mu, Q. and K. Lee (2005), 'Knowledge diffusion, market segmentation and technological catch up: the case of telecommunication in China', *Research Policy*, **34**(6), 759–83.

Mytelka, L.K. (2000), 'Local system of innovation in a globalized world economy', *Industry and Innovation*, **7**(1), 15–32.

Nelson, R. (1993), *National Innovation Systems: A Comparative Study*, Oxford: Oxford University Press.

Nelson, R. (1994), 'The co-evolution of technology, industrial structure and supporting institutions', *Industrial and Corporate Change*, **3**(1), 47–64.

Nelson, R. (1995), 'Recent evolutionary theorizing about economic change', *Journal of Economic Literature*, **33**(1), 48–90.

Nelson, R. (2006), *Economic Development from the Perspective of Evolutionary Economics*, New York: Columbia University.

Nelson, R. and N. Rosenberg (1993), 'Technical innovation and national systems', in R. Nelson (ed.), *National Innovation Systems: A Comparative Analysis*, New York: Oxford University Press, pp. 3–21.

Nelson, R. and S. Winter (1982), *An Evolutionary Theory of Economic Change*, Cambridge: The Belknap Press of Harvard University Press.

Nelson, R., R. Mazzoleni, J. Cantwell, C. Juma, N. von Tunzelmann, S. Metcalfe, C. Henry, B.A. Lundvall, A. Goto and H. Odagiri (2005), *A Program of Study of the Process Involved in Technological and Economic Catch-up*, mimeo, Columbia Earth Institute.

Niosi, J. (2006), 'Success factors in Canadian academic spin-offs', *The Journal of Technology Transfer*, **31**(4), 451–7.

Niosi, J., S. Athreye, G. Britto and T. Tschang (2007), 'The global computer software sector', draft, Catch-up Project.

Odagiri, H. and A. Goto (1993), 'The Japanese system of innovation: past, present and future', in R. Nelson (ed.), *National Innovation Systems: A Comparative Analysis*, Oxford: Oxford University Press, pp. 76–114.

Ramani, S., M. Derengowski Fonseca and R. Mu (2007), 'The pharmaceutical sector', draft, Catch-up Project.

Rasiah, R., X. Kong and Y. Lin (2007), 'Semiconductors: explaining variations in catch-up strategies in Malyasia, China and Taiwan', draft, Catch-up Project.

Rosenberg, N. (1982), *Inside the Black Box*, Cambridge: Cambridge University Press.

Tushman, M.L. and P. Anderson (1986), 'Technological discontinuities and organizational environments', *Administrative Science Quarterly*, **31**(3), 439–65.

Utterback, J.M. (1994), *Mastering the Dynamics of Innovation: How Companies can Seize Opportunities in the Face of Technological Change*, Boston, MA: Harvard Business School.

Viotti, E. (2002), 'National learning systems: a new approach on technological change in late industrializing economies and evidences from the cases of Brazil and South Korea', *Technological Forecasting & Social Change*, **69**(7), 653–80.

Von Hippel, E. (1988), *The Sources of Innovation*, New York and Oxford: Oxford University Press.

Wade, R. (1990), 'Industrial policy in East Asia: does it lead or follow the market?', in G. Gereffi and D.L. Wyman (eds), *Manufacturing Miracles: Path of Industrialization in Latin America and East Asia*, Princeton, NJ: Princeton University Press, pp. 231–66.

World Bank (2008), *World Development Report 2008: Agriculture for Development*, Washington DC: The World Bank.

2. Explaining divergent stories of catch-up in the telecommunication equipment industry in Brazil, China, India and Korea

Keun Lee, Sunil Mani and Qing Mu*

2.1 INTRODUCTION

The telecommunications industry is one of the fastest-growing industries in the world characterized by significant technological changes. In most countries of the world mobile communication technologies have sought to replace or overshadow fixed line technology. The industry has two segments or parts: manufacturing of telecom equipment and distribution of telecom services. The technological changes have, in essence, completely altered the landscape of this high-tech industry. Given the complexity of its technology and the consequent huge investments that were required, in the past the equipment part of the industry has been dominated by a handful of MNCs based in the developed world. But the arrival of mobile technology has allowed enterprises from the developing world to enter this otherwise oligopolistic industry based in the North. The distribution segment, on the other hand, is nationally owned, very often by a public telephone and telegraph (PTT) provider. But with the embracing of liberalization and deregulation by most countries, the distribution of telecom services has now been privatized and very often thrown open to private sector competition. The natural monopoly status enjoyed by the PTTs has been eroded. In most developing countries one could find only one part of the industry, namely the distribution segment, while the manufacturing segment was largely based in the developed world, with most countries relying on imports of this equipment. However, there are notable exceptions.

The four countries, Brazil, China, India and Korea, have sought to build some measures of innovation and manufacturing capabilities in telecommunications equipment. The history of this process could be traced back to the late 1970s when Brazil was the first among these four to design a domestic sectoral system of innovation. This was soon followed or imitated by Korea and India in the mid-1980s and by China towards the late 1980s. All four countries crafted a state-led sectoral system of innovation with a government research institute at the core of the system. The research institute developed the technology, which was then licensed to public and private domestic enterprises. Firms converted this technology in order to manufacture equipment that in turn was sold to monopoly state-owned service providers. The state thus effectively used public technology procurement as a way of nurturing and supporting this innovation capability. However, the recent wave of privatization and deregulation of the industry has completely altered the working of the sectoral system of innovation. In fact, we see two broad divergent paths. At one extreme, we have the Chinese and Korean systems that have succeeded in coping with the challenges posed by globalization and have emerged as major exporters of telecom equipments, while at the other extreme we have Brazil and India, which have increasingly become net importers of telecom equipment. Some of the enterprises from the former group have now become important world players and have become MNCs in their own right. On the other hand, neither of the latter two countries has any domestic enterprises in the industry worth the name, although both of them have become major manufacturing hubs for telecom equipment. These hubs are dominated by affiliates of the MNCs. Thus in both the countries we see a passage of innovation capability from public to private foreign enterprises.

While the four countries of China, Korea, India and Brazil present substantial heterogeneity that makes any comparison almost impossible, they share one commonality in technological development. That is, all of these four had once developed more or less 'indigenously' digital telephone switches. While this is an interesting phenomenon, probably a more interesting thing should be the divergent paths taken by the four countries after the initial development of the digital telephone switches. In this long-term trajectory, China and Korea side together with relatively more success in technological development, while India and Brazil have been going through a similar and less successful path.

Korea had a telephone service bottleneck in the 1970s and 1980s, and after much effort it succeeded in developing its own digital switches in 1981–83, taking over the markets from the imports and MNCs. Its enhanced capabilities in wired telecommunication, accumulated over the preceding decades, have led to the growth of indigenous capabilities in wireless telecommunication, too. China also had serious bottlenecks in telecommunication and used to import all its fixed line digital switches, but it succeeded in developing its own digital switches in 1991, to taking over the markets from the imports and the MNCs. It is now moving ahead with confidence with a third generation wireless telecommunication system and has developed and declared its own indigenous standards in 3G wireless telecommunication.

Now, in contrast, although Brazil also developed its own digital switches in the 1980s, it failed to sustain its capabilities over time. India's own digital switches were developed in the 1990s by C-DOT (a Government Research Institute: GRI). However, local production and R&D capabilities are still weak compared to the MNCs, both in capabilities and markets, and local units have failed to make a successful transition to the mobile telecommunication era.

How these 'common starts with subsequent divergent paths' can be explained is the central focus of this chapter. To tackle this task, we turn to the theoretical framework of the SSI (sectoral innovation system) that has been developed and evolved by a group of scholars following the neo-Schumpeterian tradition. In particular, we refer to Malerba (2004). The theoretical building blocks of Malerba's SSI consist of the regimes of knowledge and technologies, demand conditions (or market regimes), actors and networks and coordination among them, and the surrounding institutions including IPRs, laws, culture and so on. However, the book edited by Malerba (2004) deals with cases and sectors from the developed countries. This chapter, together with other chapters in this volume, extends the original SSI framework to the context of catch-up in developing or latecomer countries. Thus, while we will apply the same framework, we expect that some modification or adaptations will be necessary to make it more applicable to the specific context of developing countries.

Similar adaptations have been made by Lee and Lim (2001), Lee et al. (2005), Mu and Lee (2005) and Mani (2005a and 2005b) when they analyse the industry cases from China, Korea and India with theoretical concepts such as the sectoral innovation system or technological regimes as subcomponents. For instance, given our goal of explaining the divergent stories of catch-up or lagging behind, we will put more emphasis on: (a) the importance of arranging access to a foreign knowledge base; (b) the initial promoting and coordination role of the government; and (c) how to create and sustain competitive advantage and capabilities of local or indigenous firms. In sum, this chapter aims to explain variations among the four latecomers in, first, the (fixed line) digital switch industry and, second, the wireless telecommunication system industry, as well as their divergent evolution over time, within the framework of the SSI proposed in Malerba (2004).

In what follows, we first provide an overview of the evolution of the sectors in each of the four countries (section 2.2). Then section 2.3

discusses a theoretical framework for analysis and proposes our hypotheses to explain the variations among the four. Sections 2.4, 2.5 and 2.6 deal with three different aspects of the sectoral innovation system to explain the variations, starting with the knowledge system and access (section 2.4), demand conditions and how to sustain market success (section 2.5), and the actors and their role in sustaining growth of indigenous technological capabilities (section 2.6). Section 2.7 deals with the transition to the wireless era, and section 2.8 concludes the chapter with a summary.

2.2   EVOLUTION OF THE SECTOR IN THE FOUR COUNTRIES

The basic historical evolution of the telecommunication equipment sectors in China, India, Korea and Brazil can be summarized as follows. As explained below, there are substantial variations, and our task is to explain them in terms of the SSI framework.

2.2.1   The Chinese Story

After the People's Republic of China was founded, the telecommunication administration system was established and the communication network was built. This network connected the whole country and was centred in Beijing (Zhang, 2000). The first step-by-step telephone switch equipment factory, Beijing Wired Factory, was set up in 1957 with the help of experts from the former Soviet Union. In 1958 the Beijing Wired Factory began to produce the JZB (47 type) step-by-step telephone switch, which replaced the imported equipment in China. As step-by-step switches have some disadvantages, being slow, noisy, and requiring frequent adjustment and maintenance, the Ministry of Post and Telecommunication (hereafter MPT) decided to stop the production of step-by-step switches in 1974 (Zhu, 2000).

In 1966 the Tenth Research Institute of the MPT developed the first coded crossbar telephone switching system. This system had been widely used in telephone networks throughout the country.[1] The major models of crossbar switches developed by the Tenth Research Institute include the JT-801 switching exchange series, the HJ09 trunk-local-rural switching system and the HJ10 terminal switching system. In 1975 a slightly improved version of crossbar switches was developed by the Academy of Telecommunications Science and Technology under the MPT and was approved by the MPT. Until then, however, owing to the closed door policy, China was not able to absorb advanced telecommunication technology from the West, and the level of technological capability was very low. Only after the open door policy in May 1984, was a more advanced crossbar switching system with a capacity of more than 10 000 ports developed and produced in Tianjin; however, China had not developed or produced even an analogue electronic switch (Zhang, 1999). But in other parts of the world, fully automatic digital switches had already been widely installed. In sum, in China the step-by-step switches were mainly used in the 1960s and 1970s and the crossbar telephone switches in the 1980s.

According to Mr Wu, the former minister of the MPT, as of 1980 China lagged 20–30 years behind the developed countries as the step-by-step switches comprised about 29 per cent of the telephone network, and crossbar switches comprised 33.7 per cent, while analogue electronic switches, imported from foreign countries, represented only 6.7 per cent of the network in China (Wu, 1997).[2] Thus, it can be said that the telecommunication network in China had been dominated by the out-dated step-by-step and crossbar central office switches before the first digital automatic (SPC) switch made by Fujitsu (Japan) was imported and installed in the Fujian Province in 1981 (Wu, 1997, p. 73; Xin and Wang, 2000, p. 21; Cheng, 1999, p. 47).[3] After the first installation, all the major multinational SPC switch manufacturers started to sell their switches in China.

Realizing the attractiveness of its market size and the associated bargaining power, the Chinese government actively approached multinational suppliers for technology transfer and joint venture negotiations. In 1984, the first foreign direct investment (FDI) was approved to establish a very large joint venture (JV) in China: The Shanghai Bell Telephone Equipment Manufacturing Corporation (Shanghai Bell hereafter) formed a partnership with Bell Telephone Manufacturing Company (hereafter BTM), a subsidiary of ITT at that time and later Alcatel. Another JV agreement between Siemens in Germany and a factory owned by the Ministry of Electronics Industry (MEI) in Beijing was signed in October 1988 to establish a company called Beijing International Switching System Corporation (BISC). This company produced EWSD (Electronic Worldwide Switch Digital) switches from 1991 (IGI, 1997, pp. 143–4). Fearing that the two JVs would dominate the Chinese market, other multinational suppliers started to actively pursue JV negotiations with their Chinese partners and from 1993 they eventually established their own joint ventures in China. As a result, the involvement of FDI transformed China's switch market from a market dominated by 'direct imported goods' to a 'JV dominated' one in the early 1990s. The large-scale installation of imported switches in China's telecom networks and the presence of a large number of JVs in China fostered the diffusion of technology know-how across the country.

As section 2.4 elaborates, there was a broad-ranging knowledge transfer and exchange involving R&D, production, sub-contracting, marketing, after sales services and local human resource training (Tan, 2002; Zhang, 2000, p. 148). Domestic researchers and engineers, teamed with entrepreneurs, quickly grasped the opportunity to develop competitive products in China. A specific project to develop digital electronic telephone switches in China started in 1984, initiated by Professor Wu at the Center for Information Technology (CIT) under the Zhengzhou Institute of Information Engineering belonging to the People's Liberation Army. Wu's team at the CIT was joined by the Luoyang Telephone Equipment Factory (LTEF) under the MPT that used to produce crossbar (electromechanical) switches. Some of the specialists who used to work at Shanghai Bell also participated in this project to develop digital automatic switches (Shen, 1999, pp. 76–7).

In 1987 a contract to develop a switch with 2000 lines was signed between the CIT and the PTIC (Posts and Telecommunications Industrial Corporation) under the MPT. From then, PTIC played the role of general project manager and financial sponsor, with the CIT as the main technological force and the LTEF as a technical assistant and a test workshop. Then, it was in 1991 that this three-party consortium of the CIT, LTEF and the PITC finally developed a central-office digital automatic switch (HJD-04). Domestically designed and manufactured central-office SPC switches (a kind of digital automatic switch) started to serve the rural markets in 1992.

From the mid-1990s indigenous manufacturers began to compete directly with JVs, first in rural markets and subsequently in urban markets, with significantly improved product quality and added features. Starting from a 10.6 per cent market share in 1992, the four indigenous manufacturers – led by Great Dragon (Julong), Datang, Zhongxing and Huawei (the so-called Ju Da Zhong Hua in Chinese, which means 'great China') – accounted for 43 per cent of China's digital automatic switch market in 2000 (see Figure 2.1). Their switches even began to be exported to many developing countries in East Asia, Central Asia, Eastern Europe and Latin America.

2.2.2 The Korean Story

Korea had telephone service bottlenecks in the 1970s and 1980s. However, until the late 1970s, Korea had neither its own telecommunications manufacturing equipment industry nor a research and development (R&D) programme. As a result, the nation imported most of its equipment and related technologies from foreign suppliers (see Table 2.1), and the Korean

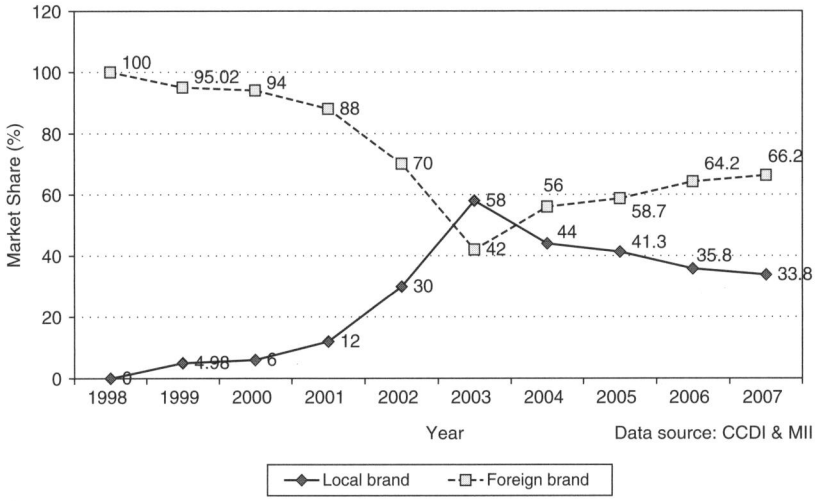

Figure 2.1 Market shares in mobile phones in China: Local vs. foreign

technicians merely installed foreign switching systems into the nation's domestic telephone networks.

With its industrial and commercial bases developing rapidly and its population growing (approaching 36 million people), Korea's telecommunications services fell far behind demand in the late 1970s. Therefore, after prudent consideration, the Korean government decided that the nation needed to develop its own manufacturing capabilities and R&D infrastructure necessary for the creation of state-of-the art digital phone switching systems.

The Korean consortium tried hard and in 1981–83 the Korean Electronics and Telecommunications Research Institute (ETRI) developed a proprietary digital switching system, called the TDX (time-division exchange) series, in collaboration with a national network of switching system manufacturers and distributors. The development of a switching system in Korea went from the manual switch and the step-by-step switch, and leapfrogged into the analogue electronic switch, then into the digital electronic switch, skipping the crossbar switch (see Table 2.1).

This indigenously developed product took over the markets from the imports and MNCs. Korea's enhanced capabilities accumulated over the preceding decades have also led to the growth of indigenous capabilities in wireless telecommunication.

Table 2.1   Development process of switching system in Korea

Model		Commercial time in the world	Installment time in Korea	Technology acquired approach in Korea
Manual switch		1880s	1896~	Equipment import
Automatic switch	Electro-mechanical switch	1890s Step-by-step switch	1935~ Strowger	Equipment import
			1960~ EMD	FDI, Technology Alliance
		1930s Crossbar switching	Not installed	–
	Electronic switch	1960s Analogue electronic switch	1979~	Technology import, FDI
		1970s Digital electronic switch	1982~1985 TDX series	Technology import, FDI Developed by Korea
		1990s ISDN	1991~	Developed by Korea

Source: Lee and Lee (1992). Cited in Mu (2002).

2.2.3   The Indian Story

The telecom equipment industry in India has been assiduously built up by the state. During the period since independence in 1947 to 2007, three distinct phases could be seen in the development of the telecom equipment industry in the country. The first phase is the period 1947–1985, when the country depended on foreign licensing and exclusive state manufacturing. There were only two telecom equipment manufacturing firms, one specializing in the manufacture and sale of switching and terminal equipment and the other specializing in the manufacture and sale of terminal equipment. Both these firms were owned by the central government, but invested very little in local technology development so production was entirely based on licensing technologies from abroad. Mani (1992) showed that these technologies were not suited to the usage patterns prevailing in the country and so these imported technologies required lengthy and costly adaptations. This phase was characterized by very low tele-densities (less than one telephone per 100 people), long waiting lists for new lines (average wait of very nearly three years) and poor quality of service (very high fault rates and low call completion rates).

The second phase corresponds to the period 1985 to 1995 when the state intervened very heavily, on the one hand in the creation of state-of-the-art telecom technologies that were suited to Indian conditions by establishing a public laboratory, C-DOT, and on the other hand by throwing open the manufacture of telecom equipment to domestic private sector enterprises. The laboratory was very successful in developing a family of digital switching systems that were best suited to Indian conditions. These technologies were of course restricted to large local switches so that the country continued to depend on foreign sources of technology essentially through the licensing mode for long-distance switches and for a variety of transmission and terminal equipment. During this second phase, the price of switching equipment fell dramatically, owing, *inter alia*, to the availability of local technologies, and this allowed the country to make some improvements in both the quantity and quality of telecom equipment in the country. Teledensities, during this second phase, increased to over 1 per 100, the waiting list was considerably reduced and there were tremendous improvements in other quality parameters including significant improvements in the digitization of the industry. The domestic manufacturing industry was at its zenith during this period: it was able to supply almost 90 per cent of the equipment requirements of the service providers. The service providers, both in the first and second phases, were state owned, and therefore public technology procurement was the main instrument used for stimulating local manufacturing.

The third phase commenced in 1995 and continues to the present day. Now, the share of fixed telephones in the total network, although increased in absolute terms, in a relative sense has stagnated. The industry is now heavily dominated by wireless technologies. The ratio of wireless (mobile) to fixed line stands at around 4, one of the highest recorded anywhere in the world. The phase is characterized by a number of important developments that have changed the complexion of the industry. The main changes could be summarized as follows.

First of all, the provision of telecom services has been effectively privatized with the private sector nudging into the market for fixed lines and concentrating very heavily in the market for wireless technologies. Thus, the manufacturing of telecom equipment has been thrown open to imports and indeed FDI. Consequently the trade balance of the industry has become increasingly negative and affiliates of MNCs have started local manufacturing facilities. In fact the telecoms industry has been one of the major recipients of FDI in the country. The two state-owned undertakings have become virtually bankrupt and had to be resuscitated using government grants and further infusion of foreign technologies.

The state's ability to practise public technology procurement has been considerably reduced and consequently the public laboratory, C-DOT, has virtually collapsed in terms of local development of technologies. Also the state failed to strategically reorient the laboratory from the manufacture of fixed line technologies to wireless ones. The laboratory has now ended up as a contract research organization to affiliates of the MNCs. But there has been a silver lining. The experience and expertise gained in developing digital switching systems has given Indian engineers such considerable software expertise that India has now emerged as an important source of software and design capabilities for the world telecom equipment industry. There are now many R&D outsourcing deals between the world telecom equipment industry and Indian software firms. In short, although the country has considerable innovation capability, even during this phase of flux, it has moved on from domestic ownership to that of foreign ownership. In this way, the Indian case is roughly opposite to the experiences recorded in China and indeed Korea.

2.2.4   The Brazilian Story

Brazil has one of the largest telecom equipment industries in the whole of Latin America. The history of the industry is divided into four phases. The first phase is the period from the 1950s up to about the mid-1970s when the industry was entirely dominated by a limited number of affiliates of MNCs with one large state-owned provider of telecom services. Access to telecom services was very difficult, the tariff too high and both the waiting list for new lines and the number of potential consumers on the waiting list were too high. This kind of shortage in access even promoted a 'black market' in telecom services. Given this state of affairs, the government decided to build local capability in telecom switches towards the mid-1970s. This manifested itself in the form of a public laboratory, the CPqD, being established in the city of Campinas, which has now emerged as one of the most high-tech areas in the country. The laboratory developed a family of digital switching systems known as the Tropico family by the late 1980s to early 1990s. Brazil has the distinction of having the first public R&D project in the telecom area anywhere in the developing world.

This leads us to the second phase, which covers the period from 1976 to the 1990s, when the Brazilian state attempted to foster the evolution of a domestic local equipment manufacturing industry through a variety of public support measures, the most dominant of which was public technology procurement. The third phase extends from the early 1990s, to the late 1990s when the industry was in a state of flux. Almost all the domestic manufacturers were taken over by MNCs, the laboratory was in a state of confusion and the largest state provider of telecom services was broken up and privatized. The sectoral system of innovation underwent several changes during this period. The fourth, or last phase begins in 1998 and continues to the present day. This is a phase with very important developments, which are summarized below.

First, the telecommunications equipment manufacturing industry in Brazil is now largely dominated by affiliates of MNCs. Almost all the wholly owned Brazilian telecommunications manufacturing firms have been either acquired by MNCs or have been closed down. This resulted in the top three in the world's leading telecommunications equipment manufacturing firms entering the Brazilian market: Alcatel and Nortel Networks in 1991 and Lucent in 1997.[4] Currently the only Brazilian manufacturer left in the industry is Tropico. Even this firm has a foreign equity holding in the form of 10 per cent of its equity being held by a foreign company, namely Cisco Systems.

Second, the R&D system of the telecommunications equipment sector has undergone a major structural shift and in 2003 it consisted of three different types of organization: stand-alone public laboratories, R&D departments attached to production enterprises (mostly foreign companies) and university departments. The main R&D organization, namely the Telebras-owned CPqD, has been made into a private foundation. This means that, for a large proportion of its budget, the laboratory will increasingly have to engage in income-generating activities, which can affect its forays into long-term research issues. However, the Brazilian state has put in place a number of legal and fiscal instruments to assure a steady and minimum market for the output of this laboratory. Another notable feature is the entry of private laboratories to telecom research in the country. It is also equally interesting to note that of the four foreign labs, three are attached to foreign equipment manufacturers and one to a leading new fixed line provider. The only Brazilian private sector lab is the Genius Institute of Technology.[5] The institute has at least one collaborative research venture with CPqD on an R&D project in the area of digital terrestrial television. Nevertheless CPqD continues to be the major component of the R&D system and has put in place a number of strategies designed to continue its research activities within the constraints imposed by the changed external environment.

The main changes in the distribution of telecom services can be summarized as follows.

First of all, the distribution sector has been privatized and hence the new telecom operators, some of them affiliates of foreign providers, are not really obliged to procure their equipment from local sources, although a recent legal instrument has improved the probability that they will indeed consider domestically manufactured equipment with Brazilian technology. More on this point is to be found in a later section where the role of the government is discussed. Second, the major growth area is in the equipment for cellular telephony. This is an area where most of the Brazilian R&D organizations, including CPqD, do not have much capability. As a consequence of privatization, the centre of gravity in decision-making has changed to the regulator, ANATEL, from the Ministry of Communications. Almost all the major decisions with respect to the industry were made by ANATEL, together with the responsibility for monitoring its effectiveness, although after the elections of 2002 the newly constituted Ministry of Communications is slowly attempting to regain its lost 'position' with respect to decision-making. There are now two directorates in the Ministry, dealing with industry and technology and the other dealing with services and universalization. The financing of R&D projects in the telecommunications equipment sector has been stream-lined with the establishment of the Fund for Technological Development of Telecommunications (Fundo para Desenvolvimento Tecnológico das Telecomunicações, FUNTTEL) in 2000. The service providers contribute to the fund and it is jointly administered by BNDES and FINEP. In addition to this fund there are of course the R&D incentives provided under the Informatics Law 8248 of 1991 and the more recent Law 10176 of 2001.

2.3 THEORETICAL FRAMEWORK AND HYPOTHESES

2.3.1 Modifying the SSI Framework for the Catch-up Context

A starting point in these joint studies on catching up in sectors is that the catch-up process in income per capita has been associated with the emergence and growth of some leading sectors that have spurred the growth in the country (Malerba, 2006). Malerba (2006) finds that the same success or failure factors found at the level of countries as a whole are also behind the emergence and growth of a sector in a country. Those factors include: learning and capabilities by domestic firms, government policy, a highly skilled labour force, entrepreneurship and small and medium-size firms, some key large firms. Actually, these factors are the key building blocks of the theoretical concept of the SSI.

Drawing from several intellectual precedents, such as the innovation system literature (Edquist, 1997), the national systems of innovation

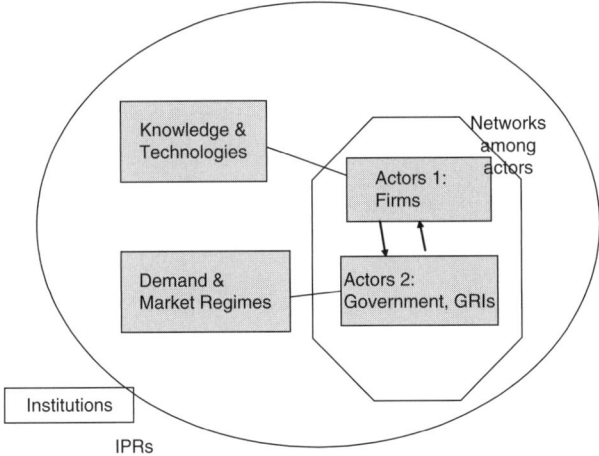

Note: GRIs = government research institutes.

Source: Adapted from Malerba (2004).

Figure 2.2 *Building blocks of the sectoral innovation system (SSI) of Malerba*

literature (Freeman, 1987; Nelson, 1993; Lundvall, 1993), and the technological systems concept (Carlsson and Stankiewitz, 1995; Hughes, 1984; Callon, 1992), Malerba (2002, 2004) defines a sector as a set of activities that are unified by some linked product groups for a given or emerging demand and that share some common knowledge. Firms in a sector have some commonalities and at the same time are heterogeneous in terms of learning processes and capabilities. Then, as explained in Figure 2.2, the building blocks of Malerba's SSI consist of: (a) the regimes of knowledge and technologies; (b) demand conditions (or market regimes); (c) actors and networks and coordination among them; and (d) the surrounding institutions including IPRs, laws and culture. These elements are supposed to interact to generate variety subject to selection and co-evolution.

This chapter, together with others in this volume, extends the original SSI framework to the context of catch-up in developing or latecomer countries. Thus, while we will apply the same framework, we expect some modification or adaptations to be necessary to make it friendlier to the context of developing countries. Similar adaptations have been made by Lee and Lim (2001), Lee et al. (2005), Mu and Lee (2005) and Mani (2005a and 2005b) when they analyse the industry cases from China, Korea and India with theoretical concepts such as the sectoral innovation system or

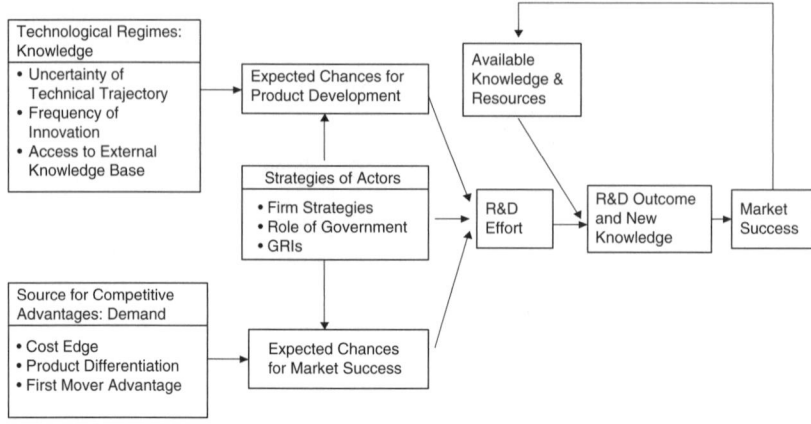

Source: Lee and Lim (2001).

Figure 2.3   Model of technological and market catch-up and SSI

technological regimes as its subcomponents. Figure 2.3 shows a modified SSI framework with more concrete elements relevant to the context of catching up. Let us call the 'theoretical framework' in Figure 2.3 a model of technological and market catch-up. That implies first that the degree of success in catching up is primarily measured by catch-up in market shares which should be, if it is to be sustained, backed up by technological catch-up or learning. The three key building blocks of the SSI are here with more specific connotations for catch-up. The first block, or regimes of knowledge and technologies, is related to the probability of successful development of specific technologies or products by the latecomer firms or actors. The second block, or demand conditions, determines whether the technologies or products developed by the latecomers can succeed in markets and thus increase their market share. The third block, or actors, primarily includes firms, governments and other supporting actors, including the financial system. It is basically firms' strategic decisions on how to respond to the demand conditions and existing knowledge systems. Because the ultimate criteria for successful catch-up relate to the level of technological capabilities of firms, the focus in this chapter is also about what is happening to the firms in charge of the whole process.

Now in Table 2.2, we can examine more specific differences between the SSI of developing countries and advanced countries. First, in the context of catch-up, which tends to have a low probability of success given the fierce competition from the incumbent firms from the developed countries, more often than not, the role of the government is critical during

Table 2.2   Comparing SSI blocks in the advanced and developing countries

SSI blocks	Advanced countries	Developing countries
Knowledge regime actors	Property of knowledge base (appropriability etc.) Private firms	Access to foreign knowledge base Firms, Governments, GRIs
Institutions	Financial systems	Public–private coordination
Demand conditions	First mover advantage & differentiation (high end)	Cost advantages & differentiation (low end)

Source: Authors' own elaboration.

the initial stage of technological and market development. The literature has found many cases in which governments provide a substantial portion of initial R&D expenditure or protection for the indigenous products. Thus, actors in the SSI of developing countries tend to include not only firms but also the government and GRIs (government research institutes). This emphasis on the role of the government is different from the usual situation in advanced countries, where the focus on the actors is more on private firms. Next, regarding external institutions, financial systems and overall national innovation systems (NIS) are important in the advanced countries. But in most developing countries financial markets are often deficient, which calls for more intervention by the government in the form of credit rationing by the state-assisted banks.

Regarding demand conditions or market regimes, important considera-tion in the catching-up context should focus on the grounds for market competitiveness of the products by the latecomers. Competitiveness can be based on cost edge, product differentiation, or first mover advantages. Among these three, in the case of advanced countries, the focus would be more on first mover advantage and product differentiation for higher-end markets. But, in the case of catching-up economies, more often than not the products by the latecomers start with price advantages which are sometimes combined with product or market differentiation for lower-end markets. That was the case for the digital switches indigenously developed in China or Korea. In China the segmented nature of domestic markets or rural markets combined with a limited number of MNCs acted as an initial protected market domestic for manufacturers producing differentiated commodities suitable for rural or low-end markets.

Next, regarding regimes of knowledge and technologies, we perceive this block as the determinants of the probability of the physical develop-ment of specific technologies or products. Then among these determi-nants, the developing countries should focus on the ease of arranging access to a foreign knowledge base (see Table 2.2). This focus differs from the case of advanced countries where the focus in the knowledge regime would be more on the general property of the sector's knowledge base. Given that catch-up is basically a process of reducing the knowledge gap between the forerunners and the laggards, the possibility of learning and opportunity for knowledge transfer is a critical element. The importance of knowledge access has been confirmed by many cases including Lee and Lim (2001) for six industries in Korea, and Lee et al. (2005), Mu and Lee (2005) for China. As explained in Lee (2005), the access can be arranged in various forms including informal learning, licensing, FDI, strategic alliance, co-development, and so on. In sum, given our goal of explaining the divergent stories of catch-up or lagging behind, we will put more emphasis on: (a) the importance of arranging access to a foreign knowledge base; (b) the initial promotion and coordination role of the government; and (c) how to create and sustain competitive advantage and capabilities of local or indigenous firms.

2.3.2   The Regime of Knowledge and Technology of the Telephone Switches and Hypotheses

In the introduction to this chapter, we noted that all the four countries had succeeded in developing fixed line telephone switches by indigenous efforts. We interpret this fact as being a result of the unique technological regime of telephone switch technology. As analysed in Mu and Lee (2005), the technological regime of telephone switches is characterized by a relatively predictable technological trajectory and infrequent innovation, at least as of the 1980s, which was the time the four countries were starting or completing their catch-up effort.

In Mu and Lee (2005), the nature of this technical trajectory was addressed by examining the ages and life-cycles of new technologies in switches and the frequency of innovation by counting the number of patent applications. Given the history of telephone switches from the manual switch (1880s–1920s) to the electromechanical switch (1920s–1960s) and then to the electronic switches such as the stored program control (SPC) switch (1965–now), we can see that the life spans of generations of telephone switches are relatively long. The average age for an electromechanical switch in service was roughly 35–40 years, while some individual users had adopted the electromechanical switches for as long as 55 years (Dittberner, 1977). It is over 35 years since the inception of the digital automatic switch but this switch is still used worldwide. This shows that the telephone switch industry is characterized by a more predictable technical trajectory compared to other industries, such as the computer industry. Whereas computer products are characterized by life cycles of about six years, telecommunication switch equipment has traditionally had life-cycles of 20 to 40 years, and transmission equipment has been replaced every 10 to 20 years (Duysters, 1996).

Next, the patenting trend in telephone switches shows that the regime is featured by a low frequency of innovation (see Table 2 of Mu and Lee, 2005). When we checked the number of patents related to telephone switches by keyword search on the USPTO website, we found that during the 1977 to 1992 period[6] the average annual growth rate of the related patents was only minus 0.6 per cent, while other emerging technologies, such as DRAM (dynamic random access memory chips), showed much higher growth rates (30 per cent in the case of DRAM over the same period); the same is true of wireless communication technologies, among others.[7] Frequency of innovation is also related to the age of technologies, such that old technologies tend to exhibit a more stable technological trajectory.

Thus, given a more predictable technological trajectory and less frequent innovation, we can reason that the fixed line telephone switch is a relatively easy target for latecomers to emulate and develop. But the greater opportunities cannot be realized unless effective access to foreign knowledge is available and/or there is planned determination to achieve the target. Furthermore, this kind of technological regime is predicted to lead to stage-skipping catch-up because the latecomer can more easily aim to skip some stages and target later stages. This prediction is our first hypothesis. Although it will be elaborated in the next section, here let us mention briefly that this was the case in Korea and China. China had only limited experience of developing or producing electromechanical switches but skipped development and production of analogue electronic switches to jump directly to producing digital automatic switches (Mu and Lee, 2005). Similarly Korea gained experience in developing the manual switch and the step-by-step switch and leapfrogged into analogue electronic switches, and then into digital electronic switches, skipping the crossbar switch (Mu, 2002).

The second hypothesis is about the importance of access to a foreign knowledge base, as access to foreign knowledge bases is an important component in the success of the indigenous development of digital switches in latecomer countries, with some variations in each country. Section 2.4 is devoted to this hypothesis.

Next, another important, or third, hypothesis is about how to explain the divergent trajectories of catch-up in the four countries, and our hypothesis is that the difference between India and Brazil vs. China and Korea is a result of the different roles of the actors (government) regarding whether or not they provided the initial market protection and coordinating roles. Section 2.4 will focus on this hypothesis by examining the role of the government. In this regard, an important and related issue is the role of private companies and their capability building. In an *ex-post* sense, a more clear-cut difference between the relative success of China and Korea as against the lack of success of both Brazil and India, appears to be the different role and strength of the business enterprises in each country and whether or not they were an integral part of the SSI.

The leading telecom equipment manufacturers in both Korea (Samsung and LG) and China (Huawei, Datang and ZTE) had strong in-house R&D capabilities and as such they were able to participate very effectively in the technology development process. On the other hand, in the cases of Brazil and India, the local equipment manufacturers were very weak technologically and therefore had to depend almost entirely on their respective GRIs. The GRIs themselves failed to make strategic choices regarding technology. However, why the strengths of private enterprises were different should be explained *ex ante* because they were not strong initially, but gained strength gradually. The question is, why was that possible? This is a difficult question to answer and, for this reason, we need to look at the role of the government concerning whether or not it provides protection for 'infant industries'. This issue is worth further exploration. Lastly, we will closely examine the difference between China and Korea in the modes of access to the foreign knowledge base (through foreign JV in China vs. licensing in Korea), and modes of market protection (segmented market in China vs. closed markets in Korea).

The next important hypothesis is about what could happen to the latecomer countries when there is a major technological change or discontinuity. Here our hypothesis is that if the indigenous actors succeed in developing their own capabilities, they can even overcome the difficulties imposed by uncertainty and discontinuity associated with shifts in technologies. The cases of mobile telecom in Korea and China show this as they have made a successive transition from digital switches (fixed lines) to the mobile telecommunication technology era. More interestingly, they have even taken advantage of the emergence of the new era to manage a path-creating catch-up, such as the commercialization of CDMA technology in Korea and development of the 3G wireless standard (TD-SCDMA) in China. This is in contrast to the stage-skipping catch-up which they had made in developing digital switches. On the other hand, if the latecomers fail to develop their own capabilities, the shift of technological paradigm can act as a further barrier to catch-up, as has happened in the case of Brazil and India.

Finally, we notice that there might be two models of catch-up in terms of which types of firms will be leading the catching-up process of catch-up (Lee, 2005). The first model is the Korean style catch-up, which is led by big firms pursuing more or less independent roads with regard to the MNCs. In this model of catch-up, indicators can be market shares in domestic or world export markets. The other model is the Taiwanese style catch-up, which is led by smaller firms that are pursuing more interdependent roads with regard to the MNCs. These firms will be more integrated with the global value chain or global production network run by the MNCs. In this model of catch-up, productivity can be an indicator of catch-up as the latecomers might move up the ladder of value chains toward higher value added segments. In the telecom sector, while China seems to be conforming to the first model of independent catch-up, India, as we will discuss, is showing some promising signs of behaving according to the second, interdependent model of catch-up.

2.4   SSI BUILDING BLOCK 1: TECHNOLOGIES AND ARRANGING ACCESS TO FOREIGN KNOWLEDGE

The technological regime of digital switches can be characterized by low frequency of innovation and low uncertainty (mature technologies) and thus it was not that difficult for the latecomers to try to develop them by indigenous effort. But, despite this, obtaining access to critical foreign knowledge has been important for the successful development of switches in all four countries.

2.4.1   China

In China, the initial access was arranged via a JV (Shanghai Bell), and the huge market size of China provided the government with a strong bargaining position when dealing with MNCs regarding obtaining the necessary technology and learning opportunity provided (Mu and Lee, 2005). Details follow below.

Setting up a joint venture, Shanghai Bell[8]
While the Chinese government had allowed the imports of large-scale digital switches to alleviate the immediate bottleneck in the telecommunication infrastructure following the reform, it thought that direct imports of finished foreign digital automatic switches should be only a short-term solution for China. As the most populous country with a huge potential market, transferring technologies by setting up joint ventures was

considered necessary for China, with the benefits of increased local value added and job creation. More importantly, China hoped that joint ventures would stimulate technological learning in the country and encourage a build-up of indigenous technological capabilities. The MPT approached almost all the major telecommunications companies around the world to explore opportunities for technology transfer by setting up joint ventures. At that time, several state councillors and premiers paid official visits to industrialized countries and explored the possibility of establishing joint ventures (Zhang, 2000, p. 228).

However, at that time, most of the telecommunications companies were only interested in exporting their finished products to China. Bell Telephone Manufacturing Company (BTM), a subsidiary of ITT and later Alcatel, was one of the few firms who were willing to exploit the potentially huge market, together with some technology transfer in manufacturing components by conducting a comprehensive 'turnkey' project.[9] Obviously, the attractions of a potentially large market and the opportunity for a long-term partnership with local manufacturers were the key elements for BTM's interest in the project (Shen, 1999, p. 64).

As the huge size of the domestic market provided the government with a strong bargaining position in dealing with multinational corporations (MNCs), the Chinese government made a requirement that three conditions must be satisfied when a foreign firm enters China to establish a joint venture in the telecommunication business. The first condition is that the Chinese side must hold a majority share of more than 50 per cent (in the case of Shanghai Bell, the share is 60 per cent); the second is that the foreign side must transfer important technology to the Chinese side, and the third is that the custom large-scale integrated (LSI) chips used in telecommunication equipment must be produced within China (Zhu, 2000). Following these conditions, Bell Telephone Manufacturing Company (BTM) agreed to transfer the technologies that the Chinese requested in its joint venture, Shanghai Bell. The first preliminary agreement between BTM and the Posts and Telecommunications Industrial Corporation (PTIC) was therefore signed in Luoyang in November 1980.[10]

Indigenous R&D consortium

Now, before discussing the specific linkages between Shanghai Bell and the indigenous Chinese firms, let us provide a first introduction to the three organizations constituting the R&D consortium which were jointly responsible for the indigenous development of digital switches (HJD-04) in China. The three organizations are: the Center for Information Technology (CIT) under the Zhengzhou Institute of Information Engineering (ZIIE) belonging to the People's Liberation Army, the Posts and Telecommunications

Industrial Corporation (PTIC), and the Luoyang Telephone Equipment Factory (LTEF) of MPT. The CIT was the research arm of the Army and played the role of initiator of the project; the PTIC was originally the procurement unit of the MPT and played the role of general project manager and financial sponsor, and the LTEF used to be a producer of crossbar switches and later emerged as the initial producer of the HJD-04. These three organizations had different motivations and backgrounds when joining this consortium.

Although this tripartite R&D consortium played a key role in the development of indigenous digital electronic switches in China, diffusion of knowledge from Shanghai Bell to this consortium was critical. Let us illustrate this point. First of all, the designers of HJD-04 absorbed the knowledge of Shanghai Bell's System-12, and the main manufacturer, LTEF, sought technical help from Shanghai Bell. This was possible as LTEF is a PTIC subsidiary factory, and PTIC is Shanghai Bell's major shareholder.

First, Professor Wu, the key designer for HJD-04 at the CIT, acquired information about System-12 and other foreign systems through publicly available documents. Some of the other engineers, who had experience in helping the System-12 project, also contributed to the development of HJD-04. Second, many local Chinese were involved in the process of adapting the System-12 to the Chinese environment and contributed with their learned knowledge and skill to the development of indigenous switches. When producing, installing and maintaining System-12, the consortium always sought help from the MPT engineering teams and experienced engineers in local PTAs (Post and Telecommunication Authorities) in provinces (Zhang, 2000, p. 230). The MPT brought to Shanghai Bell a group of highly skilled staff from MPT's R&D institutes, universities and factories across the country. Among them there were many experienced senior engineers and professors who were knowledgeable in the field. They played a crucial role in building up the company in the early stages. Thereafter, most of them returned to their institutes and some subsequently used the knowledge they had obtained from the System-12 to carry out various R&D projects for Shanghai Bell. Some of these specialists participated in the development of the HJD-04 technology (Shen, 1999, pp. 76–7). This process of technology diffusion gave birth to, and led to the operation of new types of digital automatic exchanges developed by the indigenous units (Zhang, 2000, p. 232; Wu, 1997, pp. 75–6). Third, the LTEF sought help by sending delegations to Shanghai Bell to explore suitable solutions when developing its production facilities and management approaches (Shen, 1999, p. 153). As a result, the LTEF was able to upgrade its technological capabilities. Finally, as Shanghai Bell brought its components production facilities in line with world quality standards and technologies, the manufacturers of HJD-04 were able to buy these components readily and cheaply within China.

To summarize, the designers of the indigenous switch, HJD-04, first started by conducting research on Shanghai Bell's System-12, using publicly available documents. Also, some of the other engineers participating in the development of HJD-04 were recruited from those who had participated in the Shanghai Bell System-12 project. Moreover, the main manufacturer (LTEF) of the HJD-04 sought direct technical help from Shanghai Bell. Therefore, with some experience of computer technology and telecommunication technology, together with an array of available foreign technologies from JVs, the institute (CIT/ZIIE), in cooperation with LTEF and PTIC, developed the first successful central-office-level digital switches in China in 1991. It should be noted that the project was initiated by engineers led by Professor Wu working in CIT. The CIT invited first the LTEF, and later sought help from the PTIC as a financial sponsor (Shen, 1999, p. 174; Mu, 2002, pp. 233–4).

As a next step, to produce the HJD-04 on a large scale, the consortium cooperated with the joint initiatives by the MPT and MEI (Ministry of Electronics Industry) to establish a manufacturing company, called Great Dragon (Julong). Great Dragon was actually a business group comprising nine affiliated companies including the LTEF (Zhang, 2000, p. 151). With the joint sales activities of the nine affiliated companies, the HJD-04 has experienced rapid growth in sales since 1992. The average annual growth in sales has been over 200 per cent for the past three years. In 1994, the market share of HJD-04 went from zero to 16 per cent. The annual single shift capacity for HJD-04 in late 1995 was 4.6 million lines. By October 1998, cumulative sales of HJD-04 were 16 million lines, next to Shanghai Bell's sales of 23 million lines.[11]

After the development of the HJD-04 in 1991, knowledge diffusion grew further through the collaboration of engineers and other personnel, which finally led to the successive development of four other types of digital automatic switches (C&C08, EIM-601, ZXJ-10 and SP-30) by other indigenous firms. The later development of other types of digital switch by firms such as ZTE (Zhongxing), Datang, and finally Huawei, all benefited from knowledge diffusion via inter-firm mobility of skilled engineers. For example, Huawei's location at Shenzhen and higher salary levels attracted skilled manpower from Great Dragon (original manufacturer of HJD-04). Many skilled young engineers, who had mastered or who at least had knowledge of the HJD-04 system, left Great Dragon for Huawei (or ZTE).[12] They had contributed to the R&D of another digital switching system, C&C08, in Huawei.

2.4.2   Korea

In Korea, in the process of indigenous development of digital switches (the so-called TDX), some technology was absorbed by licensing with ITT, AT&T and LM Ericsson/Erifon, and was augmented by their prior experiences with producing analogue switches by licensing agreements.

The development of Korean's own digital switching system TDX series was on the basis of purchased technology from advanced countries which goes back to the 1970s. Before developing and producing its own digital switches, the Korean government decided to purchase or license analogue switching technology at first because of its weak technological and financial capability. In order to purchase manufacturing technology on analogue switching and to produce switches in Korea, in September 1977 the state-owned company Korea Telecom Co., purchased M10CN technology from Bell Telephone Manufacturing Company (BTM), the subsidiary of ITT (Korea Telecom Co (KTC) was acquired by Samsung Semiconductor & Telecom which was integrated with Samsung Electronics). Because one company alone was not able to meet the market demand for switches, another joint venture, GoldStar Semiconductor, was established by the Lucky GoldStar Group and AT&T. GoldStar Semiconductor imported No.1A technology from AT&T in November 1979 (Hwang, 1993).

Two years later, KTC continued to license digital switching S1240 technology from ITT, and GoldStar imported digital switching 5ESS technology from AT&T. Although the establishment of JVs and technology imports have helped the Koreans access switching system knowledge, they have not directly led to the indigenous development of the digital switching system in Korea. By 1979, under the guidelines set by the government's fourth five-year national economic development plan, 300000 new telephone lines were being activated each year. The effort, however, still left Korea farther and farther behind in meeting its own explosive growth in telephone services. As a result, in 1982 the government decided that the manufacturer of its own TDX switches would not be able to meet demand and that it would have to nurture its telecommunication technology. It hoped that such a movement would help the nation to devise a more effective strategy for satisfying its demands for advanced information technologies, particularly the phone system networking technologies.

The Ministry of Post and Telecommunication's strategy was therefore that imports and domestic development should be implemented simultaneously during this period. In the early 1980s the Korean government was not sure that its domestic technology was able to develop its own digital switching system, so the ETRI publicly purchased digital switching design and engineering technology from Ericsson (Hwang, 1993). Based

on the imported digital switching design and engineering technology of
Ericsson's AXE-10, the ETRI first developed a prototype called model
TDX-1X in July 1982 (Kim, 2000, p. 136) and this achievement enabled
Korea to become the tenth country in the world to develop an electronic
switching system. Thereafter, the Korean team succeeded in developing
a differentiated product, TDX-1, in December 1983, which was more
effective than the AXE-10 (Mu, 2002).

The ETRI transferred the technology of the TDX-1 to four manufacturing firms: GoldStar Semiconductor, Daewoo Telecom, Dongyang
Electronic & Telecom and Samsung Semiconductor and Telecom. After
the successful development of the TDX-1 switching system, ETRI continued to improve the technology in collaboration with a network of actors
consisting of the ETRI, the TDX's manufacturing firms, KT and universities, to produce more advanced versions, such as the TDX-1A, which was
developed in 1986 and can accommodate up to 10240 subscribers. The
TDX-1A technology was quickly transferred to manufacturers that initially mass produced the systems mainly for rural and small city markets.
In order to improve the TDX-1's capacity and other features, in December
1988, the TDX's manufacturing firms developed the TDX-1B, with a
capacity of 20000 lines. Then the ETIR, combined with the TDX's manufacturing firms, KT and universities, developed a large capacity switching
system, TDX-10, which is a newly designed product with a 100000-line
capacity.

2.4.3 Brazil

In Brazil, the CPqD launched an R&D programme in 1977 to develop its
own digital switches, and many researchers at USP (Universidade de São
Paulo) who had produced a prototype of a small digital switch moved
to CPqD. CPqD built up considerable innovation capability in concep-
tualizing and designing digital switching systems, especially during the
period 1976–1991. The developed technology was effectively transferred
to domestic private sector manufacturers who then began to manufacture
and sell these domestically designed switches to the state-owned operating
company, Telebras. However, the opening up of the Brazilian manufacturing sector to foreign investment meant that some of these domestic
manufacturing firms were taken over by multinational companies. This
resulted in the number of wholly owned Brazilian companies being significantly reduced to just one. Despite this increased competition from MNC
manufacturers within the country and from imports from abroad, Tropico
switches were still able to maintain their market share. There is a general
feeling in the literature that the technological capability of the domestic

innovation system has decreased as a result of this liberalization of the equipment manufacturing sector, the privatization of the telecom services distribution segment, and the privatization of the main laboratory itself. However, the quantitative evidence that is used to demonstrate this is not very robust and is open to question.

2.4.4 India

In India, a GRI, or C-DOT, had succeeded in developing its own digital switches more or less indigenously. C-DOT was established as a stand-alone public R&D organization by the central government in 1984. The core team at C-DOT came from two research groups from elsewhere, namely from the Telecommunications Research Centre and the Tata Institute of Fundamental Research. It was charged with the responsibility of developing a family of digital switching systems that were suitable for the Indian usage pattern and conditions. Its scope has now been broadened to include transmission and access products as well. Over time, C-DOT has developed a wide range of switching and transmission products both for rural and urban applications. It is claimed that while the C-DOT main exchange can also function as a mobile switching centre for GSM Cellular Service, the small rural automatic exchanges developed for the rural environment can work without air conditioning. They come complete with SS7 Intelligent Network signalling systems. In addition ISDN facilities are also available; what is unique is that these switches have been designed to operate without air conditioning in harsh environments. About 45 000 exchanges with a total of about 23 million telephone lines have been installed in India. This means that approximately 50 per cent of the equipped capacity in the country is based on C-DOT designed switches. Bulk exports have been made to about 22 countries such as Vietnam, Bangladesh, Ethiopia, Nepal, Ghana and Uganda. This systematic vendor development shows that there have been considerable technology spillovers to downstream industries as well. However, over time, and especially during the period since 1995, it is clear that the GRI failed to take into account the fact that the future of the Indian telecommunications industry lay in wireless communication and consequently it did not re-orient its research strategy to encompass this technology which was to become the mainstay of India's telecom industry.

Both in Brazil and India, the respective laboratories developed the switches more or less on their own although the capability was indeed developed in an incremental fashion. Furthermore, a common pattern in the indigenous development of digital switches was the tripartite R&D consortium among the GRIs in charge of R&D, SOEs or the Ministry itself in charge of financing and coordination, and private companies in charge of manufacturing from the initial or later stages.

2.5 SSI BUILDING BLOCK 2: DEMAND CONDITIONS

In all the four cases, there was great and ever-increasing demand for modern telecommunication, but the demand was being met by imported goods or MNCs. Furthermore, to a certain extent, markets were segmented between rural and urban markets for differentiated products. Thus it can be said that the initial products developed locally by the latecomer firms or R&D units had no choice but to target low-end or rural markets with smaller capacity. Since these markets were somewhat neglected by the MNCs or not suitable for MNCs' products, they played the role of initial nurturing bases for local products.

2.5.1 China

China is a typical segmented market with respect to geography, socio-demographics and lifestyles (Schmitt, 1997; Kotler, 2001). The telecommunication equipment market in China is not only huge, but also segmented. One of the most important characteristics of this market is a kind of dualism: rural–urban dualism and core–periphery dualism. In other words, there are two different markets in China: one similar to developed countries and the other more often found in underdeveloped countries. In terms of the level of general economic development as well as the existing telecommunications network conditions, different areas of China vary to a considerable extent. Many inland districts and rural areas lag far behind the coastal, urban areas and large cities. Thus demand for telecommunication services from inland districts or rural areas is different from that in large cities as these areas are often not able to afford expensive foreign digital automatic switches. Given the knowledge about the Chinese market, Chinese firms first targeted the rural or lower-end market in China's public telecommunications network, while all foreign companies were aiming at large cities.

Apart from the three international gateways, there were five levels in the public network: levels 1 to 4 (known as C1, C2, C3, C4) were transit switches, and level 5 (known as C5) was comprised of terminal switches. There were eight level-1 (C1) transit switching centres; 22 level-2 (C2) transit switching centres were located in the capital cities of provinces or autonomous regions; level-3 (C3) transit switching centres were located in each district; level-4 switches (C4) at the county level; and level-5 (C5) terminal switches were located in every major city and town. The HJD-04 system could be used at C4 level or lower (although technologically it was designed also to meet the requirements at the C3 level). It had a capacity of approximately 30 000 (later 60 000 lines) subscriber lines and could be used as local or tandem switches. Up until 1993, the C3 and higher levels were dominated by foreign systems. However, there was a large market for the HJD-04 at the lower levels (about four times bigger than the C3 and higher markets), which foreign systems either had not yet focused on or had difficulties in entering.

This HJD-04 had a simple machine-operator interface, with a Chinese language screen menu. Due to its low development and production costs, this kind of switch was provided at much lower prices, which made it popular in rural areas at first. According to Shenzhen Special Zone Daily, in the mid-1990s, 90 per cent of Huawei's products were installed in C4 or C5; 100 per cent of Zhongxing's products were applied to C4 or C5. Since 1997, Zhongxing's products began to enter C3; in contrast, 90 per cent of Shanghai Bell's products were installed in C3 or upwards.[13]

Given the *ex-post* importance of rural markets, one might ask why the MNCs or JVs ignored this market. Our first answer is that the urban markets were large enough for the MNCs to indulge themselves in when they entered China from the mid-1980s to the early 1990s. A more important answer is that even if they wanted to go for the rural market, their products were not suitable for it. Transmission quality and transmission lines varied greatly in different areas of China. Under the low network level and the poor network conditions, foreign systems were rarely able to work. In addition, many foreign systems were designed for lower usage of lines. However, the rural market was characterized by a combination of low telephone penetration rates and intensive use of each telephone set. Thus, the foreign systems ran into problems, sometimes even leading to breakdowns in the local network.[14] Furthermore, the screen menus of all the foreign systems were in English. Outside the big cities it was difficult to find operators who could understand English. The products by the MNC and the JVs were also expensive compared to the local products. In sum, in terms of the sources for competitive advantage, the expected opportunity for market success was high for indigenous Chinese firms. On the one hand, in competition with the foreign or local JV firms within China, the indigenous firms took advantage of the segmented nature of the Chinese market. On the other hand, when later competing in the international export market, they took advantage of relatively cheap labour costs and plenty of other resources. Thus, digital automatic switches manufactured by indigenous firms enjoyed several sources for competitive advantage.

After having significantly improved product quality and added new features, indigenous manufacturers began to compete directly with local JVs in both rural and urban Chinese markets after the mid-1990s, and eventually in world markets.

2.5.2 Korea

In Korea the indigenously developed switch or TDX-1 (10 240-line capacity) first targeted rural areas or smaller cities in March 1986. The four areas where TDX-1 was installed include Gapyoung, Jeonkok, Goryung and Muju, which are all rural areas, not even cities (Kim, 2000, p. 138). It was only after success with the experimental installation in these four areas that the KT (Korea Telecom) decided on its plan to produce the model on a large scale in late 1986: from 1987 the modified model (TDX-1A) with a capacity of 10 240 lines was installed on a large scale, covering 36 areas in the nation with a total capacity of 189 000 lines. The same was true for the TDX-1B (22 528 lines), which was developed in 1989 by four private companies. The first large-capacity switch targeting urban areas was the TDX-10 (over 50 000 lines), which was developed in 1991.

2.5.3 Brazil

In both Brazil and India, the demand for telecom equipment was supported by public technology procurement in the period up to the late 1990s. In Brazil, until 1998 the state-owned service provider, Telebras, was the only consumer. Further, the demand up to this time was only for fixed line telecom equipment. However, all this was to change in that year when two important developments took place: first Telebras was privatized, which meant that there were several new – but only private – providers of telecom services. Some of them were even foreign owned. This meant that the state was unable to practise public technology procurement. But secondly, to minimize the ill effects of this change for the local industry, the state put in place an ingenious legal instrument, called Resolution no. 155 of 1999. ANATEL, through this resolution, regulated service contracting procedures and the purchase of equipment or materials by telecommunications service providers. This resolution provides further discipline regarding clauses included in the Concession Contracts and Authorization Terms for the provisioning of Fixed Switched Telephone Service, FSTS, and similar clauses contained in the Brazilian Satellite Exploitation Rights Term entered into by the Providers of Telecommunications Services and ANATEL. As regards the Concession Contracts and Authorization Terms, the provider has to base its purchase/contracting decisions, with respect to the various offers presented, on the satisfaction of the objective price criteria, delivery terms and technical specifications established in the pertinent regulations.

If proposals presented by duly qualified companies are equal, the provider will apply a tie-breaking criterion:

- preference to services offered by companies located in Brazil; or
- preference for equipment and material produced in Brazil, including, those with domestic technology.

The equivalency mentioned above will be determined when the following conditions are cumulatively present:

- the domestic price is lower than or equal to the price of the imported product, placed in the national territory, including the taxes incurred;
- the delivery term is compatible with the requirements of the service; and
- the technical specifications established in the pertinent regulations are satisfied, including relatively to ANATEL's certification patterns, when applicable.

The resolution does not apply to providers whose legal status is that of a public company or mixed capital company, as they are governed by a specific law regarding the procedures for the acquisition of services, equipment and materials.

However, it must be pointed out that the Brazilian-developed Tropico switches had a market share of only about 25 per cent as it was only in the market for local switches.

2.5.4 India

In India, too, the government stimulated demand for the C-DOT-developed switches through public technology procurement. Consequently indigenous switches had a market share of very nearly 50 per cent. But there have been many instances, especially during the 1990s, in which the state has discriminated against domestic technology. The public technology procurement can be explained as follows.

It has a decentralized telecom switches procurement policy. In order to simplify the procurement process, the department receives tenders and sets a fixed rate through a tendering process commonly known as a 'rate contract' after which the Chief General Managers of the various telecom circles are authorized to purchase their requirements from approved vendors.[15] The Telecommunications Engineering Centre (TEC) within the department sets the technical standards of all telecom products, including switches.[16] Thirty per cent of the total requirements of switching equipment are reserved for public sector enterprise. However, the price at which this 30 per cent is procured is at the lowest price quotation received for the remaining 70 per cent, for which an open tender is invited. This reservation price is referred to as the L1 price. It is thus seen that the public sector producer of switching equipment has actually to bid for 30 per cent of the switching requirements without actually knowing the price at which the bid is going to be made. Thus it is clear that the public procurement process followed in the case of switching equipments does not afford any protection to the public sector producer, which in this case is ITI Ltd in Bangalore. The price–performance ratio is thus the main criterion for selection rather than other non-technical considerations, such as deferred credit facilities. For several years at least, given the near monopoly position of the government carriers, the public procurement policy will be an effective instrument for stimulating local R&D activities. However, with the growth of private service providers, this will be less effective, especially when the private sector providers, who are in the initial years of establishment, also take into account deferred credit facilities which only the MNC vendors can offer.

2.6   SSI BUILDING BLOCK 3: ACTORS

So far, the stories look similar among the four countries, but differences are starting to emerge in the area of the role of actors – the government in particular. While the government played an active role in promotion and coordination in both China and Korea, this was not the case in either India or Brazil. This was the seed for the divergence between the two groups of countries.

2.6.1   China

In China the government gave market protection and incentives for domestic products. The role of the government also became decisive when the indigenous Chinese firms started to compete directly with the JVs in both rural and urban areas (Mu and Lee, 2005). The role of the Chinese government was basically to provide market protection and to give incentives for the adoption and use of domestic products. In 1996, the government stopped arranging foreign government loans to import digital automatic switch equipment. Instead, the Chinese government began to impose tariffs on imported communication equipment and to promote the purchase of locally made equipment. The sum of the market shares of local firms (including Sino-foreign joint ventures) was 63.1 per cent in 1995 (Mu, 2002). One year after these tariffs were introduced, the figure reached 84.8 per cent in 1996, and in 1997 it reached over 90 per cent, namely 94.9 per cent.

From 1997 the MPT organized coordinating conferences every year with the Administrative Bureaux of Post and Telecommunication. Through these conferences, the MPT encouraged the Administrative Bureaux of Post and Telecommunication to prioritize the purchase of indigenous equipment if the equipment was suitable and was priced appropriately. During the first conference, contracts for more than 5 million lines were signed, and eventually more than 7 million lines of digital automatic exchange were sold. In the second coordinating conference, contracts for 17 million lines of digital automatic switch were agreed and 18 million lines were eventually sold. These two coordinating conferences were a turning point for the growth of the communication manufacturing industry in China (Xin and Wang, 2000). For example, in the second coordination conference, Huawei gained 6.505 million lines of orders, which was 40 per cent of the total orders for 1997 and 1998 (Xu and Fu, 1997). Encouraged by the People's Bank of China, the China Construction Bank supplied Huawei buyer credit RMB 3.85 billion, which was 45 per cent of the bank's total buyer credit in 1998.[17]

As a result of the coordinating conferences and financial support, since 1998 the indigenous firms' market shares have increased rapidly and they have become the main suppliers in the domestic market. In the urban market, indigenous firms claimed 21 per cent of the market; but in the rural market, they dominated with a market share of 80 per cent.[18] The four indigenous manufacturers, Great Dragon, Datang, Zhongxing and Huawei, held more than 60 per cent of China's digital automatic switch market in 1998 (Table 3, Mu and Lee, 2005).

2.6.2 Korea

In Korea, too, as in China, government support and protection were important factors in supporting the Korean-made switching systems as the ministry or the government procured the indigenously developed switches in the 1980s. Mu (2002) provides details on the role of the government.

Government policy statements, both in writing and in public, offered valuable guideposts for outlining government priorities and trying to build citizen support. During the early stages of the Korean TDX program's implementation, in order to overcome the nation's deficiencies, the government decided that the ETRI, the KTA (Korean Telecommunications Authority)[19] and the four domestic manufacturers (LGIC, Samsung Electronics, Daewoo Telecom and Hanwha Telecom) would join the project, fully sharing and utilizing their resources. With the government acting as 'grand coordinator', the combined ideas and actions of researchers, users and manufacturers were brought to bear in an effort to meet the project's goals. The synergy that this partnership created largely accounts for the success of the innovative experience.

After the TDX-1 was successfully developed, the Korean government began to implement some policies to support indigenous firms' growth. For example: (a) in the mid-1980s, the Korean government limited imports of foreign switches as often as possible; (b) in order to encourage manufacturing firms to learn technology and promote investment, the Korean government implemented a quota mechanism for the four firms' market shares. The Korean government passed a special law to promote investment in the TDX project, which guaranteed domestic manufacturers a market for the TDX through KT's purchases of the technology's by-products for early network modernization. The law also created a financial mechanism for continuous funding of ETRI research by requiring a portion of the profits earned by the domestic TDX manufacturers (Hwang, 1993).

Moreover, KT also provided the R&D funds for the TDX series. It also prepared user requirements that specified the desired capacities for the TDX series – TDX -1, 1A, 1B, 1B/ISDN, 10, 10/ISDN, 10A – and the functions required for commercial telecommunication services.

2.6.3 Brazil

Brazil initially pursued clear industrial policies for the promotion of indigenous products but gave up owing to political instability and later moves to liberalization (for example, the elimination of market guarantees for local products and local content requirement in the 1990s). Nevertheless, after a period of flux around the late 1990s, the state has stepped in with a number of instruments to support local technology development. These could be summarized as follows.

These instruments could broadly be divided into: (a) those leading to more R&D investment through essentially fiscal instruments; and (b) those leading to an assured market for the output of this R&D essentially through legal instruments stipulating the procurement of these products by service providers. Historically speaking, the latter type of instruments were more important during the pre-privatization phase while in the post-privatization phase the former were more important. While this categorization is, by and large, watertight and these categories are mutually exclusive, there are notable exceptions. For instance, the Laws of Informatics of 7232 and especially its amended version of 8248 involve both public technology procurement and provision of fiscal incentives for R&D. But since it is more of a legal instrument, although with fiscal implications, we treat it in the former category. Since some of the legal instruments for promoting innovation were discussed above, here we restrict ourselves to a discussion of the fiscal instruments.

Provision of research grants for technological development of telecommunications

Although the Brazilian government had privatized CPqD, it did put in place a national fund, called the Fund for Technological Development of Telecommunications (Fundo para Desenvolvimento Tecnológico das Telecomunicações, FUNTTEL), which was established by Law 10,052 of 28 November 2000, in order to stimulate the process of technological innovation, enhance human resources capacity, generate new jobs and promote access for small and medium-sized companies to capital resources, and amplify the competitiveness of the Brazilian telecommunications industry. Contribution to FUNTTEL by all telecommunication services companies started on 28 March 2001, at a rate of 0.5 per cent of the amount of gross operating telecommunication services' revenue.

Subsequently Decree 4733 of 2003, concerning the telecommunications sector development, provides guidelines for the use of FUNTTEL for R&D as well as for incentives for research institutions to develop technologies that improve access to telecommunications services.[20] The decree also announced policy goals, to become effective on 1 January 2006, concerning methods for setting and adjusting rates, billing procedures, portability of local numbers for residential and non-residential customers, defining a 'locality' and clarity as to direct or indirect stockholdings by Brazilian or foreign legal entities so as to permit knowledge of the composition of the capital of the company and to verify compliance.

FUNTTEL is managed by BNDES and FINEP. Thirty per cent of its funding is to be given to CPqD. The fund became operational from mid-2001, so it is too early to assess its performance. Based on the initial data available, up to the end of 2004, 16 projects had been approved, of which two belonged to CPqD. Based on the value of approved projects, it could be seen that 88 per cent of the total budget was already allocated and with a portion of the remaining projects which are under evaluation becoming successful, the total budget for the year would be successfully allocated. This rather high success rate for applications may also be an indirect measure of the innovation capability that is resident in the country.[21]

As noted before, the amount of funds available under FUNTTEL is a function of the sales revenues of the service providers. Since these are bound to increase in the future, there should be no problem financing this scheme. Thus, it can be seen that the establishment of this financial instrument is yet another support mechanism used by the Brzilian state to maintain its innovation capability.

Provision of deferred credit facilities

It is well known that the sales of equipment and machinery are not only based on price–performance criteria, but are also based on the availability of credit facilities. Small equipment manufacturers based in developing countries do not usually have the financial wherewithal to access such deferred credit access and this can hamper the sale of products based on domestic technology in particular. The issue is all the more complicated by the availability of bilateral credit as the Telemar–Japan Bank for International Cooperation loan episode of 2001 shows.

However, it must be noted that during 1999–2002, the BNDES has put in place a credit facility known as 'Programme for Support of Investments in Telecommunications'. Over two-thirds of the amount sanctioned under this credit facility has gone towards purchase assembly and installation of equipments by both fixed line and cellular providers (BNDES, 2000).

Tariff protection

Although Brazil joined the World Trade Organization (WTO) in 1995, it has yet to sign the WTO's Information Technology Agreement which reduces tariffs on information and communications products to zero. The average import duty for telecommunications equipment is 15–17 per cent, although it is expected to come down over time (the average mean applied tariff for all goods was 11.8 per cent in 2002). In switching equipment it ranged from 8–21 per cent in 2003 and is expected to decrease to 8–16 per cent by 2006. This lowering tariff means that the Brazilian telecom equipment industry will have increasingly to compete with foreign imports. Imports of switching and other telecommunication equipment have shown significant increases during this period.

Thus it is seen that Brazil's efforts to maintain its innovation capability through the operation of legal and fiscal instruments are sometimes effectively challenged by the availability of bilateral credit and the continued reduction in import duties. This may accentuate as the country gets effectively absorbed into NAFTA.

2.6.4 India

In India, in contrast, there are instances in which the Indian state positively discriminated against the wider diffusion of the indigenously designed C-DOT switches by allowing imports of the same. For instance, it is clear from an answer to an 'unstarred' question in the upper house of the Indian parliament that the DoT procured almost five times the tendered quantity of switching equipment during the same period, supposedly for modernizing the network with ISDN.[22] But the number of subscribers using ISDN in the whole country was only 309.[23] So it is clear that the DoT appears to have purchased this 'overspecified' equipment far in excess of its actual requirement and this 'excess purchase' appears to have eroded the market share of C-DOT. Furthermore the Comptroller and Auditor General of India (2000) found a number of other irregularities with this tendering process. For instance, although most of the components of this switching equipment were imported by the suppliers, the DoT assumed an import content of as little as 23 per cent while working out a reduction on rates on account of the fall in customs duty in the 1995–96 budget. This inaccurate assumption by the DoT led to an excess payment of Rs 405 million to the suppliers, with a corresponding loss to the government exchequer. The DoT also had to make an unavoidable expenditure of Rs 639 million in the procurement of these exchanges against the 1997–99 tender due to the failure of the Tender Evaluation Committee (TEC) to submit its report within the bid validity period: it took 190 days to finalize its report against the prescribed limit of 42 days.

2.7 TRANSITION TO WIRELESS TELECOMMUNICATION

Wireless telecommunication technologies use radio, satellite, laser and infra-red transmissions to deliver data for networks or phone systems. There are numerous applications for wireless technologies.[24] Broadly speaking, applications of wireless technologies are divided into the following: (a) voice and messaging; (b) hand-held and other Internet-enabled devices; and (c) data networking. Mobile phones, pagers and two-way business radios come under voice and messaging services. These devices can be further divided into two categories depending on what standards they are based on. They can be either analogue or digital, depending upon the way in which they process signals and encode information. The analogue standard is the Advanced Mobile Phone System (AMPS). Digital standards are the Global System for Mobile Communications (GSM), or Code Division Multiple Access (CDMA). Compared with the digital system, the early developed analogue system had many disadvantages as a cellular communication. For instance, it didn't support encryption, compression and ISDN compatibility. So a new mobile system called GSM has been developed.

GSM utilizes a technology called the time division multiple access (TDMA), in which several different calls may share the same carrier and each call is assigned a particular time slot. GSM digitizes and compresses data, then sends it down a channel with two other streams of user data, each in its own time slot. It operates at either the 900 MHz or 1800 MHz frequency band. CDMA is another digital wireless technology that works by converting speech into digital information, which is then transmitted as a radio signal over a wireless network. Using a unique code to distinguish each call, CDMA uses spectrum efficiently, enabling more people to share the airwaves simultaneously without static, cross-talk or interference.

Wireless telecommunication technologies are divided into several generations in terms of technical functions. The first generation (1G) network is the analogue cellular system, which started in the early 1980s. It serves only voice transmission at a bandwidth of 9.6 kbit/s and has no data transmission capability. The second generation, or 2G, superseded 1G by using digital signals for the first time with a bandwidth of 9.6 to 14.1 kbit/s. Since its introduction, 2G technology has steadily improved, with increased bandwidth, packet routing, and the introduction of multimedia functions. 2Gs are divided into TDMA (Time Division Multiple Access) based and CDMA (Code Division Multiple Access) standards depending on the type of multiplexing used. The 2.5G networks, such as GPRS (General Packet Radio Services) and CDMA2000 1x, are the enhanced versions of 2G networks with data rates up to about 144 kbit/s. 2.5G is a stepping stone between 2G and 3G cellular wireless technologies. While the terms '2G' and '3G' are officially defined, '2.5G' is not. It was invented for marketing purposes only. The 2.5G provides some of the benefits of 3G (e.g. it is packet-switched) and can use some of the existing 2G infrastructure in GSM and CDMA networks. GPRS is a 2.5G technology used by GSM operators. Some protocols, such as CDMA2000 1x-RTT for CDMA, can qualify as '3G' services because they have a data rate of above 144 kbit/s, but are considered by most to be 2.5G services (or 2.75G, which sounds even more sophisticated) because they are several times slower than 'true' 3G services (Mishra, 2004).

3G also uses digital signals and has data rates of 384 kbit/s and more.[25] It is based on the International Telecommunication Union (ITU) family of standards under the International Mobile Telecommunications programme, IMT-2000. 3G technologies enable network operators to offer users a wider range of more advanced services, such as automatic global roaming, while achieving greater network capacity through improved spectral efficiency. Services include wide-area wireless voice telephony, video calls, and broadband wireless data, all in a mobile environment (Selian, 2001). Additional features include HSPA (High-Speed Packet Access) data transmission capabilities that enable transmission speeds up to 14.4 Mbit/s on the downlink and 5.8Mbit/s on the uplink.[26] Examples of the 3G networks include: CDMA2000 1x EVDO, CDMA2000 3x, TD-SCDMA, Arib WCDMA, IMT-2000 DECT, and others.

The technological regimes of wireless telecommunication feature a high frequency of innovations, highly uncertain (volatile) trajectories, a large amount of R&D required, and an ever-evolving knowledge base (Lee and Lim, 2001). Thus it can be said that it is difficult for the latecomer to attempt a catch-up. But, as the thesis of leapfrogging suggests, everybody is a beginner in this new generation of technologies; this implies some possibility for success targeting the first mover advantages. But it can also imply greater barriers to catch-up. The final outcome will depend on the existing level of capabilities and on getting the necessary access to a foreign knowledge base.

2.7.1 The Korean Case

The development of the CDMA cellular phone system and initiation of services in Korea is one of the most successful cases of a path-creating catching up or leapfrogging, led by private–public collaboration (Lee and Lim, 2001). When the Korean firms and the government authorities considered development of the cellular phone system, the analogue system was dominant in the USA, and the TDMA-based GSM system was the dominant system in Europe. However, the Korean authorities (Ministry of Information and Telecommunication) were impressed by the emerging CDMA technology with its higher efficiency in frequency utilization and higher quality and security in voice transmission. Thus, despite great uncertainty over the development of the world's first CDMA system, as well as strong reservations expressed by the telephone service provider and the system manufacturers, such as Korea Telecom, Samsung and LG, the Ministry and the ETRI (Electronics and Telecommunication Research Institute) decided to go along with the CDMA. Although it was in 1995 that the first test of the CDMA system was conducted, the Korean government first designated the CDMA system development as a national R&D project as early as 1989. This also meant that the Korean authorities were quite well informed of the trend in telecommunication technology and had foresight.

In 1991 the contract was drawn up to introduce the core technology from, and to develop the system together with, the US-based Qualcomm. In 1993 the Ministry declared CDMA to be the national standard in telecommunication. Korean subscribers (more than 6 million now) accounted for more than 75 per cent of worldwide CDMA subscribers in the mid-1990s, and Korea also started the CDMA-based PCS service in 1997.

With its high frequency of innovation and high fluidity of trajectory, the telecommunication industry does not give latecomers any incentives for R&D effort. Expected profits and other related gains from first mover advantages served as a strong attraction, and the high risks were shared by the government-led R&D consortium and knowledge alliance with Qualcomm. The ETRI also contributed to reducing technological uncertainty by providing accurate and up-to-date information on technology trends and by identifying the correct R&D target that was more promising than alternatives.

In achieving the leapfrogging by taking a different path, the role of the government was very critical in taking the initiative to form a R&D consortium with private firms and pushing them ahead. However, it should be noted that the core technology was bought from Qualcomm, and thus Korean producers still have to pay heavy royalty fees, the equivalent of 5.25 per cent of sales revenue per mobile phone unit, in addition to a lump sum for the technology licensing. The localization ratio in the mobile phone was only 30 per cent, and most of the core part including the MSM electronic chip is imported. However, in 1997, ETRI succeeded in developing the MSM chip by itself, and subsequently in 1999 Samsung declared that it could produce most of the core chips required in CDMA mobile phones. That meant the completion of the core part assimilation stage by mean of reverse engineering. Korean firms are now worldwide leaders in CDMA-based phones, and they are now entering the final stage of the creation and design of the new product concept using reverse engineering.

The Korean success in the world-first development of the CDMA system co-developed with Qualcomm (US-based venture company at that time with the core CDMA technology) indicates the importance of knowledge access which helped to overcome the disadvantages posed by uncertainty facing CDMA technology which emerged only after GSM technology developed in Europe (Lee and Lim, 2001).

2.7.2   The Chinese Case

Situation up to the 1G and 2G era: foreign dominance and catch-up
The mobile handset industry has entered a boom stage in China since 1998. From 1998–2003, the annual market growth rate reached more than

50 per cent. By the end of 2003, the number of mobile handset users in China reached 270 million, making it the largest user of handsets in the world. The mobile handset industry is also one of the fastest-growing industries in China.

However, in terms of technology, in the period of the first generation (1G), the Chinese market was completely controlled by foreign products, from base stations and switches to handsets. For example, in the early years of the Chinese handset market, Motorola and other foreign companies controlled the whole market. Later on, Nokia and Ericsson joined Motorola as dominant firms. In 1999 foreign brands had a 92.2 per cent share of the market. Local brands only had 5.3 per cent. During this time, mobile phones were very expensive: the price was about RMB 50 000 to 60 000 (or USD 6000 to 7000) per set. Indigenous makers, such as Eastern Telecom, could only produce the handset through OEM (own equipment manufacturing) for Motorola in the form of SKD (semi-knockdown) and CKD (complete knockdown) production in which all parts and modules were imported. There were about 6 million users in China in 1999.[27]

However, efforts in learning and R&D by indigenous companies began as early as 1995, and their initial target was learning the 2G technology. Huawei developed the sample equipment GSM900 handset in October 1997. ZTE succeeded in the commercialization of its GSM product ZXG10 series in 1999. Zhongxing Company (ZTE) developed the Chinese-based dual-band handset in May 1999. In March 2000, this handset model passed the FTA test and became the first indigenous brand in China with its own intellectual property rights (IPR) in the handset field. By 2001 Huawei had developed all GSM systems and CDMA-ystems (Xia, 2001). Regarding CDMA-based wireless telecommunication technology, in 1995 ZTE imitated R&D on the key technology of CDMA. In November 1999, ZTE succeeded in the development of a mobile switching system, in June 2000, in the development of base stations, and in October 2000 it succeeded in the development of a handset (Lu, 2001). By September 2001, Huawei applied CDMA-related patents to 132 items at home and 18 items abroad (Zhou, 2001).

Based on this effort, indigenous manufacturers came to produce mobile communication equipment for 2G products. However, in 1999, the market share of base stations, switches and handset produced by indigenous makers was still negligible at 2 per cent, 4 per cent and 3 per cent respectively (Fang and Yu, 2002).

For the 2.5 generation wireless telecommunication technology, Huawei had been using its four R&D institutes in Shenzhen, Beijing, Shanghai and India since 1998, and was able to develop the system and handsets successfully by September 2001. Similar efforts bore fruit at the ZTE company around 2001.

As can be seen above, indigenous manufacturers have made strenuous efforts to learn and enhance their capabilities. These efforts began to yield fruit with steadily increasing market shares, initially from the handset markets. In 2001 the market shares of indigenous manufacturers exceeded 20 per cent (Figure 2.1). Then, in 2003, local firms overtook foreign firms for the first time, capturing 58 per cent of the domestic market in handsets. But, with 2003 as the peak, the shares of indigenous manufacturers started to decline again, finally to around 34 per cent in 2007, as shown in Figure 2.1. That was a big surprise and disappointment for the Chinese public and policy-makers, who became anxious to know the reasons for this sudden setback as well as why there had been a rise in the past. This pattern of catch-up and retreat by Chinese manufacturers contrasts with the catch-up by the Korean manufacturers who had not experienced such a setback during the course of the catch-up.

Lee et al. (2009) give a good explanation of the reasons for the catch-up and setback. The regimes of technologies and knowledge in mobile phones are characterized by frequent innovation and high rates of demand for new and more technologically sophisticated products (Lee and Lim, 2001). These features do not give latecomers any strong incentives regarding R&D effort nor do they suggest they would be likely to succeed in the catching-up process. However, there are other elements of the technology/knowledge regime that encouraged latecomers to attempt catch-up. These elements include the high modularity of mobile production combined with a reasonable degree of knowledge accessibility. Given this high modularity, indigenous Chinese manufacturers relied on core technology parts (main platforms and core software) from foreign suppliers and then combined them with their own development efforts in peripheral technologies.

However, the high frequency of innovation has begun to give Chinese manufacturers more problems. Every day new functions are added and upgraded to phones, in addition to generation changes to 3G. Such an ever-changing environment requires greater and faster in-house R&D capabilities, and, moreover, the module-based production allows only limited response due to its low flexibility and heavy reliance on upstream suppliers. Indigenous handset manufacturers in China were not able to control the whole production process, including the types of components used. Given this situation, it is natural for the MNCs to enjoy a strong upper hand over indigenous manufacturers who had limited R&D capabilities and relied on module-based production. In other words, while higher modularity tends to lower entry barriers, it does not guarantee the automatic upgrading of competences at later stages. For a number of years after successful entry, Chinese mobile phone producers have remained occupied with mostly peripheral technologies such as MMI design, packaging and module-based production configuration. Advance to the core technologies embedded in 'hidden' modules appears to remain a challenge for them.

Indigenous development of 3G wireless telecommunication system (TD-SCDMA)[28]

In China, the era of the first and second generation wireless telecommunication industry and markets was dominated by foreign companies or GSM standards. However, from the emerging third generation of mobile telecommunications, the scenes are expected to be different, with a more prominent role assumed by Chinese actors. The Chinese agencies, the Chinese Academy of Telecommunications Technology (CATT), have developed their own standards (TD-SCDMA) for the third generation of wireless telecommunications in cooperation with Siemens. The Chinese have been promoting this standard and competing against two other standards (WCDMA and CDMA 2000) initiated by foreigners. Below, we explain the process of indigenous development of 3G wireless technology.

SCDMA was an embryonic form of TD-SCDMA, and this technology was listed in the 'Ninth Five-year Science and Technology Development Program' by the Chinese government. Xinwei Company, a joint venture established by USA-based Cwill and the CATT (the former body of the Datang Group), was the company that first developed SCDMA. This company received a grant of 15 million yuan from the Ministry of Post and Telecommunication, and 10 million yuan from the Planning Commission of the Chinese government.

The pioneering scientists that first developed SCDMA in 1994 were Wei Chen, who graduated from Stanford University, and Guanghan Xu, who was a professor at the University of Texas at Austin. The two of them set up a company named 'Cwill'. Wei Chen and Guanghan Xu had worked with Sihe Li before they went to the USA. After several rounds of negotiation with Cwill company, in November 1995 the CATT was able to set up a new joint venture with Cwill, named Xinwei Company. This is the company that developed SCDMA with a large grant from the government. The company also scouted many engineers from Huawei and ZTE.

The birth of TD-SCDMA (Time Division Synchronous CDMA)

In January 1998 a meeting was held jointly by the Ministry of Posts and Telecommunications and the Ministry of Science and Technology to discuss whether or not China could submit its own 3G standard to ITU, and it was finally decided to develop TD-SCDMA on the basis of the

SCDMA technology. For this reason, the SCDMA teams in Xinwei were called upon by the CATT to develop the TD-SCDMA technology. Also, the CATT began to look for new partners to work with. They decided to collaborate with Siemens, and the team speeded up the process greatly by using Siemens' advanced computer emulation system. After being revised several times, the TD-SCDMA system was developed on 20 June 1998 and approved by the ITU in 1999.

In order to commercialize the TD-SCDMA technology, Datang Mobile Communication Equipment (also called Datang Mobile) was set up in March 2002. The company was composed of three parts. The first part was the TD-SCDMA development team from CATT; the second was made up of engineers who had participated in the research and development of the GSM products at the Shanghai Datang Mobile company. The third was comprised of engineers and managers from the WCDMA Business Unit of the Datang Telecom Technology and Industry Group.

By the end of 2001, the President of the company proposed the idea of the TD-SCDMA alliance. On 30 October 2002, the TD-SCDMA Industry Alliance was formed in Beijing with the participating members of Datang, South High-Tech, Huali, Huawei, Lenovo, ZTE, China Electronics group, and PTIC, the eight famous local telecom manufacturers. There was great demand for such an alliance. For instance, Huawei had already invested a substantial amount of R&D money for WCDMA and CDMA 2000 but had not been very successful. Thus, it was even more difficult for Huawei to invest in TD-SCDMA. However, with the arrangement of the TD-SCDMA alliance, the member companies could share the R&D costs and intellectual property rights of the TD-SCDMA technology. More new members joined the alliance every year. By the beginning of 2006, there were 26 companies in the alliance, including Sino-foreign joint ventures of Shanghai Alcatel, Dingqiao (a joint venture established by Huawei and Siemens in 2004) and Punuo Mobile (a joint venture established by PTIC and Nokia in 2006).

In this TD-SCDMA industry alliance, two indigenous telecom companies, Huawei and ZTE, had played key roles. This was possible because they had strong bases in fixed telecom and 2G wireless technology. In Huawei, the R&D team that developed the mobile system was the same one that had developed the fixed line system. With the lead and help from these key players, the indigenous telecom companies were able to supply most of the component products constituting the whole TD-SCDMA system. Within the industrial value chain, Huawei, ZTE, PTIC and Datang were in charge of supplying the system equipment, and Spreadtrum Communications Inc, Tianji Communication, COMMIT Incorporated, ADI and CQCYIT (Chongqing Chongyou Information Technology Group) were in charge of supplying the chips. Finally, Datang, ZTE, Bird, Hisense, Lenovo, TCL and Haier supplied the handsets for the market.

Although MII officially announced TD-SCDMA as the 3G standard in China on 20 January 2006 after testing in several cities, TD-SCDMA has not yet been commercialized to any great extent. However, efforts towards commercialization have been in progress, and on 5 December 2006 the minister of MII declared that the 3G certificate would be authorized before the 2008 Olympic Games (Yu, 2007).

The success factors: knowledge access, governments and market conditions
As can been seen above, the indigenous development of 3G wireless technology was made possible by the arrangement of appropriate access to foreign knowledge in directly forming an alliance as well as by inviting participation by scientists trained abroad.

On top of this, there was a great deal of assistance from the government, who provided not only overall coordination and leadership, but also cash. The Ministry of Information Industry, the State Development and Reform Committee, and the Ministry of Science and Technology have set up a joint project, the '3G TD-SCDMA Mobile Communication Standard and Product Development', to support the TD-SCDMA Industry Alliance. From this project, in 2003, a special fund of RMB 700 million was supplied to the Alliance, and Datang Mobile received RMB 200 million. After that, members of the alliance received financial support every year. In 2005 the alliance obtained RMB 240 million from the Electronic and Information Industrial Development Fund. In addition, the China Industrial and Commercial Bank (CICB) signed a strategic cooperation agreement with Datang Group in September 2005, in which CICB promised to give financial support to the TD-SCDMA business of Datang Group.

Finally, one particular feature of the Chinese market also needs mentioning as the story is quite similar to the case of digital telephone switches explained in preceding sections. As often noted, in absolute size the low-end market is quite large in China. The low-end market, however, requires low-price technology. Bird Company, for example, grew as a result of its pagers business, which thrived in the rural regions of Western China, a market that the multinationals ignored. Bird saw this type of region as a niche market which it could enter easily (Xie and White, 2005). This was the same for Huawei, whose initial approach was to capture rural markets first and city markets later so that it could get rid of tough competition from multinationals in the city. Compared to multinationals with technological advantages, local companies in developing countries have the advantage of local market knowledge. For example, the multinationals were slow to offer the clam shell design which Chinese customers preferred, and Chinese manufacturers quickly captured that market; now this design accounts for 80 per cent of the Chinese domestic market. Similarly, many local companies have adopted a strategy of winning markets based on design; for example, Haier's pen-shape handsets and TCL's rhinestone-studded handsets.

2.7.3 The Brazilian Case

Compared to a number of other developing countries, mobile communications entered the network in Brazil as far back as 1990. However, the real growth of the network took place only after the privatization of the network in 1998. This is indicated by the sharp increases in the ratio of mobile to fixed lines since that period, and the ratio began to be greater than unity from 31 July 2003 onwards. This growth in mobile communication is due not only to an increase in the number of service providers, but also to the types of technologies and the consequent reduction in prices that ensued. For instance in June 2000, ANATEL announced the adoption of the 1.8 GHz spectrum band for the national wireless system, bringing Brazil into the global GSM wireless community.[29] Brazilian consumers have three different technologies to choose from, thus increasing competition not only among service providers but also across different technologies. Another important feature of mobile communications is the fact that it will have adverse consequences for the demand for equipment for fixed line telephony.[30] Given the fact that domestic technology is available only for fixed line telephony, the growth of mobile communication has important implications for the future building of innovation capability in the fixed line telephony sector. This is especially so because almost all the equipment used in mobile telephony (switching, transmission and terminals) is supplied by MNC manufacturers.

2.7.4 The Indian Case

The C-DOT and other local companies in India failed in general to make a successful transition to the mobile era due to their low R&D capacities, compared to the MNCs. The same is true in Brazil as the CPqD failed to develop large-scale switches and mobile systems. In India mobile telephones began to diffuse around 1997, and by 2007 the country had five mobile telephone subscribers for every one fixed line subscriber (see Table 2.3). In fact, it is the phenomenal growth of mobile phones that has increased the teledensity in the country from less than 1 per 100 in 1991 to over 23 per 100 in 2007.

Table 2.3   *Growth of wireless communication in India, 1991–2009 (in millions)*

Year	Fixed	Growth rate (%)	Mobile	Growth rate (%)	Total	Growth rate (%)	Teleden-sity	Ratio of mobile to fixed
1991	5.07				5.07		0.6	
1992	5.81	14.60			5.81	14.60	0.67	
1993	6.8	17.04			6.8	17.04	0.77	
1994	8.03	18.09			8.03	18.09	0.89	
1995	9.8	22.04			9.8	22.04	1.07	
1996	11.98	22.24			11.98	22.24	1.26	
1997	14.54	21.37	0.34		14.88	24.21	1.56	0.02
1998	17.8	22.42	0.88	158.82	18.68	25.54	1.94	0.05
1999	21.59	21.29	1.2	36.36	22.79	22.00	2.33	0.06
2000	26.51	22.79	1.88	56.67	28.39	24.57	2.86	0.07
2001	32.44	22.37	3.58	90.43	36.02	26.88	3.58	0.11
2002	41.48	27.87	13	263.13	54.48	51.25	4.3	0.31
2003	42.58	2.65	33.58	158.31	76.16	39.79	5.1	0.79
2004	45	5.68	50	48.90	95	24.74	7.04	1.11
2005	49	8.89	76	52	125	31.58	10.66	1.55
2006	40.43	−17.49	149.5	96.71	189.93	51.94	17.16	3.70
2007	39.25	−2.92	233.63	56.27	272.88	43.67	25	5.95
2008	37.9	−3.44	346.89	48.48	384.79	41.01	33.23	9.15
2009	37.06	−2.22	525.15	51.39	562.21	46.11	47.89	14.17

Source: Telecommunications Regulatory Authority of India (various issues).

In fact, the growth of mobile communications has been phenomenal over the last three years or so when the monthly sales of handsets have averaged around 8 million sets. Such a high volume of domestic demand has prompted all the major mobile handset manufacturers in the world to establish their manufacturing plants in India. Domestic manufacturing on such a large scale has now resulted in the demand for semiconductor devices such as Digital Signal Processors. This has led to a semiconductor manufacturing industry evolving in India. Thus, although India has no history of successful development of mobile standards (as in the case of Korea and China), the mobile handset industry is having a significant spillover effect on the rest of the economy. In addition, as mentioned earlier, there are considerable private innovation capabilities in wireless technologies essentially due to India's capability in chip design technologies.

2.8   SUMMARY AND CONCLUDING REMARKS

This chapter has tried to explain both initial commonalities and later divergence among the four countries of China, Korea, India and Brazil in the telecommunication equipment sector. The commonality was the fact that all of these four countries had once developed more or less 'indigenously' digital telephone switches. The later divergence is that the initial success in fixed line technology has led to the successful transition to the mobile telecommunication technology in Korea and China, whereas India and Brazil have failed to make this transition to the mobile era.

The findings or arguments of the chapter can be summarized as follows. First, one of the reasons why all the four latecomers were able to develop their own digital switches has to do with the fact that the nature of the knowledge system of digital switches was mature and of a stable trajectory, and arranging access to knowledge was not difficult, whether it was in the form of licensing/JV or through study of the literature in the public domain.

Second, the later variations among the four should then be explained in terms of the strategies of the actors and the networks among them. The first dimension of the critical difference was in the role of governments in providing coordination and protection with a strategic vision; this was the case in China and Korea whereas no sustained state activism existed in the cases of India and Brazil. The second dimension of the critical difference was the fact that the initial success had led to a build-up of capacities of private firms in China and Korea, whereas this was not the case in India and Brazil. Thus, in the mobile era, more roles were played by manufacturing companies in Korea and China, whereas in the fixed line era, R&D was mainly conducted by the GRIs and then transferred to manufacturing companies.

Third, once the indigenous actors acquired some mass of capabilities, they could even overcome the difficulties associated with abrupt technological changes or discontinuities. The cases of mobile telecom in Korea and China show this as they show a transition from digital switches (fixed lines) to mobile telecom. More interestingly, Korea and China have taken advantage of the emergence of the new era to even manage a path-creating catch-up, such as the commercialization of the CDMA technology in Korea and the development of the 3G wireless standard (TD-SCDMA) in China. This is in contrast to the stage-skipping catch-up which they had made in developing digital switches. On the other hand, if the latecomers fail to develop their own capabilities, the shift of the technological paradigm can become a further barrier to catch-up, as has happened in the cases of Brazil and India. In sum, paradigm (or generation) shifts can represent either a window of opportunity (as for China and Korea) or a further entry barrier (as in India or Brazil) for latecomers' successive endeavours. This indicates that the evolution of the SSI is a function of both technological changes and the changing levels of actors' capabilities, namely the co-evolution of technologies and actors.

Finally, the chapter notes the possibility of two models of catch-up in terms of which types of firms will be leading the process of catch-up (Lee, 2005). One model is the Korean-style catch-up that is led by big firms pursuing a more or less independent road with regard to MNCs. The other model is the Taiwan-style catch-up that is led by smaller size firms that are pursuing a more interdependent road with regard to MNCs. These firms will be more integrated with the global value chain or global production network run by the MNCs. In the telecom sector, while China seems to be going along the first model of independent catch-up, India has been showing some promising signs of going along the second, interdependent model of catch-up.

NOTES

*   Earlier versions of this chapter were presented at the three workshops on 'SSI and catch-up' held in Milan and Maastricht. The authors would like to thank Franco Malerba and Richard Nelson, editors of this volume, as well as other participants for valuable comments.

1.   The Tenth Research Institute of the Ministry of Posts and Telecommunications, http://www.xdz.com/wenzhang/zlzy/kyjg/leaf/html/2290_0.html.

2.   In his original text Wu (1997, p. 13), used the words 'electronic telephone switches (including electronic and semi-electronic telephone switches)' which must be referring to imported analogue electronic switches as he also stated that digital switches were not installed in China until the 1980s, in other words until the introduction of the device made by Fujitsu in 1981.

3.   This is why the telecommunications system in China was one of the poorest in the world as it had merely 3 972 000 telephone lines compared with a population of over 900 million, with about four phones for every 1000 people in 1978 (Wu, 1997, pp. 7–8; Xin et and Wang, 2000, p. 7; Shen, 1999, pp. 16–17).

4.   Of these three, Nortel Network's Brazilian subsidiary is very active in data transmission and wireless markets in the country. It is not an active player in central office switching equipment.

5.   Genius is part of a large Brazilian consumer electronics company, Gradiente.

6.   We look at this period because the Chinese project to develop domestic digital electronic telephone switches started in the mid-1980s to succeed in 1991.

7.   For comparison of growth rates of US patents in several technology categories, see Lee and Lim (2001).

8.   This section draws upon another work by the authors (Mu and Lee, 2005).

9.   In the early 1980s, when Shanghai Bell was established, BTM was a subsidiary of ITT (International Telephone and Telegram Corporation in the USA) (Zhang, 2000, p. 138). In 1987, Alcatel of France took over ITT's telecommunications business. Thus, Alcatel became the parent company of BTM, and then BTM was renamed Alcatel Bell Telephone Manufacturing Company (http://www.alcatel.com/atr/DATR_about.jhtml).

10. In 1980, BTM was convinced that its technology could be successfully transferred to China, given China's skilled personnel, sound financial policies and a suitable partner, PTIC (Zhou and Kerkhofs, 1987, p. 186).

11. See 'Woguo Juyong Jiaohuanji Chanye de Fazhan Xianzhuang yu Qianjing Zhanwang' [Development and prospects of central office SPC switches in China], available at http://202.96.31.133//information/industryy.nsf.

12. This is from personal experience. On one hand, the first author's colleagues at MPT 513 Factory, who had participated in producing HJD-04 switches in MPT 513 Factory, left for Huawei or ZTE in 1992 or 1993. One of them had become a core engineer of Huawei's R&D division. On the other hand, one of the first author's university, class-mates is now working at Huawei as a senior engineer. Before joining Huawei, he had worked for several years at a local PTA office and had experience in imported SPC switch operation. According to him, many of his colleagues had a similar professional background.

13. 'Guanyu Woshi Chengkong Jiaohuanji Chanye de Sikao' [Thinking about SPC switch-ing industry in Zhenshen city], *Shenzhen Special Zone Daily*, 13 May 1997.

14. Interview (in July 2001) with Ms Zhou Hongjie.

15. The Department of Telecommunications (DoT) receives and evaluates bids from domestic firms (including affiliates of MNCs) and awards rate contracts based on price and performance.

16. TEC, through its core group, is responsible for drawing up the Standards' and Generic Requirements (GRs) for networks, systems, equipment and products to be used in the Indian telecommunications network. The Centre, through its regional offices, is also responsible for coordinating and evaluating these products, equipment and systems. TEC also provides advice to the DoT in respect of products and networks used by the DoT. The switching division of TEC is responsible for all activities related to the switching products, either working in the DoT's network or interworking with the DoT's network. This includes preparation of specifications of state-of-the-art digital switching systems, validation of switching systems to be inducted in the DoT's network, interface testing of PABX and switches for GSM and basic service, testing of hardware and software, upgrading of various switching systems, providing software maintenance support and field support to switching systems working in the DoT's network.

17. Including Zhongxing and other telecommunication manufacturing firms, the volume of buyer credit supplied by the China Construction Bank was RMB 8 billion in that year (*Shenzhen Special Zone Daily* [*Sehnzhen Tequ Bao*], 30 July 1998).

18. Source: China telecommunication, US Department of Commerce – National Trade Data Bank, 3 November 2000 (http://www.tradeport.org/ts/countries/china/isa/isar0024.html).

19. KTA was created to expand and manage basic telecommunications facilities in 1981, and was incorporated as Korea Telecom (KT) in July 1990.

20. See http://www.natlaw.com/brazil/topical/cm/dcbrcm/dcbrcm20.htm/.

21. This is of course based on the assumption that both FINEP and BNDES employ very rigorous selection criteria for choosing research projects.

22. See Rajya Sabha Unstarred Question No: 4125, http://164.100.24.219/rsq/quest.asp?qref=21560. According to the answer given by the Ministry of Communications, the DoT actually ordered 0.91 million lines of digital switching equipment in reponse to a tender for just 0.2 million lines.

23. See the response to the same question no: 4125. From the same response it is also clear that the number of ISDN subscribers even in developed countries ranges from 0.5 million in the USA to only 40 000 in Italy.

24. Science Mathematics Technologies: Telecommunications, Wireless & Network Information Technology (TCOM), http://www.smccd.net/accounts/skyline/smt/TCOM.html.

25. See '3G and UMTS Frequently Asked Questions', http://www.umtsworld.com/umts/faq.htm.

26. http://en.wikipedia.org/wiki/3G.
27. Interview with Shihe Li by *Journal of Telecommunication Technology*, 'TD-SCDMA' Li Shihe, Chief Technical Consultant of Datang Mobile Communications Equipments, *Journal of Telecommunication Technology*, No.2, 2006.
28. Based on Nan and Lu (2006). Nan Qiao and Yixuan Lu have interviewed Sihe Li, senior consultant of Datang Mobile; Ku Wen, Director of Science & Technology department of MII; Cao Shumin, Vice President of MII Telecom Academy; Mofang Li, chief engineer of China Mobile; Huan Zhou, Chairman of the Datang Telecom Technology and Industry Group; Yigang Yang, Vice Chairman of the Datang Telecom Technology and Industry Group; Ruan Tang, Vice President of the Datang Telecom Technology and Industry Group, and President of Datang Mobile; Hua Yang, general secretary of TD-SCDNMMA Industry Alliance, among others.
29. According to the World GSM association, the choice of 1.8 GHz for the 'C' band in Brazil preserves the 1.9 GHz frequency for Third Generation (3GSM) technology, allowing for full-scale evolution of the wireless Internet. ANATEL has said that this decision would allow Brazil to adopt 3GSM technology within two to three years via a smooth evolutionary path from GSM today, to wireless multi-media networks of the future. See the Press Releases Archive of the Association at http://www.gsmworld.com/.
30. In 1998 the largest share in mobile switching centres is accounted for by NEC (40%), followed by Nortel (25%), Ericsson (24%), Lucent (6.5%), Motorola (4%) and Alcatel (0.5%). See Melo and Gutierrez (2002, p. 7).

REFERENCES

BNDES (2000), *BNDES News, Quarterly Report for BNDES Partners*, No. 9, January–March.

Callon, M. (1992), 'The dynamics of techno-economic networks' in R. Coombs, P. Saviotti and V. Walsh (eds), *Technical Change and Company Strategies*, London: Academic Press.

Carlsson, B. and R. Stankiewitz (1995), 'On the nature, function and composition of technological systems', in B. Carlsson (ed.), *Technological Systems and Economic Performance*, Dordrecht: Kluwer.

Cheng, S. (1999), *Jiedu Minzu Xinxi Chanye [Analysis on National Information Industries]*, Beijing: Huawen Press.

Comptroller and Auditor General of India (2000), *Report of the CAG on Union Government for the year ended March 1999*, Union Government Post & Telegraph Department.

Dittberner, D.L. (1977), 'Telephone switching: technologies in conflict', in P. Paul and M.A. O'Bryan (eds), *Telecommunications and Economic Development*, Dedham: Horizon House International.

Duysters, G. (1996), *The Dynamics of Technical Innovation: The Evolution and Development of Information Technology*, Cheltenham, UK and Brookfield, VT, USA: Edward Elgar.

Edquist, C. (1997), *Systems of Innovation: Technologies, Institutions and Organizations*, London: Pinter/Cassell.

Fang, X. and J. Yu (2002), 'The application of integration innovation on the 3G industry', *China Soft Science*, **12**.

Freeman, C. (1987), *Technology Policy and Economic Performance: Lessons from Japan*, London: Frances Pinter.

Hughes, T. (1984), 'The evolution of large technological systems', in W. Bijker, T.

Hughes and T. Pinch (eds), *The Social Construction of Technological Systems*, Cambridge, MA: MIT Press.

Hwang, E.G. (1993), *The Korean Economies: A Comparison of North and South*, New York: Oxford University Press.

IGI (1997), 'Switching market and opportunities in China', Boston: IGI Consulting Inc.

Kim, L. (2000), 'Korea's national system of innovation in transition', in L. Kim and R.R. Nelson (eds), *Technology, Learning, and Innovation. Experiences of Newly Industrializing Economies*, New York: Cambridge University Press.

Kotler, M. (2001), 'Distribution in China', Kotler Marketing Brief, Kotler Marketing Group.

Lee, J. and J. Lee (1992), 'Technological development process and technological innovation strategy of telecommunication industry in Korea: case of electronic switches' development', *Telecommunication Review*, 2(11) [*in Korean*].

Lee, K. (2005), 'Making a technological catch-up: barriers and opportunities', *Asian Journal of Technology Innovation*, 13(2), 97–131.

Lee, K. and C. Lim (2001), 'The technological regimes, catch-up and leapfrogging: findings from the Korean industries', *Research Policy*, 30(3), 459–83.

Lee, K., S. Cho and J. Jin (2009), 'Dynamics of catch-up in mobile phones and automobiles in China: a sectoral systems of innovation perspective', *China Economic Journal*, 2(1), 25–53.

Lee, K., C. Lim and W. Song (2005), 'Emerging digital technology as a window of opportunity and technological leapfrogging: catch-up in digital TV by the Korean firms', *International Journal of Technology Management*, 29(1–2), 40–63.

Lu, J. (2001), 'The process of ZTE's mobile telecommunications R&D', *China Radio Management*, No. 4.

Lundvall, B.Å. (1993), *National Systems of Innovation*, London: Frances Pinter.

Malerba, F. (2002), 'Sectoral systems of innovation and production', *Research Policy*, 31(2), 247–64.

Malerba, F. (2004), *Sectoral Systems of Innovation: Concepts, Issues and Analyses of Six Major Sectors in Europe*, Cambridge: Cambridge University Press.

Malerba, F. (2006), 'Catch-up in different sectoral systems of innovation: some introductory remarks', paper presented at the IV GLOBELICS Conference, Trivandrum, Kerala, 4–7 October.

Mani, S. (1992), *Foreign Technology in Public Enterprises*, New Delhi: Oxford and IBH Publications.

Mani, S. (2005a), 'Innovation capability in India's telecommunications equipment industry', in A. Saith and M. Vijayabaskar (eds), *ICT's and Indian Economic Development*, New Delhi: Sage Publications, pp. 265–322.

Mani, S. (2005b), 'The dragon vs the elephant. Comparative analysis of the innovation capability in the telecom industry of China and India', *Economic and Political Weekly*, 40(39), 4271–83.

Melo, R. and M.A. Gutierrez (2002), 'Telecomunicações pós-privatização: Perspectivas Industriais e Tecnológicas', Rio de Janeiro: BNDES.

Mishra, A.R. (2004), *Fundamentals of Cellular Network Planning and Optimisation: 2G/2.5G/3G. . . Evolution to 4G*, Chichester: John Wiley and Sons.

Mu, Q. (2002), 'Market segmentation, knowledge diffusion and technological leapfrogging in China: the case of telephone switch'. Ph.D. thesis, Economics Department, Seoul National University, December.

Mu, Q. and K. Lee (2005), 'Knowledge diffusion, market segmentation and technological catch-up: the case of the telecommunication industry in China', *Research Policy*, **34**(6), 759–83.

Nan, Q. and Y. Lu (2006), 'TD-SCDMA Zhengzhuan (Biography of TD-SCDMA)', *Telecommunication World Weekly*, 17 March.

Nelson, R. (1993), *National Innovation Systems: A Comparative Analysis*, New York: Oxford University Press.

Schmitt, B.H. (1997), 'Who is the Chinese consumer? Segmentation in the People's Republic of China', *European Management Journal*, **15**(2), 191–4.

Selian, A. (2001), '3G mobile licensing policy: from GSM to IMT-2000 – a comparative analysis', International Telecommunication Union, case study for 3G Mobile Workshop, 19–20 September 2001, available at: http://www.itu.int/osg/spu/ni/3G/casestudies/GSM-FINAL.doc.

Shen, X. (1999), *The Chinese Road to High Technology: A Study of Telecommunications Switching Technology in the Economic Transition*, New York: St. Martin's Press.

Tan, A. (2002), 'Product cycle theory and telecommunications industry: foreign direct investment, government policy, and indigenous manufacturing in China', *Telecommunications Policy*, **26**(1-2), 17–30.

Wu, J. (1997), *Zhongguo Tongxin Fazhan Zhilu* [*The Development Road of Telecommunication in China*], Beijing: Xinhua Press.

Xia, S. (2001), 'Exert the potential advantages and build up the national brand: the process of Huawei's mobile telecommunications R&D', *China Radio Management*, No. 6.

Xie, W. and S. White (2005), 'Windows of opportunity, learning strategies and the rise of China's handset makers', INSEAD Working Paper, Singapore.

Xin, X. and Y. Wang (2000), 'Kuayue Shikong: Zhongguo Tongxin Chanye Fazhan Qishilu [Crossing time and space: revelation from the development of telecommunication industry of China]', Beijing: Youdian daxue Chubanshe Beijing: University of Post and Telecommunication Press.

Xu, R. and J. Fu (1997), 'Huawei became the largest supplier of indigenous SPC switching' [Huawei Chengwei Guochan jiaohuanji Zuida Gongyingshang], Sehnzhen Tequ Bao [Shenzhen Special Zone Daily].

Yu, Q. (2007), 'Forecasting the destiny of 3G in China' [Bama Zhongguo 3G Mingyun], *Contemporary Marketing* [*Xiandai Yingxiao*], No. 3.

Zhang, M. (1999), 'Chronicle of events in telecommunication industry in China' [Zhongguo Tongxin Chanye Fazhan Dashiji], available at: http://www.electron.cetin.net.cn/w1999/nrxs.php3?lsh.

Zhang, X.P. (2000), *Dianxin Yewu Shiyong Quanshu* [*The Complete Knowledge of Telecommunication*], Beijing: Taihai Chubanshe [Taihai Press].

Zhou, H. and M. Kerkhofs (1987), 'System 12 technology transfer to the People's Republic of China', *Electrical Communication*, **61**(2), 186–93.

Zhou, X. (2001), 'Implement the high starting point developing strategy: Huawei's CDMA system R&D', *China Radio Management*, No. 10.

Zhu, G. (2000), '*Zhongguo Dianxin Jishude Fazhanyu Zahnwang*' [Development and Prospect of Telecommunication Technology in China], *Zhonguo Tongxin* [China Telecommunication], No. 1.

3. The global computer software sector

Jorge Niosi, Suma Athreye and Ted Tschang

3.1 OVERVIEW OF THE SECTOR (1950–2007)

The computer software and service industry (CSS) is now a global sector with multiple product and service niches. In the United States it is comparable to the automobile industry in terms of employment, sales, value added, or market capitalization. Its core is composed of three related activities: software publishing, computer systems design and services, and data processing services.[1] Other related activities are telephone call centres, which may or may not be related to software.[2] Companies active in these sectors often include several classes and move from one class to another within their main activity. Of course, publishing packaged software for large markets and designing software for specific clients are much more demanding than entering data or responding to technical telephone calls from clients.

3.1.1 Evolution of the Sector

The CCS industry has moved through different stages. The industry was born in the United States, the cradle of the computer, and the CSS sector progressively detached itself from the computer manufacturing industry. The main stages were as follows (Hoch et al., 2000). The first era (1950–59) was the period of the birth of independent programming services: IBM had a virtual monopoly on the sale of mainframes computers, and usually sold programs embedded in their machines. However, large corporations and government departments using mainframes required programs that IBM did not provide. Professional service companies appeared at this time; most of them were based in the US. A few of these firms also appeared in Western Europe, Japan and India, such as Cap Gemini (France). The role of the US government was key in the birth of this new industry (Mowery, 1996). The second era (1959–69) was that of packaged software products. It was launched by DEC and its popular minicomputers. New companies appeared, selling packaged software products to a mass market, instead of custom software for specific clients. The third period (1969–81) was that of independent enterprise solutions providers. IBM, following antitrust lawsuits, decided to sell software unbundled from their mainframes. Several major competitors entered the market. The fourth phase (1981–94) started with the personal computer (PC). It was a new mass market, not with thousands of clients, but with millions of them. In 1981, IBM had launched the PC, and decided to outsource its operating system to a new company, Microsoft, founded in 1975. Microsoft DOS, and then Windows, became the most popular operating system. DOS attracted new entrants to the CSS industry. Several other operating systems appeared to compete with it in the market, including advanced generations of UNIX and Solaris (Sun Microsystems), MacOS (Apple), OpenVMS (DEC, then HP) and Linux. Thousands of applications competed for the many markets created by the ubiquitous PCs. In era 4, the industry was growing at the rate of 20 per cent a year, mostly in the United States. The present era (1995–) was launched by the arrival of the Internet. The development of a world wide web made possible the creation of a new range of companies selling browser products, as well as a new niche, that of e-commerce. Also, in this era, IBM became a software service company (after its sale of their PC division to China's Lenovo), many of the early entrants became MNC, and the industry became truly global. Concentration in the CSS is low today, as compared with most other industries, but it is rapidly increasing, as the largest corporations try to dominate niches other than their original ones. Also, the present era is now changing radically, as packaged software gives way to the sale of software service applications online.

3.1.2 Segmentation of CSS and Some Main Characteristics

Providers of computer software are basically two different types of companies. The older and (on average) larger producers of software are the computer hardware providers, such as IBM, HP, Apple, Sun Microsystems and Unisys. The newer entrants are the so-called independent software vendors; they are the most numerous competitors, and there are thousands of them in every industrial country.

The CSS has two main segments: the packaged software segment and the software services segment. Conversely to popular perception, packaged software represents maybe 30 per cent of the total software produced, and at most 60 per cent of computer software. Customized software written for computers is produced both in-house by the customer's programmers, or under contract for large users such as banks, insurance companies and manufacturing corporations. It is usually divided into 27 segments (see Table 3.1). Among the key niches, one finds accounting and finance, business intelligence, customer relationship

Table 3.1   Computer software and service niches and representative firms

Niche	Representative firms
Accounting & finance	Cognizant, Intuit
Asset management	McDonald, Dettwiler and Associates
Billing & service provisioning	Flextronics Software Systems
Business intelligence	SAP, Cognos
Collaborative	Lotus Development/IBM, PalmSource, MKS
Content & document management	EMC, FileNet, IBM, OpenText
Customer relationship management, marketing and sales	Claritas, LexisNexis Interaction, Oracle, Pivotal Corporation, SAP, FirstWave
Database & file management	Oracle, Novell
Development tools, operating systems & utilities	Apple, IBM, Microsoft, PalmSource, Oracle
E-commerce	GlobalWare Solutions, IBM
Education & training	Adobe, The Learning Company
Engineering, scientific & CAD/CAM	The MathWorks, UGS Corp.
Enterprise application integration	SAP, Software AG
Enterprise resource planning	SAP, Oracle, Sage, Microsoft
Entertainment & games	LucasArt, Ubisoft, ElectronicArts
Financial services, legal and government	SunGard, Sage Software, Intuit, Misys.
Health care management	Cerner, IDX, 3M Health Information Systems
Human resources & workforce management	Ceridian, Sage Software, Kronos
Manufacturing, warehousing and industrial	SAP, Oracle, IFS, SYSPRO, Microsoft
Messaging, conferencing and communication	Comverse, IBM, Genesys, Nuance
Multimedia, graphics & publishing	Adobe, Corel, Novell
Networking and connectivity	Computer Associates, BMC, Keynote
Retail, point-of-sale, & inventory management	Epicor, CoreIMS, NetSuite, TrakerSystems
Security	Symantec, SuftControl, NetScreen, ActiveCard
Storage & systems management	Symantec, EMC,
Supply chain management & logistics	Manugistics, GlobalWare Solutions, TGI, SAP
Wireless	iWay, SunGard, Symbian, Webex, ZipLip

Source: Authors' own elaboration of Hoovers, Computerworld, InfoWorld News articles.

management (CRM), e-commerce, enterprise resource planning (ERP), entertainment and games, health care management, manufacturing and warehousing, multimedia, security and supply chain management (SCM). Competition is strong within and among niches, as the larger companies deploy efforts to move from one niche to the next in order to gain economies of scale and scope. New competitors, such as some of the largest CSS Indian companies, have emerged serving this segment of the industry.

The production of embedded software is not included within the definition of CSS.[3] This is because embedded software is usually not sold separately from its hardware support, such as aircraft, cars, electrical appliances, game consoles, numerically-controlled machines, robots, watches and many different types of electronic equipment. Although some telecommunication software is sold separately from its equipment, most of it is 'bundled' with its hardware. The same companies that manufacture the hardware usually produce embedded software through their captive software subsidiaries and/or exclusive suppliers. The fact that it is also subcontracted and outsourced to independent software companies blurs the frontiers between the CSS and other IT sectors. In other words, the size of the CSS depends on how much companies internalize or outsource the production of software that will be subsequently sold within some type of specialized digital machine.

The two dominant segments also have different economic paradigms associated with them. Hoch et al. (2000) observe that the software product segment and customized services segments of the market operate to a very different competitive logic. Product provision in software is akin to the commoditization of software, and requires investment in anticipation of demand. Software product providers, however, have mostly fixed costs. The only variable cost that they incur is the cost of additional units, which for software is the cost of reproduction. When there is a large dominance of fixed costs, standard economies of scale accrue to the producer. Total profits increase as market share grows.

Service providers in software, in contrast, have very few fixed costs. Typically their costs are incurred as they produce, and often the client incurs these costs. Most of their costs are the costs of labour and they maximize their profits by utilizing their labour resources fully. Their objective is to develop their human resources and to utilize the human capital created as fully as possible. Achieving large scales of output is not necessarily a goal, although large providers may realize economies of scope across different kinds of service provision.

Athreye (2003) points to two more differences between the two market segments: differences in the nature of demand and the role of marketing effort. A key difference between the two types of markets revolves around the degree of client/customer concentration for a typical firm operating in these markets. Customized service markets are generally outsourced markets with a large element of customization and tend to need only a small number of buyers to become viable. The average value of transaction for each buyer, however, can be high, making the scale of demand large enough for market-based production even though customer numbers are often small, ranging from five to eight customers a year.

In contrast, firms create software package product markets by anticipating and bundling software products for many users, whether in the area of operating systems or software applications. We have already alluded to the large fixed costs in the development of products: R&D expenditures, testing of prototypes and marketing expenditures. Such products are successful when there are many users willing to buy them. This high demand allows producers of packaged software to spread the fixed costs of developing the product over many units and brings down the price of each unit. The identity of the customers is relatively anonymous and there are usually many of them. Client concentration is low and in this sense product markets are more like arm's-length, commoditized markets.

A final difference between the customized service and product segments as against packaged software is in the way that marketing is actually carried out in the two segments. Tailor-made and service software is customized and its selling is closely tied to how well the software producer understands the business domain of the client firm. Close and repeated interaction with the user is useful in expanding the credibility of the service producer, and a successful project with one user will often create a market by establishing a reputation for the service producer. Package/product segments rely on different modes of marketing, depending upon the nature of the product they are selling. Information about the uses of the product is first created through advertising, usually in trade magazines. Trial promotions of the software product usually take place through retailers of hardware who distribute some software free with the computers sold by them. More specialized software (for example computational programs, specialized database products) are usually advertised through the educational press in a manner similar to the promotion of textbooks. Similarly, the marketing of games borrows the instituted selling arrangements that are often used for the selling of films. Thus, depending upon the nature of the product, the method of actually marketing the product borrows from the institutions that exist to market other similar products.

In microeconomics terminology, we can say that the two segments are different in terms of:

Table 3.2   US packaged software industry (NAICS 5112), (1998–2006)

	1998	1999	2000	2001	2002	2003	2004	2005	2006
Revenues ($B)	84	94.3	102	105.5	103.5	104.7	112.3	119.6	131.5
Employment (000)	214.9	235	260.6	268.9	253.3	237.9	235.9	237.9	243.4
Establishments	11 689	11 132	10 599	10 353	10 089	9157	9085	NA	NA

Note: NA: Not available

Source: US Bureau of Labor Statistics, Census Service, Annual Survey and County Business Patterns.

- the balance of fixed and variable costs;
- the scale and homogeneity of demand (itself affected by the speed of computerization in the economy);
- the extent of endogenous sunk costs (e.g. marketing and advertising costs).

Not surprisingly this affects the market structure and the nature of barriers to entry in each segment. The package product segment has relatively high barriers to entry, larger profit margins, a more concentrated structure and significant first mover advantages. As Malerba and Torrisi (1996) showed even in the early 1990s, Europe lagged behind America in the relative size of this sector. In contrast, the software design and services sectors tend to be characterized by lower concentration and easy entry in niches, and to some extent the heterogeneous nature of the demand for customized applications also insulates the sector as a whole from being exposed to a high degree of price competition. Rather, what proliferates is the number of application areas and niches that new firms can exploit to grow.

The three features that distinguish the two segments also map onto several observed characteristics of the CSS sector. The first of these is the observed *low barriers to entry in a fairly fragmented (customized services) sector*: a few programmers and personal computers are all that is needed to launch a new company. The CSS displays a continuous movement of entry of new firms but also high levels of exit and turbulence often created by employees leaving existing companies to create new ones. Today most entrants are now in catching-up countries, while OECD nations, conversely, see a decline in the number of companies and establishments. The latest US figures appear in Table 3.2.

Catching up in this industry means being able to increase participation in the production of software (that is, designing and/or publishing software), as opposed to simply entering data for clients or creating technical call centres. The rise of domestic capabilities can be inferred by the participation of domestic firms in software exports. Such countries as India, Ireland and Israel are now major exporters of software, even if most often they contribute only to specific modules of the software they export. The share of the domestic software market held by local producers gives an indication of the extent of their capabilities.

Several countries are now moving up the ladder. Some of them did this through the attraction of foreign direct investment (FDI) by large independent software vendors (ISV) that located in the country and produced software. Local spin-offs emerged from these MNCs. This is the case for Ireland. Other countries both attracted FDI and nurtured the development of a local industry. This is the case for China, India and, above all, Israel. These countries also upgraded their telecommunication infrastructure, implemented legislation that attracted FDI and provided incentives for R&D. They also invested in human capital. Some of them created software parks in order to lure both local and international software producers.

For catching up, human capital is not enough. The policy environment must also be suitable in order to stimulate R&D (through tax credits, direct subsidies, venture capital or other measures), facilitate the establishment of new firms, attract international producers, and provide market access to public and private consumers.

A second key feature is that this is a *labour-intensive industry*, and in the customized segment it requires little capital but vast numbers of highly skilled personnel. These university-trained professionals transfer knowledge and skills from niche to niche and from one industry to the next. They are highly mobile, and the demand for them outstrips supply in all industrial countries, but also in emerging competitors, such as Brazil, China, India, Israel and Russia. This is the main force behind another characteristic: rapid internationalization.

A third attribute of the CSS is the *localization of the core design capabilities in developed nations and the continuing dominance of American producers*, even if Western Europe, Canada, Japan, and several developing countries have consistently been catching up. Trade statistics on software and related services are not very reliable, but they all show that the United States is the origin of over 50 per cent of software exports. In the OECD only the United States, Austria, Germany, Ireland and the Netherlands claim a surplus in their international software trade. Outside the OECD, India and Israel are among the few net exporters.

A fourth characteristic of the CSS is the relatively *low need for public support*. In the early days of the CSS sector, public support by the US government was key: the public sector provided R&D funds and markets for products, through procurement contracts. US federal government support was also crucial in the development of ARPANET, the ancestor of the Internet (Fabrizio and Mowery, 2007). Today markets for software products and services are well established, funding of R&D comes mainly from the private sector, and the main lever that governments need to supply in order to support the development of the CSS is quality higher education in computer science, and telecommunication infrastructures.

The fifth trait is that *increasing returns and network externalities are overwhelming*. The value of any piece of software for any customer increases if other customers use the same software. Network externalities tend to consolidate the position of incumbent companies and make it more difficult for new entrants to penetrate the market. Also, increasing returns to scale are paradigmatic. The upfront cost of developing software is high and increasing; conversely, the cost of reproduction of the same piece of software is almost negligible. Thus, one witnesses the continuous effort of the established companies to sell as many copies as possible in order to reap those economies of scale. We can also witness the mergers and acquisitions wave that spans the entire history of the fourth period (1980s to the present day), as companies try to advance their standards, increase market share and reduce R&D costs. However, as the open source movement has shown, and Bonaccorsi and Rossi (2003) have explained, it is possible for newcomers to invade a market dominated by increasing returns and network externalities, by selling support and maintenance for free software. For each packaged software type of application, there is now an open software alternative, which is usually less costly than proprietary alternatives, as the buyer only pays for the after-sale services, not the software itself. Proprietary software typically has the most advanced features, but sometimes it has too many features, thus encouraging the entry of simpler, user-friendlier open source rival applications.

The sixth feature, linked to the above-mentioned point, is the *emergence of large multinational corporations* (MNCs) in the most mature segments of the industry such as office software (Microsoft), electronic commerce (IBM), databases and enterprise software (Oracle and SAP), and software services such as customized software, technical support and maintenance (Tata CS, Infosys, Wipro). Recently, multinationals from developing countries are appearing, the most conspicuous of them being nurtured in India. These multinational companies look for international markets and pools of highly skilled labour in order to increase sales, speed innovation and reduce manpower costs. MNCs transfer organizational and technical knowledge from country to country, generating international knowledge spillovers that increase the local absorptive capabilities of the host countries.

The activities of these MNCs in host countries are as variegated as the sector itself. They include outsourced IT services such as data processing (data entry, transaction processing), contract programming, operation and support of data centres, system integration, support operations (maintenance, data recovery), and other services (training, technical call centres) (Sahay et al., 2003). They also include in-house localization of existing software, expatriate R&D, and other activities (see Table 3.3 for a glimpse of recent CSS and outsourcing investments by MNCs in India).

A seventh major feature is that *the development and protection of technology in this industry is highly idiosyncratic.* First, technology changes very fast: new computer languages appear, as well as new operating systems, new applications, new markets and niches. Second, copyright and trademarks are the most common institutions used to protect software, even if large companies try to defend their intellectual property in this industry through patents. Historically, the first software patentees were the large computer hardware companies (IBM, HP, Apple, Sun Microsystems, Unisys), but in the mid-1980s the largest independent software vendors entered the trail and started applying for and being granted computer software patents, most often in the United States and Western Europe. In a study of over 22 000 US computer software patents, Chabchoub and Niosi (2005) found that only 18 companies, out of over 1300 publicly traded computer hardware and software firms, owned 90 per cent of the patents.

Eighth, the development of software is *highly modular*, and after the general design is complete, different modules may be developed in parallel. This characteristic explains the major process of outsourcing, as computer designers send different modules to be developed elsewhere. The rapid internationalization of the sector in the fourth era includes the overseas outsourcing of the development of some of its processes, different modules and entire software programs, but also the localization of software publishing and maintenance, data entry, technical call centres, and other activities abroad. Business process outsourcing (BPO) is not always related to the CSS, and is not always outsourced overseas; but the overseas BPO of some CSS activities is an integral part of the international diffusion of the sector and the related catching-up process.

Finally, offshoring has become ubiquitous in the industry. While outsourcing has been around for many years, the offshoring of services is relatively more recent. Following from India's NASSCOM convention, it is useful to categorize software and services into software services, IT-enabled services (including business process outsourcing and call centres),

Table 3.3 India, CSS and related BPO investment announcements, 2000–2007

Invester	Country	City	Goal	Data announced	Amount
Accenture	USA	Bangalore Mumbai	ITES & BPO	Jan. 2006	NA
Adobe	USA	Bangalore & Noida	Growth of software R&D centre	March. 2007	100 million
AMD	USA	NA	Chips factory	Dec. 2005	3 billion
Ciena	USA	Gurgaon	Growth of embedded telecom software R&D centre	Apr. 2007	NA
Cisco	USA	Bangalore	R&D lab	Oct. 2005	1.1 billion
Dell	USA	Bangalore	R&D: system design of servers	Jan. 2006	NA
Dell	USA	Bangalore	Call technical centre	Jan. 2006	NA
HP	USA	Bangalore	Creation of new software lab	Feb. 2002	NA
HP	USA	Bangalore	Growth of software R&D centre	Feb. 2004	NA
IBM	USA	Delhi	Creation of software R&D centre	Apr. 1998	NA
IBM	USA	Bangalore	R&D expansion	2001	100 million
IBM	USA	Delhi	Acquisition of outsourcing firm	2004	150 million
IBM	USA	Bangalore	New software R&D centre	Aug. 2005	NA
IBM	USA	Bangalore	R&D & services labs	Apr. 2007	6 billion
IBM	USA	Bangalore	New autonomous R&D centre	Apr. 2007	NA
Intel	USA	Bangalore	R&D, venture capital, services	Dec. 2005	1 billion
Microsoft	USA	Bangalore & Hyderabad	R&D software lab expansion	Dec. 2005	1.7 billion
Oracle	USA	Mumbai	Acquired i-Flex software firm	Aug. 2005	900 million

Note: NA: not available

Source: Public announcements by the cited companies.

and R&D services. India was generally the first mover in each of these sectors. Much of the early work involved the maintenance on legacy software, for example software updates and upgrades. Then as the Indian industry's capability increased, higher value added work was offshored by clients. In addition, information technology enabled the offshoring of business processes, which are not part of the CSS but are often aggregated in the product and trade statistics. While many companies produce their own embedded software, including the telecom, automotive and consumer electronics companies, there was also a growing market of third party embedded software providers developing in India, Japan, Taiwan and China. One initial part of software outsourcing in India was embedded software. The embedded software activity in India started with Texas Instruments locating a facility in Bangalore in 1985. Since then, others such as Hewlett-Packard, China's telecom firm, Huawei, and consumer electronics firms like Samsung and Sanyo have located in Bangalore. While embedded software is now not classified as software services, it was a smaller proportion of the software efforts in the beginning. The term R&D services or engineering services is now used to describe all manner of embedded software along with the other related hardware and software systems involved in the product.

In the context of catch-up, an interesting feature of software development in the different countries of the world is that the different segments gave rise to different institutional environments that supported their growth. Thus, the US and UK, which had larger package software segments compared to their competitors in Europe, also developed venture capital institutions earlier. Among later countries to enter the product market, Israel stands out as an exceptional case but it too developed a venture capital industry early in its progress. On the other hand, countries and periods in which customized services grew faster tended to develop mechanisms and institutions to link into large labour markets where the required changes in training and skill were rapidly absorbed and diffused through private labour training institutions. Thus, Ireland and India developed a thriving private training market and US companies that needed a technical labour force were not averse to utilizing the diaspora connections in their companies.

However, in order to understand the catch-up of countries based on the growth of a software sector in their economy, we need to examine the processes of internationalization in this sector. This is because while the growth of software in OECD countries was largely based on domestic demand due to the spread of computerization within these countries, they soon ran into constraints surrounding the availability of skilled labour domestically. The growth of the software industry in several emerging economies was largely based on the foreign demand for software programmers and programming services. The only exceptions to this rule have been China, Russia and Brazil, who have tried to forge their software services industry on the basis of their large domestic and linguistically distinct demand for software products – a strategy not very different from that attempted by several European countries in the mid-1980s.

Also, the open source software (OSS) movement is creating a new and different type of turbulence. Open source software is a movement launched in the 1980s in the United States and Western Europe. It created new operating systems, and requested that the source code of Linux, Apache and other operating systems, and all the applications based on them, are made available to users and other programmers. Thus open source software circulates fairly freely and has produced hundreds of applications that are available at no cost (Lakhani and von Hippel, 2003). Volunteer programmers, specialized open source companies, companies operating in the packaged software subsector, academics and end users are all producing open source software (Perens, 2005). The open source software market share in the CSS is over 15 per cent today, and growing faster than the sector itself. Open source software is feasible and profitable because it is more cost effective, thus attracting cost-conscious users, and also because revenues are generated for companies not by selling software but by providing after-sale services. Many developing countries have adopted open source software for all public sector operations, including most Latin American countries and China.

3.2 THE INTERNATIONALIZATION OF THE SOFTWARE SECTOR (1980–2007)

The internationalization of the computer software sector follows patterns that roughly correspond to the product life cycle (PLC) and industry life cycle (ILC) theories (Vernon, 1966; Klepper, 1997; Mazzucato, 2003). New products and services are born in the most advanced industrial nations where innovation systems and affluent markets exist. This is an era of high turnover of firms located in the most developed countries, with many firms entering and exiting the market. Internationalization starts with the export of products in their original form, as they were produced for affluent markets. The process continues with investments of the large innovative corporations in less advanced countries for the purpose of localization (adaptation for other markets) and the transfer of parts and modules for cost reduction. Later on, the original innovators create subsidiaries in less developed nations in order to produce entire systems best suited to the needs and characteristics of those less advanced nations. In this phase, expatriate R&D activities of MNCs evolve from technology transfer units to indigenous technology units (Ronstadt, 1984). At the same time, competitors emerge based in the host countries, as knowledge externalities allow new entrants to produce similar, albeit usually simpler versions of the products for the local or regional markets. Finally, these developing country entrants become fully-fledged competitors and seize large portions of the global markets. Third world multinationals emerge (Wells, 1983). This general pattern has been observed in dozens of manufacturing industries from cement and steel to electrical appliances and computers.

The PLC and its derived ILC perspectives provide a fairly accurate description of many industries, even if it has been shown that some industries, particularly science-based ones, diverge somewhat from the general pattern. Biotechnology is still in a period when many firms are entering and exiting the market, yet it is already migrating towards such nations as China and India (Niosi and Reid, 2007). The international migration of the aerospace industry occurred only over half a century after its birth, and the sector tended not to increased dispersion but to rapid concentration in a few national or regional champions (Niosi and Zhegu, 2006).

The internationalization of the computer software sector tends to follow the PLC and ILC patterns. Innovators based in the United States exported software, then created captive subsidiaries for localization and module production in less advanced nations, then formed R&D subsidiaries in those countries while at the same time outsourcing parts and pieces of their software programs. During these phases competitors emerged, most notably from those of the first set of host countries.

Before trying to understand the internationalization of the sector, it may be useful to summarize the phases in the development cycle of software. The cycle starts with the project definition, most often made with the collaboration of the client and the prime contractor, most often a company based in an OECD country, but increasingly often an Indian firm. The client's request is analysed and the prime contractor designs the general lines of the solution. Then the work is divided into modules, some or all of which being sent for development to an offshoring country. Later, the prime contractor assembles the system and implements it again in conjuction with the client (Figures 3.1 and 3.2).

3.2.1   The First Wave: India, Ireland and Israel

The internationalization of the CSS towards developing countries started with direct investments of large MNCs in India, Ireland and Israel (Arora

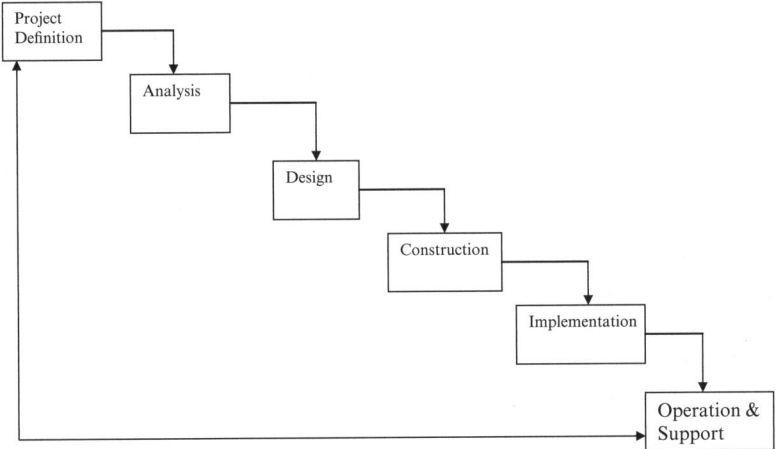

Figure 3.1   The 'waterfall' software development cycle

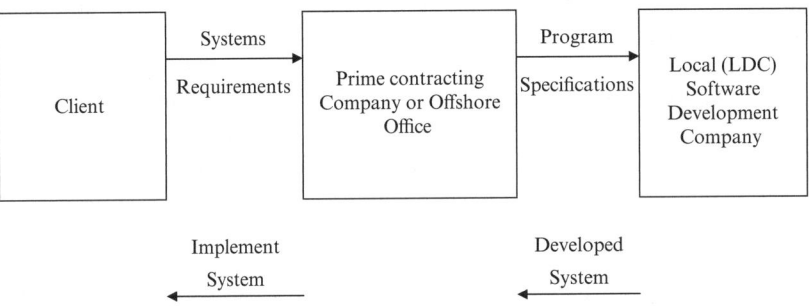

Source: Pearl2 Project (2004).

Figure 3.2   Process flow for foreign outsourced software development work

et al., 2001; Arora and Gambardella, 2005; Athreye, 2004, 2005; Banerjee and Duflo, 2000; Joseph, 2006). The three countries appeared to be substantially different in terms of the activities allocated to foreign subsidiaries, licensees and subcontractors, production and export patterns, and overall externalities that accrued to host countries.

India

India is prominent among the newcomers. Since the 1970s India has attracted information technology foreign direct investments and subcontracting. In the 1970s and 1980s, India attracted such early innovators as IBM and Texas Instruments (even if IBM temporarily left India in 1978). The software policy of 1986 and the liberalization of 1992 brought back IBM and added dozens of foreign computer software companies. India's comparative advantages were its large pool of skilled technicians and engineers (400000 professionals in 2006 and 60000 new graduates every year), widespread English proficiency, and relatively low salaries compared to North America and Western Europe. North American and Western European MNCs both outsourced work to Indian software firms and established captive subsidiaries in order to produce software modules locally, as well as to expatriate software services such as technical call centres, maintenance and localization. MNCs were forced to do so because of shortages and high prices of skilled manpower in their home markets.

Also, the Indian IT industry benefited from permanent links with expatriate personnel moving back and forth to and from North America (Joseph, 2006). In India, we witness a continuous development of the CSS sector through different organizational forms, in a clear upward capability movement from technical call centres and software subcontracting, to foreign direct investment (FDI) in captive BPO subsidiaries and both foreign owned and domestic research centres.

In India the drivers of the rapid expansion were exports, mostly to North American and Western European markets. Only in the 2000s has the internal market started to show some dynamism. Athreye (2005) underlines the fact that those Indian exports, which have been steadily rising from the late 1980s on, have almost always been the result of the activity of Indian owned and controlled firms.

Large MNCs first established themselves in India and local firms developed in parallel, mostly through international or domestic subcontracting, and they now represent a major share of the country's exports. Such names as Cisco, IBM, Microsoft, Oracle and SAP, are among the largest foreign competitors for local manpower.

India's exports have experienced a continuous rise since the early 1990s. In 1988 the Indian government created an Electronics and Computer Software Promotion Council that marked the rapid rise of exports. Exports grew from US$145 million in 1991 to US$6008 million in 2000. By 2005–2006, India's software and related service exports were worth US$13.6 billion, and they were growing at a rate of 20–30 per cent a year. India's exports are directed almost exclusively toward the US and the UK, from such major clusters as Bangalore, Mumbai, Delhi and Hyderabad. It is possible that the Indian boom in software exports that started in the 1980s will slow down, due to its own balancing loops, as the number of new graduates in computer science and engineering does not keep pace with demand, and salaries of Indian professionals become high compared

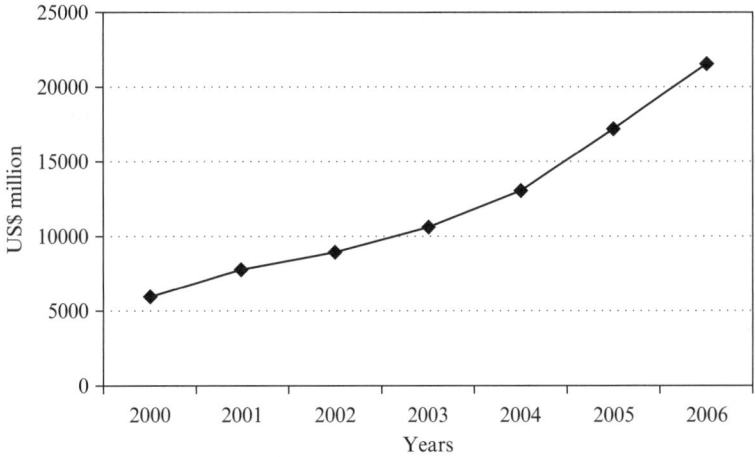

Source: National Association of Software and Service Companies, India.

Figure 3.3   India's export of CSS and related BPOs (2000–2006)

with those of China, Russia, Brazil or the Philippines. Yet, according to Athreye (2005) the growth of Indian exports may continue in the foreseeable future on the basis of rising productivity and upgrading of services into value added categories such as computer systems design (Figure 3.3).

In 2005 Cisco, Intel and Microsoft each announced investments of over US$1 billion in India to upgrade their software facilities (see Table 3.3). Oracle also bought an Indian competitor for a similar sum, and announced an additional increase in its Indian payroll from 8600 to 10000 employees. In 2006 Accenture announced the doubling of its staff in India, China and the Philippines from 24000 to 50000 over three years, most of which will be in India. MNCs based in industrial countries are now creating software centres in India in order to design, develop and test brand new software.

While foreign multinational corporations based in the United States and the United Kingdom originally launched the Indian software industry, today the country is home to several local multinational software outsourcing companies such as Tata Consultancy Services, HCL Technology, Infosys and Wipro. India is unique among the catching-up countries, due to the internationalization of many of its major domestic firms. Indian software FDI started in the late 1980s with the first subsidiary of HCL and Infosys, two of the largest domestic firms (Pradhan, 2007). By 2007 India's FDI in software represented over US$8 billion, with 165 Indian software companies that had a total of 645 subsidiaries abroad. The affiliates – most often wholly owned subsidiaries – are located in the United States and Canada (37 per cent), Europe (25 per cent), Asia (22 per cent), Middle East (5 per cent) Oceania (3.5 per cent), Africa (2.6 per cent), and Latin America (2.3 per cent) (Pradhan, 2007). On a country-by-country basis, the United States (221 subsidiaries), the United Kingdom (83), and Singapore (60), are the main destinations of India FDI in software. Germany (37), China (29) and Malaysia (20) follow. In terms of the number of foreign subsidiaries, the main MNCs from India are Tata Consultancy Services (47 subsidiaries), HCL Technology (31), Cambridge Solutions (19) and Teledata (15).

Also, India's largest software companies are now starting to market their own products and have their own trademarks for their proprietary products (Joseph, 2006). These trademarks are now registered in the United States and European Patent and Trademark Offices. More recently, the largest Indian software MNCs are looking for cheaper locations in such countries as China, Latin America and Russia.

Ireland

It was in the late 1970s that the government of the Republic of Ireland started targeting the software industry. Ireland's competitive advantages included low salaries, an educated English-speaking labour force, a good telecommunication infrastructure and the opportunity to use the island as a base to sell software in the European Community market. In the 1980s and 1990s 200 North American multinational companies created subsidiaries in Ireland which in turn invested in upgrading their university system. Several international software companies moved up from localization to computer software design, and the process of upgrading of their activities is far from complete (Sands, 2005). Due to massive FDI, the cost advantage of Ireland declined over time, and the industry – both foreign and domestic – moved up in the value chain towards design activities and brand new software.

By 2004, according to official figures, Ireland had exported US$19 billion worth of software and was the number one country in terms of its software exports. The industry was composed of some 900 companies, of which 130 were MNCs and 760 were local firms, the latter being responsible for US$1.4 billion in exports. Irish domestic firms were mostly niche companies with a small but increasing international presence, and reduced support of national or international venture capital. The Irish software industry employed 25000 people, down from the 30000 it employed in 2000, but its export figures kept moving up after the 2000 collapse of the IT markets. Falling employment and increasing value of exports are a signal of the increasing value added of the Irish software production.

In sum, Ireland is a much smaller player than India in the software market, but due to its considerable public investments in education and infrastructure, it has been able to continue moving up the technological ladder. However, future obstacles to growth include the increasing cost of its university graduates in computer sciences, shortage of skilled personnel, competition from India and other low-cost countries, the trend towards a decline of software sales from package to Internet services, and the rapid concentration of software niches under the control of such companies as IBM, Microsoft, Oracle or SAP.

Israel

Israel developed its computer software industry in the 1980s and 1990s. The Israeli industry emerged on the basis of strong government support for education, and public and private investment in telecommunication infrastructure and venture capital. Over 400 software companies exist in the country, including both the subsidiaries of large American multinational corporations and domestic firms.

The country possesses some major comparative advantages besides education, infrastructure and venture capital. These include massive immigration of educated computer scientists and engineers from Russia and other Eastern European countries after the fall of the Berlin wall in 1989, and also continuous immigration from Argentina and Western Europe. On the basis of these advantages, Israel very soon attracted large R&D centres of software multinationals; their mission was to design and develop, not just localize, computer and embedded software.[4]

Unlike Ireland, Israel has a very strong local sector competing in the world markets with its own computer software products and internationally recognized brands in management systems. Some 120 Israeli software firms are quoted in NASDAQ and other North American stock exchanges. Israel, like India, has its own software multinational corporations, such as AMDOCS (sales of US$2.6 billion in 2006, present in 50 countries with 16 000 employees). Over 100 software Israeli firms have been granted patents in the US up to 2002 (Giarratana and Torrisi, 2004). Also, software is the largest ICT industry in Israel in terms of sales, accounting for almost 40 per cent of all sales in 2000.

In spite of its high rates of growth in the 1980s and 1990s, the Israeli industry experienced lower rates of growth in the 2000s, due to its small labour pool, increasing costs of programmers and software engineers, and competition from lower cost nations, such as India, China and Russia (see Figure 3.4). Also, competing in management, e-business and other industrial software proves increasingly difficult as these niches are rapidly concentrating under the leadership of such industry giants as HP, IBM, Microsoft, Oracle and SAP.

Exports (US$ million)

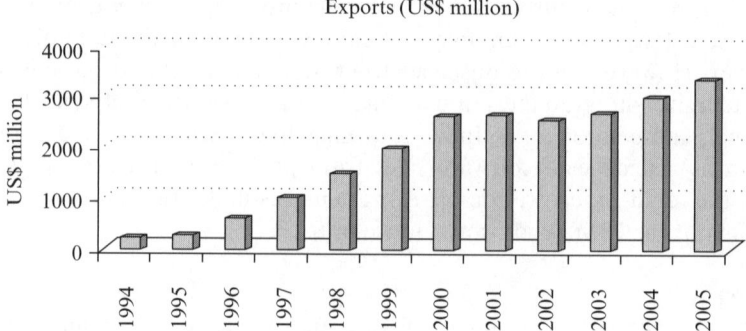

Source: Israel Association of Electronics and Software Industries, 2006.

Figure 3.4   Israel's software industry

The three I's of the first wave have followed very different paths and seem to have created a dynamic export sector from the CSS-related BPO sector. Tables 3.4 and 3.5 compare the countries and their MNCs.

3.2.2   The Second Wave: China and the Philippines

In the 1990s a small group of new countries entered the international markets. China and the Philippines are paramount among them.

China
China is the emerging giant in the software industry. China's strengths include a large labour pool (330 000 professionals in 2002, and 37 000 graduates every year), government support in the form of both tax incentives and infrastructure, and low salaries. The software industry was given priority in the 10th Five Year Plan, in the late 1990s; governments introduced several types of tax rebate and, since 2001, massively increased the university resources for software education.

Foreign universities were invited to create programs. Technology parks were created or revamped to accommodate the new firms. Currently, China has six software exporting clusters in Beijing, Shanghai, Tianjin, Shenzhen, Dalian and Xian, and is planning to create nine others by 2010. Under these incentives, over 10 000 companies were created according to the Chinese Software Industry Association. Also, China, like India, takes advantage of externalities gained by the large number (some figures put that number close to 100 000 per year in all disciplines) of Chinese students in advanced education in foreign universities, even if the majority of them

Table 3.4   The three Is compared

	India	Ireland	Israel
Population (million, 2006)	1095	4	6.3
GDP per capita (US$ PPP 2006)	3700	43 600	26 200
Total exports 2006 (US$ billion)	112	120	43
Software exports 2005 (US$ billion)	17.3	28.2	3.3
Software exports as per cent of total exports	17%	16%	7%
Software industry employment*	570 000	25 000	35 000
Firms with US software patents**	1	5	108
National association	NASSCOM	NSD	IASH

Notes:
*   Excluding BPO and information technology enabled services (ITES)
**   Up to 20

Source: NASSCOM, Israel Association of Electronics and Software Industries, and Irish Software Association.

do not return to China. Yet, like Russia, China suffers from low English proficiency, weak understanding of Western business practices and a reputation for poor intellectual property protection (Sahay et al., 2003). For example, the largest Chinese companies, such as UFSoft, KingSoft and Kingdee, all sell Chinese versions of Western software. We are not aware of Chinese firms becoming international competitors from their overseas subsidiaries, like the largest Indian firms. Thus, the Chinese computer software industry is mostly oriented towards the burgeoning domestic market, including the huge government market. In terms of exports, and for cultural, geographic and linguistic reasons, Chinese companies are today more oriented towards outsourcing for Japanese and Korean companies in the area of embedded software. Among MNCs, Adobe, Intel, Lucent Microsoft, Oracle and Nortel have R&D labs in China. Microsoft has signed a Memorandum of Understanding for a massive technology transfer to China, and conducts R&D in China for the internal market. Intel has also created a major software lab. By 2005, China's software exports were worth US$3.6 billion (see Figure 3.5) and the Chinese Ministry of the Information Industry forecasted exports in the US$12–13

Table 3.5 *Software multinationals (end 2005)*

Name	Founded	No. of country presence	Revenue (US$ bn) 2006	Employees 2006	Country head office	US patents as of 1/1/2006	Stock Exchange	Activity
Microsoft	1975	101	44.28	71 553	USA	6613	NASDAQ	Software services
IBM (software)	1911		15.8	ND	USA	>15000	NYSE	Software services & hardware
Oracle	1977		14.4	56133	USA	940	NASDAQ	Software & services
SAP	1972	50	10.9	36600	Germany	140		Software & services
Tata C. Services	1968	34	3.0	62832	India	6	NSE (India)	Outsourcing, IT services, & software
Infosys	1981	12	2.52	58409	India	0	NASDAQ	Consulting & IT services
Wipro	1946	16	3.47	66000	India	1	NYSE	R&D service provider
Formula Systems	1983		0.5	5000	Israel	7	NASDAQ	Proprietary software, IT services
UFIDA	1988	2	0.1	5000	China	0	SSE(China)	Proprietary software, integration
Stefanini IT Solutions	1987	10	NA	4000	Brazil	0	NA	Outsourcing & integration
Luxoft	2000	5	0.046	2300	Russia	0	NA	Software development & maintenance

Source: Authors' own elaboration of company annual reports, websites and USPTO (United States Patents and Trademark Office).

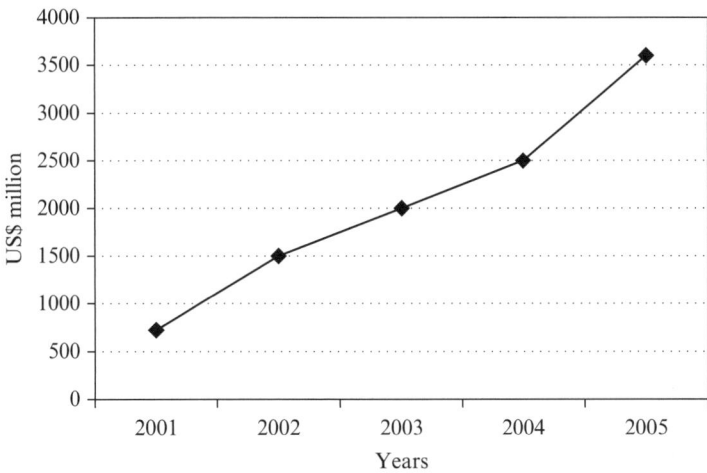

Source: China Software Industry Association.

Figure 3.5 *China's exports of CSS and related BPOs (2001–05)*

billion range by 2010 (*China Daily* online, 22 June 2006). Some 80 per cent of China's exports come from multinational corporations operating in China (China Economic net, 1 December 2006).

China has been promoting software aggressively for a number of years, and more recently, outsourcing, as the means of internationalizing its software industry. Ironically, while the state promoted R&D-based projects initially, those have had limited success, being 'flagship' companies more than anything else, and flagship R&D-based companies are often small, with 100 to 500 employees. The real growth has come from investments by MNCs and also from Chinese firms outside of the state sponsored sector, in the private sector with companies that initially made finance, accounting and other kinds of software that could be customized and sold to many thousands of customers. Eventually, some of these succeeded even against some of the larger foreign MNEs.

An even newer breed of company spawned in the private sector – the outsourcing-based company – rose in the late 1990s and mid-2000s, to create yet another major subsector.

● While very few firms had success with the export mode, some companies found that servicing Western firms that had local Chinese needs for subcontracting was a good way to enter the market.

- More recently, other Chinese companies have been having great success in Japan, again by servicing Japanese systems integrators.

The Philippines

The Philippines is another country that is aiming at the outsourcing computer software market. The Philippines has managed to develop a business process outsourcing and other IT-enabled services capability not unlike India's, albeit on a smaller scale. Since its entry into the broader BPO market took place not long after India's, this suggests that a follower, if not a fast follower, still has opportunities. Its strengths include low salaries and a fairly large pool of talent with English proficiency. Its weaknesses are in the area of intellectual property protection. With 300 firms and some 10000 programmers (Pearl2 Project, 2004), in 2005 the country exported US$272 million in software and its software international sales increased by 33 per cent a year in the 2000s. Also, it exported US$2.5 billion in BPO, but the country has no major domestic software company and most of its exports come from multinational corporations such as Accenture, Computer Associates, Fujitsu, Microsoft, NEC and Oracle. Most of its IT workforce and infrastructure is in the call service industry; the potential for upgrading may be there.

The Philippines has also recently gained a name for itself through its call centre work. While various kinds of BPO work like animation, and to a more limited extent, software services and R&D services, also do get outsourced to the Philippines as well, these have grown rather steadily. In contrast, call centre growth rates have been explosive, with 100 per cent growth rates not being uncommon for several firms in the mid-2000s.

Another way to look at outsourcing is as the result of actions of specific companies (i.e., MNEs). This was certainly the case in China and the Philippines, where the market has been smaller, and so the activity can be seen to be the result of single actors operating alone, at least initially. In the case of the Philippines, a single MNE, Caltex, started the 'subsector' for petroleum and gas-based MNEs, while another, AIG, started it for insurance, and P&G started by locating its human resources services in the Philippines. The fact that a single corporate takes such great risks to begin a greenfield operation suggests that the MNEs' own internal networks and knowledge transfer capabilities are so great that, other than the basic requirements of an abundant low-cost, highly skilled labour pool, other factors in the local 'setting' may not be as important.

While the two larger exporters of the first wave (India and Ireland) are way ahead of the second pack, China has already taken third position from Israel, and if present trends continue, by the end of the decade the Philippines and Russia should also have moved ahead. Figure 3.6 shows the trends of the first two waves.

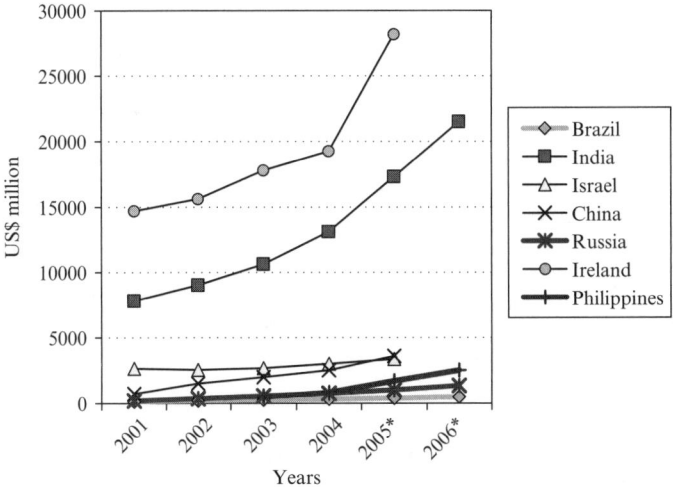

Sources: National associations of software companies.

Figure 3.6   CSS exports, main countries

3.2.3   The Emerging Third Wave: Russia, Eastern Europe and Latin America

Russia

In spite of the fact that it was only in 1987 that cooperatives and private firms were allowed to operate in the country (Katkalo and Mowery, 1996), Russia is already the third largest software outsourcing destination in the world (*Businessweek*, 2006). With main clusters in Moscow and St Petersburg, Russia has several strengths, including a large pool of engineers and computer scientists numbering about 250000 professionals in 2005, low salaries and a good communication infrastructure. Some 45000 university IT graduates enter the workforce every year. Besides, government support is flowing into the industry. In 2006 the federal government announced an initiative to create four large software techno parks by 2010, located in Dubna (near Moscow), St Petersburg, Nizhny Novgorod, and Novosibirsk. Each park will receive a grant of about US$80 to 100 million in infrastructure. In 2006 salaries of a programmer were on average US$12000 per annum, 20 per cent of US salaries, but slightly higher than those of Indian professionals. Obstacles to international outsourcing of computer software include low English proficiency, lack of knowledge of Western business practices, and widespread

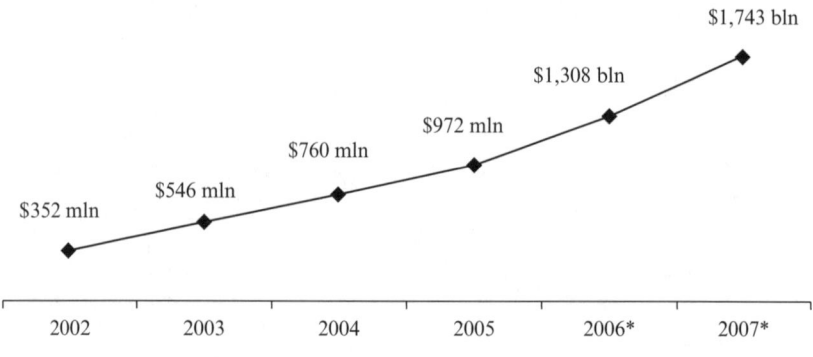

$352 mln $546 mln $760 mln $972 mln $1,308 bln $1,743 bln

2002   2003   2004   2005   2006*   2007*

Note: * forecast figures.

Source: Third Annual Survey of the Russian Export Market for Programming Services, Solutions and Products. RUSSOFT Association and Outsourcing-Russia.com, 2006.

Figure 3.7   Russia's exports of software by volume (2002–2007)

counterfeiting. However, foreign companies with software labs in Russia are mushrooming, and include Alcatel, Boeing, Dell, HP, IBM, Intel, Motorola, Nortel, SAP and Sun Microsystems. In 2004, Russia exported US$750 million in software, US$1 billion in 2005, and US$1.3 in 2006, 17 per cent of which came from the subsidiaries of multinational corporations (RUSSOFT, 2005a). Boasting an annual growth of 30–50 per cent a year for the domestic industry, the Russian Information and Communication Technologies Minister forecasted some $US1.7 billion in exports during 2007. The United States and Canada are the two key destinations, absorbing about 65 per cent of Russian exports (see Figure 3.7).

Also, Russia is developing its own software companies, such as EPAM (Russia's number one with 1700 employees, US$57 million in sales in 2005) and Luxoft (Russia's number 2 with 1600 employees and US$46 million in sales in 2005).

Bulgaria and Romania
Bulgaria and Romania are positioning themselves as new software outsourcing nations. Bulgaria's comparative advantages are, first, a fairly large pool of software engineers at low salaries, a pool increasing by over 5000 a year. Also, the country has a fast-improving telecommunication infrastructure and obtained accession to the European Union in 2007. Already hundreds of small Bulgarian software companies are doing contract work for large customers such as Boeing, BMW and Nortel.

Several large MNCs installed development centres in the country. The first, in 2000, was SAP, which installed an expatriate R&D lab in Sofia (*Businessweek*, 1 November 2004). In 2006, Microsoft, HP and Software AG followed suit. Other companies installed BPO centres, including IBM. Key markets for Bulgarian software are the United States, Canada, Germany, France, the United Kingdom, the Netherlands, Austria, Italy, Japan and China. However, language and cultural barriers persist, and skills and quality controls are variable.

Romania is another Eastern European competitor. Salaries of programmers are low (US$6000 a year on average), the country has a labour pool of some 45 000 developers, and the annual graduate cohort is around 8000. Its entry into the European Union is also a major plus for the country. By 2000, it was exporting close to US$100 million to North America and the European Union. At that time, there were some 350 companies, most of them small and medium sized firms. The country is becoming a specialist in security software, where both Microsoft and Symantec subcontract anti-virus software production. Other companies have created expatriate labs in Bucharest, including Oracle in 2004 (Saleh et al., 2004; McGee, 2005). In 2005 software exports, consisting mostly of outsourcing, passed the 250 million euro threshold.

Latin America (Argentina, Brazil and Mexico)
Latin America belongs both to the earlier and to the later wave. In fact, the idea and embryonic development of the industry had started way before China, the Philippines and Russia. As early as in the late 1980s, some authors were writing about the importance and the potential future benefits of the software industry for the region (Correa, 1990; Schware, 1992). But regional governments were far more interested in the nurturing of basic staples (food, minerals, oil and gas) than in such a sophisticated industry as software. Something may now be changing. Governments have discovered the promise of the software industry at least in a few countries. It may be too little, too late: Indian and other software multinationals are now very active in the area. Tata CS now has 5000 employees in Latin America, in Argentina, Brazil, Chile, Mexico and Uruguay. US multinationals are already creating support, maintenance and R&D centres in the region. The potential of knowledge spillovers from multinationals to local firms is thus present.

The next major catch-up country may be Brazil. Its software and related services production is close to US$9 billion. With some 6500 firms, Brazilian competitive advantages include its large pool of 160 000 IT professionals and 15 000 new graduates entering the workforce every year. Salaries are low and comparable to South-East Asian competitors. However, English proficiency is poor, and business relationships with North America and Western Europe are weak, as is the reputation for IP protection. Besides, the largest Brazilian-owned software producers are most often either government firms or the subsidiaries of financial institutions, thus they are not very active in the export markets (Junqueira Botelho et al., 2005). Brazilian domestic companies lack the qualifications to compete in the high end of the market. All these factors explain the weak dynamism of the Brazilian software export activities and the confinement to local markets.

However, in 2004, from its clusters in Rio, Sao Paulo, Campinas and Recife, the South American country was exporting US$314 million worth of software. The bulk of these exports came from 14 domestic companies and 9 subsidiaries of multinational corporations and went to other Latin American markets. Recent MNC investment announcements in Brazil were far more modest than those recorded in India or China.

Argentina is catching-up. . .with Brazil. In 2004, some twenty years after India, Argentina unveiled a plan for the development of the software industry (2004–14). By 2005 its production had grown to US$1.1 billion, its exports to US$170 million, and employment is growing at 25 per cent a year, fuelled by the low cost of programmers and technical manpower, at about US$11 an hour for a university-level programmer. Also, Argentina has more university students per capita than any other Latin American country. The industrial association of the software industry seems very active. However, the English proficiency of the population is not high. The kind of industry developing in that country is a mix of call centres and software development subcontracting. Among the new multinationals investing in Argentina's software, one finds Intel with a new R&D centre (in Cordoba in 2007), TCS and Firstsource Solutions from India (support services), Exact Software (Netherlands, localization) and others.

In the software industry, Mexico benefits from a certain number of advantages. It has the largest Spanish-speaking population in the world; it is part of NAFTA and can export Spanish software to both the US and Latin America; it is close to the US sources of expertise and the main outsourcing market. Also, the Mexican government has targeted the industry through PROSFT (a program for the development of the software industry). Yet in 2003 the industry produced only US$840 million in software out of which 8 per cent (US$64 million) were exported, including US$30 million in services. A few MNCs have located their facilities in Mexico, including IBM in Jalisco, Oracle in Mexico DF, and more recently Tata CS in Guadalajara to employ 500 engineers. Thus Mexico follows the decades-long Latin American tradition of focusing its production on the domestic market. A few companies such as Aspel (accounting software) and Hildebrando (systems integration) are among those with international exports and presence (Ruiz Durán, 2004). Also, the number of graduates in Mexican universities is not high, and the best of them can move north of the border to high paid positions. The telecommunication infrastructure is poor (19 lines per 100 people, against 22 in Argentina and Brazil, or 29 in Uruguay). Finally, the Mexican Association of Information Technology (AMITI) has, according to Computerworld[5], mostly concentrated on hardware and not attended the interests of the software industry as such.

3.3 NATIONAL MODELS OF CATCHING UP

As noted earlier, the growth of the software industry in several emerging economies was largely based on the foreign demand for software programmers and programming services. This trend has now spread to a range of R&D services and business process activities 'enabled' by the use of IT. The only exceptions to this rule have been China, Russia and Brazil, who have tried to forge their software services industry on the basis of their large domestic and linguistically distinct demand for software products – a strategy not very different from that attempted by several European countries in the mid-1980s.

The software industry presents several avenues and models of catching up: independent software development in the country with the highest absorptive capabilities (Israel); path-dependent development under the foreign direct investment of multinational corporations (Ireland, Philippines) and export-oriented development with both foreign direct investment and entry of local companies serving largely foreign and not local demand for software programming and IT skills.

The development path favoured for catch-up points to the influence of different initial conditions and favourable institutions. Initial conditions include domestic market size and human capital stocks. Favourable institutions include mainly venture capital and the rapidity with which the educational sector was able to respond to fine changes in the skill composition of software labour demand and thus maintain the competitiveness of the national industry.

Due to the size of their internal markets, Brazil and China could develop the computer software sector with products and services aimed at domestic demand. This option was less attractive to Ireland and Israel due to their small population, but also to countries with large but poor populations, such as India and the Philippines, because of the small size of their internal markets. By 2006, India, with a population of 1.1 billion had only 4.25 computers per 1000 people and 60 million Internet hosts, while China had 41 computers and 85 Internet users per 1000 people; the Philippines had a population of 91 million, but only 16.8 computers per 1000 people and 5 million Internet hosts.[6] However, the case of Israel shows that this was not an insurmountable problem if one could capture a sizeable share of the worldwide market. Israel succeeded in its chosen niche of security products. However, Athreye (2005) notes that Indian firms fell behind in the race to develop an ERP product in the late 1980s. The Indian version, developed by Ramco, was superseded by a superior product from SAP two years ahead of them. Like West European firms that had tried the same in the mid-1980s, they found their marketing skills inadequate for a large international market.

In terms of human capital, the differences amongst the catching-up countries are also huge. In 1995, the school life expectancy was still low in most catching-up countries: that of an Irish 5-year-old was 16 years (and 17 years in 2003), against 13.5 years in Brazil, 12 in China and the Philippines, and 9 in India.[7] Except in Brazil, where it had increased by almost three years, it had barely increased by 2003 in other catching-up countries. But relative numbers hide the more important total numbers: in 2000, China had a tertiary educated population of 20.4 million, compared with 20 million in India, 13.6 million in Russia and 4.5 million in Brazil (NSF, 2006). Similarly, by 2006, total employment in the software and services sector was 1.2 million in India, and projections were about 1.6 million in 2007 (NASSCOM, 2007). IDC estimates that total employment in the Chinese software industry was well over 600 000 by 2005, and growing at a rate of 20 per cent a year (Gantz, 2006). In Brazil the industry had some 220 000 employees in 2005 (Tigre and Marques, 2007).

Institutions also matter. Those related to science and technology, including technical training, matter the most. In all these catching-up countries governments have increased the support to education in general and higher education in engineering and computer science in particular. Where the support was weaker, the industry has found serious obstacles in its development (Pearl2 Project, 2004). Governments have in a few cases created technology parks, attracting firms with tax incentives and advanced technology infrastructure (China, India and Russia). Technological incubators and public venture capital also fostered the software sector and accelerated catching up (Israel). National authorities have also implemented preferential procurement policies (China, Israel) and e-government (Brazil) (Behrens, 2003; RUSSOFT, 2005b; Saxenian, 2003).

A second look at the different paths followed by catchers up reveals some advantages and disadvantages in each of them. The Indian path is one that starts in low value added services, such as custom-made software, BPO and incipient proprietary products. A big advantage of this path is that it avoids head-on confrontation with established firms. It also allows scaling up with a conservative financing structure and large international presence – all advantages that a capital-poor, labour-abundant and poor economy can exploit. Such a trajectory may be more adequate to countries such as the Philippines with a potential for a larger, but less skilled, labour pool and a relative shortage of venture capital. Its main disadvantage is its longer trajectory until the new entrants move into high value proprietary products, and the role of reputation as a barrier to new entry. The strong reputation of existing (Indian) firms may mean the scope for new independent entry into this sector may be limited and any growth that occurs will be through the setting up of captive branch plants by Western and now Indian multinationals.

The Israeli path is somewhat at the opposite end of the Indian one. Very early, Israeli firms started launching their own products, developing their own trademarks and trying to carve some niches for themselves. Israeli firms could grow in the context of abundant venture capital, highly skilled engineers and solid public support in terms of R&D subsidies and procurement. The main advantage of this path was that it established a presence in some niches in the initial phases of their development. Time will say whether this catching-up trajectory can keep its momentum in a context where the industry starts to concentrate and US competitors are acquiring some of the top Israeli companies. In the meantime, few countries besides Israel will be able to follow this path. The Chinese path is more reminiscent of that followed by many West European countries but there are features that suggest that China may be more successful in gaining large market shares. The vast majority of Chinese software exports are made of embedded software (which enjoys a higher IPR protection), produced and exported by Japanese, South Korean and Taiwanese firms. China has the geographical advantage of proximity to East Asia and the linguistic advantage of its characters so that it can potentially think of a large market (Greater China) where its products could be used and exported to with little customization. If successful the Chinese will have forged a path no different from the US firms with their package software products.

However, this catching-up path may be difficult to export to other countries. Although Brazil has adopted a similar path to China, its success is less assured. Several decades of inward-looking industrial growth in Latin America have shown that developing products for domestic markets is not the fastest and surest way of learning and catching up. With exports representing some 3 per cent of sales, the Brazilian computer software industry could become trapped in its own internal market and experience only sluggish growth. Internal markets, sophisticated as they may be in some sectors (i.e. finance), can support only limited occasions for learning and expansion. Unlike in the case of China, this market is not large and is in sectors of weak appropriability, such as application software.

3.4   POLICY IMPLICATIONS

Some policy implications for developing countries are straightforward. Countries trying to catch up in this information technology should learn from the experiences of previous entrants. The first lesson, maybe, is that several routes are available and others are possibly yet to be discovered.

My sense is that the two main paths of growth have different policy implications. Going down the product route requires the government to subsidize the use of IT and create a large domestic market for its use. The subsidy required to promote IT use and cross the digital divide within the economy is likely to be very large because low labour costs mean that the price advantages of computerization are low in the domestic sector. However, this is one way to encourage the discovery of new uses, for example the revolution wrought by Skype, the usefulness of centralized information on prices resulting in new information services providers in rural areas and so on. In the past, much effort in developing domestic software products has gone into import substitution efforts. More useful would be a generalized subsidy that encourages use of IT and thus stimulates demand for a new range of products based on novel uses of IT.

A less expensive way to promote the growth of a software industry is to leverage the positives about software services growth. Unlike other industries where catching up requires heavy fixed capital investments and imposes long payback periods and high risks, software services and more recently BPO and R&D services require mostly human capital and communication infrastructure. Many niches, most of which are still contestable markets, and where the passage from one niche to others is still feasible, also constitute this sector. In other words, it is a flexible industry with many doors and many communicating vessels.

For catching up, human capital is not enough. The policy environment must also be suitable in order to stimulate R&D (through tax credits, direct subsidies, venture capital or other measures), facilitate the establishment of new firms, attract international producers and provide market access to public and private consumers.

Key policy elements along this route to growth of the industry include the following:

- Applying both horizontal R&D incentives, such as R&D tax credits, for all types of firms, and direct R&D subsidies for small firms, as in Israel, if they do not already exist;
- Nurturing large labour pools through higher education and selective immigration;

- Supporting entrepreneurship and new technology firms through different inducements.Technology parks are effective ways of sending signals to specialized markets, and reduce barriers to the entry of new technology-based companies through low-cost buildings, tax holidays, and effective telecommunication infrastructure.
- Corporate incubators may also help to bring together technological innovation, entrepreneurial and organizational competence, financial resources and capabilities.

3.5   BACK TO THEORY

The PLC and ILC theory is one of the cornerstones of present day administrative science. It provides a fairly good approximation to the internationalization of the CSS. However, the detailed analysis of several industries has shown that each sector unfolds its own life cycle pattern (Klepper, 1997). The computer software industry also displays idiosyncratic characteristics. One is that the sources of international spillovers include not only exports and FDI from early innovative nations, as the PLC–ILC model has emphasized, but also the international two-way mobility of programmers and entrepreneurs from catching-up to innovative nations, as the cases of India, Ireland and Israel have shown.

A second characteristic is that the institutional framework of the sector must also be included in order to understand its international development. The presence or absence of high quality tertiary education institutions, a venture capital industry and policy incentives for the promotion of a software industry are also part of the explanation of why catching up occurs in some nations and not in others, and of the path that countries follow in order to catch up.

Finally, the PLC–ILC theory does not allow for several paths of catching up, but assumes that catching up is available for all developing countries. Our study has shown that this is not the case.

3.6   CONCLUSION: COMPUTER SOFTWARE AS A WINDOW OF OPPORTUNITY

The computer software industry in a broader sense, including the BPO and information technology enabled services (ITES), is a major window of opportunity for developing countries. It does not require major domestic investment in laboratories and long periods of time before developing countries obtain results, as is the case for biotechnology or nanotechnology. However, it requires national investment in education and telecommunication infrastructure. This is the first and most evident policy implication. Also, a 'two leg approach' (learning from incumbent corporations) seems advisable: the three initial offshoring nations (India, Ireland and Israel) and the two most successful newcomers (China and Russia) are benefiting from important knowledge inputs from large established multinational corporations, which also provided commercialization channels for the software outputs. These multinationals represent the vast majority of exports in both Ireland and China. Only Israel and India have grown a sizeable number of large and successful domestic firms with international scope. Thus, the second policy implication is that foreign software multinational corporations should be invited to participate in the growth of the local software industry in developing countries.

The third implication is that domestic firms need to be supported by local and international venture capital firms. Israel has followed this path and India is now receiving substantial amounts of international venture capital.

Many developing countries are locked in inferior institutions and organizations yielding low levels of both public (education, R&D outputs and incentives) and private goods and services (new products and processes). Institutional inertia is the most frequent situation in most LDCs (Mokyr, 2002, p. 222). Also, cultural environments may have positive or negative impacts on the supply of institutional innovation (Ruttan, 2001, p. 131; Kuran, 2004) and on the climate for learning.

Should developing countries entering the CSS sector search for domestic or international markets? The issue, presented fifteen years ago in a comparison between Brazil and India (Schware, 1992) now seems ludicrous. Demand comes from rich advanced nations; looking for exports, India has moved far ahead of Brazil, a country that gave priority to domestic markets; in fact, Indian multinational software corporations are now looking for cheap labour and new markets in Latin America. Also, the computer software sector may be one among other factors promoting balanced growth across the economy. One sector, even if dynamic, cannot pull the entire Indian economy out of secular stagnation. But the computer software industry may serve as a model for other related IT and service sectors in India or elsewhere in the developing world.

The domestic market may be a springboard for catching up, inasmuch as domestic firms in developing countries do not use their national market as a private fief and rapidly move from the home to the international marketplace. During the import substitution period (1950–90) many companies in developing countries, particularly in Latin America, contented themselves with producing for the home market. Of course, any local market, even in large countries such as Brazil or Mexico, is only a small fraction of the world market; by locking themselves into the domestic market such companies missed the opportunity to gain knowledge from users in different places and lost economies of scale and scope.

Local entrepreneurship has been a major element in the origin of any national software industry. This was the case in Brazil, China, India and Israel, and it is becoming increasingly important in other countries such as Ireland and Russia.

As both ISV and equipment producers grow, they tend to outsource increasing proportions of their software. Most observers (including IDC, McKinsey, PriceWaterhouse and UNIDO) are unanimous in forecasting a steady rise of international software outsourcing. This trend involves an increasing number of international networks and value chains, as well as increasing opportunities for developing countries to learn and participate in the industry.

Common factors in catching up are government support for the industry, technological competency and cost competitiveness of the labour force. Specific growth factors for particular countries have been the role of the military (in the first periods of the industry in both Israel and the United States), cultural and geographic proximity (China with regards to Japan), or the entry of Ireland into the European Community. Even in those countries where the military has played a role, it was only in the early stages of the industry. Civilian software applications are a hundred times more important than military applications.

Developing countries are displaying several different paths to catching up in the software sector (see Table 3.6). The largest Indian multinationals move through the service–to custom design–to product path. Some of the largest Chinese firms move from products for the local market to products for international markets. Israeli firms chose a strategy of niche products for both national and international markets from the start. In other terms, as in the food industry there is no single virtuous path to catching up, but several. The choice of catching-up strategy is related to the factors that developing countries can more easily obtain: hundreds of thousands of fairly skilled computer scientists in India, a less plentiful, but more skilled labour pool as in Israel, combined to easier access to venture capital, or large internal and neighbouring Asian markets in the case of China. Figures 3.8 and 3.9 summarize the catching-up ladders for India and China. Note that there are two different ladders in China: some firms are learning through outsourcing and exporting modules, and others through selling in Asia packaged software conceived for China.

Key common elements in the catching up were the access to large markets, either domestic or international, a large pool of computer

Table 3.6 Comparing the new entrants

	Ireland	India	Israel	China	Philippines	Russia	Brazil
Origins of demand	External	External	External	Internal and external	External	External and internal	Internal
Exporters	Foreign and local firms	Local and foreign firms	Local and foreign firms	Foreign firms	Foreign firms	Local and foreign firms	Foreign and local firms
Institutions: associations	Irish Software Association	NASSCOM	IASEI	NA	NA	RUSSOFT	SOFTEX, APEX
Clusters	Dublin, Galway	Bangalore, Delhi, Madras Hyderabad	Haifa, Tel Aviv	Beijing, Chongqing Shanghai Tianjin	Manila Quezon City	Moscow, St Petersburg	Sao Paulo, Rio, Brasilia
Competitive advantages	English proficiency, Innovation EU market	Labour cost; English proficiency	English proficiency; innovation; external links	Labour cost	Labour cost	Labour cost; high skilled personnel	Labour cost
Competitive disadvantages	Increasing labour costs	Increasing labour costs	Small market; crowded niches	Low English proficiency & skills	Low English proficiency & skills	Low English proficiency	Low English proficiency & skills

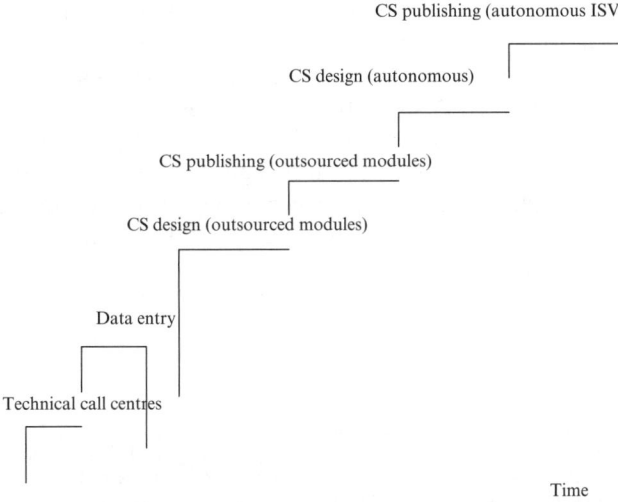

Figure 3.8   The Indian catching-up ladder

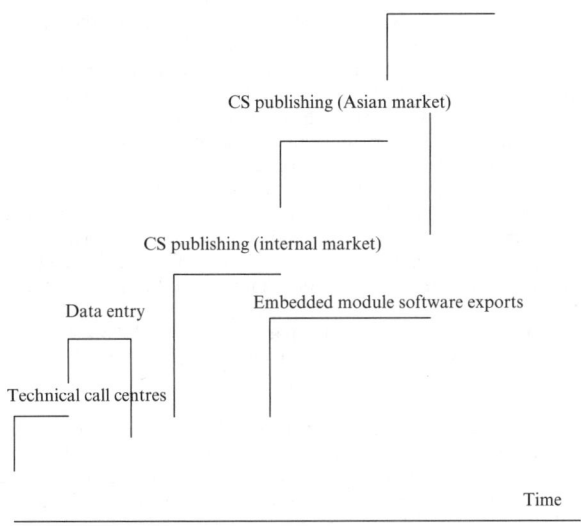

Figure 3.9   The Chinese catching-up ladders

scientists and programmers, as well as economic and innovation policies facilitating both FDI from multinational firms and R&D activities from both local and international corporations. Idiosyncratic catching-up factors include the role of the military and the role of imported labour

(Israel), and internal private market demand (China). It is also worth noting that in the Indian software industry, as in pharmaceuticals, large Third World multinationals grew out of serving the international market, not the internal market. Also, in both cases, these large Indian corporations moved from mass production of low-innovation products and services (generics, software services) towards higher-innovation products, not on the basis of sophisticated domestic technology policies (as in the case of Israeli software), but through a long process of learning and competing in the international markets.

NOTES

1. Software publishers (NAICS 511210 in the North American industrial classification code) 'carry out the operations necessary for producing and distributing software'. Computer designers (NAICS 541510) 'comprise establishments primarily engaged in providing expertise in the field of information technologies through one or more activities, such as writing, modifying, testing and supporting software to meet the needs of a particular customer'. Data processing, hosting and related services comprises establishments primarily engaged in providing infrastructure from data supplied by clients or provide automated data processing and data entry services.
2. Telephone call centres (NAICS 561420) include computer and mathematical science occupations (group 15) but also sales, legal, management, building and other occupations.
3. Embedded software is a program inserted into a special-purpose computer device. It differs from independent software, which can be uploaded into a general-purpose computer (such as a PC) that can perform different tasks. Special-purpose computer devices are part of such diverse equipment as aircraft, automatic telling machines, cars, electrical appliances, nuclear reactors, numerically controlled machines, telecommunication equipment or watches. The ubiquity of the semiconductor, in thousands of various applications, has generalized the production and incorporation of computer programs into many different types of apparatus. The producer of the machines often creates such software, but the programs are increasingly outsourced to independent software companies. China, for instance, has become a major producer of embedded software for Japanese firms.
4. In 1972 IBM created in Haïfa the first expatriate software laboratory in Israel. In 1989 Microsoft installed its R&D laboratory in Israel (Haïfa). Other software MNCs include BCM Software (1999), HP (1994) and SAP (2000).
5. http://www.computerworld.com/.
6. CIA Factbook and Nationmaster statistics. As a matter of comparison, in 2006 the US had 544 computers per 1000 population, Canada 393 and France 295.
7. OECD (2005) and World Bank Indicators. Equivalent figures for 1995 were: 19.5 in Australia (21.1 in 2003), 17 in the United Kingdom (20.4 in 2003) and 13.5 in Sweden (20.3 in 2003).

BIBLIOGRAPHY

Abramovitz, M. (1986), 'Catching-up, forging ahead and falling behind', *The Journal of Economic History*, **46**(2), 385–406.

Arora, A. and S. Athreye (2002), 'The software industry and India's economic development', *Information Economics and Policy*, **14**(2), 253–73.

Arora, A. and A. Gambardella (eds) (2005), *From Underdogs to Tigers: The Rise and Growth of the Software Industry in Brazil, China, India, Ireland, and Israel*, Oxford: Oxford University Press.

Arora, A., V.S. Arunachalam, J. Asundi and R. Fernandes (2001), 'The Indian software services industry', *Research Policy*, **30**(8), 1267–88.

Athreye, S. (2003), 'Multinational firms and the evolution of the Indian software industry', Economics Study Area Working Papers no. 51, East–West Center, Economics Study Area.

Athreye, S. (2004), 'Role of transnational corporations in the evolution of a high-tech industry: the case of India's software industry', *World Development*, **32**(3), 555–60.

Athreye, S. (2005), 'The Indian software industry', in A. Arora and A. Gambardella (eds), *From Underdogs to Tigers: The Rise and Growth of the Software Industry in Brazil, China, India, Ireland, and Israel*, Oxford: Oxford University Press, pp. 7–40.

Banerjee, A.V. and E. Duflo (2000), 'Reputation effects and the limits of contracting: a study of the Indian software industry', *Quarterly Journal of Economics*, **115**(3), 989–1017.

Bardhan, A.K. and C. Kroll (2006), 'Competitiveness and an emerging sector: the Russian software industry and its global linkages', *Industry and Innovation*, **13**(1), 669–95.

Behrens, A. (2003), 'Brazilian software: the quest for an export-oriented business strategy', London Business School, DRC Working Papers no. 21.

Bonaccorsi, A. and C. Rossi (2003), 'Why open source software can succeed?', *Research Policy*, **32**(7), 1243–58.

Breznitz, D. (2005), 'The Israeli Software Industry', in A. Arora and A. Gambardella (eds), *From Underdogs to Tigers: The Rise and Growth of the Software Industry in Brazil, China, India, Ireland, and Israel*, Oxford: Oxford University Press, pp. 72–98.

Businessweek (2004), 'India: now it's hardware's turn', 17 May.

Businessweek (2006), 'India: more than just call centres', 27 December.

Campbell-Kelly, M. (2003), *From Airline Reservations to Sonic the Hedgehog: A History of the Software Industry*, Cambridge: MIT Press.

Carmel, E. (2003a), 'Taxonomy of new software exporting nations', *Electronic Journal on Information Systems in Developing Countries*, **13**(2), 1–6.

Carmel, E. (2003b), 'The new software exporting nations: impacts on national well-being resulting from their software exporting industries', *Electronic Journal on Information Systems in Developing Countries*, **13**(3), 1–6.

Chabchoub, N. and J. Niosi (2005), 'Explaining the propensity to patent software', *Technovation*, **25**(9), 971–78.

Chudnovsky, D. and A. Lopez (2002), 'The software and information services sector in Argentina', United Nations University, WIDER Discussion Paper 2002/92.

Correa, C.M. (1990), 'Software industry: an opportunity for Latin America?', *World Development*, **18**(11), 1587–98.

Cusumano, M. (2006), 'Where does Russia fit in the global software industry? Exploring how Russia's nascent software industry measures up to other countries', *Communications of the ACM*, **49**(2), 31–4.

Cusumano, M. and S.A. Smith (1997), 'Beyond the waterfall: software development at microsoft', in D. Yoffie (ed.), *Competing in the Age of Digital Convergence*, Boston, MA: Harvard Business School Press, pp. 371–412.

D'Costa, A.P. (2002), 'Software outsourcing and development policy implications: an Indian perspective', *International Journal of Technology Management*, **24**(7–8), 705–23.

D'Costa, A.P. (2003), 'Uneven and combined development: understanding India's software exports', *World Development*, **31**(1), 211–26.

Fabrizio, K. and D.C. Mowery (2007), 'The federal role in financing major innovations: information technology during the postwar period', in N. Lamoreaux and K. Sokoloff (eds), *Financing Innovation in the United States, 1870 to the Present*, Cambridge: MIT Press, pp. 283–316.

Gantz, J. (2006), 'The contribution of software and IT services to the Chinese economy', IDC No. 200756, Framingham, IDC.

Giarratana, M. and S. Torrisi (2004), 'Entry and survival from emerging countries: technology, brand building and external linkages', Working Paper.

Hoch, D., C.R. Roeding, G. Purkert and S.K. Lindner (2000), *Secrets of Software Success*, Boston, MA: Harvard Business School Press.

Joseph, K.J. (2006), *Information Technology, Innovation System and Trade Regime in Developing Countries: India and the ASEAN*, New York: Palgrave Macmillan.

Junqueira Botelho, A.J., G. Stefanuto and F. Veloso (2005), 'The Brazilian software industry', in A. Arora and A. Gambardella (eds), *From Underdogs to Tigers: The Rise and Growth of the Software Industry in Brazil, China, India, Ireland, and Israel*, Oxford: Oxford University Press, pp. 99–130.

Katkalo, M. and D.C. Mowery (1996), 'The emerging Russian software industry' in D.C. Mowery (ed.), *The International Computer Software Industry*, New York: Oxford University Press, pp. 240–71.

Klepper, S. (1997), 'Industry life cycles', *Industrial and Corporate Change*, **6**(1), 145–83.

Kuran, T. (2004), 'Why the Middle East is economically underdeveloped: historical mechanisms of institutional stagnation', *The Journal of Economic Perspectives*, **18**(3), 71–90.

Lakhani, K.R. and E. von Hippel (2003), 'How open source software works: "free" user-to-user assistance', *Research Policy*, **32**(6), 923–43.

Lee, K. and C. Lim (2001), 'Technological regimes, catching-up and leapfrogging: findings from the software industry', *Research Policy*, **30**(3), 459–84.

Malerba, F. (2004), *Sectoral Systems of Innovation: Concepts, Issues and Analysis of Six Major Sectors*, New York: Cambridge University Press.

Malerba, F. and S. Torrisi (1996), 'The dynamics of market structure and innovation in the Western European software industry', in D. Mowery (ed.), *The International Computer Software Industry: A Comparative Study of Industry Evolution and Structure*, New York: Oxford University Press, pp. 165–96.

Mazzucato, M. (2003), 'Risk, variety and volatility: growth, innovation and stock prices in early industry evolution', *Journal of Evolutionary Economics*, **13**(5), 491–512.

McGee, M.K. (2005), 'Move over, India', *Information Week*, Issue 1064.

Mokyr, J. (2002), *The Gifts of Athena: Historical Origins of the Knowledge Economy*, Princeton, NJ: Princeton University Press.

Mora, A. (2004), 'Software companies making it: case study of Costa Rica', paper presented at the Strategies for Building Software Industries in Developing Countries Conference, Honolulu.

Mowery, D.C. (ed.) (1996), *The International Computer Software Industry*, New York: Oxford University Press.

NASSCOM (2007), 'Industry fact sheet 2006–7', Delhi.

National Science Foundation (NSF) (2006), 'Science and engineering indicators', Washington, DC: NSF.

Nelson, R.R. (1993), *National Innovation Systems: A Comparative Analysis*, New York: Oxford University Press.

Niosi, J. and S. Reid (2007), 'Biotechnology and nanotechnology: science-based industries as windows of opportunity for developing countries?', *World Development*, **35**(3), 426–38.

Niosi, J. and M. Zhegu (2006), 'The co-evolution of industries and regional innovation systems', paper prepared for IV GLOBELICS Conference, Trivandrum, Kerala, India.

OECD (2005), 'Education trends in perspective, analysis of the world education indicators', Paris: OECD.

Pearl2 Project (2004), 'State of the industry report: Philippines software development', Manila.

Perens, B. (2005), 'The emerging economic paradigm of open source', Washington, George Washington University, available at: http://perens.com/Articles/ Economic.html.

Perez, C. and L. Soete (1988), 'Catching-up in technology: entry barriers and windows of opportunity', in G. Dosi, C. Freeman, R. Nelson, G. Silverberg and L. Soete (eds), *Technical Change and Economic Theory*, London: Pinter, pp. 458–79.

Pradhan, J. (2007), 'National innovation system and the emergence of Indian information and software technology multinationals', Working Paper 2007/09, Delhi: ISID.

Ronstadt, R. (1984), 'R&D abroad by US multinationals', in R. Stobaugh and L.T.J. Wells (eds), *Technology Crossing Borders*, Boston, MA: Harvard Business School Press, pp. 241–64.

Ruiz Durán, C. (2004), 'Mexico: the management revolution and the emergence of the software industry', paper presented at 'The rise of the software industry' Conference, Montreal.

RUSSOFT (2005a), 'The survey of the Russian export software market', Moscow and St Petersburg.

RUSSOFT (2005b), 'IT outsourcing destination: Russia', Moscow and St Petersburg.

Ruttan, V.W. (2001), *Technology, Growth and Development*, New York: Oxford University Press.

Sahay, S., B. Nicholson and S. Krishna (2003), *Global IT Outsourcing, Software Development across Borders*, New York: Cambridge University Press.

Saleh, N., C. Erran and T. Mroczkowski (2004), 'Becoming software exporters. The cases of three Eastern European Nations – Romania, Poland and the Czech Republic', *Journal of East–West Business*, **10**(1), 43–71.

Sands, A. (2005), 'The Irish software industry', in A. Arora and A. Gambardella (eds), *From Underdogs to Tigers: The Rise and Growth of the Software Industry in Brazil, China, India, Ireland, and Israel*, Oxford: Oxford University Press, pp. 41–71.

Saxenian, A. (2003), 'Government and Guanxi: the Chinese software industry in Transition', Working Paper, London Business School, Centre for New and Emerging Markets.

Schware, R. (1992), 'Software industry strategies for developing countries: a walking on two legs proposition', *World Development*, **20**(2), 143–64.

Softex (2005), 'Perfil das Empresas Brasileiras Exportadoras de Software', Brasilia.

Tigre, P.B. and F.P. Marques (2007), 'O sector de software e servicios no Brasil', paper presented to RedMercosur, Rio de Janeiro.

Torrisi, S. (1998), *Industrial Organization and Innovation. An International Study of the Software Industry*, Cheltenham, UK and Lyme, NH, USA: Edward Elgar.

Tschang, T. and L. Xue (2005), 'The Chinese software industry', in A. Arora and A. Gambardella (eds), *From Underdogs to Tigers: The Rise and Growth of the Software Industry in Brazil, China, India, Ireland, and Israel*, Oxford: Oxford University Press, pp. 131–67.

Vernon, R. (1966), 'International investment and international trade in the product cycle', *Quarterly Journal of Economics*, **80**(2), 190–207.

Wells, J.L.T. (1983), *Third World Multinationals*, Cambridge, MA: MIT Press.

4. Explaining variations in semiconductor catch-up strategies in China, Korea, Malaysia and Taiwan[1]

Rajah Rasiah, Xin-Xin Kong, Yeo Lin and Jaeyong Song

4.1 INTRODUCTION

The evolution of semiconductor manufacturing was very much driven by precision control demands in the United States military but because of its complementary and enabler properties it is increasingly diffusing into the manufacture and use of many different products and processes. It is therefore very common to find semiconductor chips driving central panel control systems in the manufacture of steel and cement, CAD-CAM machines in garment making, monitoring of captive salmon, storing of graphic memory in digital cameras, powering computers, and providing control to computer numeric control (CNCs) and electronic device machines (EDMs). Although the processes of manufacturing semiconductor chips vary in sophistication – from simple transistors that replaced cathode ray tubes (CRT) in the transfusion of pictures in televisions to sophisticated microprocessors that power supercomputers – the design and fabrication of chips remain high technology. Hence, catch-up attempts in the industry have required lumpy investments in large physical plants, machinery and equipment, human capital and its requisite matching demand. Scale economies have not fallen despite continued miniaturization and the decomposition of semiconductor manufacturing vertically into chip design, chip fabrication, assembly and test. Even in Taiwan Amsden and Chu (2003) and Rasiah and Lin (2005) have argued that scale requirements have driven up firm size. Despite similarities, the sources of learning and innovation in the industry, as articulated by Malerba and Nelson in this volume, are expected to be different from the routes taken by firms in the other industries in the volume. Malerba (1992),

Malerba and Orsenigo (1997), Malerba et al. (2001) and Nelson (1993, 2007) aptly address the specificity of firms and industries in understanding technological catch-up from an evolutionary perspective.

Governments in the four countries, namely China, Korea, Malaysia and Taiwan, have all taken serious steps to promote semiconductor manufacturing and therefore offer a unique set of experiences to examine variations in the catch-up process. These countries also provide enough diversity to examine variations. China, with a population of 1.4 billion in 2006, has a large domestic market and has since 1978 been integrating an essentially centrally planned economy into the capitalist world system. With a population of 47 million in 2006, Korea is the next biggest, and in Samsung the country has a shaper of the technology frontier in dynamic random access memory (DRAM) and NAND Flash chips. Malaysia and Taiwan, with populations of 25 and 19 million respectively in 2006, are smaller economies where domestic demand never acted as the major stimulant of rapid manufacturing growth. Taiwan is the smallest of the four economies but Taiwan Semiconductor Manufacturing Corporation (TSMC) is not only the first contract manufacturer of semiconductor chips that has separated chip design from chip fabrication, but has caught up swiftly to join Samsung at the DRAM frontier.

This chapter aims at explaining the key drivers among the four latecomers of China, Korea, Malaysia and Taiwan, in the origin of semiconductor manufacturing and in the pace of catch-up achieved using the framework of sectoral system of innovations (SSI) proposed in the introduction of this volume by Malerba and Nelson.

4.2   HISTORICAL BACKDROP

Unlike in the pioneering economy of the United States where the government-led military and later the domestic market were critical in the origin and spread of semiconductors using silicon (the prime material used in semiconductor devices) and gallium arsenide (see Marsh, 1981),[2] the main drivers of demand in China, Korea, Malaysia and Taiwan have largely been export markets. China is the only one among the four that had a military plan targeted at the computer and semiconductor industry during Chairman Mao's administration. The government created the Ministry of Electronics Industry (MEI) but the subsequent growth in semiconductor production from the 1980s has had little link with both instruments.

Large-scale foreign-driven semiconductor assembly emerged in Taiwan and Korea, Malaysia and China in the 1960s, 1970s and 1980s respectively, following the opening of export processing zones. Multinationals seeking low-wage, literate and disciplined workers in locations with good basic infrastructure and security relocated assembly and later test operations in these countries. Special export processing zones were created and coordinated in these countries to attract semiconductor firms. Employment creation started as the prime policy aim of the host governments in the initial phase (Lim, 1978).

Among the four countries Korea was the first to attempt integrated semiconductor production operations when Samsung acquired a local firm in 1975 to venture into chip manufacturing. Wafer fabrication subsequently began to mushroom outside the developed economies when leading semiconductor firms started to outsource fabrication because of rising production costs, quick technological obsolescence and falling profit margins from the 1980s (Rasiah, 1993; Hurtarte et al., 2007). Apart from microprocessors, where only Advanced Micro Devices (AMD) has fabrication facilities outside the United States in Dresden (Germany), since 2003 the fabrication of most other integrated circuits, diodes and transistors has increasingly been outsourced. Intel has one memory wafer fabrication plant and announced plans in 2007 to build another in China. Taiwan's United Microelectronics Corporation (UMC) has contract fabrication operations in Singapore. Infineon started power chip fabrication in Kulim, Malaysia in 2006. Osram is the other foreign firm having fabrication operations in Malaysia.

The historical evolution of the semiconductor industry in China, Korea, Malaysia and Taiwan can be summarized as follows.

4.2.1   China

Semiconductors gained strategic status when computers and semiconductor devices were classified under the category of national industries for research during Mao Zedong's leadership when the Ministry of Electronics Industry (MEI) was created. The initial stage development of integrated circuit (IC) industry in China could be traced from the mid-1960s. The first semiconductor integrated circuit device, called the digital logic (DTL) circuit, was developed successfully in 1965, which led to the successful development of TTL, ECL, PMOS, n-type metal oxide semiconductor (NMOS), and complementary metal oxide semiconductor (CMOS) technologies. The basic R&D elements related to materials, equipment, manufacturing and techniques were largely developed before the 1980s and occurred in the MEI, the Chinese Academy of Social Sciences, and the Ministry of Spaceflights. Apart from microprocessors, it can be argued that prior to 1980 Chinese IC technology was catching up with frontier firms. However, in the period 1980–95, IC industrial development began to fall behind that of firms at the technology frontier (Xin-Xin, 2008). There are many reasons to explain the stagnation in China in 1980–95. One explanation is that government focus on semiconductor R&D declined as foreign semiconductor firms relocated assembly and test operations in China from the 1980s. China enjoyed its first large-scale manufacturing of semiconductors following the relocation of American plants in export processing zones (EPZs). Flagship firms such as Intel, National Semiconductor (Fairchild now), Motorola (sold subsequently to Freescale), and Chippac relocated operations in China but regulations requiring that non-joint ventures must export all output meant that these firms had to target export rather than domestic markets. China's share of global IC and electronic components exports rose from 0.2 per cent in 1990 to 1.7 per cent in 2000 and 7.4 per cent in 2006 (computed from Table 4.1 using global export figures as the base).

While a strong FDI-led platform was evolving from the 1980s, the Chinese government also launched instruments to encourage R&D in semiconductors and to assist the opening of local firms in strategic industries that included semiconductors, computers and telecommunication equipment. The acquisition of the computer manufacturing division of IBM worldwide by Chinese firm Lenovo, and the expansion of Taiwanese-owned Acer, American-owned Dell and HP into China heralded a major breakthrough for Chinese semiconductor firms, which now have the market potential to sell chips to major users. IBM was already manufacturing computers in China before the Lenovo takeover.

4.2.2   Korea

The early EPZ-type assembly operations that began in the 1960s were superseded by the opening of the first local semiconductor firm in Korea in 1974. This firm was subsequently bought by Samsung in 1975 to start off the catch-up process in the semiconductor industry. The launching of the Heavy and Chemical Industries (HCI) by the government in 1975 was pivotal in attracting Samsung's entry into semiconductor chip manufacturing, although the firm was also motivated by its own self-expansion plans to supply its consumer electronics subsidiaries (Kim, 1997a, p. 88). Imports and adaptation of machinery and equipment and the absorption of process technologies, acquisition of ailing foreign firms, and gradually in-house development through the hiring of Korean engineers and scientists carrying tacit and experiential knowledge from foreign firms helped Samsung to reach the technology frontier in DRAM chips in 1984 (see Edquist and Jacobssen, 1987; Kim, 1997a). Samsung has since

Table 4.1   *World IC and electronics component exports, selected economies, 1990–2006*

	Value (US$ Million)			Share in national exports	
	1990	2000	2006	2000	2006[a]
World	55983[d]	307544	392345	4.9	3.3
Canada	1271	3459	2165	1.3	0.6
China[b]	128	5352	29209	2.1	3.0
Costa Rica[b]	. . .	51	1231	0.9	15.0
European Union (25)	–	58742	62237	2.4	1.4
Hong Kong, China	2562	14046	37881	6.9	11.7
Indonesia	18	739	944	1.1	0.9
Israel[c]	143	1782	1588	5.7	3.4
Japan	13391	42454	41725	8.9	6.4
Korea, Republic of	5364	24688	28486	14.3	8.8
Malaysia[b]	4321	18729	25509	19.1	15.9
Mexico[b]	. . .	3064	2159	1.8	0.9
Morocco[b]	110	480	732	6.5	5.8
Philippines[b, d]	1053	16663	16969	41.9	36.1
Singapore	3675	34436	67861	25.0	25.0
Taipei, Chinese	2435	21767	39213	14.7	18.4
Thailand	901	5877	8312	8.5	6.4
United States	13991	62824	53044	8.0	5.1

Notes:
a: to the nearest year
b: includes substantial exports from export processing zones
c: includes estimates from the secretariat
d: total of data reported.

Source: Extracted from WTO (2007: Table 11.49).

been shaping the technology frontier in DRAM and NAND Flash chips. Samsung, Hyundai and LG Electronics back-integrated into semiconductors from consumer and telecommunication products (KSIA, 2005).

4.2.3 Malaysia

National Semiconductor relocated operations in Penang in 1971 to start the semiconductor industry in Malaysia. This firm was followed by Advanced Micro Devices (AMD), Mostek (sold later to Thomson CSF in 1986 which later sold the plant to International Device Technology in 1989), Hewlett Packard, Monolithic Memories Incorporated (acquired by AMD in 1989), and Intel by 1976. A parallel relocation of American semiconductor firms also occurred in Kuala Lumpur and Petaling Jaya: Texas Instruments, Motorola, Western Digital, MEMC and Harris Semiconductor relocated operations in Kuala Lumpur and Petaling Jaya in the 1970s. [3] Hitachi and Siemens were the first Japanese and European semiconductor firms respectively to relocate operations in Malaysia in 1973. All the firms began with front-end assembly operations using labour-intensive technology. NEC, Motorola, Fujitsu (Senawang and Seremban), and ST Microelectronics (formerly known as SGS-Thomson) (Muar) subsequently started operations in Malaysia from the 1980s. Korean and Taiwanese semiconductor firms such as Samsung and ASE began assembly and test operations from the 1990s in Senawang and Johor respectively. Test activities were integrated with assembly by the MNCs from 1976. The subcontract firm of Carter Semiconductors opened operations in Ipoh in 1979.

Local investment in semiconductor manufacturing also started in assembly and test operations when Carsem (owned by Hong Leong) acquired Carter Semiconductors during the mid-1980s' industry-wide crisis. Subsequently Unisem (Ipoh) and Globetronics (Penang) started similar operations in the early and mid-1990s respectively. However, although venture capital from the government-owned Malaysian Technology Development Corporation (MTDC) has been used to support Globetronics, none of these firms have connected in any significant way with government labs (including The Malaysian Institute of Microelectronic Systems, MIMOS and public universities).

Motorola was the first to start wafer fabrication in Malaysia (in Seremban), but its scope was limited to old transistor technology, and the plant closed down in the late 1990s. The government managed to attract Infineon to start an 8-inch wafer fabrication plant in Kulim to produce power chips in 2005. Government efforts to attract similar plants from Samsung and Qimonda failed as the plants eventually went to India and Singapore respectively in 2006–07. The government subsequently acquired VLSI in the Silicon Valley, and assisted the founding of Silterra (Kulim), 1st Silicon (Sama Jaya), and a development wafer plant at MIMOS. By 2001 the labs at VLSI and MIMOS had already closed down, and the 1st Silicon plant in Sama Jaya in 2007 was only engaged in the fabrication of application specific integrated circuits (ASICs) using 4-inch wafers. Infineon is still ramping up production while Silterra is engaged in supplying fabricated wafers using complementary metal oxide semiconductor (CMOS) technology. Despite these developments almost 100 per cent of fabricated wafers used in assembly and test operations in Malaysia are imported. Only Infineon's back-end plant in Kulim has plans to supply wafers to Qimonda's front-end plant in Malacca.[4]

Semiconductor manufacturing was not targeted as a strategic industry in the 1970s and early 1980s when foreign driven assembly operations expanded sharply. Instead it fitted a typical neo-liberal hands-off strategy of inviting labour-intensive low value added manufacturing. Exporting firms located in export processing zones were offered tax exemptions and tariff-free operations on the basis of investment and employment generation. Following the launching of the Industrial Master Plan (IMP) in 1986, semiconductors was a strategic industry but no targeting was formulated to support a catch-up. The Malaysian Institute of Microelectronics Systems was established in the Prime Minister's department in 1985, which was eventually corporatized following directions given in the Action Plan for Industrial Technology Development (APITD) in 1990.

4.2.4   Taiwan

Foreign firms relocated back-end assembly operations in export processing zones in the 1960s to start semiconductor manufacturing in Taiwan. Government policy was instrumental in making the shift from simple assembly and test activities into front-end activities when the Electronic Research and Service Organization (ERSO) was established among the Industrial Technical Research Institutes (ITRI) in 1974.

However, the creation of ITRI initially did not produce significant results for the semiconductor industry as no grants were given to stimulate participation in R&D activities. The small firm structure operations, based on Marshallian knowledge flows, assisted little to spur upgrading in a highly capital- and knowledge-intensive industry (Rasiah, 2008). In addition to the science and technology project (STP) funds that were disbursed from 1979, ITRI also started to develop incubators to stimulate the birth of high-tech firms. ERSO, the division within ITRI involved in supporting R&D in electronics activities, became a key driver of incubation from 1979 but particularly after 1983 when the projects introduced a matching framework when providing grants (Rasiah and Lin, 2005). The government's extensive investment to provide the high-tech infrastructure (e.g. R&D labs and standards organizations) in the Hsinchu Science Park was also instrumental in driving incubators to world class firms such as United Microelectronics Corporation (UMC), TSMC, ASUS, Winbond, Ase and Vanguard.

Large firms such as TSMC, which is the world's leading contract manufacturer of semiconductor wafers, have subsequently forged a strong collaboration with foreign technology R&D labs, universities and purchasers to move up the technology trajectory. In 2006 TSMC was fabricating cutting edge 12-inch wafers using 0.13 micron chips using nanotechnology with R&D support from a range of foreign collaborators providing the design support. The firm also announced plans to fabricate microprocessors in 2008 (Shilov, 2007).

It can be seen that the histories of catch-up in semiconductors of the four East Asian economies are different from the path taken by the United States. Differences in the height reached in the technology ladder, organizational structures, and product types manufactured in the four countries can be established by mapping the structure and product trajectories of the different semiconductors. Figure 4.1 shows the relationship of firms: semiconductor and buyer–supplier firms (including complementary firms), and oganizations that constitute a semiconductor cluster.

4.3   CATCH-UP TRAJECTORIES

In this section we examine the trajectory paths of process and product technologies taken by semiconductor firms in China, Korea, Malaysia and Taiwan. The catch-up started with entry into the assembly manufacturing of memories by foreign multinationals in export processing zones in all four countries: 1960s in Korea and Taiwan, 1970s in Malaysia and 1980s in China. Also, the technological regime of semiconductors can be characterized by high-velocity, high-frequency devices using light emitting devices that are expensive (using gallium arsenide material base) that are used in mobile phones and related products, and low-frequency devices that do not require much light emitting functions and are also cheap and abundant (silicon as the base), which are used to fabricate memories and microprocessors. TSMC is engaged in all categories; Samsung is engaged in memories and NAND Flash.

Figure 4.2 shows selected semiconductor devices with non-scale based presentation of the value added enjoyed by each of them. The semiconductor devices value chain typically involved seven stages: capacity implant development and specifications; chip design; wafer fabrication; chip assembly; packaging and test; sales; and marketing (see Figure 4.3). These devices are then fitted into final goods electronics products such as consumer appliances, industrial electronics and information communication products (see Figure 4.1). The active semiconductor components provide the control for these products. Whereas multinationals began assembly and test operations of memory chips, the entry into chip fabrication and chip design started with government supported programmes. China had the first government programme in the 1950s but the

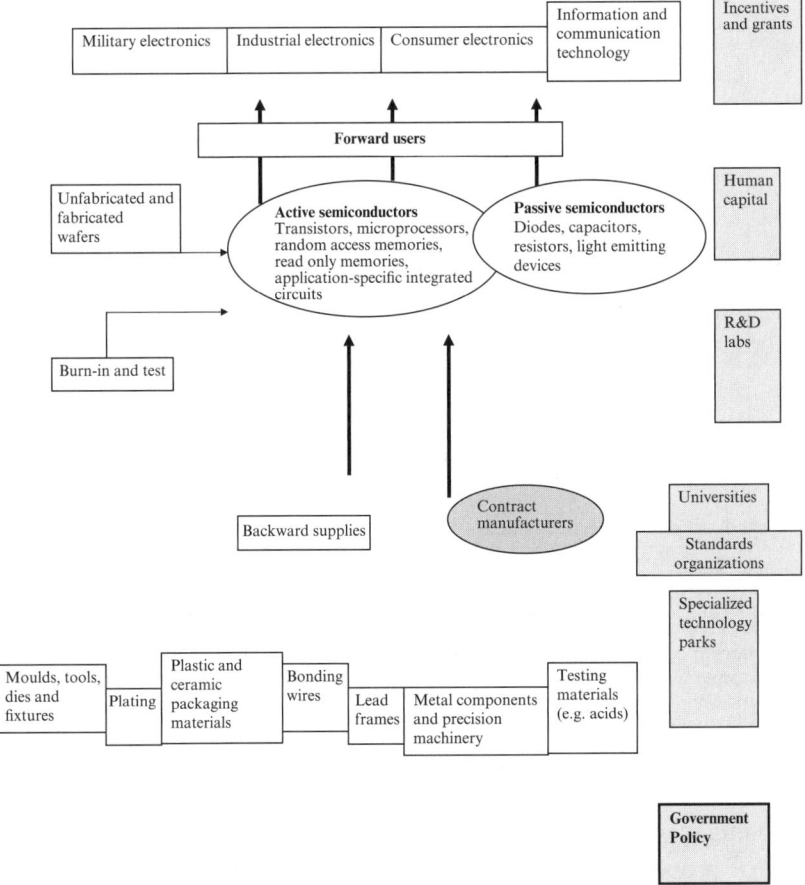

Source: Rasiah (2008)

Figure 4.1 Semiconductor cluster, East Asia, 2008

development of the industry from the 1980s has little link with that programme. Taiwan and Korea followed next, launching formal programmes
to develop semiconductor manufacturing through the establishment of
the Electronics Research and Service Organization (ERSO) among the
Industrial Technical Research Institutes (ITRI) in 1974 and 1975 and the
Heavy and Chemical Industry (HCI) programmes respectively (Mathews
and Cho, 2000; Amsden and Chu, 2003; Kim, 1997a; Rasiah and Lin,
2005). Malaysia (1986) earmarked semiconductors among its strategic
industries in 1986 when launching its first Industrial Master Plan (IMP).

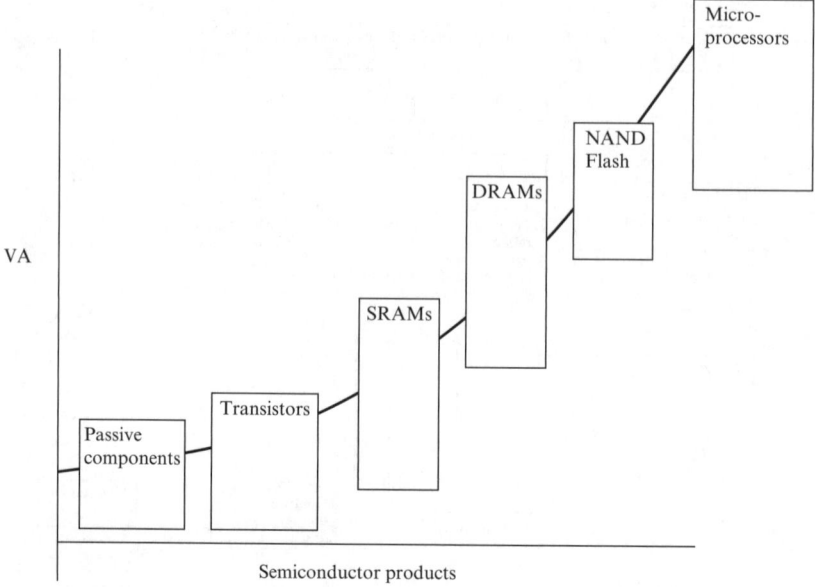

Notes: Projected not to scale; Passive component devices include diodes, resistors, capacitors and light emitting devices; Electron flow is the central dimension of active components; SRAM: Static random access memory; DRAM – Dynamic random access memory.

Figure 4.2   Selected semiconductor devices

Unlike foreign affiliates already in possession of the requisite intellectual property rights (IPRs), local firms bought licences or firms to access both product and process technologies. The regulatory framework on IPRs was first introduced with the 1989 Washington Treaty that legalized industrial layouts in addition to industrial designs and patents. The governance regime of IPRs was included in the 1995 World Trade Organization's (WTO) Trade Related Intellectual Property Rights (TRIPs) agreement. Local firms' access to most product technologies in the four countries first came through licensing and acquisition of the firms. Korean firms were the leading acquirers of technology through such a route, followed by Taiwanese firms. For a long time microprocessor manufacturing was dominated by Intel until AMD won a legal suit to enter production in the 1990s. Intel and TSMC unveiled a strategic agreement on 3 February 2009 to manufacture Intel atom based system-on-chip (SoC) microprocessors and the companies also agreed to cooperate in other areas (Shilov, 2009).

Value added

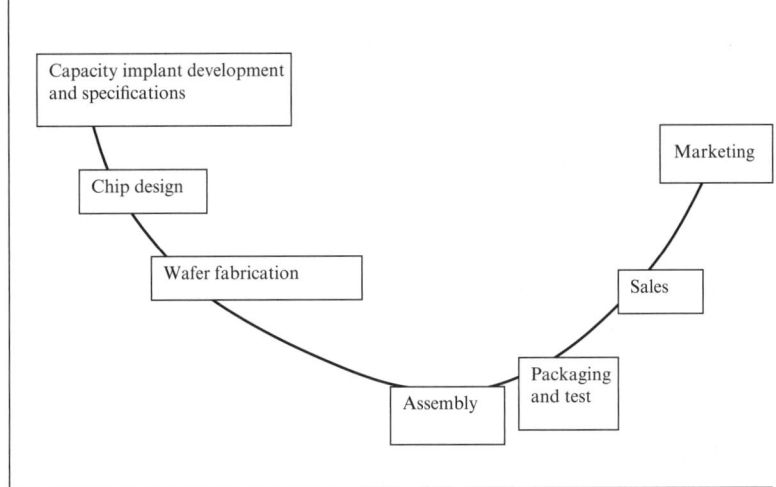

Stages in value chain

Figure 4.3 Value chain of semiconductors, 2008

Unlike foreign assemblies that started operations in the 1960s, local Korean and Taiwanese semiconductor firms went directly into integrated operations from the late 1970s. UMC was started in 1980 (Tsai and Zhou, 2006: 95; Mathews and Cho, 2000) following the acquisition of the semiconductor division of RCA in the second half of the 1970s (see Rasiah and Lin, 2005). RCA offered UMC ASICs, diodes and transistor technology. The merger of TSMC (49 per cent) and Philips (51 per cent) in 1987 gave the Taiwanese firms access to more sophisticated memory chips such as DRAMs.

Foreign and local Malaysian firms are largely specialized in assembly and test operations. Local assembly and test firms are engaged in assembly of second and third generation transistors and memory chips while foreign firms largely manufacture first and second generation memories and microprocessors. Four firms were engaged in wafer fabrication in Malaysia in 2007. Although assembly and testing dominated semiconductor manufacturing, when the first waves expanded operation in the 1980s semiconductor firms in China embarked more extensively on wafer fabrication.

Horizontal user–producer links grew between semiconductor firms and suppliers and buyers in the United States, Japan and Germany.[5] Several machinery technology semiconductor firms co-evolved as strong interactions helped machinery firms automate, refine, remodify and manufacture more efficient and effective machinery and equipment. Taiwan's world class machinery industry facilitated a similar transition. In Malaysia the machine tool industry co-evolved alongside the semiconductor industry owing to quick demand changes that forced even multinationals such as Intel, AMD, Texas Instruments and National Semiconductor to seek proximate sourcing.

4.3.1   Process Technology

Process technology refers to the processes, organization, layout and machinery and equipment modifications that are undertaken to process or assemble products. It refers to machinery and equipment, layouts, inventory and quality control systems, production organization and firm structures. Lead firms in process technology are able to drive creative destruction as they are able to lower defects, delivery times and costs while raising quality levels. Falling profit margins often drive latecomers lacking product innovation rents typically to either drive out high-cost incumbents or to fill up the vacuum left behind them. Apart from industrial layouts of chips and chemical processes, cutting edge machinery and equipment and materials, most process technologies are not subjected to IPRs and hence their diffusion is far quicker and easier than product technologies.

Rapid growth of user–producer-driven product and process specifications, with defect-free output and delivery times, also drove closer interface and technology coordination between semiconductor firms and buyer firms (e.g. computers, avionics, consumer electronics and mobile phones) in all four countries (see Rasiah, 1994, 1996; Hobday, 1995). Kim (1997a) and Kim and Nelson (2000) discussed the critical role of dynamic firms in the process technology catch-up trajectory by creatively duplicating acquired and reverse engineered technologies.

Semiconductor firms in all the four countries are engaged in state-of-the-art development of process technologies. Taiwan and Korea led in the take-up of process patents in semiconductor devices issued by the US patent office over the period 2002–06 with 2907 and 2503 patents respectively. Malaysia and China followed next, with 39 and 27 patents each over the same period.

China

Foreign-owned multinationals in China relocated significant aspects of their process technology including just-in-time (JIT) systems through their subsidiaries to facilitate better coordination between them and buyers.

China has both the Malaysian type MNC operations and a strongly emerging local base resembling Taiwan (Xin-Xin, 2006). Intel, Freescale, National Semiconductor, Texas Instruments and Chippac carry out large-scale assembly and testing of semiconductors in China targeting export markets. These firms also have back-end design and other operations that are important for improving production performance.

Foreign firms were the initial transmission channel for the movement of process technologies to Chinese semiconductor firms. Because the first wave of semiconductor firms coming to China relocated in the 1980s when flexible production systems, automation and continuous improvement benchmarks were absorbed by European and American firms, these techniques were already being used from the outset among export-oriented firms.

Although the main machinery and equipment in assembly, test and fabrication are still imported, considerable adaptations have already started in China. By the end of the 1990s Chinese firms had already started supplying robotics and automated machinery to foreign and local semiconductor firms.

Korea
Korean semiconductor firms had initially relied on knowledge embodied in the human capital they employed as well as training provided by machinery and equipment suppliers from Japan, the United States and Germany. However, as the Japanese firms became more reluctant to transfer process technology once Korean firms reached sufficient levels of maturity, they decided to invest in in-house development (see Amsden and Kim, 1985; Kim, 1997a; Amsden, 1989).

Integrated manufacturing spreading into consumer and telecommunication products and the development of the chemical industries also facilitated the diffusion of low-cost machinery and equipment, chemical materials, inventory control systems, and space utilization skills to help Korean firms lower production costs. Integrated operations enabled cross-transfers of process technology.

Incremental engineering through the absorption of Japanese JIT and kaizen practices were instrumental in the rapid diffusion of flexible specialization practices (6-sigma, TPM, SGA, teamworking, QCC and TPM) in semiconductor assembly and test in all four countries from 1980. Duplicative imitation and later creative imitation (Kim, 1997a) dominated catch-up in process technology practices. These developments took place both in local and foreign firms. Extensive improvements (including in-house modifications) in machinery and equipment (e.g. fully automated machinery and integration of die attach and die bonding), materials (e.g. changes in use of sticky tape, shipping tubes and epoxy) and layouts helped reduce cost, eliminate defects, and shorten throughput time. These developments largely diffused from automotive manufacturing in Japan. Volatile fluctuations in demand drove firms to keep inventories low and production changes swift.

The emphasis on yield management spread from Samsung to the other semiconductor firms such as Hynix in the 1990s. Yield management at the corporate level included continuous R&D to improve process technology. Samsung invested a huge amount of capital in purchasing high-end equipment and machinery, and Hynix focused on R&D of new process technology. Korean engineers were highly regarded for their deft skills and meticulous attention to detail. R&D projects were also conducted at the government level. An example is the project conducted by the Ministry of Science and Technology between 1994 and 1996, the purpose of which was to develop production and process management systems.

Despite extensive efforts by the government to stimulate the fabrication and manufacture of machinery and equipment – including the opening of the Cheon, a semiconductor equipment complex – the development of local capabilities has been slow, so that in 2005 foreign manufacturers and imports still accounted for 80 per cent of the machinery bought by semiconductor firms (KSIA, 2005).

Malaysia
Foreign assembly plants first transferred semiconductor assembly and test as well as related process technologies to Malaysia from 1971. Semiconductor assembly and test firms in Malaysia subsequently enjoyed significant transformation in process technologies from the late 1970s with the proliferation of automation, flexible production systems, and their consequent impact on skill training (see Rasiah, 1988a, 1994).

Whereas NS (Micro-Machining) and Intel (Intel Automation) started their own machinery subsidiaries, Texas Instruments, HP, Hitachi, AMD, Harris Semiconductor (renamed as Intersil and finally as Chippac) and IDT created in-house machinery workshops in Malaysia. However, by the mid-1980s, Intel closed its machinery subsidiary, while AMD, HP and Chippac reduced theirs to emergency solutions (see Rasiah, 1988a, 1988b, 1996).

Intel in Penang started prototype development from 1980 to facilitate technology transfer to local supplier firms to support its own flexibilization and use of JIT operations (see Rasiah, 1988a, 1988b, 1994, 1995). Indeed rapid technological obsolescence driven by shortening product cycles and miniaturization forced semiconductor firms in Malaysia to establish strong a interface with machinery suppliers.

Organizational change and a rise in productivity helped reduce capital and labour inputs per unit of output. Indeed, Intel expanded its output twice while reducing its workforce from 8000 employees to 4000 employees in 1984 (the plants in Barbados and Puerto Rico were closed down to appropriate production synergies from these gains) (see Rasiah, 1988b).

Driven initially by American firms to absorb cutting edge Japanese and American inventory and quality control systems, kaizen practices were introduced in both foreign and local firms manifesting in different forms – for example, small group activities, just-in-time, quality control circles, and six-sigma – and were developed in these firms to raise efficiency levels by eliminating defects and downtime, and coordinating production flexibly to meet volatile fluctuations in demand and prices.

Growth of experiential knowledge in MNCs and the American open framework helped Malaysian employees to ramp up new operations and to provide expert training and process systems in the semiconductor value chain. Indeed, Malaysian engineers and managers played an important role in the ramping of manufacturing in Intel in Shenzen and Manila, Motorola in Shenzen, and AMD in Bangkok in the 1980s.

The local firms of Carsem, Unisem and Globetronics managed to reduce production costs in semiconductor assembly and testing so much so that they were starting to capture demand from incumbent American, Japanese and German firms: creative destruction.

Locally owned Silterra, by far the most advanced Malaysian local fabrication plant, took up five process patents issued by the US Patent Office in the period 2002–06. The foreign-owned Intel and National Semiconductor subsidiaries in Malaysia led patent take-up issued by the US Patent Office over the period 2002–06 with 21 and 20 patents respectively.

Taiwan

The initial source of process efficiency improvements was recorded through technology transfer by employees gaining experiential knowledge working in American and Japanese consumer electronics firms and training provided by machinery and equipment suppliers. Taiwanese firms then internalized training and inventory and quality control systems in-house once the suppliers became reluctant to supply the latest technologies. As in the other countries, kaizen practices in different forms – for example, small group activities, just-in-time, quality control circles and six-sigma – were developed in these firms to appropriate throughput efficiency and make production agile and flexible to meet volatile fluctuations in demand and pricing.

The domestic machinery industry in Taiwan adapted well to the needs of semiconductor manufacturing, including wafer fabrication, to manufacture cutting edge machinery and equipment, and to support modifications in firms. Taiwan's OEM firms achieved global service provider (GSP) status by introducing kaizen practices to lower throughput times and defects, and meet customer requirements, which helped them experience the Schumpeterian Mark I system of creative destruction (Malerba, 1992; Rasiah and Lin, 2005).

Taiwanese domestic firms – for example, UMC, ASE, TSMC, Windbond, Asus and Vanguard – upgraded and relocated their supply base at all major buyer locations, and also introduced and refined their capacity to anticipate changes in demand from buyer firms. Network cohesion facilitated strong differentiation and division of labour in Taiwan to support large-scale manufacturing of OEM computers (only Acer is a major local OBM computer manufacturer in Taiwan), scanners, monitors, motherboards and components.

4.3.2   Product Technology

Unlike process technology, the catch-up process in product technology is much more difficult owing to the introduction of intellectual property rights, huge investments, and the leaps in path-dependent knowledge required to sustain participation in the development of products facing rapidly shortening product cycles. Semiconductor firms in the four countries have managed to move up the product technology trajectory of semiconductor chips, with those in Korea and Taiwan closest or at the technology frontier.

China
Both foreign and local firms in China are engaged in assembly, test, fabrication and R&D activities on non-optical, optical, discrete, analogue, logic, memories, ASSPs, and ASICs. While much of the R&D is confined to ASICs, some firms undertake DRAM fabrication and R&D (e.g. Intel, Freescale and Qimonda). Government-funded R&D labs in China's high-tech parks are working on DRAM R&D. Government initiatives propelled China's move to stimulate firms' movement up the technology trajectory in the 1990s.

The key drive took place under Project 909 (launched in 1996) where, with the support of both the Federal and Shanghai government, Hua Hong was established through a strategic alliance with NEC of Japan to start an 8-inch IC production line, design centre and R&D centre in 1997 (see Table 4.2). By 2003 Hua Hong had more than 10 subsidiaries supplying ICs and design services for smart cards, power meters, home networking, car electronics, and development of related application software. Hong Hua developed China's first radio frequency identification (RFID)

Table 4.2   Technology trajectory of leading local firms

	China	Korea	Malaysia	Taiwan
	Hua Hong	Samsung	Silterra	TSMC
1975		Started		
1976–1981		Acquisitions, hiring and licensing		
1982		64K DRAM		
1984		256K DRAM		
1986		1M DRAM		
1987				Incorporated
1988		4M DRAM		Hiring personnel and contract fabrication
1990		16M DRAM		
1992		256M DRAM		
1996		1G DRAM		
1997	Founded			
1999	DRAM, ASICs	256MB NAND		
2000		516MB NAND	Started with 0.25 CMOS	
2001		1G NAND	0.22 CMOS	Range of DRAMs
2002	IC Foundry	2G NAND	0.18 CMOS	
2003		4G NAND		
2004		8G NAND		12' wafer
2005		16G NAND	8MB SRAM	Nand Flash
2006	Plans for 12-inch wafer	32G NAND	0.13 CMOS	

Source: Compiled from Kim (1997a: 88); Authors' interviews (2007); Samsung website; TSMC website; Silterra website.

chip in 2001 followed by chips for SIM cards in 2002 and high security microcontroller chips in 2003. In 2004 the company was authorized as the chip supplier of the China National ID Card Generation II Project. In 2007 Hua Hong was recognized internationally as having a world class capability in layout engineering of digital, digital/analogue, electrical erasable, programmable, read only memory (EEPROM), embedded MCU, and deep submicron digital ICs.

Although there were over 500 IC design houses in China in 2007, most of these firms focused on ASICs rather than the more lucrative market provided by DRAMs and microprocessors. The acquisition of IBM computers by Lenovo is widely considered to be driven by initiatives to quicken entry and acquisition of IC technology and markets. Hence, although the Chinese experience so far remains behind the frontier, the aggressive acquisitions alongside strong government support for learning have given Chinese firms the confidence to rapidly scale the routes of upgrading in semiconductor design, fabrication, and R&D.

Korea

Korean companies started with memory products as their specialization; memory products have a large and fast-growing market, and have the advantage of mass production (see Kim, 1997a). Since the competitive advantage in the memory market lies in the production technology and equipment, late entrants can also catch up in a short time if provided with sufficient capital and human resources. Also, the microprocessor industry is dominated by Intel, with stringent patent laws shielding it against new entrants.

Through a series of hiring of Korean human capital embodied with tacit knowledge working in foreign firms, and acquisition of ailing but strategic foreign firms and licensing agreements, Samsung started fabricating and manufacturing 64K DRAM chips in 1982 and by 1984 had reached the frontier of DRAM technology to manufacture 256K DRAM chips (Edquist and Jacobssen, 1987; Kim, 1997a). LG Electronics, Hyundai and Hynix followed similar patterns in acquiring product technology.

The product technology trajectory of Samsung is shown in Table 4.2. Samsung's strategy of seeking its human capital, technology and markets globally alongside its own internalized development facilities – which included R&D labs and its own university – drove the firm to quicken the process of integration so that Hwang's (the CEO of Samsung) law enabling the doubling of memories every 12 months replaced Moore's (CEO of Intel) law that achieved this only in 18 months. By the mid-1980s Samsung had become a driver of creative accumulation in semiconductor memory chips. Table 4.2 shows Korea enjoying the highest position in the product technology trajectory of semiconductor firms among the four countries.

Malaysia

Foreign and local Malaysian firms are largely specialized in assembly and test operations – the former in the latest product lines. The local firms of Carsem, Unisem and Globetronics are engaged in contract assembly and testing of low-end microchips. Carsem was acquired from foreign-owned Carter Semiconductor in 1984, Unisem was started new by a group of Malaysians who left American semiconductor firms in 1990, and Globetronics was started by Intel's local managers in 1992. Semiconductor multinationals acted as a training ground to expand experiential knowledge.

In 2007 there were two foreign (Infineon and Osram) and two local (Silterra and 1st Silicon) fabrication houses in Malaysia. These firms are engaged in low-end 4-inch and 8-inch wafer technology. Infineon fabricates power chips while the local firms are engaged in the fabrication of complementary metal oxide semiconductors (CMOS in the case of Silterra) and application specific integrated circuits (ASICs in the case of 1st Silicon), both using silicon wafers.

At least seven semiconductor firms seeking to relocate ASIC and DRAM fabrication in Malaysia chose not to after negotiations with MITI, Malaysia. The prime reasons were the lack of human capital and insufficient capitalization.

The Malaysian government corporatized MIMOS in the early 1990s and established Silterra in late 2000. Silterra was the second largest South-East Asian fabrication factory in 2006 and its main production operation was the fabrication of 0.25 micro CMOS chips. There were a number of management changes over this period up to 2004. It was in 2004 that the government-linked investment company, Khazanah, acquired control of Silterra, providing the much-needed capital for expansion. Being still new to the industry, Silterra forged a strategic alliance with IMEC, one of Europe's leading independent research centres, which led to the successful fabrication of 8MB SRAM chips using 0.13 micron CMOS technology in 2005 (Silterra, 2006) (see Table 4.2). Silterra then established a strategic partnership with Key ASIC in 2006 to provide mutual customers with access to the latter's IP portfolio and design services on the former's 0.18- and 0.13-micron CMOS process technologies. The firm reported having expanded market shares following the acquisition of access rights to Key ASIC's design facilities, and is seeking to expand its size to appropriate scale economies.

Taiwan

Local Taiwanese semiconductor firms went directly into integrated operations when UMC was started in 1980 (Tsai and Zhou, 2006, p. 95; Mathews and Cho, 2000) from the acquisition of the semiconductor division of RCA in the late 1970s (Rasiah and Lin, 2005). RCA offered UMC ASICs, diodes and transistor technology.

The merger between TSMC (49 per cent) and Philips (51 per cent) in 1987 gave the Taiwanese firms access to DRAM technology. From 1983

ERSO helped the incubation and creation of several high-tech firms e.g. Windbond, ASUS, Vanguard and ASE, including assistance with R&D and wafer fabrication capabilities.

The collapse of RCA coincided with the acquisition of the company's semiconductor division by ERSO in the late 1970s. ERSO gave birth to United Microelectronics Corporation (UMC) in 1980, which started producing ASICs for consumer electronics firms (Ernst, 2000; Mathews and Cho, 2000; Mathews, 2002). Taiwan Semiconductor Manufacturing Corporation (TSMC) started subsequently in 1987. TSMC was the first contract semiconductor chip manufacturer to separate chip design from chip fabrication, to specialize in the latter. With strong R&D support from ERSO, Taiwanese firms began to participate in front-end operations such R&D and wafer fabrication. The front-end firms did not integrate with the old back-end firms in Taiwan as the companies were different. In the more integrated Taiwanese semiconductor companies, such as UMC and ASE, the back-end activities of assembly and testing were eventually relocated in China and Malaysia. UMC has also relocated wafer fabrication abroad in Singapore and the United States.

Although UMC was the first Taiwanese fabrication plant to open in Taiwan, TSMC has become the leading Taiwanese fabrication house since the 1990s and hence the focus here is on the latter. Once the government successfully negotiated a joint venture with Philips holding 51 per cent of the share, Morris Chang, who had gained tacit and experiential knowledge working in American firms and left Texas Instruments as its Senior Vice President, was appointed as its founding CEO. Using his knowledge and linkages with R&D centres, universities, buyers, suppliers and rival firms, he played a key role in charting the direction of the firm.

Not only have the leading local semiconductor manufacturers in Taiwan (UMC, TSMC, ASE and Winbond) and China upgraded to participate in R&D and wafer fabrication, but they have also targeted production at important national manufacturers – especially computer manufacturers (e.g. Acer and Lenovo and the contract manufacturing firms such as Tatung, Vanguard and Asus) as well as exports (Mathews and Cho, 2000; Amsden and Chu, 2003; Rasiah and Lin, 2005). Some large American multinationals have also set up R&D and wafer fabrication plants in China and Taiwan. In Taiwan especially, considerable R&D offshoring has occurred from the late 1990s – something that began with TSMC, a joint venture between Philips and Taiwanese capital that was started in 1986. The top three leading semiconductor manufacturers in Taiwan are also among the top ten DRAM producers in the world. Taiwan's world class machinery industry has also helped the complementary development of semiconductor machinery and equipment.

Table 4.3   Product technology capabilities of leading firms, selected economies, 2007

Closeness to frontier	Capabilities of firms
Frontier operations	Korea: OBM R&D and fabrication of DRAM/NAND Flash
Frontier operations	Taiwan: OEM fabrication capability of frontier DRAM/NAND
Previous generation	China: OEM fabrication capability in 0.13 and 0.18 micron CMOS, NMOS and DRAMs
Previous generation	Malaysia: OEM fabrication capability in 0.13 0.18 CMOS

Source: Compiled from Kim (1997a, p. 88); Authors' interviews (2007); Samsung website; TSMC website; Silterra website.

TSMC was the first to specialize in IC fabrication, separating it from IC design. By 2007 TSMC had become completely Taiwanese owned. From being the world's first independent contract manufacturer of memories entering the manufacturing of 12-inch wafers using nanotechnology, the firm unveiled a strategic agreement to manufacture the Atom system on chip microprocessors for Intel in 2009 (Shilov, 2009).

Overall, semiconductor firms are at the technology frontier in process technology in all the four countries examined. However, only firms in Korea and Taiwan are at the product technology frontier. Although semiconductor firms in Taiwan are not involved in integrated operations and are still heavily but horizontally reliant on strategic alliances for markets and technology, they are engaged in cutting edge product technologies in the segments they have entered. Korean semiconductor firms are dominated by fairly independent access to markets and technological capabilities. Chinese firms come after that, followed by Malaysia, where fabricating firms are heavily reliant on foreign markets and technology and are still far from the technology frontier (Table 4.3).

4.4   BUILDING BLOCKS

Having established the technological paths, this section analyses the drivers behind them using the broad net expounded in the introduction in this volume by Malerba and Nelson. The unfolding of these paths will help explain the differences, if any, of the catch-up patterns of firms in China, Korea, Malaysia and Taiwan.

4.4.1   Access to Foreign Knowledge

Semiconductor assembly and testing began with the transfer of technology by multinationals to their subsidiaries in Korea and Taiwan from the 1960s, in Malaysia from 1972, and in China from the 1980s. Flagship semiconductor firms such as Intel, AMD, National Semiconductor, Hitachi and HP relocated the assembly and testing of the cutting edge production technology to Malaysia and China. These early phases were associated with employment generation in export processing zones with little focus on catch-up.

Two major and more minor routes to accessing foreign sources of knowledge in the semiconductor catch-up track can be identified from the four countries. In the first route all four countries 'used' foreign firms as training grounds to access tacit knowledge. In the second route Korean, Taiwanese, Chinese and Malaysian firms accessed foreign technology through licensing. In the third route Taiwanese and Chinese firms merged or acquired foreign firms to access technology and markets.

Korea and Taiwan led the way among the four countries in driving a catch-up in the semiconductor industry. The Korean government encouraged local firms to license technology from foreign companies and to invest abroad to access technology from foreign labs. Foreign direct investments made by Korean companies in the US mainly include setting up local R&D labs to learn cutting-edge technology such as ASIC design technology. Samsung and Hyundai set up R&D labs in Silicon Valley in 1983, which helped the development of DRAM technology. Korean and Taiwanese semiconductor companies established strategic alliances with leading foreign companies. The purpose of Korean alliances with Japanese firms was to learn process, management and memory technologies, whereas alliances with the US and European companies were mainly intended to learn memory technologies and capture market shares. Licensing from Micron Technology provided the early entry into DRAMs for Samsung in 1983 (Edquist and Jacobssen, 1987) while UMC grew from ITRI's acquisition of RCA in 1979. TSMC started as a joint venture with Philips in 1987 (Rasiah and Lin, 2005). Samsung accessed Sharp's 16K SRAM and 256K ROM technologies (Kim, 1997b). Dependence on foreign firms fell in the 1990s in the vertically integrated Korean firms but the de-verticalized Taiwanese firms remained strongly linked to strategic alliances with foreign firms.

Technological partnerships have been formed between foreign and

Korean and Taiwanese companies since the 1970s. Lucky Goldstar and LG Electronics from Korea acquired 5 per cent and 58 per cent of equity in Zenith in 1991 and 1994 respectively. LG Electronics owned Zenith and retained its name as a subsidiary in 1999 (Zenith, 2008). Unlike in consumer and industrial electronics where mergers and acquisitions drove significant learning, Korean firms moved up the value chain in semiconductor manufacturing largely through licensing and the development of in-house technology. Korean firms signed cross-licensing, royalty and technological alliance agreements with foreign companies. Between 1983 and 1988, Korean semiconductor firms entered 101 technology licensing agreements; 66 cases of these were with US firms. The early fabrication houses of UMC and TSMC in Taiwan merged first with RCA and Philips respectively in 1979 and 1987 before acquiring them. However, whereas Korean firms had reduced their dependence on strategic alliances by the mid-1990s, the highly de-verticalized Taiwanese firms remain strongly but horizontally attached to their strategic partners.

Korean and Taiwanese firms took advantage of the mid-1980s' downswing in the industry: prices of 64K DRAM chips had fallen from US$50 to US50 cents in 1980–85, and the EPROM fell from US$18 to US$4 in three months in 1985 (Rasiah, 1988b). This Schumpeterian (Schumpeter, 1934) Mark I entry – the displacement of ailing incumbents (Malerba, 1992; Mathews, 2006) such as Mostek (sold subsequently at a low price to Thomson CSF before International Device Technology acquired it) and the phasing out of old product lines in AMD, Intel, Texas Instruments and National Semiconductor – coincided with the entry of Taiwanese contract semiconductor manufacturers. Whereas Korean firms licensed technology from foreign firms directly, much of the early Taiwanese forays into foreign technology were done through ERSO. The early acquisitions in Taiwan and licences in Korea allowed a key point of entry, which was then transformed to drive frontier research especially in memories – *à la* the Schumpeterian Mark II development of creative accumulation (see Malerba, 1992).

Chinese and Malaysian firms have also accessed foreign technology through licensing agreements but with less success. However, whereas the focus in Korea and Taiwan has been on accessing foreign technology by local firms moving up the product technology trajectory, in China and Malaysia foreign firms still dominated exports largely in the low value added production stages of assembly, packaging and test operations. Initiatives to follow the Taiwanese framework started in Malaysia and China. The Chinese government allowed total foreign equity when all output was exported. The focus in China shifted subsequently in the 1990s as technological deepening became important. Hence, both local and foreign firms have managed to attract incentives to start R&D operations and wafer fabrication. Attempts to move up the value chain in Malaysia have again benefited from two foreign wafer fabrication subsidiaries of Infineon and Osram, who relocated their technology from abroad. The local firms, Silterra and 1st Silicon, established strategic tie-ups with design technology from foreign technology suppliers and purchasing firms, R&D labs and universities. The acquisition of VLSI technology in the Silicon Valley in 1997, however, did not materialize because the management then at MIMOS did not have a strategy to use the knowledge for the design and fabrication of wafers.

Whereas there was only one local firm engaged in IC design and two local firms in wafer fabrication in Malaysia, there were over 500 local firms engaged in IC design and over 10 wafer fabrication plants in China in 2007. Although Silterra has IC design and a roadmap for expansion, its future has remained uncertain as its owners are detached from its actual activities. Chinese firms are better placed with strong domestic demand and committed government support. The acquisition of the IBM personal computer division by Lenovo has also given Chinese firms a major boost for the acquisition of technology and markets. Hence, Chinese rather than Malaysian firms are better positioned to pursue a catch-up to the frontier in semiconductors.

4.4.2   Demand Conditions

Export markets were the critical initiator of large-scale semiconductor manufacturing in Korea, China, Malaysia and Taiwan and remain important (see Tables 4.1 and 4.4; Figure 4.4). China's semiconductor market nevertheless had become the third largest in the world by the end of the 1990s. Ownership regulations in electronics required that foreign-controlled firms export most of their output. These regulations were the same in Malaysia; at least 80 per cent of output had to be exported for firms to hold 100 per cent foreign equity (Rasiah, 1995). Although the initial efforts to acquire semiconductor manufacturing operations were motivated by the desire to ensure quality support for their consumer electronics plants and to expand into fabrication and chip design and R&D, Samsung and LG Electronics relied extensively on export markets to generate demand. The imposition of export quotas in return for subsidized credit by the government of Korea and the difficulty in obtaining dollars to import machinery and equipment and materials were also instrumental in driving export orientation by these firms (Amsden, 1989). Whereas local firms are also important buyers in Korea, Taiwan and China, foreign firms remain the main purchasers in Malaysia.

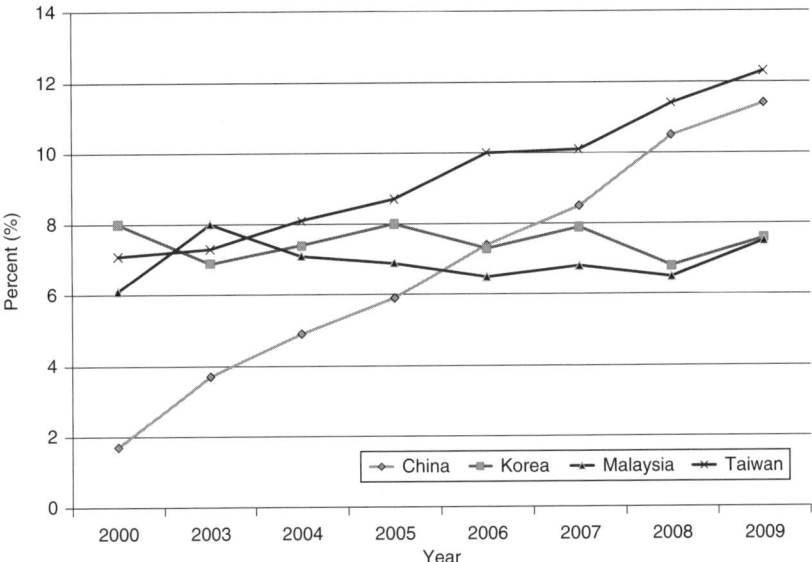

Figure 4.4   World share of IC exports, selected economies, 2000–2009 (%)

Korean and Taiwanese consumer and information hardware electronics firms purchase the bulk of their ASICs and DRAMs from local semiconductor firms. User–producer relations have been strong in driving wafer fabrication in all four countries as lock-in plays a key role in the wafer fabrication start-ups. Booking–billing ratios are important in low margin fabrication where yield is critical because of the lumpy nature of investment involved. The bulk of semiconductor chips are sold to lock-in contractors; the rest in open markets. The strong interface between semiconductor firms and electronics firms that use chips has been an important element driving and shaping the flow of knowledge between them. However, 1st Silicon in Malaysia has been losing buyers. Silterra has managed to reverse its fortunes in export markets since 2003 and has shown a steady rise since then.

The acquisition of IBM's computer manufacturing division has also expanded the Chinese-owned Lenovo market share in computers and, with that, demand for Chinese semiconductor firms. In Korea, as of 1990, export demand accounted for 92.5 per cent and domestic demand accounted for the rest. Since the size of the domestic market was negligible, companies focused on the export market. Strong export demand has led to the trade balance involving the industry to reach positive figures

Table 4.4   Trade balance, semiconductors and electronics, selected economies, 2006

| | Value (US$ billion) | | Trade balance |
	Export(X)	Import(M)	(X−M)/(X+M)
Semiconductors			
China[a]	29.2	121.7	−0.613
Korea, Republic of	28.5	24.7	0.071
Malaysia[a]	25.5	31.1	−0.099
China, Taipei	39.2	31.8	0.104
Electronics			
China[a]	287.3	197.9	0.184
Korea, Republic of	83.7	40.3	0.350
Malaysia[a]	67.9	46.1	0.191
China, Taipei	64.5	41.1	0.222

Note: a: to the nearest year.

Source: WTO (2007: Tables 11.36 and 11.48).

in Korea and Taiwan (see Table 4.4). The trade balance of China and Malaysia was negative. The high import figures for China and Malaysia are accounted for by imports of wafers (especially by foreign firms located in export processing zones) and machinery and equipment. Nevertheless, the hugely positive trade balance in the overall electronics industry in China and Malaysia shows that consumer and industrial electronics firms in these countries acquire most of the components produced in their countries.

Whereas semiconductor firms in Malaysia and China have largely remained in assembly and test activities, their counterparts in Korea and Taiwan have upgraded strongly to wafer fabrication, designing and R&D activities. In addition to export demand, the OEM contract manufacturers – especially in export-oriented computers and peripherals – provide considerable demand for the sale of high value added chips in Taiwan. Hence, domestic firms (including Taiwanese firms that have relocated front-end activities in China) have since the second half of the 1980s become major buyers of Taiwanese DRAMs and ASICs. The vertically integrated operations of Korean firms have facilitated internal transfers of semiconductors. Both the Malaysian type and the Taiwanese types of activities and demand conditions have evolved in China.

The lack of upgrading has driven down Malaysia's export shares in world exports of integrated circuits in the period 2000–05 when those of

Taiwan and China have continued to rise. Exports as a share of world integrated circuits exports from China rose from 1.7 per cent to 3.7 per cent and 5.9 per cent in 1990, 2000 and 2005 respectively (WTO, 2006: Table 59). The commensurate figures for Taiwan were 7.1 per cent, 7.3 per cent and 8.7 per cent respectively. The Malaysian share rose from 6.1 to 8.0 per cent in 1990 and 2000 respectively, but fell to 6.9 per cent in 2005. Malaysian figures are expected to fall further following a hollowing out currently taking place in the semiconductor industry in the country.

While export markets essentially provided the demand for semiconductor firms in Malaysia, China, Korea and Taiwan, access to sell fabricated wafers or assembled and tested semiconductor devices from domestically fabricated wafers relied extensively on connecting with buyers. In Malaysia the two local wafer fabrication plants enjoy market access through a lock-in agreement with consumer and telecommunication electronics firms located abroad. Indeed, the wafer fabrication plants were begun after the lock-in deals were struck. These demand arrangements are similar to the experience of Taiwan and China. The vertically integrated structure has, in addition, provided strong demand from within Korean firms. Despite the presence of downstream flagship firms such as Intel, Motorola and Dell in Malaysia, Silterra exported all the wafers it fabricated in 2006, with 70 per cent going to North America and the remainder to Asia and Europe.

4.4.3   The Role of Government

Government policy in the promotion of semiconductor manufacturing has also differed. From simply offering incentives to attract MNCs' direct operations in the 1960s and early 1970s, the Korean and Taiwanese governments directly promoted the growth of local firms. While the human capital gained experiential knowledge working in the MNCs, government research institutes failed to assist technological catch-up in Korea (Kim, 2001).[6] In Taiwan, government-led ITRIs, which were started in 1974 (and the electronics labs at ERSO), played a central role in driving R&D in local firms. The heavy and chemical industries programme offered Samsung and LG Electronics subsidized credit and support for seeking licences from foreign firms, while in Taiwan the STP grants of 1979 (particularly after they had to be matched by grants from the private sector in 1983) and the Hsinchu Science Park offered tremendous R&D synergies (Ernst et al., 1998; Mathews and Cho, 2000; Amsden and Chu, 2003; Rasiah and Lin, 2005).

Korea's and Taiwan's technology transfer agreements also actively screened *ex ante*, monitored the use and diffusion, and undertook *ex post* appraisal to ensure licensing fees were brought down, diffusion occurred, and mistakes were not repeated. The government in Taiwan launched an active education policy, at one level driving expansion in human capital supply from technical schools and universities, and at another level imposing levies on unskilled labour imports to pressure firms to upgrade (Tseng et al., 1994). Governments in both countries also launched a brain gain programme to attract back citizens enjoying experiential and tacit knowledge.

China's national S&T plan started to play important roles in enhancing linkages between industry and academia. For instance, the main S&T Plans – like the 863, the 973 and supporting plans – encouraged firms, research institutes and universities to work together. Since 2000, in particular, China launched 12 significant S&T-specific projects, which included super large-scale IC and software. By 2007, seven national IC industrialization bases had been established, including those at Shanghai, Xi'an, Beijing, WuXi, Chengdu, Hangzhou and Shenzhen.

China has an FDI attraction policy similar to that of Malaysia. Its large labour force supports assembly and testing in MNC operations in locations such as Pearl River Valley and Shenzen, and local integrated firms located in high-tech parks. Public R&D labs play an important role in supporting the knowledge base of local firms in China.

Several domestic IC manufacturing plants were launched through the national seventh, eighth and ninth five-year plans. By the end of 1999, there were five large domestic and joint venture companies – Huajing, Huayue, Beiling, Xianjin and Shougang NEC Electronics – and by 2007 there were over 500 IC design houses in China (Xin-Xin, 2008). In addition, there were also 10 specialized and 871 electronics factories in GanSu province enjoying support from the Microelectronics Industrial Centre of the Chinese Academy of Sciences. IC manufacturing industry developed rapidly after the late 1990s. Shougang NEC Electronics started production of the 0.56 64M DRAM in 1996. Huajing started production in its 0.96 CMOS line in 1998. Shanghai Huahong started production of the 0.58 MOS line in 1999. Compared with the IC manufacturing industry and IC design industry, the IC packaging and testing industry was much larger in China.

Huada IC Design Centre, which was set up in 1986 as the first IC design company in China, became important after the government resumed interest in promoting local firms from 1996. Document 18 issued by the State Council in 2000 has been instrumental in driving IC design development in China. IC design output rose from 1.48 billion yuan in 2001 to 18.62 billion yuan in 2006, expanding by around 13 times (see Table 4.5). By the end of 2006, the number of IC design firms in China had reached 488. The

Table 4.5   Composition of IC value chain, China, 2001–2006 (billion yuan)

Year	Design	Manufacturing	Packaging and testing	Total
2001	1.48	2.77	16.11	20.36
	(7.3)	(13.6)	(79.1)	(100)
2002	2.16	3.36	21.33	26.85
	(8.0)	(12.5)	(79.4)	(100)
2003	4.49	6.05	24.6	35.14
	(12.8)	(17.2)	(70.0)	(100)
2004	8.18	18	28.35	54.53
	(15.0)	(33.0)	(52.0)	(100)
2005	12.43	23.29	34.49	70.21
	(17.7)	(33.2)	(49.1)	(100)
2006	18.62	32.35	49.66	100.63
	(18.5)	(32.1)	(49.3)	(100)

Source: China (2009).

share of industrial IC design sales in overall industrial IC sales reached 18.5 per cent in 2006. IC design human capital also increased in numbers from less than 5000 to more than 20000 in 2006. The share of the low value added packaging and testing segment in total sales of ICs in China fell from 79.1 per cent in 2001 to 49.3 per cent in 2006.

Because it costs US$3 billion to ramp up a wafer fabrication plant and US$10 billion for the plant to enjoy the scale necessary to make profits, in 2000 governments have either directly or indirectly funded the founding of the early fabrication plants in the four countries. The Korean government offered subsidized credit to Samsung. The Taiwanese government took 49 per cent equity in 1987 when TSMC was founded and since 2008 has taken control of the firm. The Chinese provincial governments have invested extensively to start IC design and fabrication houses. The Malaysian government controls Silterra in Malaysia through its investment arm, Khazanah. Even foreign fabrication plants in Malaysia have obtained upfront capital subsidies. The Korean government formulated a six-year plan to develop semiconductor manufacturing within the heavy and chemical industries (HCI) programme that was launched in 1975 (Kim, 1997a, p. 88). The *chaebols* were initially reluctant to enter semiconductor manufacturing owing to the heavy dependence on a foreign technology that experienced shortening product cycles. The subsidized credit and market access in the domestic market were the initial spur that drove Samsung to begin semiconductor manufacturing in 1975.

The private and public sector in Korea has invested intensively in R&D since 1986, facilitating the movement of Samsung to a shaper of the globe's DRAM technology from the mid-1980s. In order to promote balanced development of both memory and non-memory semiconductors and to improve the technological competence of the equipment and materials industry, the Korean government put forward the System IC Development Project in December 1998. The Korean government and local companies ran the IC Innovation Partnership Program from 2001 until 2005 to strengthen the design field and the non-memory sector. However, infrastructure-related investment, especially in the non-memory sector, is still quite low compared to competing countries.

While strong governmental support dominated semiconductor manufacturing until the early 1980s, mainly in the DRAM sector, support for IC manufacturing by the 1990s had been limited to three types. The first type of support is offered directly for systems IC development, while the second finances venture companies, and the third is for the construction of infrastructure building and training system designers. Examples of such governmental support include the System IC 2010 Project, the 'ASIC Joint Development Project', and 'IT Core Parts Development Project' run by the Ministry of Science and Technology and the Ministry of Commerce, Industry and Energy. Owing to the failure of government research institutes (GRIs) until the turn of the millennium (Kim, 2003), Samsung internalized the development of DRAM chips with strong links to R&D centres and other firms. Nevertheless, reforms after the turn of millennium helped transform GRIs into productive complements for generating R&D, which has assisted the strengthening of university–industry linkages in Korea (see Lee, 2011). Hence, the Korean semiconductor industry has increasingly relied on strong coordination between government GRIs and private industry for its growth.

In Malaysia the government provided generous incentives from 1971 (following the Free Trade Zone Act) to attract export-oriented firms, in which semiconductor firms such as National Semiconductor, AMD, Motorola, HP, Intel, Hitachi and Texas Instruments were among the pioneers. The objective then was simply to create jobs. Then through the Industrial Master Plan of 1986 the Malaysian government initiated the promotion of upgrading in manufacturing, including in semiconductors. The Malaysian Institute of Microelectronics Systems (MIMOS) was created in the Prime Minister's Department in 1985 to spearhead catch-up and innovation in semiconductors and related devices. Unlike the experience of Taiwan, China and Korea, MIMOS failed to incubate any successful high-tech firms in the industry. Its attempts to seek direct participation by the multinational firms failed as these firms were only engaged in assembly and test activities in the 1980s. The ethnic-coloured New Economic Policy (NEP) that targeted largely Bumiputera participation in government-run firms discouraged any possibility of giving special incentives to Chinese-controlled firms such as Carsem and Unisem, both of which had successfully entered contracts for semiconductor assembly and test in the mid-1980s and early 1990s. Although Globetronics eventually enjoyed capitalization from the Malaysian Technology Development Corporation (MTDC), the government appeared reluctant to engage in lumpy investment to drive the introduction of wafer fabrication in these firms.

The Malaysian government acquired VLSI in Silicon Valley, which opened opportunities for a Mark I entry as the firm was ailing in the mid-1990s. However, instead of using it as a vehicle to acquire technology for catch-up, lacking a clear strategy MIMOS quickly sold the plant. MIMOS was to spearhead the opening of two local wafer fabrication plants, Silterra in Kulim in 1999 and 1st Silicon in Sama Jaya in 2000, both of which operated without a clear catch-up plan and made losses until 2007. Nevertheless, Silterra has shown signs of early catch-up as the firm has since established a roadmap and has identified other firms to acquire and partners with whom it wishes to collaborate. Hence, with the possible exception of Silterra, government policy effectively failed to provide the impetus for a catch-up to take place in the semiconductor industry in Malaysia.

The government shifted its framework of coordinating MIMOS activities in 2005 when it hired the former vice president of Motorola to head it. The government also approved Silterra's efforts in hiring foreign experts to stimulate upgrading. This development, along with the hiring of human capital with experiential knowledge in the industry (Bruce Guy and subsequently a Taiwanese national) to lead Silterra through an expansionist capital financing to drive up its designing support and scale capabilities helped turn the firm around by 2006.

Foreign multinationals were attracted initially in the late 1960s with incentives to undertake export-oriented assembly and test activities. These firms provided jobs that were important during the 1960s. RCA was one of the firms to relocate operations in Taiwan. The government then targeted the semiconductor division of RCA for the acquisition of strategic technology. The government was also involved in the development of incubators at ERSO to undertake wafer fabrication activities, which started semiconductor manufacturing in Taiwan. UMC was the first to be launched by ERSO. ERSO subsequently helped the incubation and creation of several

Table 4.6 *World market share of top 15 semiconductor firms based on sales, 2005–2006*

Firm	Headquarters	Ranking		Sales (US$ Millions)			
		1H2006	2005	1Q2006	2Q2006	1H2006	2005
Intel	United States	1	1	8040	7215	15255	35395
Samsung	South Korea	2	2	4365	4581	8946	17838
TI	United States	3	3	3260	3505	6765	11300
TSMC	Taiwan	4	8	2389	2522	4911	8217
Infineon	Germany	5	6	2395	2477	4872	8297
ST	Italy	6	5	2363	2491	4854	8870
Toshiba	Japan	7	4	2317	2154	4471	9045
Renesas	Japan	8	7	1963	2050	4013	8266
Hynix	South Korea	9	10	1522	1635	3157	5599
Freescale	United States	10	11	1465	1535	3000	5598
Philips	Netherlands	11	11	1465	1534	2999	5598
NEC	Japan	12	12	1386	1381	2767	5593
Micron	United States	13	13	1242	1328	2570	4954
AMD	United States	14	16	1332	1216	2548	3936
Qualcomm	United States	15	18	1018	1133	2151	3457

Note: Q – quarter; H – half.

Source: Global Sources, available at: http://www.globalsources.com/SITE/QUALITY. HTM, accessed 20 February 2010.

high-tech firms, including R&D and wafer fabrication capabilities, for example Windbond, ASUS, Vanguard and ASE from 1983.

Grants were initiated through incubators in the Hsinchu Science Park, which originally started in 1979 but became successful after a 1:1 matching condition was attached from 1983 (when firms had to match government grants) and after the hiring of professionals brought back under the brain gain programme from the United States. These grants were instrumental in the launching of TSMC, Winbond, Vanguard, Asus and UMC. Hence, in Taiwan front-end wafer fabrication and R&D eventually took over from the original assembly and test operations undertaken by foreign multinationals from the late 1960s. TSMC had become the fourth largest seller of semiconductor devices in the first half of 2006, rising from eighth place in 2005 (see Table 4.6).

Mathews (2006) argues that the government also timed its intervention to enter the semiconductor industry during an industry-wide global crisis when incumbent firms were facing severe downswings in the mid-1980s.

Table 4.7   *R&D scientists and engineers per million people, selected countries, 1996–2006*

Country	1996	1998	2000	2002	2004	2006
China	657	605	730	806	882	1143
Japan	4907	5162	5098	5072	5299	5148
Korea	2190	2005	2317	3002	3276	4162
Singapore	2538	2986	4140	4352	4997	5713
Taiwan	3326	3794	3922	3103	3579	4159
Malaysia	90	154	276	295	503	367

Source: UNESCO (2010); World Bank (2010).

Subsequently in 1991 the government formally approved relocation of labour-intensive low value added assembly and test activities to mainland China, which helped Taiwanese firms lower manufacturing costs while better coordinating market expansion (Rasiah and Lin, 2005).

4.4.4 Human Capital

Semiconductor manufacturing became knowledge intensive from the late 1970s. Hence, minimum statistical numeracy, communicative, cognitive and judgemental skills are important before firms hire even operators. Intel's super-operators in all four countries enjoy a wage premium. The use of JIT and kaizen-type practices has raised the demand for skilled workers. Schooling in Korea, Taiwan, China and Malaysia provide such labour. In addition, participation in wafer fabrication and new product development requires good supplies of R&D engineers and technicians. However, labour markets for skilled labour tightened in Korean and Taiwan, and in Malaysia from the 1980s and 1990s respectively. Taiwanese and Korean firms relocated labour-intensive assembly and testing in Southeast Asia from the 1980s, and Chinese firms have done the same since the 1990s. Malaysia has suffered a slowing down in upgrading because of a tightening labour market as well as lack of R&D human capital. As shown in Table 4.7, the share of R&D engineers and scientists in the population showed an improving trend in Korea, Taiwan and China over the period 1996–2006. The commensurate figures for Malaysia not only contracted but the intensities per million persons have been extremely low.

    China's conversion from centrally planned economy to a market economy has also provided enough human capital to drive catch-up in both product and process technologies. The engineering intensity of

GanSu High Tech Park in China exceeded that of Hsinchu Science Park in Taiwan in 2005.

The importance of knowledge-based managers in driving the upgrading in semiconductors can be seen from the approach Samsung took to start its semiconductor operations. Samsung ventured into semiconductor manufacturing when it acquired Korea's first local semiconductor firm. The acquisition of this firm, which opened in 1974, not only helped Samsung acquire its operational facilities but also added the tacit and experiential knowledge embodied in its founder, who obtained his doctorate from Ohio State University and gained experience working in Motorola (Kim, 1997a, p. 88).[7]

To hire those who did not wish to come back to Korea, Korean companies established R&D labs in the United States to tap their resources. Korea, Taiwan, China and Malaysia also launched a talent attracting programme, which has been very important in the management of high-tech semiconductor firms and in connecting them with buyer–supplier firms and foreign R&D centres. Among the four, Korea and Taiwan were first to launch a formal policy to attract their own national human capital from abroad and especially to provide the tacit knowledge to run high-tech firms. However, whereas well-trained human resources were scattered across different industries in Taiwan, the Korean semiconductor industry, backed by the investment of *chaebols*, hired a pool of well-trained graduates from science and engineering disciplines. Since the enactment of the Immigration Law in 1965, Korean engineers have been working in the United States. Korean *chaebols* hired them back in the 1980s, offering salaries even higher than those of CEOs. However, while Korea, Taiwan and China managed to attract a critical mass of human capital with tacit and experiential knowledge to lead or work for local semiconductor firms, the Malaysians have not been very successful in this. Some Malaysians returned to work in local firms but have either been overshadowed by ethnic policies or have left because of restrictive management practices.

For example, Samsung Semiconductor Incorporated (SSI), Samsung's R&D institute in Silicon Valley, played a key role in assimilating 64K DRAM designs and production processes just six months after Samsung's announced entry in 1983 into the DRAM business. SSI began producing Silicon Wafers in 1985 with 300 engineers. SSI was expanded in 1987 to study IC applications in computers, office and telecommunications (Kim, 1997b). Samsung's Tokyo design centre was opened in 1987. Both centres became important platforms for recruiting and training human capital to serve Samsung. In a peak year, SSI hired 260 local engineers, including a substantial number of Koreans. Hyundai set up an R&D lab in Santa Clara in 1983 and at one time employed 430 local engineers. LG established a relatively small-scale R&D outpost in Sunnyvale in 1984 and roped in 115 local semiconductor engineers. New product development in those companies often involved joint work connecting human capital in both the Korean and the foreign bases. Knowledge-sharing facilitated Samsung to develop the 1M DRAM, 4M DRAM and the 64M DRAM chips in 1986, 1988 and 1995 respectively (Kim, 1997b).

Wafer fabrication and R&D, the two having a strong connection, are highly knowledge intensive. Engineers, scientists and R&D scientists and engineers are critical drivers of these operations. Taiwan supplemented demand for such human capital by stepping up their supply as well as through talent-attracting programmes. Taiwan is by far the most successful among the four as it has managed to attract back Taiwanese specialists who had gained tacit and experiential knowledge working especially in American multinationals, R&D labs and University R&D centres. TSMC, ASUS, Vanguard and Winbond are examples of high-tech firms run by these experts. Morris Chang has been the CEO of TSMC from its founding until the present day.

In Malaysia automation under conditions of productive and innovation-driven flexibilization helped raise demand for skills. Semiconductor firms, especially American-owned firms were the first to use their connections with the state government of Penang to canvass for the starting of skills development centres. MNCs funded the Penang government's move to open the Penang skills development centre in 1989 to conduct off-firm training.

While skilling (through in-house learning-by-doing and utilization of the Penang Skills Development Centre, PSDC) has been a success, Malaysia has faced severe demand–supply shortfalls that have restricted upgrading in the industry. Indeed, Malaysia's universities have failed to supply the requisite numbers and quality of scientists and engineers to firms such as Intel, AMD, Hitachi, Motorola (Freescale), HP, ST Microelectronics, Texas Instruments and Chippac, who reported being keen on hiring more engineers and scientists to undertake R&D activities since the 1990s. Seven multinationals reported dropping Malaysia when considering relocating wafer fabrication in Malaysia over the period 1997–2007. Foreign-owned Infineon embarked on an ambitious programme to train engineers and scientists in its fabrication plant in Kulim in 2007 while the locally owned Silterra has scouted the globe since 2000 to seek human capital to participate in its expansion plans.

4.4.5 Networks, Alliances and Consortiums

Consortiums and strategic alliances have been important in the development of a number of firms in the four countries. The independent local fabrication and assembly plants of China, Malaysia and Taiwan have relied extensively on formally registered strategic alliances with foreign firms and R&D centres for key technologies and markets. Enjoying large-scale and integrated consumer and industrial electronics, Korean firms attempted to work together to undertake joint R&D, but intense competition in product markets often derailed these agreements. Strategic alliances with foreign firms and labs were critical in the catch-up stage of integrated Korean firms, and have remained important in the de-verticalized Taiwanese firms. Strategic alliances are also critical in Chinese and Malaysian firms but it is too early to predict their direction.

The government has been the chief architect in helping to establish a consortium to pool R&D efforts in 1986. Samsung, Hyundai, LG Electronics and Hynix participated in this consortium to coordinate their R&D and production internalization efforts until the late 1990s when intense competition in product markets caused this relationship to break down. Korean firms have since internalized R&D and marketing efforts, thereby reproducing what Kim (1997a) classified as the old Japanese zaibatsu framework. Large vertically integrated firms, such as Samsung and LG Electronics, manufacture most of the chips they use in their consumer and industrial electronics plants. The large integrated structure of Korean firms discouraged the evolution of de-verticalized alliances *à la* Taiwan. Nevertheless, the success of Korean firms suggests that both frameworks can coexist.

Korean companies chose standard memory products as their strategic target in order to capture the large and fast-growing memory market, and also to enjoy the benefit of mass production. Since the competitive advantage in the memory sector comes from the manufacturing technology embedded within equipment, late entrants can catch the leaders up relatively easily, as long as they are supported by sufficient capital and well-trained human resources. Korean firms never feared making large-scale investments in order to rise as the leader in the future market. Samsung Electronics is building the second semiconductor complex in Hwa-Sung with an investment of US$33 billion, which will be finished by 2012. Ki-Heung Hwa-Sung Cluster will become the world's largest semiconductor complex, and will facilitate swift decision-making and market reaction.

Taiwan provides the alternative de-verticalized route to reaching the technology frontier. The establishment of TSMC's Design Center Alliance has been highly strategic in attracting access to new technology, which is vital for it to specialize in foundry-based fabrication. Accent joined this alliance in 2004 to supply complex customer designs for TSMC's process technologies.

Membership in TSMC's Design Centre Alliance allows Accent to service companies wishing to utilize TSMC's foundry operations. Accent supplies design support for OEM, fabless and chipless small-to-medium sized enterprises (SMEs), as well as start-ups.

Recent projects by Accent for TSMC include the analogue mixed signal IC, capacitive interface sensors, a multi-million gate integrated circuit for wireless applications, the hardening of an ARM CPU, systems with large memories and analogue blocks and a very complex IC for networking applications, which include 0.13μm, 0.18μm, and 0.25μm technologies. Accent also supplies its very deep submicron (VDSM) design for the delivery of incoming 90 and 45 nanometer designs.

TSMC announced in February 2008 that it was establishing production lines to start fabricating central processing units on a 45 nanometer high-end process for low-cost personal computers with a target of starting sales by the second half of the year. TSMC has developed an efficient method to produce microprocessors for Intel, which has opened the way for catch-up for Asian firms whose stringent copyright and patent laws have long threatened to restrict new entrants in the product line. Entry into micro-processors also offers Taiwanese firms the opportunity to leapfrog Korean semiconductor firms, which have dominated in the production of DRAM and NAND Flash chips.

Malaysia's Silterra, 1st Silicon, and Chinese local firms remain strongly linked with foreign technology suppliers and markets for wafer fabrication activities, though the large local market has given the latter less depend-ence on foreign firms. Silterra's alliance with Imec and Key Asic, and Hua Hong's access to technology from NEC have been strategic in upgrad-ing for both firms. Both firms are de-verticalized fabricators of wafers equipped with design and process technology R&D capabilities.

4.4.6 Co-evolution: Driver and Driven

Taiwanese firms have benefited most by far from the co-evolution of industries. Machinery and chemicals had emerged on a large scale by the early 1980s in Taiwan (Fransman, 1985; Rasiah and Lin, 2005). The co-evolution of these industries as well as the plastics industry through support from ITRI helped to provide the complementarities essential for process and product technology improvements in Taiwan's semiconduc-tor firms. Indeed a number of latest technologies that were developed at ERSO quickly found their place in the chips fabricated by Taiwanese firms. A number of such complementary technologies were developed in the chemical, plastics, and machinery and equipment labs. One such example is the thin membrane developed to separate transistors in wafers.

In Taiwan the semiconductor industry has simultaneously been the driver, as well as being driven by other industries. On the one hand, major developments in chemicals and plastics, and machinery and equipment have enhanced semiconductor product technologies and process technologies respectively. On the other hand, the proliferation of semiconductor technology as the driver has enormously benefited the development of automotive parts, computer numeric control (CNCs) and electronic device machinery (EDMs), and fish tracking equipment. Microchips fabricated by Taiwanese firms also power the industries that manufacture chemicals and plastics.

None of the remaining countries have actually appropriated significant synergies from the co-evolution of other industries. Local machine tool and plastic injection moulding firms co-evolved with upgrading and flexibilization in semiconductor firms in Penang from the 1980s, and in Shenzhen, China, from the 1990s. Korea and Malaysia remain major importers of machinery and equipment to the semiconductor industry. Wafers are also primarily imported to China and Malaysia. However, whereas semiconductor firms provide significant fabricated wafer supplies to consumer and industrial electronics firms in Korea, firms in Malaysia import all their fabricated wafers. The existing wafer fabricators in Malaysia export all production.

4.5 CONCLUSIONS AND IMPLICATIONS

Of the four countries, Korean firms are at the global frontier of product technology in DRAMs and NAND Flash products. Despite acquiring the OEM capability to fabricate cutting edge DRAMs, NAND Flash, and other CMOS products on 12-inch wafers, Taiwanese firms still rely on R&D and design support from abroad. Chinese firms are in the same situation but have not acquired the OEM capabilities to fabricate the latest chips. Malaysian foreign and local semiconductor fabrication firms are still engaged in second and third generation power chips and CMOS technology on 4-inch and 8-inch wafers. Korean and Taiwanese firms have relocated much of their assembly and test activities in China and South-East Asia, while Chinese and Malaysian firms still largely specialize in these activities.

The paths taken by firms in the two leading countries on the manufacturing of semiconductor chips, that is Korea and Taiwan, are very different. Whereas the Korean firms eventually became independent through zaibatsu-type integrated operations back-integrating from consumer and telecommunication electronics manufacturing into semiconductors, and internalizing R&D activities, Taiwanese firms have remained highly specialized in wafer fabrication or vertically integrated operations within semiconductors while continuing to depend strongly on R&D support from ERSO and foreign firms. Taiwanese firms also continue to enjoy strong collaboration particularly when participating in design and R&D activities among themselves as well as with foreign research labs and design companies. In addition, some Taiwanese firms, such as TSMC and UMC, have continued to specialize in contract wafer fabrication foundries without participation in assembly and testing. These firms have also continued to rely extensively on strategic alliances for both technological support and markets. Being highly vertically integrated, Korean firms have gradually reduced their dependence on strategic alliances as they have moved to the technology frontier.

While multinationals started the first large-scale assembly and testing of semiconductor devices, local firms spearheaded the first critical mass of fabrication activities in all the four countries. China's initial experience with the spawning of semiconductor technology within the computer industry in the 1950s did not trigger subsequent manufacturing for export markets. Despite the similarities, the evidence amassed in this chapter using the lenses provided by Malerba and Nelson in the introduction of this volume shows significant differences in the channels that drove catch-up in the four countries. The one major similarity across the four countries is the role that governments played in the initial regulatory environment as well as in investment – either through direct ownership or subsidized credit – to fabricate wafers and support technological catch-up.

The prime drivers of catch-up in the four countries have been: (1) multinationals; (2) export demand, government policy and human capital. Networks and strategic alliances and the co-evolving industries were strategically important only in Taiwan. Strategic alliances have been important in China and Malaysia but local fabrication and design houses are still in their infancy. The catch-up in the four countries has benefited substantially from links with multinationals through the development of experiential and tacit knowledge of local human capital, which has then been transferred to run local firms, licensing and the acquisition of firms. In addition, Korean firms also benefited from knowledge synergies appropriated from locating subsidiaries in key semiconductor conurbations.

Export demand initiated semiconductor manufacturing in all four countries, including in China in the 1980s. Domestic demand only became important as expansion into consumer and industrial electronics shifted significant exports for use in firms located in these countries. However, only Korea and Taiwan have managed to enjoy a positive trade balance in semiconductors in 2006. China and Malaysia experienced a negative trade balance in 1990–2006. The development of technological capabilities in wafer fabrication and other inputs helped Korean and Taiwanese firms record a positive trade balance. Slow catch-up explains the negative balance in Malaysia. Despite China's infancy and the specialization of foreign firms primarily in assembly and test operations, local firms are showing signs of catch-up. Nevertheless, all the countries recorded a positive trade balance in the broader electronics industry, demonstrating that domestic demand has grown for semiconductors.

Government policy has been central in the emergence and growth of the semiconductor industry in all four countries. However, the nature of state intervention has differed. Korea and Taiwan shifted from their policies of attracting FDI to create jobs in the 1960s to supporting the development of local firms by the 1970s. Hence, the leading semiconductor firms in Korea and Taiwan are local firms, while those in China and Malaysia are foreign firms. Both Korean and Taiwanese firms accessed technology through acquisitions and licensing. However, whereas Korean firms internalized much of their R&D activities because of the initial failure of the GRIs, Taiwanese firms accessed R&D directly from the ITRI labs. By the time the GRIs were reformed to better coordinate the link between R&D and economic performance, *chaebols* such as Samsung had already internalized such activities. Nevertheless, although the early *chaebols* such as Samsung have highly developed R&D labs within their plants, the reformed GRI framework connecting R&D allocations with performance has helped raise industry–university R&D linkages. The government has also been a critical pillar in the provision of human capital (including attracting experts from abroad), R&D grants and in Taiwan the provision of high-tech facilities such as R&D labs. The lack of human capital and performance standards has undermined the capacity of subsidized local wafer fabricators in Malaysia to upgrade. Chinese wafer firms demonstrate better capacity to upgrade because of large reserves of human capital and better coordination with performance standards. However, having emerged only after 1997, Chinese design firms are still engaged in the manufacture of low-end EEPROMs, ASICs and ASSCs and have yet to participate in the higher end of semiconductors.

Only in Taiwan is the evidence clear that the co-evolution of other industries and strategic alliances have been important. Strategic alliances through R&D consortia have been important in driving the utilization of state-of-the-art technology to support the de-verticalized structure of Taiwanese semiconductor firms. The participation of ITRI's world class labs in several different industries and its smooth integration with firms have also facilitated the appropriation of complementary knowledge synergies from chemical, machinery and plastics labs. The highly integrated structure of Korean firms has discouraged such collaboration despite initiatives by the government in 1986. The de-verticalized firms of China and Malaysia appear to be following the Taiwanese framework but this only appears promising in the former. The rising share of sales contributed by IC design and fabrication in overall IC sales over the period 2001–06 is a good indicator that semiconductor firms are catching up in the value chain. The lack of human capital and an uncertain ethnically based political structure threatens to discourage similar catch-up in Malaysia.

NOTES

1. Comments from Richard Nelson, Franco Malerba, Suma Athreye, Syama Ramani, Sunil Mani, Keun Lee, Jorge Niosi, Ted Chang, and other participants on previous drafts at the PASTAS workshops are gratefully acknowledged.
2. Gallium arsenide technology is sometimes still preferred over silicon owing to the higher frequency and light emitting functions it allows. Government financed research in the military labs (e.g. Bell Laboratory), key universities such as MIT, University of Chicago and Purdue University were instrumental in the development of diodes and transistors in the United States. Fairchild was the first private semiconductor firm created to fabricate and manufacture transistor chips following the transfer of technology from the Bell Laboratory in 1948 (see Marsh, 1981).
3. Motorola sold its semiconductor division to Freescale in 2002.
4. Infineon acquired the semiconductor division of Siemens in the 1990s. This firm uses both the names Infineon and Qimonda.
5. See Lundvall (1988, 1992) for a lucid account of the influence of producer–user interactions in driving innovation.
6. Penrose (1959) and Polanyi (1962) introduced the concepts of experiential and tacit knowledge respectively. The former refers to the acquisition and deepening of knowledge from experience while the latter also includes innate characteristics that cannot be transferred.
7. Ki-Dong Kang's firm failed to weather the first oil crisis of 1973–75 and hence sold the firm to Samsung.

REFERENCES

Amsden, A.H. (1989), *Asia's Next Giant: South Korea and Late Industrialization*, New York: Oxford University Press.

Amsden, A.H. and W.W. Chu (2003), *Beyond Latecomer Development: Upgrading Policies in Taiwan*, Cambridge, MA: MIT Press.

Amsden, A.H. and L. Kim (1985), 'The acquisition of technological capability in Korean industries', World Bank mimeo.

China (2009), *Industrial Trends of Semiconductor Industry and Components Industry, Industrial Values on Mainland Semiconductor Industry, 2004–2008*, Institute of Microelectronics Development, China Center for Information Industry Development, Beijing: Social Sciences Academic Press.

Edquist, C. and S. Jacobssen (1987), 'The integrated circuit industries in India and South Korea in an international techno-economic context', *Industry and Development*, **21**, 1–62.

Ernst, D. (2000), 'Global production networks and the changing geography of innovation systems: implications for developing countries', East–West Center working papers, Economics series no. 9, Hawaii.

Ernst, D., T. Ganiatsos, and L. Mytelka (eds) (1998), *Technological Capabilities and Export Success: Lessons from East Asia*, London: Routledge.

Fransman, M. (1985), 'International competitiveness, technical change and the state: the machine tool industries in Taiwan and Japan', *World Development*, **14**(12), 1375–96.

Hobday, M. (1995), *Innovation in East Asia*, Aldershot, UK and Brookfield, VT, USA: Edward Elgar.

Hurtarte, J.S., E.A. Wolsheimer and L.M. Tafoya (2007), *Understanding Fabless IC Technology*, Oxford: Elsevier.

Kim, L. (1997a), *From Imitation to Innovation*, Cambridge, MA: Harvard Business School Press.

Kim, L. (2001), 'The dynamics of technological learning in industrialization', *International Social Science Journal*, **53**(168), 297–308.

Kim, L. (2003), 'The dynamics of technology development: lessons from the Korean experience', in S. Lall and S. Urata (eds), *Competitiveness, FDI and Technological Activity in East Asia*, Cheltenham, UK and Northampton, MA, USA: Edward Elgar pp. 143–67.

Kim, L. and R.R. Nelson (2000), *Technology, Learning and Innovation: Experiences of Newly Industrialized Economies*, New York: Cambridge University Press.

Kim, Y. (1997b), 'Technological capabilities and Samsung Electronics' international production networks in Asia', BRIE Working Paper 106.

KSIA (2005), 'The outlook of the semiconductor equipment industry', paper presented at The IV Vacuum Technology Conference, Korea Research Institute of Standards and Science, Korea Semiconductor Industry Association (KSIA).

Lee, K.R. (2011) 'Public research system under the people's participatory government of Korea', *Asia Pacific Business Review*, **11**(2), 175–92.

Lim, L.Y.C. (1978), 'Multinational firms and manufacturing for export in less-developed countries: the case of the electronics industry in Malaysia and Singapore', unpublished doctoral thesis, University of Michigan, Ann Arbor.

Lundvall, B.A. (1988), 'Innovation as an interactive process: from user–producer interaction to the national system of innovation', in G. Dosi, C. Freeman, G. Silverberg and L. Soete (eds), *Technical Change and Economic Geography*, London: Frances Pinter, pp. 349–69.

Lundvall, B.A. (1992), *National Systems of Innovation: Towards a Theory of Innovation and Interactive Learning*, London: Frances Pinter.

Malaysia (1986), *The Fifth Malaysia Plan 1986–1990*, Kuala Lumpur: Government Printers.

Malerba, F. (1992), 'Learning by firms and incremental technical change', *Economic Journal*, **102**(413), 845–59.

Malerba, F. and L. Orsenigo (1997), 'Technological regimes and sectoral patterns of innovative activities', *Industrial and Corporate Change*, **6**(1), 83–117.

Malerba, F., R.R. Nelson, L. Orsenigo and S. Winter (2001), 'Competition and industrial policies in a "history friendly" model of the evolution of the computer industry', *International Journal of Industrial Organization*, **19**(5), 635–64.

Marsh, H. (1981), *Silicon Chip Book*, London: Pelican Press.

Mathews, J.A. (2002), 'The origins and dynamics of Taiwan's R&D consortia', *Research Policy*, **31**(4), 633–51.

Mathews, J.A. (2006), 'Electronics in Taiwan – a case in technological learning', in V. Chandra (ed.), *Technology, Adaptation and Exports: How Some Developing Countries got it Right*, Washington, DC: The World Bank, pp. 83–126.

Mathews, J.A. and D.S. Cho (2000), *Tiger Technology: The Creation of a Semiconductor Industry in East Asia*, New York: Cambridge University Press.

Nelson, R.R. (1993), *National Innovation Systems: A Comparative Analysis*, New York: Oxford University Press.

Nelson, R. (2007), 'Economic development from the perspective of evolutionary theory', paper presented at the Sanjaya Lall Memorial Conference, UNCTAD, 8–9 March, Geneva.

Penrose, E. (1959), *The Theory of the Growth of the Firm*, New York: John Wiley.

Polanyi, M. (1962), 'Tacit knowing: its bearing on some problems of philosophy', *Reviews of Modern Physics*, **34**(4), 601–16.

Rasiah, R. (1988a), 'Production in transition and its impact on the semiconductor industry in Penang', *Kajian Malaysia*, **6**(1), 85–111.

Rasiah, R. (1988b), 'The semiconductor industry in Penang: implications for the new international division of labour theories', *Journal of Contemporary Asia*, **18**(3), 44–69.

Rasiah, R. (1993), *Pembahagian Kerja Antarabangsa: Industri Separa Konduktor di Pulau Pinang*, Kuala Lumpur: Malaysian Social Science Association.

Rasiah, R. (1994), 'Flexible production systems and local machine tool sub-contracting: electronics transnationals in Malaysia', *Cambridge Journal of Economics*, **18**(3), 279–98.

Rasiah, R. (1995), *Foreign Capital and Industrialization in Malaysia*, Basingstoke: Macmillan.

Rasiah, R. (1996), 'Institutions and organizations: moving towards the technology frontier in electronics industry in Malaysia', *Industry and Innovation*, **3**(2), 79–102.

Rasiah, R. (2008), 'Ownership, institutions and technological intensities: automotive and electronics firms in East and Southeast Asia', in J. Eatwell and P. Arestis (eds), *Issues in Finance and Industry: Essays in Honour of Ajit Singh*, London: Palgrave.

Rasiah, R. and Y. Lin (2005), 'Learning and innovation: the role of market, government and trust in the information hardware industry in Taiwan', *International Journal of Technology and Globalization*, **1**(3/4), 400–432.

Schumpeter, J.A. (1934), *The Theory of Economic Development*, Cambridge, MA: Harvard University Press.

Shilov, A. (2007), 'TSMC confirms entering microprocessor manufacturing business', 27 July, available at: http://www.xbitlabs.com/news/cpu/display/20070727063402.html, accessed 3 March 2009.

Shilov, A. (2009), 'TSMC set to make Atom System-on-Chip microprocessors for Intel', 3 February, available at: http://www.xbitlabs.com/news/other/display/20090302090548_Intel_and_TSMC_ Announce_Strategic_Partnership.html, accessed 26 February 2010.

Silterra (2006), 'Silterra "chips-in" to boost local IC R&D: wafer foundry provides free fabrication facilities to chip designers', available at: http://www.silterra.com/news/news_20061204.html, accessed 26 February 2010.

Tsai, T.S.H. and C.H. Zhou (2006), 'Taiwan's United Microelectronics Corporation (UMC)', in T.S.H. Tsai and B.S. Cheng (eds), *The Silicon Dragon: The High Tech Industry in Taiwan*, Cheltenham, UK and Brookfield, VT, USA: Edward Elgar Publishing.

Tseng, W., H.E. Khor, K. Kochhar, D. Mihaljek and D. Burton (1994), 'Economic reform in China: a new phase', Washington, DC: International Monetary Fund.

UNESCO (2010), Science and Technology, Paris: United Nations, Education, Scientific and Cultural Organization, available at http://stats.uis.unesco.org/unesco/ReportFolders, accessed 18 May 2011.

World Bank (2010), *World Development Indicators*, Washington, DC: World Bank.

WTO (2006), *International Trade Statistics*, Geneva: World Trade Organization.

WTO (2007) *International Trade Statistics*, Geneva: World Trade Organization.

Xin-Xin, K. (2006), 'The development of the computer industry in China', mimeo.

Xin-Xin, K. (2008), 'The development of the semiconductor industry in China', mimeo.

Zenith (2008), 'Zenith Electronics Corporation', available at: http://www.funding universe.com/company-histories/Zenith-Electronics-Corporation-Company-History.html, 29 September.

5. Catching up in the pharmaceutical sector: lessons from case studies of India and Brazil

Shyama V. Ramani and Samira Guennif

5.1 INTRODUCTION

Taking off with the discovery of antibiotics, the pharmaceutical industry emerged as a distinct sector in the developed world in the last century, when research and development (R&D) activity by firms greatly increased in order to find solutions to the problems and demands created by the two world wars. Since then, it has continued to be a highly R&D-intensive industry with technological competencies and innovation creation being important determinants of firm survival and growth. Such trends were reinforced with the emergence and integration of biotechnology during the 1980s[1] and the commercial success of radical innovations such as recombinant insulin, human growth hormone, interferon, TPA and EPO (Achilladelis and Antonakis, 2001; Malerba and Orsenigo, 2002).[2] Major innovators of the pharmaceutical industry are to be found in only five countries: USA, Germany, Switzerland, the UK and France, where they were greatly supported by favourable national policies in terms of public and private research (McKelvey et al., 2004). Nevertheless, some emerging economies have developed significant industrial capabilities over the last 50 years. The objective of this chapter is to unravel the determinants of the catching-up process of this group through a case study of two such countries: India and Brazil.

India and Brazil are interesting countries to compare because they share some common features. Since the mid-twentieth century, the national objective of both these countries has been to develop industrial capabilities in essential sectors. The two countries also enjoyed a considerable period of lax intellectual property rights (IPR) regimes, when product patents were not allowed in the pharmaceutical sector. Both countries are very large and have a reasonably strong cadre of scientists and engineers. However, over fifty years, India has had much more success in building indigenous capabilities in pharmaceuticals than Brazil, at least to date. Why? Are the different patterns of catching up related to differences in the accumulation of capabilities by domestic firms and their strategies? If they are, what explains these differences? These are the questions we intend to explore in this chapter.

Pharmaceutical products of today broadly fall under one of three types: drugs, vaccines, and diagnostics. For the purposes of this chapter, we focus only on drugs, and refer to industrial capabilities as the capacity of domestic firms to satisfy national and international demand in terms of the quantity, quality and variety of drugs locally produced. We further consider industrial capabilities to include two components: manufacturing capabilities and innovation capabilities.

The manufacturing of drugs involves three main operations and the associated capabilities are different in terms of technological complexity. The least complex step is 'formulation' of drugs, which refers to the processing and packaging of the basic ingredients called 'bulk drugs' into a consumable form such as a tablet, capsule, syrup, injection, plaster, and so on. The production of 'bulk drugs' containing the therapeutic molecule in powder or liquid is a more complex process requiring a higher level of scientific and technological capabilities. But the most complex step is to produce the core component of bulk drugs, termed the 'active pharmaceutical ingredients' (or API).

In defining innovation capabilities, we distinguish between 're-engineering skills' and 'new drug discovery skills'. Usually a latecomer country firm starts by building re-engineering skills, that is by independently developing new processes to produce copies of existing drugs. Once a firm learns to manufacture bulk drugs, and eventually API, it can envisage investing in the development of 'new drug discovery capabilities'. Capabilities in new drug discovery can take the form of integration of biotechnology and/or research capabilities in one or more of the steps in the new drug discovery process. To date, no developing country firm has patented a new chemical entity.

Furthermore, developing country firms have to build up complementary competencies that go beyond technology if they want to commercialize drugs. The regulatory procedure to commercialize a copy of a branded drug is relatively simple. Firms just need to submit proof of their chemical and therapeutic equivalence with the proprietary drug; though some additional information and technical support need to be provided to the regulatory authority to enter the market, and such requirements vary from country to country. On the other hand, to commercialize a new drug, data has to be generated on preclinical tests on animals followed by a three-phase series of clinical testing on human beings, at the end of which a new drug application can be made with the concerned regulatory authority. At present, very few developing countries have a patent or regulatory bureaucracy that can deal with an application for the commercialization of a new proprietary drug, especially if it involves biotechnology.

At this point, before continuing further, we would like to highlight three caveats. First, we focus in what follows on how India and Brazil built their pharmaceutical industries. However, such an analysis cannot be used to draw any conclusions on whether or not a lower- or middle-income country should invest in the creation of manufacturing or innovation capabilities. There are many countries with manufacturing capacity in formulations, and limited or no competence in the production of bulk drugs, which still rely on imports to satisfy their demand. And there are also countries, mainly in Africa, which have no manufacturing capacities and are totally dependent on imports of drugs. Improvement of the health status of its citizens is a common objective of all countries, but the way it is to be done – whether through investment in the creation of manufacturing capabilities, investment in a national healthcare system, or provisions for health insurance – is a national prerogative, to be determined by policy makers, as a function of the country's specific demographic, institutional, economic and geopolitical realities.

Second, caution must be exercised in drawing conclusions on the role of IPR in the catching-up process of developing countries from our case studies. Catching up through copying, that is developing re-engineering capabilities, was indeed the traditional route pursued by most developed countries (including the USA) to build manufacturing and innovation capabilities in their knowledge-intensive sectors in earlier centuries (OTA, 1986). This was possible because the Paris Convention of 1883, followed by most countries until the end of World War II, gave freedom to the signatories to set up their own IPR systems, according to their nation's individual needs. Thus, nations that are lagging technologically usually chose to have a loose IPR regime with process rather than product patents during their period of catching up. At the same time, clearly, the accumulation of innovation capabilities does not depend only on the prevalent IPR regime, being a function of a number of complementary factors, such as the resource base and the scientific, industrial, innovation and social capabilities of a country (Fagerberg and Godinho, 2004; Abramovitz, 1986). Therefore, the results that we present and discuss in this chapter on India and Brazil cannot be used to formulate policy recommendation for another country without consideration of the possible interactions between the IPR regime and other country-specific factors and geopolitical constraints.

Third, catching up in pharmaceuticals has been made more complex since 1995 with the creation of the World Trade Organization (WTO) and the international homogenization of IPR regimes. The Trade Related Intellectual Property Rights agreement (TRIPS), signed by all member countries of the WTO, imposes product patents in all sectors, including pharmaceuticals. Under this new international legal framework, branded drugs cannot be re-engineered except under specific conditions. This means that catching up via the accumulation of re-engineering capabilities is still possible only for drugs whose patents have expired. The impact of TRIPS on the future trajectories of countries committed to a catching-up process in pharmaceuticals cannot be deduced from our case studies. This will depend on a host of other factors, such as the understanding of flexibilities embedded in TRIPS, the functioning of the regulatory bureaucracy, the engagements of the country in bilateral agreements (TRIPS+ agreements), and geopolitical constraints.

The methodology adopted in the present chapter is that of the 'national systems of innovation' (NSI) approach, which has emerged as a useful framework to study the catching-up process of countries (Lundvall, 1992; Nelson, 1993; Freeman, 1995; Edquist, 1997). It provides a useful tool to organize historical evidence on the building of different capabilities. The NSI structure has also been refined along a number of dimensions, such as sectoral specificities (Malerba, 2002) and features of developing countries (Rodrigo and Sutz, 2000), both of which are incorporated in the present chapter.

The rest of the chapter is organized as follows. Section 2 examines the process of catching up in India, followed by section 3, which traces the evolutionary trajectory of Brazil. Then section 4 identifies the major differences between the two trajectories and proposes explanations for the same. Section 5 concludes with further insight on catch-up theories and policy recommendations.

5.2   INDIA[3]

When India attained its independence in 1947, its pharmaceutical industry was of a very modest size. Western multinationals (MNCs) held about 80 per cent of the market with the remainder being served by several Indian-owned companies operating on a much smaller scale. No Indian company had manufacturing capabilities in either bulk drugs or formulations. There was heavy dependence on imported drugs, which were marketed directly by the MNCs established in India and local agents of MNCs that did not have a local presence. MNCs mainly formulated their drugs in India, importing the bulk drugs from their home countries; their contention being that the locally available bulk drugs were not of the desired quality. In the process, not only were technological externalities and knowledge transfer absolutely minimal but Indian drug prices were among the highest in the world (Ramani and Venkataramani, 2001; Greene, 2007). Thereafter, the evolution of the Indian pharmaceutical industry can be divided into four phases.

5.2.1 First Attempts to Reduce Dominance of Foreign Firms

In order to reduce the dependence on imports and Western MNCs, at least for vitally needed antibiotics, the government of India undertook large investments to establish public sector enterprises (Singh, 1985). The most important among these were 'Hindustan Antibiotics Limited' (in 1954) and 'Indian Drugs and Pharmaceuticals Limited' (in 1961). The move was useful and timely, but it was not a comprehensive response to the country's healthcare needs.

Inspired by the economic growth models of Russia and China, throughout the 1960s and 1970s, India, like most other developing countries, adopted inward-looking trade and investment policies. The objective was to minimize dependence on imports and develop an industrial base to serve the needs of its citizens, while promoting market competition and curbing monopolistic and oligopolistic tendencies. The ensuing 'import substitution' policy took the form of a complex system of price controls, high import duties and export subsidies.[4] In addition, under the guise of controlling profiteering by the private sector, the Indian government practised the 'Licence Raj', that is, the 'rule by licence' by which any firm wanting to expand its manufacturing base, export or import, had to get a licence from the government to proceed.

The system of price controls was particularly stringent on pharmaceuticals as compared to other sectors, in the interests of social welfare. In the wake of the Sino-Indian war in 1962, in order to ensure accessibility of drugs to serve wartime needs, the 'Drug display of Prices Order' (DPO) and the 'Drug Price and Control Order' (DPCO) were passed under the 'Defence of India Act' in 1962 and 1963 respectively. Over time, these two Acts were merged into one and price control was introduced in 1970 for a long list of 'notified' drugs that were deemed essential (Kaushal, 2007). The objective was to curb profit margins and promote access to drugs.

This system of regulation was continually opposed by both MNCs and fledgling Indian companies in the pharmaceutical sector. They argued that, while high import duties were responsible for pushing up domestic prices, price ceilings were discouraging the flow of investment into the industry by depressing the earnings of companies. Besides, the 'Licence

Raj' promoted public corruption and diverted the efforts of firms towards securing fiscal and tariff concessions, permits and licences, from the government rather than seeking support for R&D in any form.

Against this backdrop, India still adhered to a very tight system of IPR. At the time of independence in 1947, India's IPR system was defined by the 'Indian Patents and Designs Act of 1911', which itself was based on the British 'Patent Act of 1852'. Under this regime, patent holders were allowed exclusive rights to make, sell and use both new processes and products for 14 years from the date of filing in India. Re-engineering of branded drugs was not allowed and almost all patents of branded drugs were held by MNCs.

Thus, after twenty years of the 'Licence Raj' and an import substitution policy, 80 per cent of the market share was still held by foreign controlled firms in 1970. Indian firms had capabilities only in formulations. Prices of drugs remained among the highest in the world, partially due to import duties, but mostly because firms were focused on brand competition and promotional activities (Lall, 1974a, 1974b). Indian consumers suffered from a shortage of essential drugs and a crisis in terms of healthcare provision. MNCs, on the other hand, fared well: they were in India 'not only the most profitable among manufacturing firms in the country generally but also among all types of foreign controlled enterprises, including those in non-manufacturing sectors' (Lall, 1974b; p. 163).

5.2.2   Development of Re-engineering Capabilities and Conquest of Internal Markets

There were two possible solutions to the healthcare emergency at the beginning of the 1970s. Either medicine could be imported in large quantities as essential commodities, or incentives could be provided for the development of the local pharmaceutical industry. The Indian government opted for the latter solution.

By the mid-1950s it had been brought to the attention of the Indian government that most of the developed countries had put in place a strong IPR system with full product and process patents only after having acquired a certain level of technological competence in knowledge-intensive sectors and a good competitive position in the international market in targeted fields. Accordingly, in 1957, the Indian government appointed Justice Ayyangar to investigate this matter, and his report, submitted in 1959, recommended that only process patents be recognized for essential commodities like food and drugs. But it was after a little more than a decade that his recommendation saw the light of day in the form of the new Patent Act of 1970, which came into force in 1972. It is to be noted that even in 1972, developed countries such as Sweden, Switzerland, Spain, Italy and Japan, did not allow for product patents in pharmaceuticals, thus revealing the lateness of the Indian government in opting for this much practised option of industrial development in other parts of the world.

The Indian Patent Act of 1970 essentially constituted a 'narrowing' of the IPR regime with provisions for commercializing independently developed copies of branded drugs, if the production process was significantly different from that used to manufacture the branded product. Thereby, the incentives for Indian firms to become second innovators were increased. At the time, neither MNCs nor scholars expected the industrial organization to change much; it was essentially viewed as a possibility for the public sector to accumulate technological capabilities and serve the low-income communities directly (Lall, 1974b; Redwood, 1994).

However, Indian firms correctly sized up the 'window of opportunity' opened by the new process patent regime. Leading Indian pharmaceutical firms began to invest in building re-engineering capabilities and started producing essential drugs, slashing market prices heavily. Indian firms even entered into production contracts with the original MNC inventors, permitting them also to enjoy lower costs and a greater mark-up. As a result, slowly but surely, the market shares changed, bearing witness to the downfall of the previous market leaders, namely MNCs.

In 1970 eight of the top ten firms in the Indian market were MNCs, but, by 1995, only four of the top ten firms were MNCs (Athreye et al., 2008). The share of MNCs in the Indian market was 68 per cent in 1970, 60 per cent by 1978 and 50 per cent by 1980 (Chaudhuri, 2005). By the mid-1980s leading Indian pharmaceutical firms were producing both bulk drugs and formulations for the domestic market. By the end of the 1980s, India was exporting bulk drugs and final therapeutics, supplying many parts of the developing and developed world at lower prices and edging towards a positive trade balance. But most important of all, with the increase in market supply, the Indian public healthcare system was finally able to stand on its feet, and the proportion of the poor with access to basic drugs increased.

To conclude, the change in the IPR regime, coupled with the dynamic response of local firms to acquire capabilities in all stages of drug production, led to a sharp reduction in import dependence and MNC domination. But this would not have been possible had India not been equipped already with scientific capabilities in the form of public laboratories skilled in creating new processes and universities producing large numbers of science graduates. The demand side also supported the new trajectory as Indian consumers revealed themselves to be extremely price sensitive.

5.2.3 Development of Regulation Handling Capabilities and Assault on International Markets

The 1990s saw a number of extreme changes in the Indian regulatory environment which influenced the accumulation of technological capabilities in almost all sectors, including pharmaceuticals. In 1991 the economy was liberalized and the pharmaceutical sector was de-licenced: it was no longer necessary to get a licence from the concerned Ministries to expand the manufacturing base, export or import goods. The price control regime, DPCO, was modified and 50 per cent of the drugs were removed from price control in 1995, and only 76 drugs (26 per cent) remained under price control by 2004 (OPPI, 2004). A new regulatory agency, The National Pharmaceutical Pricing Authority, became functional in 1997 to coordinate the regulation of prices.

Economic liberalization had a remarkable effect on the growth of the pharmaceutical industry, with more firms entering the market, and the established ones increasing their manufacturing base. Production, exports and imports shot up and the industry grew rapidly in the 1990s, with an average annual growth rate of 15 per cent for bulk drugs and 20 per cent for formulations (OPPI, 2001).

Interestingly, the rise of exports was partly due to the foray of Indian firms into regulated markets of Western countries, with the principal target being the USA. During the 1980s, American policy makers had become sensitive to the need for improving access to medicines and curbing the growth of health expenditures in the USA. With this objective, the Hatch–Waxman Act was passed in 1984 to stimulate the market for generics, and, as a result, generics manufacturers no longer had to go through a lengthy period of extensive clinical trials. Demonstration of bio-equivalence was sufficient to acquire marketing approval for a generic drug. Ironically, the concerns that prompted the Hatch–Waxman Act were quite similar to those that had provoked the Indian Patent Act of 1970.

Indian firms with foresight, like Ranbaxy, recognized that the Hatch–Waxman Act in the USA, in combination with the liberal economic policies in India, was opening up new windows of opportunity. Such leader firms immediately attracted followers, which also attempted to penetrate the regulated markets of the USA and Europe (Athreye et al., 2008). In addition to exporting medicines to unregulated Southern markets, from 2000 onwards Indian firms began to get supply contracts from international organizations (e.g. WHO, PEPFAR program,[5] Global Fund) that were supporting public health programmes in developing countries, thus responding effectively to yet other windows of opportunity.

In order to sell generics in these regulated markets, Indian firms had

to upgrade their regulation handling capabilities, that is they had to ini-
tiate routines to document the entire production process under specific
formats. To enter a Western market, say that of the USA, Indian firms
had to upgrade their 'Drug Master Files' procedure by increasing the
comprehensiveness of the details supplied on the manufacturing and distribution process, to satisfy the requirements of the US Food and Drug
Administration (FDA). The generics producer also had to prove that its
manufacturing methods conformed to current 'good manufacturing practices' (GMP), as defined in the US Code of Federal Regulations. Then it
could apply for an ANDA or 'Abbreviated New Drug Application' under
four types of filings termed 'paragraphs', the last even permitting entry
of generics before patent expiration. Ranbaxy was the first Indian firm to
use the ANDA filing route to enter the US generics market, leading others
to follow. It used the steady but low return Paragraph I to Paragraph III
approach of ANDA filings, whereby the generic manufacturer entered the
market only after expiry of the product patent to secure a niche in the US
antibiotics segment.[6] Such building of regulatory handling capabilities
resulted in India having the largest number of manufacturing units vali-
dated by the FDA outside the USA by 2007: India had 75, Italy 55, Spain
25 and China 27 (Tribune des droits humains, 2007).

Similarly, after 2000, in order to supply public health programmes in
developing countries supported by international organizations such as
the WHO, Indian firms had to comply with a prequalification process of
product selection and regulations related to WHO-GMP. Thus, though
these requirements did not affect the small- and medium-scale suppliers
of intermediate or bulk drugs, the leading pharmaceutical firms that supplied international markets adopted GMP, even when it was not required
within India. The WHO also demanded other complementary practices,
such as submission of 'Drug Master Files' giving details of the firm and
its system for ensuring quality, documentation, validation, self inspection
and internal audit. The success of the Indian firms in acquiring regulation
handling capabilities is illustrated in the fact that on antiretrovirals, out of
the 85 products selected by the WHO to treat the HIV/AIDS epidemics in
the developing world, Indian firms such as Ranbaxy, Cipla, Aurobindo or
Matrix Laboratories prequalified for the supply of 60 products in 2009.[7]

5.2.4 The Quest to Build New Drug Discovery Capabilities in the Post-TRIPS Era

Hot on the heels of liberalization, India became a member of the WTO
in 1995 and thereby changed its regulatory framework to comply with
TRIPS. Between 1994, when TRIPS was ratified, and 2005, when it came

into effect, three amendments to the patent law of 1970 were passed in the Indian Parliament in 1999, 2002 and 2005 successively, to make it TRIPS compliant. On the one hand, the rising prowess of the Indian pharmaceutical sector was noted: India ranked thirteenth in terms of value and fourth in terms of volume of pharmaceuticals produced in the world by 2005 (Gehl-Sampath, 2008). On the other hand, the Indian pharmaceutical market being extremely competitive with very low margins over cost, the elimination of innovation through re-engineering initially seemed daunting and many scholars predicted a gloomy future.

For the moment, shifting to a TRIPS compliant regime does not seem to have hurt the industry. Indeed, the Indian industry is adapting in a number of ways, and probably would have gone in these directions anyway, even in the absence of TRIPS. In particular, Indian firms are noted to exercise three types of strategic responses to TRIPS. First and foremost, R&D is targeted towards the copy of drugs, vaccines and diagnostics that are off-patent or are soon to be off-patent, especially in regulated Western markets. Second, Indian firms are vying to participate in the international division of labour for the creation of new drugs by Western MNCs by offering contract research and custom manufacturing services, bioinformatics services for genomics-based drug research, and carrying out clinical trials. Indian companies realize that they cannot match the deep pockets of Western MNCs as far as R&D budgets are concerned but want to avoid exclusion. By providing contract services to Western MNCs in the latter's new drug discovery endeavours, they hope to build new dynamic capabilities either in the pre-competitive upstream research stage or in the downstream clinical trials stage (Ramani and Maria, 2005). Third, and in a smaller measure, Indian firms are initiating strategic alliances (more in the US) and outright acquisitions (more in Europe) for a variety of objectives, ranging from access to technology assets, market penetration, and a better understanding of local regulation (Greene, 2007).

Indian firms at present are still facing the heavy challenge of catching up in terms of developing drug discovery capabilities. While pursuing this course, two new kinds of threats from MNCs are rearing their heads.

First, Indian firms have become so capable that they are becoming attractive to global players. For instance, the Indian industry has been very much marked by the buying-out of its star performer, Ranbaxy, by the Japanese company Daiichi-Sankyo, making the threat of foreign buyouts a credible one for all major Indian firms. Daiichi-Sankyo has business operations in 21 countries, while Ranbaxy is present in 56 countries, including emerging and transition economies in which Daiichi has not entered. Ranbaxy is among the international leaders in generics with a renowned low-cost manufacturing infrastructure, but it is struggling to gain expertise in biotechnology and new drug development. Daiichi is weak in generics, but has a good R&D expertise and a solid position in patented drugs. A cash infusion of about US$1 billion brokered under the deal will presumably enable Ranbaxy to retire debt and increase growth. The growth potential for generics, especially in Japan, is high. These complementarities led the founding family of Ranbaxy to accept the offer of Daiichi-Sankyo to buy out their 34.8 per cent stake and make open offers as per Indian regulations for an additional 20 per cent of Ranbaxy's share in June 2008, with the assurance that Ranbaxy will operate as an independent subsidiary of Daiichi under the leadership of its current CEO, Malvinder Singh.

The acquisition of Ranbaxy, a jewel in India's pharmaceutical crown, by the Japanese firm, struck an emotional blow to the Indian public, even as the business pundits pointed out the rationality of the merger. It is not unlikely that other such acquisitions will occur in the future (Singh, 2008; Basheer, 2008). Thus the threat of some more leading Indian pharmaceutical firms losing their 'Indian citizenship' is a challenge to be reckoned with.

Second, under the stronger IPR regime ushered in by TRIPS, there is a growing concern about the conflict between pursuit of monopoly profit and satisfaction of public interest in terms of access to life-saving drugs. In India, there is an increasing number of patent disputes regarding life-saving drugs between patent owners, generic producers and the public. There are inherent tensions at the moment in courts between MNCs, which want to protect their branded drugs, and civic associations and NGOs, which demand better access to drugs for the poor through the production of generics. The MNCs call for legal clarity on what can be patented, what can be considered evergreening of patents and what kind of patents can be bypassed in the interests of the public.[8] For instance, using a pre-grant opposition mechanism introduced in 2005 in the patent law, Indian firms and a civic association challenged Novartis' application for a patent on its anti-cancer drug Glivec. The patent was rejected on the grounds that the API was based on a derivative of a molecule known before 1995, which 'does not result in the enhancement of the known efficacy of the substance' as stated in Section 3(d) of the Indian Patent Act (Srinivasan, 2007). Furthermore, these problems are exacerbated by a lack of coordination between governmental bodies. For example, Cipla gained marketing approval for a generic version of a lung cancer drug from the Central Drugs Standard Control Organization (CDSCO), which operates under the aegis of the Ministry of Health and Family Welfare, while the original innovator Roche was granted a patent by the Indian patent office at the same time for its branded drug Tarseva (Gehl-Sampath, 2008). Again, in the interests of the public, the Indian court sided with the generic producer.

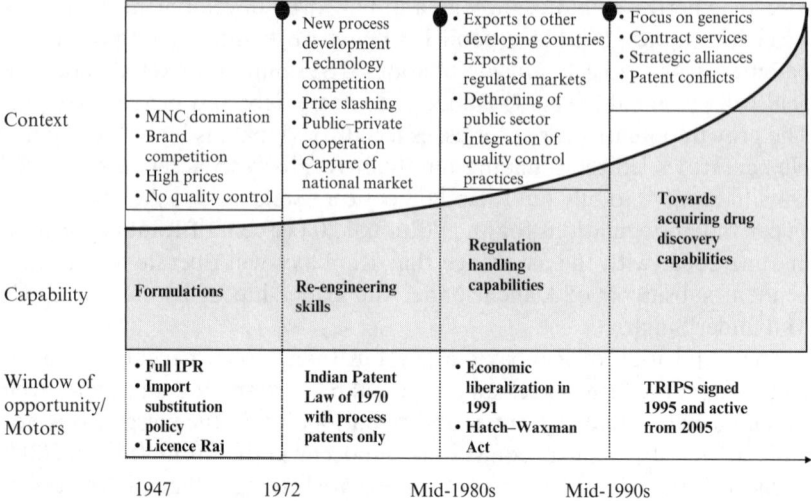

Source: Authors' own elaboration.

Figure 5.1   Evolution of the Indian pharmaceutical sector

Only the future will tell how the interests of the public will continue to be upheld under the TRIPS regime given the pressure from the MNC pharmaceutical lobbies. In turn, such cases are also often cited by MNCs to justify their lack of enthusiasm to introduce new products in India.

Thus, the future of the Indian industry will depend on how the triple challenge, namely of catching up in terms of new discovery capabilities, surviving in a global market and being socially responsible in a poverty stricken country, is played out. The evolutionary trajectory of the Indian pharmaceutical sector as presented in this section is summarized in Figure 5.1. To sum it up, by identifying and catering to several windows of opportunity opened by regulatory shifts in India and abroad, Indian pharmaceutical firms have successfully lowered the domination of MNCs in the domestic market, and built manufacturing capabilities, integrating backwards from the formulation stage to the production of APIs.

5.3   BRAZIL

Brazil had a head start over India in industrialization, thanks to attaining independence from colonial rule in 1822, more than a century earlier than India. By the beginning of the twentieth century, it had a nascent pharmaceutical industry and some public laboratories. Yet, today, unlike India, Brazil suffers from two major handicaps with respect to the pharmaceutical sector: market domination by foreign multinationals and a lack of backward integration of local firms to incorporate manufacturing capabilities in API. Both these limitations are likely to worsen in the future given the increasing presence of new players from emerging countries headed by India and China. Why? This is the question we seek to answer in this section.

5.3.1 No Industrial Policy During Critical Technical Shift

By the end of the nineteenth century, as in Europe and USA, a handful of Brazilian firms were involved in the production of mineral-based medicines on a small scale. In addition, due to the suffering inflicted by the spread of epidemics among the urban population, Brazil established a set of public laboratories between 1892 and 1927, such as the Bacteriological Institute, the Butanta Institute, Oswaldo Fiocruz Institute and the Biologic Institute, with the mission of developing and producing serums and vaccines. Thus, by the 1930s, the Brazilian pharmaceutical market consisted of: (a) public institutions devoted to the development and production of vaccines and serums to abate epidemics of plague, smallpox and yellow fever and to treat snakebites; (b) national firms involved in the production of medicines; and (c) foreign firms also committed to the production of medicines. The last group accounted for only 13.6 per cent of the pharmaceutical market at this time (Queiroz, 1994).

This situation changed dramatically with the ushering of the antibiotics revolution triggered by the spectacular success of penicillin during World War II. Leading Western pharmaceutical firms began to explore the possibilities of creating other antibiotics and drugs based on biological survey, assays and chemical synthesis. They developed technological capabilities in chemical synthesis and commercialized an array of drugs for a variety of infections that were superior to any produced by a developing country firm, including the existing Brazilian ones. The Western firms expanded their scale of production and continued to reap economies of scale as market demand in their nations got a boost with the introduction of systems of universal insurance (both public and private) and state health security schemes. Then they began a serious offensive of internationalization with augmentation of manufacturing capacity worldwide.

This expansionist trend of MNCs conflicted with the aspirations of Brazilian firms, which were striving to promote industrialization and self-sufficiency through adopting the 'import substitution model of industrialization'. In this perspective, the patent system was over-hauled in Brazil in 1945 to permit only process patents and encourage re-engineering. However, these positive incentives were nullified in the 1950s by a macroeconomic policy that attempted to attract foreign direct investment (FDI) through deferentially low exchange rates. As a result of particularly low exchange rates in the pharmaceutical sector, Western MNCs found it in their interest to import raw materials and equipment from their home countries on a large scale and expand their operating base in Brazil. On the other hand, the measures taken to facilitate the import of equipment could not be exploited by local firms because the scale of imports of equipment that was needed to be competitive with MNCs was beyond what any Brazilian firm could afford.

As a consequence of the absence of an industrial policy to protect national industries and the overwhelming presence of foreign firms armed with superior drug manufacturing technologies, Brazilian firms were caught in a difficult position and ceded their place to foreign firms. Frenkel (1978, quoted by Urias and Furtado, 2009)[9] notes that the policy to attract foreign capital inflow, combined with the competitive advantages of large firms from the USA and Europe, brought about a denationalization of the pharmaceutical sector through the exit of local firms and buyouts by MNCs. Between 1958 and 1972, 43 domestic companies were acquired by foreign firms, mostly American (Bermudez, 1992, quoted by Urias and Furtado, 2009).

This change in market composition was the beginning of a long period of steadily rising domination by foreign MNCs, which furthermore did not involve themselves in R&D activities or local production of raw materials. By the 1950s the country had about 500 pharmaceutical companies, of which very few were Brazilian, while the market shares of the foreign firms rose to about 47.1 per cent. This figure increased drastically to 73.3 per cent by 1960, with only four national firms being among the top twenty (Queiroz, 1993).

Such trends were perceived to be leading to a real problem in terms of access to medicines with prices being too high and some essential drugs not being available in large enough quantities. Therefore, the state moved in to intervene in the pharmaceutical sector in several ways to remedy this situation:

- A system of price controls was put into place in 1968. An Inter-Ministry Council for prices was charged with limiting price hikes and ensuring that the price increases in medicines were in general lower than the inflation rate (Romano and Bernardo, 2001, quoted by Urias and Furtado, 2009).

- Even process patents were removed in 1969 to provide further incentives for the development of re-engineering capabilities and the production of a greater variety of drugs (Frischtak, 1989; Queiroz, 1993; Robine, 2008; Urias and Furtado, 2009).
- A public procurement agency, the CEME (Central de Medicamentos) was created in 1971. At first its mission was to purchase and distribute medicines in hospitals. Two years later the CEME was also charged with diversifying the public provision of medicines and in the process supporting the development of a '100 per cent Brazilian' pharmaceutical industry. It was instructed to practise this policy right from the purchases of raw materials to final products, encouraging national initiatives and technology transfers (Queiroz, 1993).

Still, by the beginning of the 1980s, a veritably autonomous local industry, capable of producing its own API and finished products, was nowhere in sight. Foreign MNCs continued to dominate, catering to about 82.7 per cent of the Brazilian market (Queiroz, 1994). Visibly, even the total absence of patent protection, coupled with the operations of public agencies like the CEME, had not been sufficient to stimulate local production. Why?

A singular lack of consistency in the implementation of industrial policy thwarted the entire process. For instance, the CEME passed under the aegis of different organizations over time, with each having a distinct immediate target. In 1971, the CEME operated under the Ministry of Health but in 1974 it was moved to the Ministry of Planning and Social Welfare. According to Queiroz (1994), this shifting status resulted in a reduction of CEME's powers to act effectively as a public procurement agency and intervene in the market.

Indeed, from the 1960s to the 1980s, there was constant confrontation between the advocates of two types of logic (Andréa-Loyola, 2009). One pushed for an 'autonomous' route to development, which favoured the building of a national pharmaceutical industry committed to the production of raw materials, as well as finished products, to increase self-sufficiency. The other argued that satisfying local demand, whether through the production of local firms or the production of foreign MNCs, was primordial. This more 'neo-liberal' or 'dependant' logic was largely supported by MNCs (via the lobbying of ABIFARMA, the Brazilian pharmaceutical association made of MNCs). Thus the turbulent operations of the CEME basically revealed the competition of these two groups. More generally speaking, the 'come and go' policy exercised during the 1970s and the early 1980s by which the structure and ordering of public agencies shifted according to the whims of the government also reflected the struggle between the two lobbies.

5.3.2 Lagging Industrial Policy in a Turbulent Macroeconomic Context

During the 1980s industrial policy on the whole was largely constrained by the vicissitudes of macroeconomic policy (Suzigan and Furtado, 2006). The Brazilian economy entered into a grave economic crisis as a result of serious external debt. Being feebly competitive in many sectors, Brazil tried to improve its balance of payment through reduction of public investment and institutional changes. As a result, even while Brazil made great progress in terms of expansion of manufacturing capabilities in the pharmaceutical sector, such progress hid a strong dependence on imports in some niches. In the end, the problem of lack of backward integration over the different operations of production was never solved, but simply displaced.

For instance, budget cuts were imposed on nodal bodies such as the National Scientific and Technical Development Fund, and the discretionary power of the Economic Development Council in the decision-making process was steadily lowered.[10] Moreover, public investments in education and infrastructures were also slashed. Brutal stopping of plans for scientific and technological development as well as programmes for sectoral development led to a serious skills' constraint in terms of qualified scientists, technicians and engineers. These serious drawbacks undermined the 'social capabilities' of Brazil and also acted as a brake on industrial development during the so-called 'lost decade'.

To top it all, the government initiated protectionist measures to reduce imports and lighten the external debt. These had maximum impact on the pharmaceutical industry. The government established a system of 'market reservations' for products that could be locally manufactured, fixing high tariffs or banning imports, and preventing the duplication of industrial projects by limiting market competition in favour of domestic firms (Queiroz, 1994; Urias and Furtado, 2009; Robine, 2008).

Finally, while waiting with anticipation for the pharmaceutical industry to contribute to an improvement of the trade balance, the Brazilian government launched a back-up plan. The public sector moved forward to attempt to develop technological capabilities needed to produce important API in collaboration with the private sector. In 1984, the CEME instigated a collaboration with the CODETEC[11] and some private pharmaceutical firms. The objective of this project was to identify research output from universities with commercial potential and explore ways in which they could be brought to the market.[12] CODETEC agreed to develop a set of targeted technologies related to the API. In return, the CEME assured purchases of the same and the associated firms could manufacture and sell the concerned products on the final market. With an investment of US$5 million up to 1990, the know-how to produce about 60 API was developed, but among these only 13 reached the production phase. Even after the production process had been developed as a pilot project using public funds, the rest of the targeted API were never produced by the small firms associated with CODETEC (Queiroz, 1994).

Thus the policy measures, which were expected to draw the local industry into the catch-up process in terms of production of API and finished products in the short run, and to provide incentives for augmentation of innovation capabilities in the medium term, were only partially successful. Indeed, against all odds, the mix of state macroeconomic and industrial policies during the 1980s only contributed to widen the fundamental fragility of the Brazilian pharmaceutical industry.

For instance, while the weak degree of backward integration was still apparent and foreign firms still held more than 80 per cent of the market, there was mixed success in reducing dependence on imports. Imports of medicines stayed on average at US$15 million between 1981 and 1989, that is at less than 1 per cent of the local production, and imports of API decreased from US$310.7 to US$278.3 million between 1981 and 1987 (Queiroz, 1994; Urias and Furtado, 2009). Furthermore, domestic production of API steadily increased from US$268 to US$521 million between 1982 and 1987. However, imports of intermediary products requiring one or two processes to be converted into API increased significantly. Thus, the fall in the imports of API hid and was largely matched by an increase in the imports of intermediate products (required for the production of API) from US$37.4 to US$115.5 million, though on the whole there was an improvement in the trade deficit.[13]

Public–private cooperation, though well intentioned, was a failure due to institutional constraints and ineffective responses of firms. At the outset, any API production was subject to regulation on the margin over costs. Keeping this in mind, the consortium targeted API astutely as a function of their (low) cost of development and their (high) potential demand. The last few stages of the production process of API were not capital intensive and therefore compatible with low profit margins. But there were other intermediate steps which required high fixed cost to enjoy returns to scale and such fixed costs could not be borne given the regulation on profit margins. Therefore, more often than not, the local firms renounced the production of API and, instead, concentrated on the production of finished products, for which MNCs' imports were highly taxed or banned. Moreover, the production of such finished products was enabled by large imports of raw materials for which tariffs were still low, given the absence of local production.

To top it all, the most unexpected outcome of the gamut of regulatory changes was the responses of the Brazilian firms. Even though all technologies could be freely imitated, there was no large-scale investment in the acquisition of re-engineering skills. Being severely constrained by a lack of funds, local firms could not invest in costly equipment to expand their manufacturing base. Consequently, under a 'market reservation' system, instead of giving competition to Western MNCs, Brazilian firms began to imitate them. Local firms imported raw materials to manufacture finished products just like the MNCs and then competed in the final market by focusing on the quality and quantity of their medical sales force. A 'commercial logic' was adopted, partially imitating the behaviour of MNCs. The commercial logic followed by MNCs was based on the premise that the development and commercialization of new medicines had to be ensured by a high investment in marketing and advertisement. In contrast, the commercial logic followed by Brazilian firms was founded solely on the dedication of considerable resources to exploring the best strategies for product differentiation with competing brands (Frenkel, 2001, quoted by Urias and Furtado, 2009). Against the backdrop of high inflation rates, besides marketing outlays, Brazilian firms invested their modest resources in treasury bills offering high rates of interest, rather than in R&D.

5.3.3   Time for Critical Regulatory Shifts with Mitigated Effects

The 1990s witnessed three types of radical regulatory changes in Brazil: (a) liberalization; (b) a reinforcement of IPR; (c) a new drug policy and public procurement. Going beyond sectoral specificities, these institutional shifts offered little room for the consideration of local industry, and thus failed to trigger a large-scale rectification of the structural defects of the Brazilian pharmaceutical industry.

Burdened with excessive debt, Brazil was obliged to borrow and adopt a set of economic liberalization policies as decreed by the IMF, including the opening and the deregulation of markets. For instance, import restrictions were decreased, lowering the tariff on pharmaceutical products from 70 per cent to 14 per cent (Sweet, 2007). At the industry level, this had the serious consequence of forcing the exit of local firms on a large scale and induced a second wave of denationalization. The Brazilian economy, already marked by a strong dependence on foreign markets, was made even more vulnerable by the closure of about 1700 production units of intermediary goods destined for the pharmaceutical industry in the first half of the 1990s (Orsi et al., 2003).

Under pressure from the US Trade representatives, from 1991 onwards there was a collective reflection on how to reinforce the IPR regime to attract FDI. In 1996, without even making use of the transitional period permitting a developing country to implement TRIPS by 2005, Brazil proceeded with a new reinforcement of its patent regime to comply with TRIPS.[14] By a Presidential decree both product and process patents were reintroduced with a 20-year validity period. Moreover, a pipeline protection was implemented ensuring patent protection for medicines developed prior to 1997 under the condition that these medicines were already patented in another country and had not been marketed previously in Brazil. Accordingly, instead of following the minimum standards required by TRIPS to provide patent protection to medicines after 1995, the Brazilian Law introduced a legal possibility for firms to gain patent protection and exclusive marketing rights for medicines before this date, forcing firms manufacturing copies of the same to stop production.

Starting from 1991, the drug policy was progressively changed. First, the 1980s price control scheme was dismantled and price ceilings on many of the drugs were removed. As a consequence, firms were inclined to raise their prices so that they could reconstitute their profit, which had been seriously affected by the crisis of the previous decade.

In turn, against the backdrop of repeated devaluation of currency and soaring inflation and hyperinflation, access to medicines was made even worse. In this context, to induce competition and improve access to essential drugs, a formal system of public bidding via the so-called 'Law of Tenders' was put in place in 1993. This procedure channelled public procurements representing 26 per cent of domestic market sales through 'open auctions' (Sweet, 2007). Only price was taken into account without much attention being paid to quality, leading to very stiff price competition in the market. Four years later, the mandate of the public procurement programme was further refined by the 'basic pharmacy programme', which was set up with the specific objective of improving access to 40 essential drugs in compliance with the 'right to health' instituted in 1988 in the Brazilian Constitution.

The last pillar of the new drug policy consisted of the promulgation of the Generics Act of 1999 following the recommendation of an experts' group. On the supply side, the objective was to improve the quality of drugs sold and to fuel market competition. On the demand side, the purpose was to increase the consumption of generics (cheaper than branded drugs), with the help of public authorities investing massively in campaigns to inform people about the quality of generics. In the same year, ANVISA, the counterpart of the US Food and Drug Administration, was created to monitor the security, efficiency and quality of drugs marketed in the country.[15]

Furthermore, the law insisted that generics be at least 33 per cent cheaper than branded drugs. Finally, the promotion of the national industry was taken into account. The government's implicit argument was that, though the fixed costs of production would increase due to the implementation of higher standards with respect to quality of drugs, local firms which complied could enter a larger generics market. Predictably, the Generics Act provoked strong reactions from MNCs, which saw in it a move designed to challenge their local market shares.[16]

In practice, the Generics Act regulates the promotion, packaging and marketing of generics in Brazil. It must be noted that, until then, as in other developing countries, Brazil authorized the production and marketing of copies of branded drugs or 'similar'. These medicines contained the same API, displayed the same therapeutic indications, the same strength, or the same mode of administration as the branded drug patented abroad. However, local producers did not have to demonstrate the equivalence of their products with the branded drugs through the provision of bioequivalence data. Now, the Generic Act raised the standards by requiring firms wanting to launch new copies to get marketing approval through completing bioequivalence studies. Only in this manner could the generic be deemed equivalent to the branded drug (Sweet, 2007). Thus, three types of drug are currently available on the Brazilian market: branded drugs, generics and similars. But only similars that were launched before 1999 can be in the market till 2014, being permanently banned thereafter.

Definitely, Brazilian firms recognized the Generics Act as a window of opportunity to develop technological capabilities. The Generics Act is inducing Brazilian firms to move towards a 'technology based competition logic' (Frenkel, 2001, quoted by Urias and Furtado, 2009), under which they are modernizing their production units and developing innovation capabilities. For instance, between 2000 and 2003, generic producers in Brazil invested nearly US$1 billion in the construction and modernization of units (Bermudez and Oliveira, 2004). About 1140 new pharmaceutical products were granted marketing approval between 2000 and 2005. The generics market itself increased from 1 per cent of the total pharmaceutical market in terms of both value and volume in 2000, to 10.7 per cent in terms of value and 13.5 per cent in terms of volume by 2006. The increase in market size has clearly benefited the Brazilian firms as the number of local firms among the top 20 generics producers in Brazil increased to seven holding about 25 per cent of the market share by 2005.[17]

To conclude, where does Brazil stand today in terms of catching up in the pharmaceutical sector?

Brazil ranks today among the top ten largest pharmaceutical markets of the world with retail sales in 2006 of US$8.1 billion, but 70 per cent of the market is still held by foreign firms (Cohen, 2000). However, there has been a marked evolution in the composition of foreign firms dominating the market. In the last century, foreign firms referred uniquely to Western MNCs. Today this group has been joined by Chinese and Indian pharmaceutical firms. For instance, 11 Indian firms have established local affiliates with some manufacturing capacities (Sweet, 2007). Indian firms hold 10.3 per cent of the Brazilian generics market today and intend to continue their offensive to increase their market shares.

Dependence on foreign imports continues. The industry continues to import more than 90 per cent of its raw material and in 2007 Brazil recorded the huge deficit of US$2.7 billion, more than double the value in 1997 (Urias and Furtado, 2009). Its dependence on imports is not due to lack of technological competencies, but due to the fact that the initial and intermediate stages of the production of API require a huge capital investment which cannot be amortized given the final market prices and the dynamics of the market.[18] Therefore, instead of investing the manufacturing capabilities in all segments of the drug production process, it makes financial sense to import whatever is necessary.

On the positive side, since 2000, there has been a real effort to renew sector-specific industrial policy and facilitate capacity-building. To promote spin-offs and technology transfer from universities, a Brazilian version of the US Bayh–Dole Act of 1980 has been enacted. In addition, other measures have been put in place, such as tax breaks for R&D investment, subvention for purchase of machines, funding of public–private joint research projects, and, to a small measure, funding of corporate research projects. Yet there are discrepancies. For instance, Tenders Law and the Generics Act aimed at improving competition in the pharmaceutical market and accessibility of drugs do not necessarily work for national firms. In particular, the buying of generics to fund the public health programmes at the cheapest prices favours new actors (firms from emerging countries) and imports. Indeed Brazilian firms feel discriminated against because they have to comply with GMP edicts which do not apply to imports (Hasenclever and Paranhos, 2008).

The public sector and public–private cooperation still reign. Far-Manguinhos, a public research institute in pharmaceuticals, is the nodal organization around which a strong and dense network of public institutions and private firms has been constructed. The private firms and public laboratories in this network are involved in R&D programmes, aimed at reverse-engineering and copying existing molecules. For instance, Nortec (a spin-off of Far-Manguinhos) is involved in a long-term agreement with Far-Manguinhos whereby it produces the API that Far-Manguinhos uses for the formulation of antiretrovirals (Cassier and Correa, 2008). Further downstream, the state provides steady demand for these drugs. As a result,

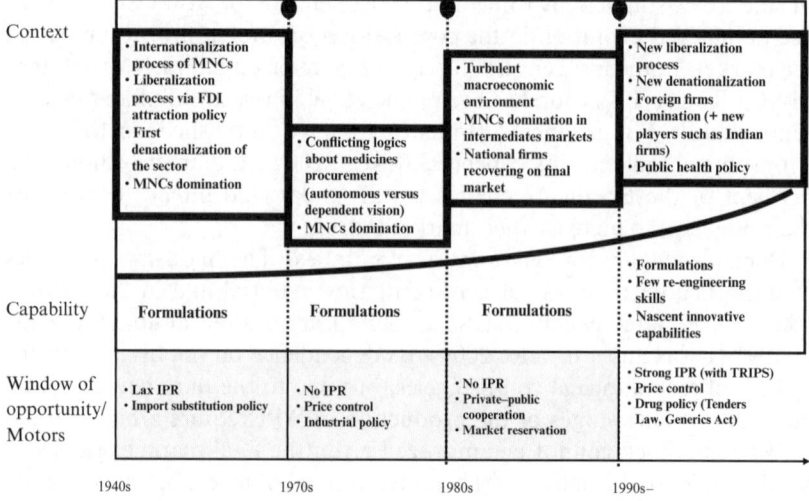

Source: Authors' own elaboration.

Figure 5.2   Evolution of the Brazilian pharmaceutical sector

the public sector today is a provider of serums, vaccines and medicines and also intends to become a provider of diagnostic kits, which is emerging as another social need.

The evolution of the Brazilian pharmaceutical sector is illustrated in Figure 5.2. As it reveals, the future of Brazilian firms will depend on the extent to which government policy and public–private cooperation are able to face the challenges posed by the strong presence of foreign (European and Asian) MNCs and the lack of backward integration over all phases of drug production.

5.4   DISCUSSION OF RESULTS

Why did two countries such as India and Brazil, starting with a similar resource base and policy rationale, exhibit such different trajectories of accumulation of industrial capabilities over time? To answer this question, we start by identifying the pillars of state policy and their rationale. Then we examine the responses they provoked within the industry. We show that the endogenous responses consisted of two parts. On the one hand, most of the time, the predicted and desired outcome was partially realized and, on the other hand, there were invariably other unpredicted responses that emerged. The latter unexpected elements, which were specific to the two countries, pushed them along distinctive trajectories.

5.4.1 Similar Priors but Different Outcomes

The starting objective of the governments of India and Brazil was to achieve self-sufficiency and autonomy in the pharmaceutical sector. Towards this end, they began by constructing scientific capabilities through investment in higher education. One of the first tasks of the Government of India after independence was to create institutes of higher education and research.[19] In Brazil also, the state invested in higher education with the creation of a network of universities and public laboratories.[20]

Then, to translate scientific capabilities into re-engineering capabilities, a lax system of IPR permitting the accumulation of re-engineering capabilities was necessary. Thus India shifted to a loose IPR regime, allowing for only process patents between 1972 and 2005. Similarly, Brazil had a loose patent system with only process patents from 1945 to 1969, and it did away with the entire patent regime between 1969 and 1997.

Finally, given the large internal size of their domestic markets, for both countries the policy of import substitution was a reasonable strategy to adopt. Each embraced it to a different degree to curb imports and promote exports and local industries. Thus, in terms of capabilities and public policy, Indian and Brazilian pharmaceutical markets resembled each other by the mid-twentieth century. Nevertheless, despite these similarities, the final outcomes after 50 years diverged greatly in terms of the degree of backward integration of local firms, the domination of MNCs in the domestic market, and the role of public sector.

A different achievement in backward integration
Both India and Brazil started by creating 'basic manufacturing capabilities' in formulation by importing bulk drugs and API. At this stage, they acquired 'packaging skills' or 'skills in formulations'. Then they invested in developing 're-engineering capabilities' in order to acquire 'production capabilities in bulk drugs and API'. This enabled further backward integration over the production process and reduced the costs of production, but this was much less in Brazil compared to India.

In Brazil, more than 90 per cent of the core substances of drugs, the API, are still imported and only a few local firms are involved in their production (Sweet, 2007). In contrast, leading Indian firms have successfully integrated over the different phases of the drug production process, from the formulation of finished products to the more complex production of APIs at competitive prices.

Traditional and new forms of domination by MNCs
The degree of domination of MNCs seems to be correlated with the degree of backward integration achieved in the two countries, but it is not clear which factor is responsible for the other. It is similar to trying to answer the classic question: which came first, the chicken or the egg?

In Brazil the traditional form of market domination by MNCs still reigns. Even the generics supply side contains many foreign firms. A consequence of such dependence is a steady foreign trade deficit in the pharmaceutical sector. The new element in the MNC domination is that new players have joined the big boys, namely Indian and Chinese firms.

In India, the traditional form of domination by Western MNCs was eliminated by the mid-1980s; however, new forms of potential domination are being perceived and are giving rise to concern among civic associations, policy makers and Indian firms. At the moment they are taking the form of patent conflicts concerning life-saving drugs and the threat of foreign buyouts. The risks being augured by these trends are not very clear. Will India lose its place as re-engineering capital of the world in pharmaceuticals? Will foreign buyouts again lead to India being a formulation or manufacturing centre? Will market size be reduced on the supply size with delocalization following foreign acquisition?

Internationalization
The evolutionary process in terms of internalization followed a parallel route to the building of manufacturing and innovation capabilities, similarly increasing in complexity. At present, Indian firms are ahead of Brazilian ones, not only in terms of technological capabilities but also in R&D, production and marketing capabilities outside India. They have acquired firms in the USA and Europe and have established production facilities in Latin America and Africa as well. This, in turn, has led them to also fortify their 'regulation handling capabilities' in order to be a player in the global market.

Different dynamics of the public sector
In India, during the 1960s and 1970s, the public sector was viewed by industry observers as the patron saint of the poor, but in the post-TRIPS era, it is in Brazil that the public sector remains active and vibrant.

In Brazil, from the 1970s and the mid-1990s, though public laboratories were largely committed to the development and transfer of technology to the private sector, success was not evident. However, from the end of the 1990s, the Brazilian state has engaged itself seriously in the promotion of public health and this has led to new stock-taking of R&D and manufacturing capabilities.[21] For instance, under the universal access programme to HIV/AIDS treatment, Far-Manguinhos ensures the industrial application of technologies developed in both public laboratories and private firms (mostly spin-offs of Far-Manguinhos). By so doing, public sector firms can produce drugs in their own manufacturing units and supply essential drugs to public health programmes, which offer a steady demand.

Strangely, in India, after the 1980s, once the basic demands of the public health system were satisfied, the public sector had only a minor impact on the development of innovative capabilities. Indeed, the role played by some of the CSIR labs (strong in synthetic chemistry), which had been crucial earlier, is deemed insufficient today. At present, the lacuna is in biotechnology and the focus of state policy is on building scientific capacity in targeted niches, promoting public–private cooperation, and streamlining regulatory procedures (Chaturvedi, 2007). However, despite such public investment, there have been few start-ups, outside of bioinformatics. Even as suppliers of qualified personnel, universities are found wanting today. Most science graduates have only bookish knowledge and not enough practical knowledge, communication skills, or teamwork capacity, requiring firms to invest at least a few years in training the young graduates hired in order to make them productive.[22]

5.4.2 Main Reasons for Divergent Evolutionary Trajectories: Different Policy Design and Distinct Endogenous Responses

As shown in the preceding section, in both India and Brazil, the state was motivated by the same rationale and implemented similar policies, but the outcomes were very different. Why? First, the impact of policies motivated by the same objective can be different depending on their design, that is their content, timing and implementation process. Second, in addition to expected responses, they can also provoke unexpected reactions from stakeholders, as the outcome of a policy cannot be entirely commanded in a market economy. Third, both expected and unexpected outcomes can trigger secondary effects that provoke further change through 'mimicry' and 'bandwagon effects'. It is the distinct features of these three elements: policy design, endogenous response and secondary reactions in India and Brazil that have led to the different evolutionary outcomes. We illustrate this proposition with examples.

Domination by MNCs served by inconsistent policy design?
The impact of policy is determined not only by content but also by form of implementation. In both Brazil and India the rationale of import substitution was a cornerstone of state policy. But, in India, this was followed consistently and comprehensively in the pharmaceutical sector, while in Brazil

it vacillated over time. The Indian government did not hesitate between the implementation of an import substitution model and a policy aimed at attracting FDI. Import duties were imposed on all foreign items. In contrast, throughout the period studied, in Brazil there were two lobbies confronting each other. One lobby pushed the import substitution agenda because of the existence of a large domestic market, while the other sought support for opening the market to attract FDI. The MNCs backed up the latter with disastrous effects on local firm strategy.

As a result India seems to have put more of a united front in selectively implementing the advice offered by the Washington Consensus. On the other hand,

> compared to India, the much more profound incorporation of the majority of the recommendations of the original Washington Consensus and some of the augmented ones in Brazil have not only been responsible for reducing the efficiency of the coordination of the macroeconomic policies with its National Innovation System, but also explain to a great extent the bad general economic performance expressed, notably, by slower economic growth (Nassif, 2007, p. 13),

during the 'second lost decade' (that is 1990–2000).

The above features, coupled with the realities of the Indian pharmaceutical market such as razor thin profit margins and declining prices, made India unprofitable for large-scale investment in the view of MNCs whereas the Brazilian market seems to have been simply more comfortable for the Western MNCs, which are now being joined by new players from India and China as well.

Role of perceptions and endogenous responses in catching up

A policy will achieve its desired outcome only if it provokes the targeted response. The same policy measure can lead to different perceptions of windows of opportunity among stakeholders and provoke different evolutionary trajectories (through unforeseen responses of individual actors and bandwagon effects) to exploit such windows of opportunity.

For instance, consider the impact of loose IPR in the two countries. In India a switch to a loose patent regime in 1972 was correctly perceived as a window of opportunity to increase profits through the development of re-engineering capabilities. It did not lead the Indian firms to patent new processes in the Indian patent office en masse, but it forced them to look for new methods of production compatible with local resources and constraints, since the original method could not be copied. Thus, they developed technological capabilities required for duplicative imitation and creative imitation (Kale and Little, 2007).

When some firms made huge profits via the creation and commercialization of lower priced generics, a secondary bandwagon effect was triggered within the market. In 'winner takes all' tournaments, often the incremental technological innovations continued, with a second or third innovator improving upon earlier re-engineered products and grabbing the market share yet again, lowering the prices even further and increasing consumer welfare. As a consequence, Indian drug producers faced continual gales of Schumpeterian technological competition in which only the most diversified or the most technologically competent firms could survive and the Indian pharmaceutical market became very dynamic and competitive.

In Brazil, without any form of IPR, all new products and processes could be freely imitated. However, this did not induce Brazilian firms to invest in acquiring re-engineering skills. As a business strategy it was more profitable to focus on the last stages of formulations that required little capital investment and technical skills rather than undertake the costly project of building manufacturing capabilities in all stages of drug production. Indeed, the Brazilian firms found it profitable to mimic the Western MNCs rather than compete with them. So they also imported raw materials, bulk drugs and API, focused simply on the commercialization process, with special care being bestowed on advertising and marketing routines. Even when public research organizations developed new technologies and transferred them to the private sector at the laboratory or pilot scale, Brazilian firms were reluctant to invest resources to learn to scale up the process technology to a manufacturing level. And this reluctance continued to be exhibited despite the willingness of the Brazilian state to buy their products to meet social needs.

Such 'commercial logic' of Brazilian firms had a secondary effect on the innovation system; it pushed the public sector to become active and attend to the needs of the citizens. As mentioned previously, from the late 1990s, when industrial policy was geared to support the public health system, government laboratories developed generics and incremental innovations for the public sector pharmaceutical firms. Today about twenty public laboratories, which are very active in national research programmes, contribute to 10 per cent of national production in terms of volume (Bermudez et al., 2004).

Unexpected impact of policy in catching up
Policy formulated for a particular purpose can provoke an unforeseen response both within the country and abroad. For instance, while loose IPR designed to facilitate accumulation of re-engineering skills had little impact in Brazil, the Generics Act promulgated in 1999, in the interest of public health and safety, had a tremendous impact on catching up.

Until the Generics Act, as in other developing countries, three types of medicine were available in the Brazilian market: branded drugs, generics and similars.[23] From this date, however, the Brazilian government chose to discriminate against similars in order to improve drug quality and also to minimize competition through brand differentiation as the similars were sold under local brand names. This regulatory change pushed firms to switch to the production of generics from similars and in the process pushed them towards a technology-based competition.

Similarly, the Generics Act in Brazil and Hatch–Waxman Act of 1984 in the USA, which were not at all designed with the objective of promoting foreign firms, did exactly that. For astute Indian firms these regulatory changes opened up new windows of opportunity and contributed to their becoming multinationals.

5.5 CONCLUSIONS

From the start our findings have confirmed some basic tenets of the evolutionary literature on catching up in terms of technological change and industrial growth. The national environment and national system of innovation, in combination with the responses of the actors concerned, determines the country-specific industrial trajectory in any sector, which is also path dependent. Public investment and state policy are at the heart of the catch-up process, but public investments alone will not yield desired outputs if the underlying set of scientific, technological, institutional and social capabilities is inadequate. Moreover, as Nelson (2008) points out, an accumulation of scientific and technological capabilities through investment in human and physical capital alone is not adequate as a successful assimilation of technologies requires effective institutions.

Beyond this, do the case studies yield any new insight on the processes of catching up? We propose three inferences by way of contribution to the catch-up literature on accumulation of industrial capabilities.

Our case studies demonstrate that radical regulatory changes can create windows of opportunity (Soete, 1985) and generate positive externalities, in a way very similar to radical technological discontinuities. Thus the origins of windows of opportunity for the accumulation of technological capabilities need not always be associated with a technological discontinuity, as is usually considered in the catch-up literature. Indeed, in the pharmaceutical sector, regulatory changes related to industrial competition, IPR, drug safety, or public health may also open up windows of opportunity.

They also show that windows of opportunity may or may not be exploited. Final outcomes are uncertain, unpredictable, endogenous phenomena. They are guided by the beliefs and expectations of the different economic actors in the innovation system, which play a very important role in technological capacity-building.

Finally, the experiences of India and Brazil prove that even accumulation of institutions and scientific and technological capabilities need not be sufficient for catching up. In addition, the institutions must induce appropriate endogenous responses from the concerned stakeholders. In other words, there is a need to ensure 'perceived incentives' or conditions, which give rise to a set of expectations that lead stakeholders to take actions that support the desired outcome of policy. By their very definition, a system of appropriate incentives is necessarily ad hoc, idiosyncratic, and context dependent.

Now developing countries are again facing a radical regulatory change, namely TRIPS. So the question is: will TRIPS open up new windows of opportunity for some players from developing countries?

Let us understand that TRIPS imposes the same rules for participating in the technology race for all countries. However, developing countries have far fewer resources to allocate for the preparation of such a race. Moreover, the opportunity cost of each unit of money invested in the technology race is higher for developing countries compared to developed countries, because of higher poverty burdens. They also suffer from technology lag. Therefore, in 'winner takes all' technology races of the post-TRIPS era, the chances of poor countries emerging as winners are quite dim. Effectively this might mean a return to the neoclassical framework, where policy and institutions have a minimal impact on catching up and firms have to create their own windows of opportunity through own R&D, regardless of the environment. Then, in this new context, what recommendations can be made for state policy and firm strategy in pharmaceuticals?

5.5.1   Make Policy Design More Rational

Given financial constraints, more than ever policy makers and other stakeholders in developing countries have to interact to design policy that matches the expectations of the different stakeholders to the maximum extent possible. Only with more dialogue and explicit bargaining can there be fewer surprises and more coordinated development. This implies that the different stakeholders, in particular policy makers, have to get out of their ivory towers to interact more with one another and contribute to a policy formulation that induces the desired responses to the maximum extent possible. Here civic associations need to be particularly active to ensure that catching up in the pharmaceuticals is also increasingly inclusive.

5.5.2   Invest in Public Research and Improve its Contribution to Catching Up

The case studies highlight that investment in universities and public research is not only necessary to ensure pools of qualified labour and technology transfer to private firms, but also to create a vibrant public sector that can fill in crucial niches underserved by private firms whenever necessary. In countries such as India there is a real decline in the role of universities and public sector laboratories in the catching-up process in pharmaceuticals. Given the challenges of biotechnology (and now nanotechnology), the contribution of public institutions is more important than ever.

5.5.3   Build Regulation Handling Capabilities

Catching up in terms of regulatory bureaucracy could also impinge on the accumulation of technological capabilities in the future. For instance, at present, in India a lack of effective regulatory bureaucracy in patenting of new chemical entities or drugs is definitely an institutional problem. Therefore Indian firms tend to seek EPO and USPTO patents, which are far most costly and risky propositions for developing-country firms.

5.5.4   Explore Options for International Cooperation

A myriad of possibilities can open up with a strategic exploration of South–South and North–South cooperation to develop common R&D programmes, a common patent granting body, cross-licensing agreements, or sharing of patent pools.

Coming now to firm strategy, we propose two main recommendations:

1. Continue to reinforce comparative advantage in generics and soft innovations. Many developing countries have more qualified personnel or/and personnel who can be hired at cheaper rates. Therefore, possible secondary windows of opportunity may also open up while investing to create new generics or incremental innovations in terms of drug delivery, dosage and software to complement an original innovation. Much will also depend on how flexibilities in TRIPS are exploited, for instance whether developing country firms can innovate

around a known molecule exploiting provisions that allow for patenting, if the efficiency of the drug is significantly improved.

2. Watch out for new opportunities. New or previously unexploited windows of opportunity may contribute to further accumulation of technological capabilities. Some possibilities are new uses of old technology, traditional knowledge and traditional medicines.[24] Another black window of opportunity, through which we cannot see at present, is associated with new forms of collaboration that are emerging between Western MNCs and leading developing country firms.

To conclude, what is the future likely to hold for Indian and Brazilian pharmaceutical firms? At first glance, since Indian and Brazilian firms have accumulated basic technological and innovation capabilities, the future should only look rosy for them in terms of further catch-up. However, the rate of accumulation of innovation capabilities is unlikely to be as high as in the past and the pecking order between India and Brazil may change.

In terms of challenges, both Indian and Brazilian firms have a great technological lag in recombinant technology and new drug discovery skills, and, in addition, Brazilian firms do not have manufacturing capabilities in API. Moreover, like all developing country firms, both Indian and Brazilian firms are simply strapped for money to invest in R&D capabilities, and also the market does not generate enough incentives for firms to invest much in R&D. For instance, even the sum of the R&D expenditures of the top 11 companies in India in 2005–2006 was only US$379 million, while that of Pfizer was almost 20 times more, at US$7440 million (Chaudhuri, 2007). Similarly, in Brazil, the overall R&D expenditure on pharmaceuticals in the country touched a low US$125 million in 2005 (De Lemos Capanema, 2006). Finally, the opportunity cost of resource allocation to R&D may be amplified by the fact that both Indian and Brazilian firms have lost a lucrative source of profit with TRIPS. They can no longer earn second innovator rents from re-engineering branded drugs.

In the above context, can India rise to the new challenge and one day create a blockbuster? As of now, no Indian firm has patented a new chemical entity, and therefore their innovative achievements in the future will depend on how their individual R&D initiatives and their participation in the international division of labour with Western and Japanese MNCs on the latter's drug discovery projects bear fruit.

Can Brazil ever achieve complete backward integration? With its current scientific capabilities, the main problem in Brazil is the lack of funds to buy the equipment that would make the necessary research and its commercialization a worthwhile business proposition. This constraint is made doubly difficult as their main competitors, the MNCs, already exploit these economies of scale at a global level and export massively to the Brazilian market.

Will the Indian and Brazilian trajectory ever cross each other or will they still be divergent in future?Though nothing can be pronounced with certainty, some parameters which will play a role in determining the outcome can be identified. In India the innovation leaders in pharmaceuticals are the private sector firms, while in Brazil the public sector labs and firms are the motors of accumulation of innovative capacity. The competition will therefore be between private sector Indian firms and public sector Brazilian units (which will transfer technology to their firms).

The hotspots of the race will be in 're-engineering generics', 'creating incremental innovations', and 'learning from international technology alliances'. TRIPS has pushed the focus of innovation investment away from pure re-engineering to re-engineering of drugs that are off-patent or will be off-patent protection in the near future, that is, generics. Firms of both countries are making forays into 'soft' innovations around new drugs, in terms of improvements in dosage, drug delivery, new uses for known molecules, and cost-reducing process innovations for generics. Again, firms in India and Brazil are collaborating with Western and Japanese MNCs in the upstream labour-intensive research segments and in the risky downstream clinical trials, and the returns are not yet clear. Currently India is in the lead in terms of re-engineering of generics, creation of incremental innovations and initiation (and participation) in international technology alliances, but, as Brazil builds capabilities in biotechnology, it is imminently possible that Brazil will leapfrog over India, unless the Indian public sector becomes more dynamic and public–private cooperation becomes more fruitful.

NOTES

1. Biotechnology refers to techniques that involve manipulation or change in the genetic patrimony of living organisms. They emerged from advances in the life sciences from the mid-1970s.
2. For instance between 1980 and 1990 the radical innovations to be commercialized were: Insulin (by Eli Lily in 1982); Human growth hormone (by Genentech in 1985, Eli Lily in 1987, Novo-Nordisk in 1988, Ares-Serono in 1988, Biotechnology General in 1989); Alpha 2 Interferon (by Schering-Plough in 1986, Hoffman La Roche in 1986); Monoclonal Orthoclone OKT3 (by Ortho Biotech in 1986); Tissue Plasminogen Activator TPA (by Genentech in 1987); Erythroprotein EPO (by Amgen in 1989); Hepatitis B vaccine (by SmithKline Beecham in 1989).
3. Some parts of this section draw upon previous articles by Ramani: Athreye et al. (2008), Ramani and Maria (2005), Ramani (2002), Ramani and Venkataramani (2001).
4. See Burton (1998) for a survey of import substitution policies adopted by India and other developing countries.

5. The US President's Emergency Plan AIDS Relief.
6. On the other hand, Dr Reddy's Laboratories adopted the aggressive strategy of Paragraph IV filings, which involves invalidating existing patents or producing non-infringing process through a costly process of litigation; a high-risk strategy due to the litigation costs involved and the 180-day market exclusivity that the firm wins on a successful challenge. Though Dr Reddy's Laboratories got six-month exclusivity for selling Fluoxentine 40mg capsules in US, it also received a severe setback when it lost the AmVaz case to Pfizer. Thus, the two early entrants differed quite markedly in their propensity to take risks. Other Indian firms then began to follow the example set by Ranbaxy and Dr Reddy's Laboratories, but the low-risk strategy of Paragraph I–III applications is the more commonly followed model. Such entry into Western regulated markets meant that the Indian pharmaceutical firms also had to set up litigation teams and invest in paying for the corresponding dispute settlement procedures.
7. For more information, see http://apps.who.int/prequal/, last visited in September 2009.
8. 'Evergreening' refers to strategies followed by firms to extend the duration of patents and retain rents from them through the filing for new patents for the same molecule on the basis of minor innovation.
9. All references that are quoted by Urias and Furtado (2009) are in Portuguese, a language that is not known to either of the authors of this chapter. Hence, these articles are not cited in the references.
10. The former was responsible for the financing of scientific and technological projects, while the latter had been charged with the mission of defining the targets for economic development.
11. The CODETEC (Company for technology development) was created in 1976 through collaboration between the State University of Campinas (UNICAMP), the Ministry of Industry and Trade, and a group of firms, mostly from the public sector.
12. In 1994 CODETEC had its own installations in the campus of the High Technology of Campinas ($3500m^2$, 12 laboratories and some pilot plants specifically for the development of processes of fine chemicals). Out of 100 employees, 60 were researchers (Queiroz, 1994).
13. Besides, this increase in the imports of API and intermediate products can be explained by the activity of MNCs present on Brazilian territory. In the face of constraining national fiscal policy, MNCs were often tempted to opt for advantageous transfer prices, that is to repatriate a part of the profits realized by billing at unduly high prices the intermediate products and API supplied to their Brazilian subsidiaries. In addition, the period was marked by high inflation rates and several devaluations of the real currency, which generated a dramatic increase in the value of imports.
14. During the Uruguay Round and even before the ratification of TRIPS in 1994 by the country members of the World Trade Organization, Brazil was the target of pressure and commercial sanctions from the United States from the end of the 1980s.
15. The mission of ANVISA also covers price control and counselling of the 'National Agency' in charge of granting patents, regarding the assessment of drug novelty.
16. With campaigns proclaiming the quality of the original API, while hinting that the quality of generics could be mediocre.
17. See www.progenericos.org.br, last accessed in February 2010.
18. Interviews with C. D'Almeida and B. Fialho, who have extensive work experience in the Brazilian public sector in pharmaceuticals.
19. It expanded the network of universities; it set up institutes for technical training such as the Indian Institute of Technology (IIT). It also established research institutions for advanced research outside the university system such as the Indian Council of Medical Research (ICMR), the Indian Council of Agricultural Research (ICAR) and the Council of Scientific and Industrial Research (CSIR).
20. Among others, Fiocruz is a public institution in charge of the promotion of public health and social development, through the creation and the diffusion of scientific and technical knowledge. In addition, the National Council for Scientific and Technological

Development (CNPq) is a public agency linked to the Ministry of Science and Technology, which works for the promotion of scientific and technological research and for the formation of human resources for research in the country. It works in close relation with the Federal University of Rio de Janeiro and its 'Chemical Institute' founded in 1963 with the support of the BNDE, the National Bank for Economic Development, and the Ministry of Planning.

21. As a result, the Brazilian government could bargain price reductions for HIV/AIDS drugs with MNCs advantageously and scale-up the universal access programme, which today covers 180 000 people living with HIV/AIDS (Guennif, 2007; De Albuquerque Possas, 2008).
22. Comments during interviews with four leading pharma firms in December 2008.
23. Referred to above.
24. In future, the exploration and exploitation of the rich Brazilian biodiversity may offer new opportunities for national players to be part of the next generation of new drug development one way or another (Fialho et al., 2004).

REFERENCES

Abramovitz, M. (1986), 'Catching-up, forging and falling behind', *The Journal of Economic History*, **46**(2), 385–406.

Achilladelis, B. and N. Antonakis (2001), 'The dynamics of technological innovation: the case of the pharmaceutical industry', *Research Policy*, **30**(4), 535–88.

Andréa-Loyola, M. (2009), 'SIDA, sante publique et politique du medicament au Brésil: autonomie ou dependence', *Sciences Sociales et Santé*, **27**(3), 47–74.

Athreye, S., D. Kale and S.V. Ramani (2008), 'Experimentation with strategy and the evolution of dynamic capability in the Indian pharmaceutical sector', *Industrial and Corporate Change*, **18**(4), 729–59.

Basheer, S. (2008), 'Ranbaxy–Daiichi merger: an emerging ardhnarish-war model?', DNA (India), available at: http://sify.com/finance/fullstory.php?id=14712790.

Bermudez, J.A.Z. and M.A. Oliveira (2004), *Intellectual Property in the Context of the WTO TRIPS Agreement*, Rio de Janeiro: WHO/PAHO Collaborating Center for Pharmaceutical Policies, National School of Public Health, Sergio Arouca and Oswaldo Cruz Foundation.

Bermudez, J.A.Z., M.A. Oliveira and E. Andrade de Oliveira (2004), 'Expand access to essential medicines in Brazil: recent regulation and public policies', in J.A.Z. Bermudez and M.A. Oliveira (eds), *Intellectual Property in the Context of the WTO TRIPS Agreement*, Rio de Janeiro: WHO/PAHO Collaborating Center for Pharmaceutical Policies, National School of Public Health, Sergio Arouca and Oswaldo Cruz Foundation, pp. 129–51.

Burton, H.J. (1998), 'A reconsideration of import substitution', *Journal of Economic Literature*, **XXXVI**, 903–36.

Cassier, M. and M. Correa (2008), 'Scaling up and reverse-engineering: acquisition of industrial knowledge by copying drugs in Brazil', in B. Coriat (ed.), *The Political Economy of HIV/AIDS in Developing Countries: TRIPS, Public Health Systems and Free Access*, Cheltenham, UK and Northampton, MA, USA: Edward Elgar, pp. 130–49.

Chaturvedi, S. (2007), 'Exploring interlinkages between national and sectoral innovation systems for rapid technological catch-up: case of Indian biopharmaceutical industry', *Technology Analysis and Strategic Management*, **19**(5), 643–59.

Chaudhuri, S. (2005), *The WTO and India's Pharmaceuticals Industry*, New Delhi: Oxford University Press.

Chaudhuri, S. (2007), 'Is product patent protection necessary in developing countries for innovation? R&D by Indian Pharmaceutical Companies after TRIPS', Calcutta: Indian Institute of Management Calcutta, Working Paper Series: WPS No. 614/September 2007.

Cohen, J.C. (2000), 'Public policies in the pharmaceutical sector: a case study of Brazil', Washington, DC: The World Bank, Latin America and the Caribbean Regional Office, Human Development Department, LCSHD Paper Series.

De Albuquerque Possas, C. (2008), 'Compulsory licensing in the real world: the case of ARV drugs in Brazil', in B. Coriat (ed.), *The Political Economy of HIV/AIDS in Developing Countries: TRIPS, Public Health Systems and Free Access*, Cheltenham, UK and Northampton, MA, USA: Edward Elgar.

De Lemos Capanema, L.X. (2006), 'A industria farmaceutica Brasileira e a atuação do BNDES', Rio de Janeiro: BNDES Sectorial.

Edquist, C. (1997), *Systems of Innovation: Technologies, Institutions and Organizations*, London: Pinter.

Fagerberg, J. and M. Godinho (2004), 'Innovation and catch-up', in J. Fagerberg, D. Mowery and R. Nelson (eds), *Handbook of Innovation*, Oxford: Oxford University Press, pp. 514–43.

Fialho, B., L. Hasenclever and J.M.C. Mello (2004), 'The geography of innovation in the pharmaceutical industry: assessing implications for developing countries', in D. Gibson, M. Heitor and A. Ibarra (eds), *Connecting People, Ideas and Resources across Communities*, West Lafayette, IN: Purdue University Press.

Freeman, C. (1995), 'The national system of innovation in historical perspective', *Cambridge Journal of Economics*, **19**(1), 5–24.

Frischtak, C.R. (1989), 'The protection of intellectual property rights and industrial technology development in Brazil', Washington, DC: The World Bank, Industrial and Energy Department, working paper, Industry Series.

Gehl-Sampath, P. (2008), *India's Pharmaceutical Sector in 2008: Emerging Strategies and Global and Local Implications for Access to Medicines*, London: Department for International Development, DFID.

Greene, W. (2007), 'The emergence of India's pharmaceutical industry and implications for the US generic drug market', Washington, DC: Office of Economics Working Paper, US International Trade Commission.

Guennif, S. (2007), 'Droits de propriete intellectuelle et sante publique dans les pays du sud: l'enjeu des medicaments antisida', *Transcontinentales*, no. 5, 19–37.

Hasenclever, L. and J. Paranhos (2008), 'The development of the pharmaceutical industry in Brazil and India: technological capability and industrial development', mimeo.

Kale, D. and S. Little (2007), 'From imitation to innovation: the evolution of R&D capabilities and learning processes in the Indian pharmaceutical industry', *Technology Analysis and Strategic Management*, **19**(5), 589–611.

Kaushal, L.M. (2007), 'Drug price control order and recent developments', available at: http://pharmexcil.com/data/uploads/5.DrugsPriceControlOrderandRecent Developments.pdf.

Lall, S. (1974a), 'International pharmaceutical industry and less-developed countries', *Economic and Political Weekly*, **9**(47), 1990–96.

Lall, S. (1974b), 'The international pharmaceutical industry and less-developed countries, with special reference to India', *Oxford Bulletin of Economics and Statistics*, **36**(3), 143–72.

Lundvall, B.-Å. (1992), *National Innovation Systems: Towards a Theory of Innovation and Interactive Learning*, London: Pinter.

Malerba, F. (2002), 'Sectoral systems of innovation and production', *Research Policy*, **31**(2), 247–64.

Malerba, F. and L. Orsenigo (2002), 'Innovation and market structure in the dynamics of the pharmaceutical industry and biotechnology: towards a history-friendly model', *Industrial and Corporate Change*, **11**(4), 667–703.

McKelvey, M., L. Orsenigo and F. Pammolli (2004), 'Pharmaceuticals analyzed through the lens of a sectoral innovation system', in F. Malerba (ed.), *Sectoral Systems of Innovation: Concepts, Issues and Analyses of Six Major Sectors in Europe*, Cambridge: Cambridge University Press, pp. 73–120.

Nassif, A. (2007), 'National innovation system and macroeconomic policies: Brazil and India in comparative perspective', paper presented at the United Nations Conference on Trade and Development.

Nelson, R. (1993), *National Innovation Systems: A Comparative Analysis*, Oxford: Oxford University Press.

Nelson, R. (2008), 'Economic development from the perspective of evolutionary economic theory', *Oxford Development Studies*, **36**(1), 9–21.

Office of Technology Assessment (OTA) (1986), 'Intellectual property rights in an age of electronics information', Washington, DC: US Government Printing Office, p. 228.

OPPI (2001, 2004), 'Organisation of Pharmaceutical Producers of India: Pharmaceutical Compendium', Mumbai.

Orsi, F., L. Hasenclever, B. Fialho, P. Tigre and B. Coriat (2003), 'Intellectual property rights, anti-AIDS policy and generic drugs: lessons from the Brazilian public health program', in J.P. Moatti, B. Coriat, Y. Souteyrand, T. Barnett, J. Dumoulin and Y.A. Flori (eds), *Economics of AIDS and Access to HIV/AIDS Care: Issues and Challenges*, Paris: Edition de l'Agence Nationale de Recherches sur le SIDA.

Queiroz, S.R.R. (1993), 'Os determinantes da capacitaçao tecnologica no sector quimico-farmaceutico Brasileiro', Ph.D. thesis, Department of Economics, UNICAMP.

Queiroz, S.R.R. (1994), 'Un transfert reussi et contrarie par une politique de developpement national: la production pharmaceutique', in C. Durand (ed.), *La Coopération Internationale et les transferts de Technologie*, Brussels: De Boeck.

Ramani, S.V. (2002), 'Who's interested in biotechnology: R&D strategies, knowledge base and market sales of Indian biopharmaceutical firms', *Research Policy*, **31**(3): 381–98.

Ramani, S.V. and A. Maria (2005), 'TRIPS and its possible impact on the biotech based segment of the Indian pharmaceutical industry', *Economic and Political Weekly*, 12–18 February, pp. 675–83.

Ramani, S.V. and M. S. Venkataramani (2001), 'Rising to the technological challenge: integration of biotechnology in the Indian pharmaceutical industry', *International Journal of Biotechnology*, **3**(1/2), 95–115.

Redwood, H. (1994), *New Horizons in India*, Suffolk: Oldwicks Press Limited.

Robine, A. (2008), 'Transfert et acquisition de la technologie dans les pays émergents: l'exemple bresilien de l'acces aux medicaments contre le sida', Ph.D. thesis, Department of Economics, Université Paris 1 Panthéon-Sorbonne.

Rodrigo, A. and J. Sutz (2000), 'Looking at national systems of innovation from the south', *Industry & Innovation*, 7(1), 55–75.

Singh, N. (2008), 'A win win deal', Biospectrum (India), available at: http://biospectrumindia.ciol.com/content/BioBusiness/10807111.asp.

Singh, S. (1985), *Multinational Corporations and Indian Drug Industry*, New Delhi: Criterion Publications.

Soete, L. (1985), 'International diffusion of technology, industrial development and technological leapfrogging', *World Development*, 13(3), 409–22.

Srinivasan, S. (2007), 'Battling patent laws: the Glivec case', *Economic and Political Weekly*, 15 September, pp. 3686–91.

Suzigan, W. and J. Furtado (2006), 'Industrial policy and development', CEPAL Review.

Sweet, C. (2007), 'Regulating the tigers: the institutional dynamics of Indo-Brazilian trade reflections from the pharmaceutical sector', paper presented at ELSNIT Conference on Institutional Dimensions of Integration and Trade, Barcelona.

Tribune des droits humains (2007), 'L'industrie Indienne n'aide pas les Indiens', available at http://www.humanrights-geneva.info/article.php3?id_article=2152.

Urias, E. and J. Furtado (2009), 'Institutional changes and their impacts on the Brazilian pharmaceutical industry', paper presented at VII GLOBELICS conference, Dakar, Senegal, 6–8 October, 2009.

6. The agro-food sector in catching-up countries: a comparative study of four cases

Shulin Gu, John O. Adeoti, Ana Célia Castro, Jeffrey Orozco and Rafael Díaz

6.1 INTRODUCTION

6.1.1 The Importance of Agriculture and Research Objective

This study looks into the development of the agro-food sector from a sectoral innovation systems perspective, focusing on dynamics and mechanisms that brought about changes to the sector in the circumstances of technological progress and globalization.

Human beings have been engaging in agriculture for thousands of years. This sector uses land to produce foodstuffs and the output is used as raw materials in an increasingly wide range of manufacturing. The agro-food sector makes up a crucial part of developing economies. It is the basis securing the food supply for the increasingly huge population in the developing world.

In total 3 billion, half of the 5.5 billion people of the developing world, live in rural areas (The World Bank, 2008, p. 3) and most of them are involved in agriculture for their living. What is happening to the sector in catching-up countries? What about the prosperity of the vast pool of the agricultural population in the developing world? What lessons can be drawn from their experiences in order to improve policy-making for the development of the sector?

Mainstream development thinking, from Lewis (e.g. Lewis, 1954) to Prebisch (1959), put modern sectors at the centre of catch-up in developing or 'backward' countries, with agriculture being assigned a passive role. These lines of thought have been influential up to the present time. Important progress has been achieved in the past fifty years (Sisler and Oyer, 2000; The World Bank 2006, 2008), arguing, based on plentiful experience, that the agricultural sector has played important 'catalyst' roles for sustainable development. However, these works have been largely restricted to the analysis of agriculture itself and have been made in the sphere of agricultural economics. There have been few works that have incorporated the insights developed in innovation economics and innovation systems into the study of the agro-food sector in either developed or developing countries, with some exceptions such as Cusmano et al. (2008) and some works in World Bank (2006).

Our study attempts to fill this gap by employing a sectoral innovation system approach to the investigation of selected agro-food sectors in four developing countries: cassava in Nigeria, vegetables in China, coffee in Costa Rica, and soybeans in Brazil. We wish to shed light on the understanding of factors and processes that caused the changes in the studied sectors from a new angle of innovation and change. We also explore the evolutionary paths and modes which show great diversity among the cases but with a rationale. A coherent research framework makes it possible to compare cases evolved in different country contexts and generalize findings from them, which hopefully contain relatively more dedicated policy implications.

The remaining part of the introduction section presents the theoretical background and analytical framework and the research method. This section also gives the basic information for the case countries. Section 2 discusses the case of cassava in Nigeria, section 3 vegetables in China, section 4 coffee in Costa Rica, and section 5 soybean in Brazil. Section 6 discusses findings; finally a short section 7 concludes the chapter.

The work presented in this chapter is a result of a collective effort. The authors have been working as a team over a two-year period. We developed the analytical framework for the agro-food sector together, under the very good project leadership of Richard Nelson and Franco Malerba. John O. Adeoti, Ana Castro, Jeffrey Orozco and Rafael Díaz, and Shulin Gu wrote the country cases on cassava (Nigeria), soybean (Brazil), coffee (Costa Rica), and vegetables (China) respectively and independently first, whereupon the team members made cross-comments and the authors revised again. Shulin Gu worked as the coordinator, integrated the cases and wrote up the chapter.

6.1.2 Theoretical Background and Analytical Framework

Sectoral innovation systems

This study takes a sectoral innovation system (SIS) approach. The perspective of innovation systems (IS) puts the creation, diffusion and application of knowledge as key to growth that takes place through interactions between various actors of an innovation system (Lundvall, 1992; Nelson,

1993). Initially the focus of the IS perspective was on the level of the nation state; later focus was on the industrial sector, which became an important and informative branch of IS studies.

A sector implies (Malerba, 2004, pp. 13–17) a set of activities that are unified by some related product groups for a given or emerging demand and that share some basic knowledge. A sectoral innovation system considers innovation as an interactive process central to the growth of sectors, in which learning and capability-building transform the actors. Innovation and learning is assumed to take place in the bearing of institutional settings and linkages/networks of the sectoral actors; technologies and knowledge regimes and R&D centres characterize the learning modes and process. Policies are considered important in triggering or impeding learning and transformation. In short, by focusing the investigation on specificities of an industrial sector, the SIS approach is apt to prove sector-specific details. It is obvious therefore that a sectoral IS approach is not alien to the insights developed in agricultural economics and development economics, instead, it will surely be complementary to the latest advances in these disciplines. We expect that the analysis following the SIS approach will shed light on why and how the agro-food sector is active in development, by exploring the dynamics and mechanisms underpinning the learning and innovation and transformation processes.

In particular the Catch-up Project, of which the work reported in this chapter is part, has set up a 'learning-capability and knowledge-base interactions' framework (Nelson, 2006; Malerba, 2004, 2006). The major dimensions of the framework adapted to the agro-food sector are the following.

Evolution and characteristics of the sector   We outline the main composition and features of the sectoral system; the producers, distributors, processors, and the network and institutions that shape the interactions among the actors in the development process of the sector. A survey of the process of institutional change is illuminating. This shows how certain institutions emerged and were adapted through selection and dissemination, which constitutes an institutional learning trajectory.

We examine distinctions between large-scale farms and smallholder farms, because features of networks, distributional channels and poverty reduction effects may differ wildly in different producers' and other actors' organizations. In most of the cases – Costa Rica, China and Nigeria – smallholder farms dominate, and in Brazil, large farms dominate while smallholder farms are on the increase. We examine distributional agents including international traders and local traders; we examine their role in bridging supply and demand and in transferring technical information.

This is especially relevant to export-oriented sectors. We outline major institutional changes, including those which help the market to work, given that the development of market mechanisms is one of the most crucial aspects for the agro-food system in the context of developing and transition economies.

Sources and opportunities for growth   come from both the demand and supply side. We pay particular attention to the demand side of the agro-food sector; in contrast, for high-tech sectors, scientific breakthroughs and inventions at scientific laboratories have been observed as having more direct importance. Expanding and ever more sophisticated demands, increasing concern about food safety and living standards drive learning and technological upgrading and institutional change in the agro-food sector. We investigate the driving forces of the growth of the sector from the demand side such as: where did they come from – from the international market or domestic consumers? What changes have occurred in this regard in the past ten years or so under the WTO regime? How did the changes in the demand side convey or express themselves to technological learning and institutional change? What were the differences in demand factors from the international or local market? What were the connections of international and domestic markets in their impact on the growth of the sector? From the supply side in terms of technological progress, the agro-food sector as well as other 'traditional' sectors often uses general-purpose technologies developed somewhere outside the sector (von Tunzelmann and Acha, 2005); the sector, notwithstanding, is important in the national innovation systems as a massive 'carrier' in the application of new technologies and harnesses the benefits of technological progress. The 'induced innovation' theory (Hayami and Ruttan, 1971) captures this feature well. This theory argues that the characteristic natural endowments and other factors of a certain country determine or lead to which technologies are appropriate for that country to develop, and hence it acknowledges the different trajectories of agricultural development in different countries that are cast by differentiated factors.

If so, how did this process happen? Where did the technologies come from and what was the adaptive process? Also, is there any evidence that the agro-food sector is itself becoming more active in the creation of knowledge frontiers?

Acquisition of technology: local R&D versus the supply of international companies, and transformation of the knowledge base   We distinguish between: (a) product technology (new varieties of crop seeds); (b) process technology (agronomic technology which is used in plantations); (c) technologies for quality control and distribution; and (d) technologies for food process-ing. Product technology is often embodied in seeds, and is increasingly incorporated in modern bio-scientific and technological knowledge result-ing from professional R&D, but farmers' breeding through on-the-spot seed selection remains a useful contribution. Agronomic technology largely involves tacit knowledge and skills, and is rather localized in plan-tation fields; meanwhile R&D in agronomy is important and indispens-able. Technologies for distribution and quality control are often provided in the form of tools and equipment, integrated with mechanical, optical and IT technologies. In our study different cases may focus on some of the most relevant, but not all, aspects of technology and knowledge as mentioned. We explore the following questions: where were the sources for the acquisition of the necessary technologies? How was the absorptive capacity developed with regard to embodied and external sourced tech-nologies? Was there an apparent transformation of the knowledge base for the sector? What were the responses by public R&D and the extension system and how did they evolve during a time span of ten to twenty years?

The role of government We divide the roles of government into direct and indirect involvement. The indirect role relates to the role of investment in knowledge and technological infrastructure services. Uniquely for devel-oping countries, the government might devote itself with massive efforts to the development of market-supporting institutions and other institutional changes. Direct involvement might be employed in the initial stages for structural change via administrative guidance and financial subsidies. What kinds of involvement have already taken place and what experiences and lessons could we draw from them?

Global value chains
The notion of the global value chain complements the sectoral IS approach in that it scrutinizes value-adding activities, which are progressively more dispersed across national boundaries at present.

Similar in ways to the IS perspective, a value chain describes the full range of value-adding activities that are required to bring a product or service from concept and design through the intermediary processes and finally to delivery to consumers. The concept and analysis of the value chain was initially popular in business management (e.g. M. Porter). In the past decade, the idea of the global value chain was explored in relation to international trade and development studies (e.g. UNIDO, 2002; Gereffi, 1999; Kaplinsky, 2000), against the background of economic globaliza-tion. The examination of the global value chain looks at the distribution of value activities between various chain participants such as producers, trading companies and consumers. It reveals that in the sectors under investigation, particularly the coffee sector, those who use intangible capabilities and knowledge increasingly create and seize higher valued segments, such as seed breeding, marketing and coordination of chain activities. These gains are 'rents', as the authors call them, from technological innovation and/or from managerial or institutional strength. Export of the final product alone may not automatically bring about fair profits to the exporter if the exporter does not care about capability-building so as to be able to move up into intangible assets-based activities. But some authors (e.g. Pietrobelli and Sverrisson, 2004) criticize the concept of the global value chain because it does not give enough consideration to the opportunities and changes at the low-value end, hence it gives little information about how the low-end actors (mostly in developing countries) can improve themselves. We believe that by combining the value chain analysis with the IS approach, their weaknesses can be counterbalanced.

Value chains are specific to certain products or services; moreover, the structure or governance of a value chain changes over time. Analysis of the global value chain offers an important reference to, particularly, export-oriented agro-food sectors, as shown in the coffee case of Costa Rica (see below).

6.1.3 Research Method

Comparative case study and synthesis
Comparative case studies are especially helpful in identifying trends, patterns and features (Mjøset, 2006a and 2006b; Flyvbjerg, 2003) of the developments of the agro-food sector provided that our observations are made in a number of distinctive policy and development areas. From an evolutionary point of view, which sees the world as heterogeneous and changing over time, we do not expect to find out the universally valid truth. Instead, we anticipate finding differentiated patterns and features, and will generalize them by comparing the underlying conditions. In order to be able to make a certain level of generalization, we have tried hard to have country cases developed as good as for corresponding to each other. It was a process that entailed a great deal of enormous dialogue among the team members, and the dialogue and discussion in turn encouraged several rounds of revision of the cases. The dialogue and mutual referring led to a synthesis that eventually we achieve, which is presented in section 6, 'Findings and discussion'.

Both the country cases and the synthesis are basically descriptive. We use quantitative and qualitative data, reports, published papers, government documents and so on from various sources, in order to

Table 6.1 Countries, cases and strategic orientations

Country	Brazil	China	Costa Rica	Nigeria
Case subject	Soybeans	Vegetables	Coffee	Cassava
Domestic demand or export orientation	Export	Domestic	Export	Domestic

Source: Authors' own elaboration.

answer the research questions following the 'learning-capability and knowledge-base interactions' framework. The authors in our group have been involved in surveys and training in the respective areas for many years, and all have accumulated rich experience which ensures that the study is high quality.

Selection of cases
Given the broad coverage of the agro-food industry – cereals, meat, and fruits and vegetables as the FAO (the United Nations Food and Agriculture Organization) categorizes it – it is difficult to analyse agro-food as a single the sector. Each segment, or even each agro-food product, is distinct in, among other things, factor composition and consumption elasticity; each is specific in driving forces and development dynamics. We chose a major, or representative product as the analytical unit, that is: soybeans for Brazil, cassava for Nigeria, coffee for Costa Rica and vegetables for China.

In the remarkable time of globalization one important gauge for the case selection is their strategic orientation: domestic needs-oriented or export-oriented. The four cases make up a balanced combination: two, the Brazilian soybeans and the Costa Rican coffee, have the international market as their most important orientation, and the other two, the Chinese vegetables and the Nigerian cassava, aim mainly at domestic needs (see Table 6.1).

6.1.4 Basic Information on Case Countries

We take several parameters to depict the basic information on the case countries.

a. The level of development, measured by per capita GDP. The more developed the economy is, the fewer people rely on the land for their living, and the more developed are the institutions and supportive

Table 6.2   Level of development, labour-to-land ratio and Gini coefficient

Country	Brazil	China	Costa Rica	Nigeria
Total national population 2004 (1000)	180 654	1 320 892	4250	127 117
Agricultural population 2004 (1000)	25 869	849 417	803	37 827
Share agricultural population in total population	14.3	64.3	18.9	29.8
Per capita GDP 2004 (US$ constant 2000 prices)	3636	1441	4333	397
Per capita agricultural GDP of the agricultural population (US$ constant 2000 prices)	1589	241	1867	364
Per capita arable land (ha)	0.32	0.10	0.05	0.22
Per agricultural capita arable land (ha)	2.23	0.16	0.28	0.75
Gini coefficient	0.59 (1998)	0.45 (2001)	0.47 (2000)	0.51 (1997/97)

Source: Various tables from FAO Statistical Yearbook (2005–2006).

industries. Brazil, Costa Rica and China are middle-income countries in terms of development, and Nigeria is in the low-income group.

b. The labour-to-land ratio, measured by per capita arable land, indicating one of the most important natural endowments for the agro-food sector. Brazil is the richest among the case countries, while China and Costa Rica are poor in arable land resources. By referring to per agricultural capita arable land, the difference between Brazil and the land-poor countries becomes even more striking; Brazil stands more than 10 times higher than China in this resource.

c. The Gini coefficient indicates the status of wealth distribution. Brazil has the most unequal society. But in recent decades income gaps in all the case countries are tending to become wider.

For parameters (a) to (c), refer to Table 6.2.

d. The structural or specialization characteristic, measured by agricultural production index (see Table 6.3). A country having a production index of a certain category equal to 1 is at the world average of the

Table 6.3   Agricultural production index

	Cereals	Meat	Fruit and vegetables
USA	3.68	3.21	1.08
France	3.28	2.53	1.51
Japan	0.26	0.58	0.53
China	0.88	1.38	1.77
India	0.60	0.14	0.84
Brazil	0.23	2.70	1.11
South Africa	0.76	1.03	0.79
Russian Federation	1.50	0.86	0.63
Nigeria	0.50	0.21	0.63
Thailand	1.26	0.70	0.82
Vietnam	1.34	0.79	0.74
Costa Rica	0.15	1.05	4.50
World	1	1	1

Note: More countries (a few typical advanced economies and a few typical developing economies) are included in this table and Table 6.4 to enable the case countries to be compared in a broader context.

Source: Reproduced based on FAO, Statistical Yearbook (2005–2006), Table A1: Total and agricultural population (including forestry and fisheries), and Tables B1, B2, B3: Production of cereals, meat, and fruits and vegetables and share of each category in world.

category production; a country with an index higher than 1 produces more than the world average of that category. Likewise, a country with an index of a certain category smaller than 1, at, say, 0.5, produces that category of agricultural product at half the world average. The index is made following the UNFAO classification; it divides the agro-food sector into three categories: cereals, meat, and fruit/vegetables. Of the case countries, Brazil is specialized in meat production, soybeans having been used as an important feed for meat production; Costa Rica is specialized in fruits/vegetables, coffee being in this category; China is specialized in vegetables; and Nigeria is lower than the world average for all indexes.

e.   International trade position is measured by net (export minus import) total trade value and agricultural net trade value (see Table 6.4). Brazil and Costa Rica have been important exporters of agricultural products. In particular Brazil's agricultural exports make up the lion's share of the total net (export) value of the country. Nigeria and China are net importers of agricultural products; the case of vegetables for China and the cassava for Nigeria are both oriented to domestic consumption.

Table 6.4 *International trade positions*

	Net total trade value (US$ million)					Agricultural net trade value (US$ million)				
	1979–81	1989–91	1999–2001	2003	2004	1979–81	1989–91	1999–2001	2003	2004
USA	−28417	−113204	−427969	−580542	−706961	23214	18284	10913	8825	4019
France	−17753	−19154	−1011	−6801	−16731	3259	9606	9948	11470	12005
Japan	−3436	64942	87083	88010	110568	−16612	−27940	−33436	−35294	−39605
China	−2717	16405	27776	34093	25741	−5571	−2727	−6896	−11427	−20862
India	−5099	−4058	−8891	−14153	−22272	1096	1879	1352	1601	1950
Brazil	−3391	10702	−2474	22419	30529	6325	6330	10351	17314	23617
South Africa	5552	5890	1293	−4380	−2520	1418	933	873	1076	771
Russian Fed.	n.a.	n.a.	57070	60500	87145	n.a.	n.a.	−7017	−8655	−10166
Nigeria	5317	5907	7732	9034	16984	−1623	−334	−995	−1561	−1778
Thailand	−2615	−8275	5389	3759	1682	2853	4183	4641	6756	8096
Vietnam	−960	−406	−848	−5051	−5051	−280	441	948	976	1345
Costa Rica	−395	−373	−477	−1585	−1971	550	716	1230	1211	1323

Source: FAO, Statistical Yearbook (2005–2006), Table C5: Net total trade value and net agricultural trade value (exports − imports).

Table 6.5   The three agricultural worlds

	Agriculture based	Transforming	Urbanized
% of rural population (2005)	68	63	26
% of agriculture in GDP (2005)	29	13	6
Annual non-agricultural GDP growth (1993–2005) (%)	3.5	7.0	2.7
Orientation of economic activities	Subsistence oriented	Moving towards market oriented and diversified activities	Market oriented and diversified activities
Public spending on agriculture/ agriculture GDP %	4%	About 10%	Higher than 10%
Infrastructure and modern inputs	Low	Improving infrastructure High use of modern inputs	Relatively modest use in chemical fertilizer
Case country in this study	Nigeria	China	Brazil, Costa Rica

Source: Compiled by authors based on The World Bank (2008), Tables 1.1, 3.2; pp. 31, 39, 75–76.

'The three agricultural worlds' of developing countries – the agriculture based, the transforming and the urbanized, as the World Bank (2008) have introduced them – summarize the above discussion and count the parameters, such as development level, population pressure, and agricultural endowments as an aggregate. Rows 1 to 6 of Table 6.5 give general characteristics of each agricultural world, and the final row puts the case countries of the study into the related agricultural worlds.

Brazil and Costa Rica are located in the 'urbanized' world, China is in the 'transforming' world and Nigeria is in the 'agriculture based' world. Although Nigeria has witnessed a dramatic reduction of its rural population in recent years, its agriculture fits the characteristics of the agriculture based group in terms of orientation of economic activity in agriculture, public spending on agriculture, infrastructure and modern inputs in agriculture.

6.2 THE CASSAVA SECTOR IN NIGERIA: GAINING STRATEGIC IMPORTANCE IN SOCIAL AND ECONOMIC DEVELOPMENT

6.2.1 Introduction

Nigeria is located on the west coast of Africa, covers 924 000 km², and has a population of 140 million (2006 Census) with a growth rate of 2.8 per cent. The country comprises the Federal Capital Territory and 36 states. The federal government is responsible for the national development policy, while the states have jurisdiction over activities confined within their state boundaries. Local government authorities of the states are responsible for development activities at the grassroots level. The economy is largely agrarian but the export structure is dominated by crude oil, which accounts for at least 80 per cent of the foreign exchange earnings. As shown in Table 6.6, the agricultural sector accounted for about 40 per cent of GDP in recent years, while the oil economy accounted for about a quarter of the GDP. The challenge of export diversification and the need to meet the growing domestic demand for food has brought into focus the need to boost agricultural production.

Cassava is the second most important African food staple, after maize, in terms of calories consumed, and is widely acknowledged as a crop that holds great promise for addressing the challenges of food security and poverty reduction (Nweke et al., 2001). In the early 1960s Africa accounted

Table 6.6   Nigeria: sectoral contribution to GDP (1999–2005)

Sector	% contribution to GDP						
	1999	2000	2001	2002	2003	2004	2005
Agriculture	43.45	42.65	42.3	42.14	41.01	40.98	41.21
Petroleum	24.45	25.91	26.04	23.46	26.53	25.72	24.33
Solid minerals	0.25	0.25	0.25	0.26	0.25	0.26	0.27
Telecommunications	0.45	0.46	0.55	0.78	0.99	1.2	1.45
Manufacturing	3.49	3.44	3.52	3.7	3.57	3.68	3.79
Financial institutions	4.05	4.03	4.02	4.97	4.12	3.96	3.82
Wholesale and retail trade	13.46	13.04	12.76	12.99	12.54	12.9	13.64
Others	10.25	10.1	10.42	11.54	10.87	11.18	11.36
Total	99.85	99.88	99.86	99.84	99.88	99.88	99.87

Source: NPC (2007: 34) based on data from various issues of Statistical Bulletin of the Central Bank of Nigeria, Abuja.

for 42 per cent of the world's cassava production. Thirty years later, in the early 1990s, Africa produced half of the world's cassava output, primarily because Nigeria and Ghana increased their production fourfold (Nweke, 2004). Nigeria, now the largest producer of cassava, characteristically demonstrates the importance of the crop, in food security, in poverty reduction, and in diversification of the economic and export structure. An exploration of the development in this sector in Nigeria would shed light on how to realize the great promise that this sector might bring about for economic and social development in an African developing country.

Section 6.2.2 introduces the importance of cassava for Nigeria. Section 6.2.3 sketches the long evolutionary path of the cassava sector in Nigeria. It examines the transformation of the sector and the driving forces behind it. In addition to the population pressure, changes in development policy, either externally imposed from international organizations, or internally by government-initiated proactive adjustments of development strategy, have played important roles. Section 6.2.4 discusses the sources of knowledge for the planting and processing of cassava. There are two types of institution active in agricultural R&D in Nigeria: international institutions and national institutions, which have been improving in recent years. By far the most important technologies responsible for the surges in the sector relate to new cassava varieties. We examine the roles of international R&D and domestic R&D and their relationship regarding the development and dissemination of new varieties among other necessary technologies, which are of key interest in this case.

Finally, section 6.2.5 examines the importance of cassava processing, given that the '2004 Presidential Initiative on Cassava' in Nigeria expects cassava to be not only a staple foodstuff but also for industrial use. Industrial use of cassava at present is primarily in the beverage and food industries. In this section we take a cassava processing company as a case to show the status of the representative local processing companies, to see how they are progressing and to see what restrictions there are to the implementation of the newly initiated cassava strategy. This case also illustrates at the micro level what local government in Nigeria is doing in the face of these bottlenecks to enhance cassava processing.

6.2.2   Importance of Cassava

Cassava is becoming increasingly important in Nigeria. Nigeria is currently the largest producer of cassava in the world.[1] It is recognized as a potent instrument of food security and poverty reduction, and has a wide range of industrial applications, which could engender small-scale industrial development and export of intermediate raw materials.

Food security and poverty reduction
Cassava fits well into the farming system in Nigeria, which is characterized by smallholder farmers using rudimentary instruments and with less developed agricultural infrastructure. Compared to grains, cassava is more tolerant of low soil fertility and more resistant to drought, pests and diseases. Its roots store well in the ground for months after maturity and can remain available the whole year round. Smallholder farmers produce cassava with simple tools like hoes and machetes on their small plots of land. Most farmers in the main cassava belts of the south-eastern, south-western and central zones of Nigeria grow cassava, which is typically intercropped as a main or minor crop.

As a staple foodstuff cassava provides a food supply for low-income rural households in the form of simple food products (for example, dried roots and leaves), which are significantly cheaper than grains such as rice, maize and wheat. Urban households are also eating more cassava as food in the form of *gari*, which need a bit more processing. Current estimates show that the per capita dietary calories derived from cassava amount to about 238kcal in Nigeria (Cock, 1985; Stoorvogel and Fresco, 1991).The current annual production level is estimated to be about 45 million tons of cassava tubers, and about 75 per cent of the production is consumed in the form of food (Adeniji, 2007).

Cassava is important, not just as a food crop but even more so as a major source of cash income for producing households. As a cash crop, cassava generates cash income for the largest number of households in comparison with other staples, contributing positively to poverty alleviation.

Cassava processing and industrial application
Cassava roots and tubers are easily perishable, and can deteriorate within two or three days after harvesting. Additionally, the roots need to have the cyanogenic glucosides contained in them reduced to a tolerable level, so that they are acceptable and safe for consumption. For these reasons, cassava is usually sold as a processed product whilst other staple roots and tubers are most frequently sold as fresh products.[2] Traditionally the processing of cassava is laborious; it is done by women for domestic consumption and as a rural enterprise for marketing opportunities.

In addition and importantly, there is broad industrial usage of cassava. Table 6.7 gives a short list to illustrate these uses, which are mostly already to some extent being implemented in Nigeria. However, in the mid-1990s, cassava starch only accounted for 5 per cent of the total 17 000 tons of starch annually used as an industrial raw material by Nigerian firms. The bulk of the imported starch was cornstarch because the cassava starch produced in Nigeria was low in quality, and private Nigerian companies

Table 6.7   Description of cassava uses

Use	Description
Staple food	Mostly consumed in the form of *gari, fufu*, tapioca, starch, *kpokpogari* and *lafun*.
Food and beverage	Cassava flour used in bakery products and cassava starch used as a general thickening agent for food industry such as salad dressings, sauces, canned and frozen foods, and infant foods. Dried cassava roots used for beer and alcoholic drinks; syrup concentrate for soft drinks.
Ethanol	Cassava chips for producing medical and industrial alcohol.
Livestock feed	Cassava chips and pellets and leaves used in compounding animal feed for livestock and farmed fish.
Monosodium glutamate	Cassava starch is a common source for making monosodium glutamate in Asia. It is used to enhance flavour in food, e.g. Ajinomoto.
Sweetener	Cassava starch used to make glucose and fructose as substitutes for sucrose in jams and canned fruits. Cassava-based sweeteners are preferred in beverage formulations.
Pharmacy	Native and modified cassava starches used as binders, fillers and disintegrating agents for tablet production.
Glue	Cassava starch used for making glue which has a wide range of usage such as in plywood manufacturing.
Biodegradable products	Cassava starch used as a biodegradable polymer to replace plastics in packaging materials.
Paper	Modified or native cassava starch used in paper making.
Textiles	Cassava starch used in textile processing.

Source: Compiled from information on IITA website on the Integrated Cassava Project.

had neither the capacity nor the incentives required for improving their technology to make a higher quality product. Therefore the improvement in cassava processing is crucially connected to the expansion of cassava for the food supply and for the use of cassava for industrial purposes. Our analysis in this chapter therefore distinguishes between cassava cropping and the cassava processing system.

6.2.3   Transformation and Driving Forces of the Sector

The evolution of the cassava sector, since it was initially introduced in the early twentieth century through population flow, such as immigration of emancipated slaves from Sierra Leone, has gone through several stages. Following the overview of the evolutionary paths of cassava in Africa presented by Nweke et al. (2001), cassava in Nigeria has experienced several phases as a rural food staple (roughly before the 1980s), a cash crop for urban consumption and limited industrial use (mainly since the second half of the 1980s to around 2000), and a livestock feed and industrial raw material promoted for export (from 2000 to the officially launched strategy, representatively the 2004 presidential initiative – see below).[3]

The driving forces include rapid population growth from the demand side, the availability of high yielding varieties of cassava and the improvement in processing technology from the supply side, and policy thrusts. At each stage there are relatively minor upward and downward trends, which we are not able to discuss in detail in this chapter.

Table 6.8 demonstrates in more detail the evolutionary stages of the sector. We focus on the population and policy factors responsible for the evolution of the sector, leaving the supply factors for the next section.

Population pressure
Population pressure has been one of the most important drivers for the increasingly widespread adoption of cassava in Nigeria since its initial introduction. Nigeria is the most populous country in Africa. Its population in 2004 was 127 million, which is the tenth highest population among the 193 nations of the world. The high annual growth rate is responsible for the dense Nigerian population, for example, it was 2.53 per cent for 2000–2005, implying that a projected 162 million will live in Nigeria by the year 2015. This population has increased from the 1950s level, which was at 31.6 million, according to the first nationwide census during 1952–53.[4]

Now the high-yielding and suitable cassava is becoming one of the most important staple crops, substituting for the traditional cocoyam in Nigeria. The vast majority of farmers in the main cassava belts grow cassava as a main or minor crop. The traditional rotation and fallow systems have been reduced to a large extent, and continuous cropping is becoming popular. However, inorganic fertilizers that should assist continuous cropping are in short supply and soil fertility is deteriorating (Fresco, 1986).

International organizations' imposed policy reform
Policy reform imposed by international organizations was responsible for the surge of cassava production and consumption in the second phase (since the second half of the 1980s to around 2000) as outlined above. As part of the World Bank/IMF economic Structural Adjustment Programme (SAP), the Federal Government of Nigeria banned importation of grains (1987–90) to conserve scarce foreign exchange. Policies related to the banning included the devaluation of the national currency

Table 6.8 Dynamics and drivers of cassava transformation in Nigeria

	Phase 1 Cassava becomes a staple food, 1910–60	*Phase 2* Laying the foundation, 1960–77	*Phase 3* Mealy bug invasion, 1978–83	*Phase 4* The surge, 1984–92	*Phase 5* Waning surge, 1993–99	*Phase 6* Renewed surge & new challenges, 2000–present day
Timing						
Key actors	Immigrants Farmers	Rural artisans IITA Shell Oil	IITA	IITA, Government, NRCRI, Private oil companies	Government, IITA, NRCRI, Farmers, Processors	Government, IITA, NRCRI, Farmers, Processors
Drivers of change	Severe rural labour shortages (the result of wars and influenza epidemic of 1918) induce a move out of labour-demanding cocoyam into cassava. Emancipated slaves from Sierra Leone introduce *gari* processing technology. Immigrants bring in new bitter varieties.	Mechanical graters imported from Benin Republic and refined by local artisans. Graters spread, releasing processing bottlenecks. TMS varieties developed (1971–77) but fail to spread rapidly.	Mealybug invasion attacks cassava crop.	Biological control of mealybug (1981 on) takes effect. Policy changes (SAP) stifle food imports: • Drop food import subsidies. • Ban on cereal imports. • Devaluation of the naira raises food import prices. Government included cassava in extension programmes. Oil companies help finance cassava production.	Rising wage rates led to labour constraints in harvesting and processing. Imported corn starch becomes cheaper than cassava starch. IFAD loan for root and tuber expansion.	Economic policy reform (NEEDS): • PICPE • 10% cassava flour in wheat flour • Agro-processing • SMI promotion • Economic diversification • Export of cassava chips. IFAD loan for root and tuber expansion.

210

Beneficiaries	Small farmers Urban *gari* consumers	Small farmers. Urban *gari* consumers.	None	Cassava farmers. Urban *gari* consumers.	Importers of corn starch	Cassava farmers. Cassava processors. Urban consumers.
Production gains	Production doubles from 1948 to 1958.	Grater induces 50% increase in production. Annual growth 2.5% per year.	Production fell by 20%. Declined 3.7% per year.	Production increased by 150%. Annual growth rate is 12% per year.	Production up 15%. Annual growth rate slowed 1.5% per year.	National output grew to 42 million tons per year. Trial export of 1000 tons of chip to China.
Impact	Cassava established as a rural food staple.	Growing urban consumers. Cassava becomes an urban staple	Massive mobiliza-tion for biological control of mealybug across Africa.	Real *gari* prices fall. *Gari*/yam price ratio falls by 50%. *Gari*/rice price ratio falls by 25%.	Consumer *gari* prices trend upward. Industrial demand for cassava starch stalls.	Cyclic glut. Cost of production and processing high. Export not yet significant

Source: Adapted from Nweke (2004) and data from author's field work.

and dropping of food subsidies. The radical change in economic policies provided incentives for the growth of cassava production as a local staple to fill the food gap that the policy created. This created a new environment for food manufacturers as well. They were forced to look at alternatives to wheat in order to remain in business. The market opportunity was given to cassava flour even though there were problems in quality and other technical difficulties (Ogun, 1995; Moser et al., 1997).

This period is characterized by the beginning of the deliberate input of scientific and technological elements into the sector. The innovative variety of TMS cassava was adopted widely from the late 1980s due to the development of effective biological control of the mealy-bug disease.[5] The spread of the TMS variety, even though it had been available earlier in the 1970s as a major output of the research work at the International Institute of Tropical Agriculture (IITA), had stagnated. Efforts to extend both cropping and processing technologies were enhanced in order to support the diffusion of the TMS variety; this initiative was promoted collectively by the Nigerian government, international R&D institutes, national R&D and extension agencies, and private oil companies.

For the 1984 and 1992 period, production of cassava increased by 150 per cent with an annual growth rate of 12 per cent, a very high rate of increase. The experience gained from the 1987–90 grain import ban period has enabled food manufacturers to keep producing cassava flour even after 1990 when the grain import ban ended. In the years after the ban, economic factors such as currency devaluation and falling per capita incomes made some experienced food manufacturers continue to produce competitive products using cassava flour, although the annual growth rate of cassava reduced to the lower level of 1.5 per cent for 1993–99, for reasons which are briefly sketched in Table 6.8.[6]

In short, the rapid increase in cassava production and consumption in the late 1980s and the whole decade of the 1990s was mainly influenced by changes in national policy and economic factors that facilitated learning by various actors. Learning took place in the adaptation of food processing industries to the changed policy and economic environment, the dissemination of new cassava varieties, the development of, and access to, suitable processing equipment, and the acceptance of cassava as a convenient food (such as *gari*) by urban and rural consumers (Berry, 1993; Nweke, 1994). These factors led to the start of the cassava cropping processing system, and laid the foundation for cassava's importance in the Nigerian economy.

New development strategy and related policy reforms

Officially announced in 2004, a new development strategy and related policy reforms boosted and renewed interest in the sector. In contrast to the policy reforms of the earlier period that were induced by the external pressure from the World Bank/IMF (SAP), the present policy thrusts were initiated proactively by the democratic government of Nigeria itself.[7]

The Presidential Initiative on Cassava Production and Export (PICPE) is ambitiously intended to raise the production level of cassava to 150 million tons by the end of year 2010 from around 40 million tons in 2004, as a result of increased awareness and experience in cassava utilization. Bread baking and beverage industries, including soft and alcoholic drinks, and animal feed are among the targeted industries, which are expected to adopt cassava-based raw material inputs. It is also expected that the country will realize an income of US$5 billion per annum from the export of some 40 million tons of dry cassava products such as starch, chips, adhesives and other derivatives (CBN, 2007).

To fulfil these goals, regulatory efforts include the setting of a mandatory minimum of 10 per cent high-quality cassava flour in bakery products and confectionaries. Other public initiated and coordinated activities range from investment in technological capabilities to the enhancement of supportive functions for dissemination of cassava production, and to the promotion of SMEs and training workshops, as illustrated below:

- organization of training workshop at the National Centre for Agricultural Mechanization (NCAM), Ilorin, for identified fabricators from various states on existing machines and equipment for peeling, chipping, flour and starch-making;
- development of equipment for the processing of various cassava products targeted for export market in collaboration with IITA;
- production and distribution of 576 000 bundles of improved cassava cuttings by the state Agricultural Development Projects (ADPs) to farmers;
- production/procurement of planting materials such as breeder, foundation and certified stocks by the Root and Tuber Expansion Programme Management Unit (RTEP-MU), National Root Crops Research Institute (NRCRI), Umudike and IITA;
- collaboration with local communities to establish pilot cassava processing centres in each local government area of the cassava-producing states for subsequent replication and adoption.

It is apparent that the Presidential Initiative has strategic importance in that it tends to deepen the cassava cropping and processing system, assigns the sector the role of a springboard for the structural and capability upgrading of the Nigerian economy and for diversification of the export structure. The full-blown result of the initiative is yet to be seen, but some positive progress has already been seen: output of cassava has increased from 35 million metric tons in 2001 to about 42 million metric tons in 2004. And this has made it possible for Nigeria to export *gari* to Sierra Leone and other West African countries without affecting domestic consumption. In addition, the Federal Ministry of Commerce and Industry has facilitated a trial export of 1000 tons of cassava chips to China.

6.2.4   Sources of Knowledge: Role of International R&D Institutions and Local Efforts

Traditional knowledge has been important for the sector. Although a few institutions for knowledge creation had been set up in colonial times, up to 1960 no scientifically developed knowledge had been put into the cropping and processing of cassava. All the activities were done with experience-based knowledge and skills. Transfer of traditional knowledge was through farmer-to-farmer or farmer-to-artisan interaction.

National R&D centres and extension services
The later decades of the twentieth century saw the facilitated institutional creation of R&D centres for cassava technologies. At present the national R&D family of cropping technologies embraces 17 research institutes; each has a major or minor mandate in genetic/variety breeding and agronomic improvement of cassava. They are establishments either under the Federal Ministry of Agriculture or in the Federal and State Universities. Of these, the National Root Crops Research Institute (NRCRI), Umudike, which was one of those established in colonial times, is now the leading institute.

In addition to the R&D centres, the National Agricultural Extension Research Liaison Service is responsible for the coordination of research and extension. The Agricultural Development Programmes (ADPs) have been assigned the roles of rural roads construction in order to facilitate market access, and of financing extension, or so-called 'On-farm Adaptive Research' (OFAR), of new product technologies developed by research institute and university scientists.

In relation to cassava processing technologies, the leading national research centre is the Federal Institute of Industrial Research, Oshodi (FIIRO). FIIRO was established in colonial times too and has been mandated to develop mechanized processors. It had developed a peeler, washer, grater, sieve and toaster all in one integrated machine, which was then manufactured in Britain. However, the development did not prove useful because it lacked the flexibility to adjust to the quantity of cassava processing and could not be adjusted in working hours; these features are needed by the majority of small-scale processors (Asher, 1980). In addition, another public institution, the Products Development Agency (PRODA), has been assigned to focus on the development of local manufacturing equipment; and the Rural Agro Industrial Development Scheme (RAIDS), established by the Federal Government, is required to test the PRODA-designed machines and to identify farmers' food crop processing problems.

By and large, the processing technologies developed by the government agencies have only been adopted to a limited extent. However, the grating machines that are actually effective were often made by semi-educated, determined young men and women who needed to make a living from this work. The processes they created were easy, convenient, cost effective and sustainable (Adegboye and Akinwumi, 1990; Adjebeng-Asem, 1990). Meanwhile, international R&D institutes have also made a useful contribution to cassava processing.

International R&D institutes and the relationship with the national system

Of the international institutions for cassava cropping technologies, the International Institute of Tropical Agriculture (IITA), located in Ibadan, Nigeria, is the most important, and it belongs to the Consultative Group on International Agricultural Research (CGIAR) family. IITA contributed to a number of new cassava varieties including the earlier mentioned TMS varieties, which have the advantages of a higher root yield (up to 30–35 tons/ha) and a tolerance of major pests (such as mealy-bug, green spider mite).

The international Root and Tuber Expansion Programme promoted the extension of new varieties of crops in African countries. Nigeria is one of the beneficiaries, where a loan came from the International Fund for Agricultural Development (IFAD) to support cassava extension. The domestic R&D institute NRCRI of Nigeria collaborated with IITA in the implementation of these extension programmes. It was reported that, as a result of the collaboration, 15 elite varieties were released all around Nigeria between 1987 and 1996 (APMEU, 1997).[8]

The division of labour between international and domestic R&D has thus far been that international R&D developed innovative cropping technologies mainly in the form of new varieties and effective control of diseases or pests, and domestic R&D provided the necessary capability for spreading improved cassava varieties. Under the thrusts of presently ongoing presidential initiatives, collaboration towards the strategic goals between the two lines of knowledge centres might be enhanced and elaborated. This enhancement is manifested in the fact that the national NRCRI pursues comprehensive objectives that embrace the whole range: plant breeding for new varieties development, the production of breeder

stock that is a part of the National Seed Service's (NSS) cassava multiplication programme, bio-control of cassava pests, and agronomic research
to evolve optimum management of new and existing cassava varieties
(NRCRI, 1992; APMEU, 1997).

The IITA has also contributed to cassava processing. It has developed
grating techniques that enable small-scale primary processors to produce
unfermented cassava flour under certain conditions (dry, sunny weather
for sun drying) with the quality that meets industrial users' specifications.
The IITA has conducted training for dissemination of the techniques
since 1994. By 1997 more than 900 primary processors had received the
training, and this made a significant contribution to the preparation of
cassava bakery products such as in Oyo town. Interestingly, an interaction
between the processors and biscuit manufacturers helped make use of the
techniques successful: the biscuit manufacturer established at their request
a quality standard indicated by pH value, and thereafter a pH value-based
system of pricing cassava flour developed. The pH value-based system has
become an accepted instrument in regulating the supply–demand relations
of cassava flour (Phillips et al., 2004).

6.2.5   Crucial Importance of Cassava Processing and Bottlenecks

For the realization of the 2004 Presidential Initiative on Cassava
Production and Export, improvement in cassava processing is of crucial
importance, because the perishable cassava roots must be processed soon
after harvesting and the toxic ingredients be reduced to an acceptable level,
as has been mentioned earlier. Cassava processing is essential for either
foodstuff or industrial materials if the consumption is to take place away
from the cropping field. Processing of cassava, which involves washing,
peeling, grinding, screening, separating, sedimentation, bolting, storing
and packaging, is water and energy intensive. Traditionally housewives
do the job of processing for domestic consumption. Machines and equipment are used intensively when such processing is conducted in factories
running on a large scale and with a high and stable quality.

The cassava processing industry

The cassava processing industry in Nigeria has a dual structure: a few
modern multinational companies and a large number of small, local
companies that process with primitive equipment. The structure might
be thought of as a triple one as well, if account is also taken of household
processing, which exists on a large scale for domestic consumption. A case
study presented below illustrates the status of the second group, the small
local processing companies.

The case company, in Ondo state, employs 40–60 monthly wage-earners and 50–60 casual workers; the casual workers are mainly women working on peeling raw cassava. Seven of the employees have a Higher National Diploma, and the technical director of the company has a Master's degree. The company was established in 1982, but closed down in 1991 because of lack of both raw cassava supply and demand for cassava flour after the grain import banning ended in 1990. It was refurbished in 2005 subsequent to the Presidential Initiative.

Bottlenecks In physical infrastructure serious inadequacies impede the development of the cassava processing industry. A 2006 survey of Nigerian firms showed that by and large electric power from the national grid is available for only about half of the production time. Specifically the case company had to run on a heavy duty generator during power outages. The water supply causes further problems. The company in investigation relies on its own borehole for water. Road construction is restricted too. For normal operation of this company, the local authority worked specifically to ensure that the road that accesses the company was graded.

Mechanical engineering causes another bottleneck, although local capabilities are improving. The company's capability is limited to maintenance of existing machines and in making minor modifications. It runs a combination of imported and domestic made machines; utilization of production capacity is not satisfactory, at 20 per cent, and is hindered by the incompatibility between the many differently sourced machines. Other bottlenecks come from the yet-to-be-established stable supply of raw cassava input.

Actions by local government In response to the bottlenecks, the local authority (the Ondo state in this case) has taken a number of steps, under the auspicious drive of the Presidential Initiative. The Ondo state government has become involved in the revival of the company by taking a joint ownership with a private limited liability company at a 49 to 51 equity share. The state invested in the company in February 2005 with N40 million (US$315000 equivalent), which enabled the company to renew its equipment including the purchase of an electric transformer. Moreover, the state government has allocated 500 hectares of land for cassava plantation, out of which the company has cultivated 60 hectares by itself. As a result, the firm seems to have moved to vertical integration in handling the problem of the unstable supply of raw cassava input.

6.3   THE VEGETABLE SECTOR IN CHINA: EMERGENCE OF A HIGHER CONSUMPTION-ELASTICITY AGRO-SEGMENT IN RAPID ECONOMIC GROWTH

6.3.1   Introduction

Located in the east of the Asia–Europe continent, China has a land area of 9.6 million km² and a population of 1.3 billion, based on 2004 statistical data. Even though the territory is the third largest in the world, the per capita arable land of China is much less than the world average as a result of its geographic and climatic complexity, with a large proportion of the area being either mountainous or affected by drought, which accounts for more than two-thirds of the land. Historically China developed a high-level civilization based on agriculture and handicraft. In modern times the People's Republic of China (PRC) adopted a centrally planned regime from 1949. Market reforms began at the end of the 1970s; from that time the Commune System for agriculture production was dismantled and small farmer families became production units based on contracted use of the land.

The emergence of a large and nationwide system for vegetable production, distribution, and technological change is a phenomenon that has been appearing alongside rapid economic growth in the past twenty years or so. Previously the sector was much smaller, weak in R&D and extension services, and poor in variety provision. Farming in this sector was primarily subsistence and, to a less extent, on a commercial basis through adjacent industrial centres. This sector had at that time run a poor second to staple cereals; the latter took priority in agriculture policy and investment before the 1980s.

Demand factors have served as the major driving force for the growth of the sector; meanwhile technological progress led to increased productivity in staple cereals, which in turn led to some of the cultivated land being used for other produce. Section 6.3.2 explains the driving forces from the demand side.

Section 6.3.3 deals with the development of market institutions, which has been central to the emergence, expansion and deepening of the sector. Market development contributed to the opening of ever-expanding participation of actors in the sector. The development of market institutions was a policy steered process, which was vital during economic transition.

Section 6.3.4 discusses technology acquisitions and the transformation of the knowledge base for the sector. A case shows that a modern S&T knowledge base is indispensable in order to withstand the pressure from

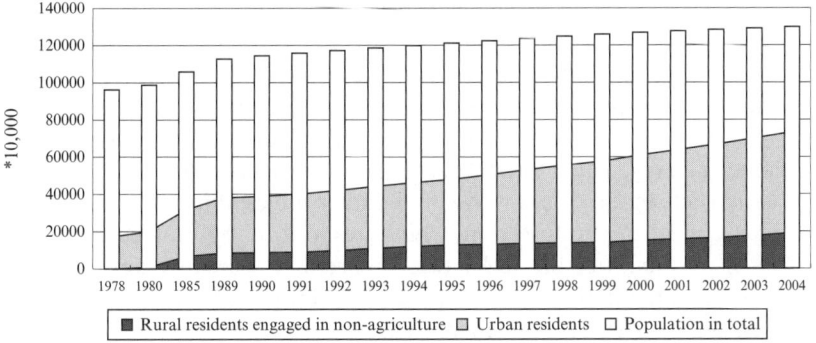

Source: Reproduced based on Tables 4.1 and 13.4, China Statistical Year Book 2005. Available at http://www.stats.gov.cn/tjsj/ndsj/2005/indexch.htm.

Figure 6.1 Urban and rural population engaged in non-agriculture

international competition and from the knowledgeable and demanding consumers as well. The agro-food industry is no longer 'traditional'. For the transformation of the knowledge base, tacit knowledge and farmers' innovation are also as important as modern technologies.

6.3.2 Driving Forces: Changed Demand in Rapid Economic Growth

One of the major drivers of the development of the vegetable sector came from the demand side. First of all, population growth contributed to the increase in demand for foodstuffs. During the last thirty years, the total population of China has grown from 900 million at the end of the 1970s to 1.3 billion in 2004, an increase of 40 per cent. In addition, the proportion of the population relying on the commercial provision of foodstuffs increased at an even higher rate; this came from two developments. The first is rapid urbanization, and the second is the massive 'temporary' migration of rural labour, which works in non-agricultural jobs in both urban and rural areas, meanwhile keeping their village homes and remaining on a permanent residential basis.[9] Altogether in a rough and conservative calculation, the proportion of the population that has left the land to live needing the commercial provision of food has increased from 20 per cent in 1978 to be more than half in 2004 (Figure 6.1).

Beyond these, there were also changes in the qualitative terms of demand. Having incomes that were continually increasing, people could afford more, and demanded fresh, tasty and healthy vegetables. In winter time, for example, consumers in North China are no longer satisfied with the few traditional vegetable commodities – Chinese cabbage, potato and turnips – which were conventionally stored after the warm season's harvests. They now desire as rich a choice as in summer time. Recently, in addition to demanding tasty and fresh vegetables, consumers are paying more attention to whether the vegetables are produced from green or organic farming. All these developments are obvious if one has visited supermarkets in the cities or observed dinner tables of households.

The agriculture industry in China responded by restructuring the production mix after the 1990s (see Figure 6.2). Cereals plantation was reduced and the plantation of 'commercial crops', as termed in China's agricultural statistics, was increased. Among the 'commercial crops' – oil and sugar crops, vegetables and fruit, and cotton – the category 'vegetables and fruit' enjoyed the most dramatic increase. The planting areas for vegetables and fruits were expanded to 17.6 and 9.8 MH (million hectares) in 2004, from 4.1 and 2.0 MH in 1983, respectively. Both expanded more than threefold, and as a result, one third (34 per cent) of the cultivated land is now used for the production of crops other than cereals; in comparison, this figure was one fifth (21 per cent) in 1983 – a historical change in China's standard. In 2004 China produced 506 million tons of vegetables and fruit, nearly eight times production in 1979–81. Nowadays, the Chinese consume twice the world average of vegetables and fruit.[10]

The rise of land output of cereals made it possible to transfer part of the land for vegetables and fruit. The average land output of cereals increased from the level of 1000 kg per hectare in 1949, to 2000 kg in 1970, 3000 kg in 1982 and 4000 kg in 1992. The figure for 2004 was 4620 kg. Seed development, together with the improvement in plantation, use of fertilizer, and infrastructure development, attributed to the growth of land output of cereals.

A final message on the overall picture, in which the vegetable sector emerges, looks at the provincial distribution of vegetable production. Production–distribution–wholesale networks of fresh vegetables are deemed to be mainly local, concentrated in areas surrounding large cities within provincial territories. However, two provinces stand out as specialized vegetable producers; they are HeBei and ShanDong provinces. Of the two, ShanDong is particularly worth noting. It is halfway down the east coast, several hundred kilometres from each of the largest cities, Beijing, Tianjing and Shanghai. In contrast, HeBei, a province that encircles Beijing and Tianjing, has geographical advantages that are deemed to be outstanding for vegetable production, but this is less interesting for our study. ShanDong has some unique strengths: including the fact that ShanDong has been ahead in the development of market institutions, it is

Land for Agricultural Plantation 1983–2004
Note: commercial crops include oil crops, cotton, sugar stuff, vegetables
and fruits

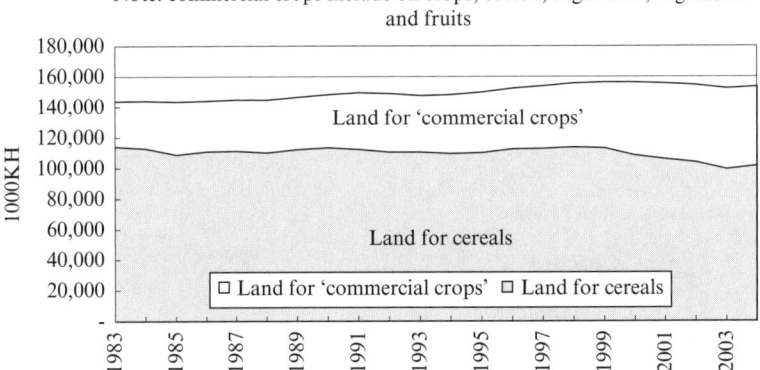

Composition of 'commercial crops' 1983–2004

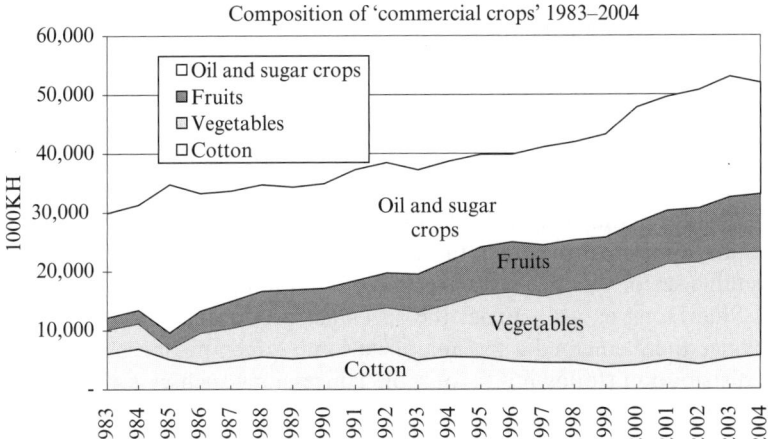

Source: Author produced based on Table 7, China Agricultural Development Report 2005, Ministry of Agriculture of China. Available at http://www.agri.gov.cn/sjzl/baipsh/2005.htm.

Figure 6.2 Change in land use and composition of 'commercial crops' (1983–2004)

the homeland of farmers' innovation in vegetable plantation technology, a kind of cheap and simple greenhouse that made effective production in winter time affordable for smallholder farmers; ShanDong is also one of the leading provinces in green and organic production of vegetables. ShanDong has therefore been an important contributor in the experimentation of technological and institutional change and has played a

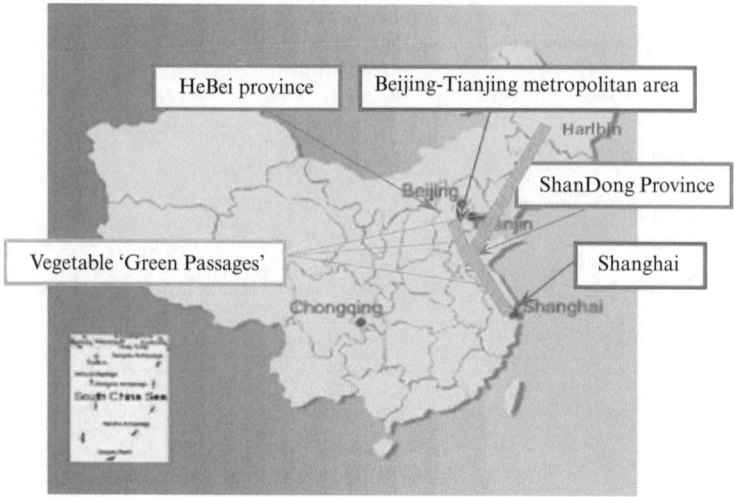

Source: Field visits to ShouGuang.

Figure 6.3   ShanDong province and its 'green passages'

role similar to that played by leading firms in industrial sectors. We will mention some of these contributions below. The formation of a nationwide vegetable sector was in a sense a result of the presence of specialist regions like ShanDong as well. From the specialist producers of the ShanDong province there emerged a few major national 'green passages' for vegetable distribution (following favourable concessions such as a reduction in highway fees in order to accelerate low-cost transport): see Figure 6.3.

6.3.3   Policy-steered Development of Market Institutions and the Evolution of the Sector

Institutional development brings about a new social construction that enables a broader participation of people, better use of existing factors, or the creation of new factors (Metcalfe et al., 2003; Nelson, 2006). In the case of the vegetable sector in China, institutional development has been focusing on the creation and deepening of market institutions. Market institutions provided new ways, other than the central planning approach, to support transactions and interactions between producers and consumers. Great strides were made in the development of market institutions, begun from very rudimental basis. Policy thrusts often prepared the way for the movement in market development.

Wholesale markets and their networks

Wholesale markets have been central in the development of market institutions. Wholesale markets sit in various nodes in the production–distribution network. Wholesale centres maintain the rules for free and fair transactions; wholesales also provide physical conditions for the conduct of transactions such as a sheltered space, transaction and storage facilities. Earlier on, following the abandonment of strict control of purchasing and marketing of agricultural products, local authorities, especially those in charge of agricultural or commercial affairs, contributed to the transformation of a small number of distribution centres that had already existed in the planned economy. Local authorities also contributed to the creation of new wholesale markets, by providing the necessary physical investment and managerial capacities. These were promoted by the government 'Vegetable Basket Programme' initiated at the end of the 1980s, which in its early stage aimed to form vegetable production and distribution networks surrounding large cities; and naturally local governments were assigned the responsibility of implementing them.[11] In some cases, villagers, in addition to vegetable producers, were collectively involved in the creation of relatively small and nearby wholesale spots too, as I learned in field visits. By the mid-1990s, wholesale markets had grown rapidly; however, they operated in segments, with little connection to each other.

A second stage emerged in the mid-1990s and aimed to integrate the segmented local markets into a nationwide system. In 1995 the Ministry of Agriculture started to grant certification to the first group of 23 markets and assigned them as 'central' or 'regular' wholesale markets. The ministry provides them with management guidance and some subsidies; these markets are required to report on market information on prices and sales' volumes, and on progress or problems they make or recognize. With this information, the Ministry Information Centre started to electronically circulate vegetable prices and supply–demand status on a daily basis, making a step towards nationwide integration of the sector. The coverage of price information soon expanded to 33 such markets located in 28 large and medium cities at the end of that year, and now the network includes more than 150 wholesales around the country.[12]

The current policy thrust (from 2002), which focuses on quality and safety provision of foodstuffs, adds more strategic roles to wholesale markets.[13] Wholesales are now assumed to play the role of monitoring the quality of vegetables against standards. The Agricultural Ministry plans that in the coming five years 500 wholesale markets, out of the several thousands in total around the country, are to be upgraded to become proficient in quality management, to be strengthened in testing and in electronic information gathering, and in encoding and delivering information.[14] The central government is playing a leading role in making the necessary investment. Starting in 2003 the government issued treasury bonds of 300–400 million yuan per annum (exchange rate between the Chinese yuan and the US dollar: about 8:1 in 2003 and 6.8:1 in 2008) for the renewal of information and test systems for key wholesales. Complementary resources are coming from local governments, private companies and wholesale markets' own funds.[15]

Specialized vendors and blockers

Specialized vendors and blockers entered the distributional network, which now accounts for dozens of millions. They are important actors in the vegetable sector.

Vegetable blockers, or middlemen, who deal with the transactions in large lots for longer distances, often came from rural areas or small towns. They are among the most active and better educated of the previously rural residents. Over time the blockers accumulated a degree of wealth, and owned physical facilities such as trucks for transportation services; some began to invest in storage facilities. The population of this group is at the level of 100 000.[16] Small vegetable vendors or peddlers, with a much larger population, came mainly from the rural area too. They run small-scale businesses and engage in urban fair trade and in rural vegetable fairs; the urban peddlers have constituted part of the above-mentioned seasonal immigrants of the rural area. Vegetable venders, both smaller and larger, are the link between the production locus, the rural fairs, the urban fairs, the wholesale centres, the supermarkets, and, in some cases, help to stretch the distributional channels directly up to organizational consumers such as university cafeterias.

Policy steering

This is a policy-steered process. Individual agents could hardly play such a role in the context of double transition – the transition of the economic regime and the transition of agricultural activities. Interestingly, the government has steered a change in which some mechanisms from the market forces are aimed to be introduced in order to replace the direct power of the government itself. Policies have been focusing on the development of mediation channels, which resulted in a wholesale harboured nationwide transaction network.

In recent years, which we would identify as the third stage, policies are giving more weight to supply and complementary parameters including R&D and testing infrastructure for quality supply, in response to the demanding domestic and international consumers.[17] Policies have also increased support for the development of seed breeding capabilities. For these purposes, a new set of legal, regulatory and institutional initiatives is taking place. Following on from the earlier developments, the ongoing S&T and safety functions could possibly be better incorporated into the production and distribution processes. This would result in a deepening of the sectoral system.

Wave-like evolutionary trajectory
By looking at the development, there appears a wave-like evolutionary trajectory. Three stages or waves that the sector has experienced thus far have had rather different momentums towards solving the earlier restriction or bottlenecks. As sketched above, the first, second and third stages, corresponding to the periods from the late 1980s to mid-1990s, the late 1990s, and the present day, concentrated on different priorities. They were, first, to solve the supply shortage problem in large cities; next, to expand the commercial supply of vegetables all over the country and build up information foundations for national integration; and thirdly was the target for quality and safe supply of vegetables. All the stages were led by government policies, called the 'Vegetable Basket Programme', and in this case it can be said that the policies were made rather instantly in response to the changing demand–supply imbalances or impediments.

The wave-like process is characterized by a non-linear, two-way relationship between policy initiative and growth outcome. A relevant policy initiative opens an opportunity for systems development and growth, but sooner or later new problems occur to which policies have to respond by constantly adjusting objectives and means. This is in essence what an evolutionary perspective presumes: growth and structural change involve complexity and uncertainty, and policy can by no means be managed as a fixed-end process (Nelson and Winter, 1982; Metcalfe, 1997).

Limits of the markets
Many limits remain regarding market institutions' development, including the following (e.g. Cheng, 2007):

- The distributional efficiency of the system is still low. It is reported that losses of vegetables during distribution could be as high as one fifth to a quarter.
- The information function of the market system, though improved after enormous efforts, is still far from satisfactory. The collection and circulation of demand and supply information is not sufficiently effective. No qualified information truly goes to small croppers to enable decision-making; they actually have to follow the suggestions by local administrations or imitate their neighbours. So sweeping

surpluses or shortages of certain vegetables happen repeatedly. Consumers also find it difficult to trace the location and process of certain supplies.

● Vegetable pricing is to an extent formed arbitrarily, in such a way that small producers are often squeezed to the lowest margins of profit.

Inadequate physical facilities, such as those for storage, transaction, transportation and communications, which are important for the distribution of perishable vegetables, cause problems. Insufficient managerial capacity is attributed to inadequacy too. Both the vendors, who came from rural areas or small towns, and the wholesale managers, many of whom were originally local officials, lack the necessary education and training. Not surprisingly therefore, traditional ways in dealing with transactions through face-to-face negotiation and cash sales are normal in most of cases, except for the most advanced such as ShouGuang (see Box 6.1). Information about the market is partial and approximate, and flows only in restricted circles.

The weak position of smallholders makes up another serious obstacle in a productive system's governance. Effective mechanisms to balance the benefits between small producers/vendors and powerful wholesale/ processing companies as addressed in Costa Rica (Orozco and Díaz, 2007) are still lacking (Gu, 2004). Farmers' cooperatives have not existed for about thirty years and regulatory efforts on fair pricing to protect the weak participants of the system are yet to be developed.

6.3.4 Acquisition of Technology and the Transformation of the Knowledge Regime

With their rapid development, the vegetable sector in particular and the agro-food in general are experiencing a transformation of their underlying knowledge base. The knowledge base that is undergoing rapid change ranges from biotechnology, which relates to seed breeding for high-yield or fine-tasting varieties; to technologies used for testing and quality monitoring which are electronic, optical and mechanical; to the knowledge and technologies that are employed for strategic management of land use and environmental protection; and the knowledge and competence for the management of a modern commercial agro-food sector.

To illustrate the necessary renewal of the knowledge base, we focus on the first two elements, that is biotechnology for the development of new varieties, and testing and quality monitoring technologies.

BOX 6.1   THE DEVELOPMENT OF MARKET
            INSTITUTIONS IN SHOUGUANG,
            SHANDONG PROVINCE

ShouGuang is a county in the middle of ShanDong province, with a population of 1 million. Traditionally ShouGuang people were adept at vegetable production; they developed some special varieties of leek, for example, which had historically served as a tribute to the Qing Emperor at Forbidden City. Now ShouGuang is becoming 'the first vegetable garden' of China, and the brand of ShouGuang Vegetable is known in China as the most prestigious.

The development of ShouGuang vegetables owes a great deal to the efforts of circulation (distribution) channels, or the creation of market institutions. Local government summarizes their experience as 'promote distribution for bolstering production'.

The central location for transactions in ShouGuang is the ShouGuang vegetable wholesale market. The city government decided to open it in 1984 in response to the difficulties that vegetable croppers were facing in selling their products. The Industrial and Commercial Bureau of ShouGuang implemented the decision with a bank loan and a small amount of personal money. Since then the market has experienced many rounds of expansion, with the investment mainly coming from the local government. In parallel, 20 or so smaller vegetable markets, some of which are more specialized in certain categories of vegetables, were created around the central vegetable wholesale market. The ShouGuang wholesale market and the smaller ones together composed a network reaching to every village. In 2003 the central market was reorganized to become the ShouGuang Vegetable Wholesale Market Co. Ltd. This reorganization introduced advanced management skills and additional capital from the Shenzhen Agricultural Products Co. Ltd. The latter is a listed company and has been one of the leading investment companies in agricultural distribution in China.

From a simple and crude transaction location, the ShouGuang Vegetable Wholesale Market Co. Ltd now possesses trading buildings of 100,000 m2, deals with not only vegetables and fruit, but also capital goods for vegetable production such as seeds, fertilizers, agricultural pharmaceuticals, and greenhouse construction materials. It provides a wide range of business services supportive to the transactions, from electronic action, storage, to exhibition and consultancy services. The first electronic vegetable auction in China was opened there in 2003. ShouGuang was probably the first region in China focusing on green production, which started as a response to problems with exporting vegetables to Japan. Up to 2006, a branch station of the National Quality and Safety Testing Services was set up in ShouGuang. The opening of the branch station willcertainly bring in technical and managerial support from the national initiative. Quality monitoring will be incorporated into the operation of the central wholesale and 16 other vegetable markets in the county.

In addition, ShouGuang established demonstration bases to secure quality vegetable production. The demonstration bases develop standard production procedures and disseminate them through training and testing services. In order to make appropriate use of land which is part of quality control, the bases are committed to take the responsibility of monitoring land environment. All these measures have begun to act just recently.

The creative management of ShouGuang in the development of market institutions has been important not only for ShouGuang itself, but also for the Province of ShanDong of which ShouGuang is part. ShouGuang is now serving as one of the nationwide distribution centres through the creation of cross-provincial-border 'green passages', including ShouGuang-Beijing Green Passage and ShouGuang-Ha'erbin Green Passage (see Figure 6.3).

Sources:
1   Author's field survey notes.
2   On the opening of Quality and Safety Testing Station of vegetables at the ShouGuang Wholesale Market, see http://www.sda.gov.cn/cmsweb/webportal/W354/A64015531.html;
3   On the Shenzhen Agricultural Products Co. Ltd, see http://www.szap.com/english/web/gsgk.asp.

Externally introduced seeds and local adaptation
The development of the sector relied heavily on externally introduced seeds, a kind of embodied product technology. Up to the present time multinational companies have supplied the lion's share, between 50–80 per cent, of new varieties of vegetables,[18] either directly through sales of their subsidiaries opened in China, or through local seed agencies' importation

and distribution. Regional agricultural R&D centres carried out the role of selection of imported varieties regarding their suitability for local soil and weather conditions. Meanwhile, the plantation skills that farmers had built up over generations paved the way for the successes in employing imported seeds in production. We have learned plentiful evidence from field visits that skilful vegetable croppers enjoyed plenty of success in accommodating new varieties into their farming and often developed small tricks to solve production problems. This explains why vegetable production is more successful in those counties or villages such as ShouGuang, where traditionally farmers were skilled in vegetable cropping.

Farmers' innovation

Compared with cereal production, vegetables are more labour-intensive and require more physical inputs. Vegetables require regular watering and shields to avoid too low temperatures or too strong sunlight. The agricultural administration in China since the 1980s had been funded for the introduction of greenhouses from abroad as part of the Vegetable Basket Programme. However, imported greenhouses, which were developed under rather different conditions, were too large for the much smaller lots of land and too expensive for much poorer farmers in China. What essentially maintained the massive production were the facilities that farmers developed themselves. A cheap and simple greenhouse was developed in 1989 from ShaoGuang, ShanDong province, and was the creation of Mr Wang Leyi and his villagers (see Box 6.2). This invention turned out to be the one most popularly employed in the provinces where the latitude and weather conditions are similar to Mr Wang's, and which cover an area populated by several hundreds of millions.

Catch-up in seed breeding capability and the establishment of bio-agricultural R&D infrastructure

China's lagging behind international suppliers in seed breeding triggered the investment in the establishment and strengthening of a modern bio-scientific and technological base for the vegetable sector, which has been part of the government's 'Vegetable Basket Programme' and other national S&T programmes. Such a base is now complete after some 20 years of effort. A system of R&D institutions for vegetables and flowers S&T has been formed, the core body of which embraces 33 units at the central and provincial academies of agricultural science. To be added to these, are some further 20 centres or branches specialized in vegetables at the lower municipal/city levels. Furthermore, around 30 vegetable and gardening departments have been established or improved in agricultural universities around the country. An additional number of research centres

BOX 6.2   MR WANG LEYI AND HIS GREENHOUSE

 He is a farmer with only four years of primary education, but he contributed greatly to the so-called 'white revolution' – 'white' because his innovation resulted in a type of greenhouse for vegetable production, which has a white roof.

Mr Wang inside his greenhouse

Mr Wang's home village, SanYuanZhu in ShouGuang county, ShanDong province, is in north latitude of 37°, experiencing frozen winters for several months. People in ShouGuang did produce vegetables in winter time in traditional coal-heated greenhouses, which use 5–6 tons of coal per MU (equivalent to 1/15 hectare) over a winter season. Not only expensive, the traditional houses were also less effective, and could only produce leafy vegetables, not fruit vegetables like cucumber. Neither the traditional greenhouses, nor the imported ones made mostly in Israel and Holland, were widely used before Mr Wang's invention.

In 1988 Mr Wang learned that a successful farmer produced fresh cucumbers in a non-heated greenhouse even in northern Liaoling province. Wang and his villagers paid him seven visits to learn from him. Based on what he learned, Mr Wang systematically tested the frame, the wall, the roof and the southern frontage to make the houses more efficient. His tests resulted in a structure which has a thick soil wall on the north side, a board and transparent plastic roof that opens in daytime and is covered with straw shade at night. It fulfils the requirement for producing fresh vegetables without heating. In 1989 the first 17 families of the village established such houses and successfully produced cucumbers. Each of the 17 families earned more than 20000 yuan in sales during the Chinese Spring Festival season. Some 200 families in the village all followed them the next year.

In subsequent years Mr Wang was asked by the county administration to teach local farmers this technology; he did this enthusiastically and, as a result, his home county became the most famous in vegetable production. He also travelled around the

country as far as XinJiang province, some several thousand kilometres away to give help to farmers there. Meanwhile, his villagers have made continual improvements to the greenhouses; they
have now developed green products with their own brands, and
have expanded activities to vegetable processing. The average
income of the villagers has now increased by two to three times
more than the national average. Mr Wang has gained an enormous reputation and has been awarded the accolade of 'model
communist party member'.

Sources:
1   renmin ribao (People's Daily), 20 January 2006
2   nongmin ribao (Farmer's Daily), 5 December 2005
3   Author's field visit to ShouGuang, ShanDong Province 2003, 2004

that are more generally engaged in life sciences have been created or
improved in the prestigious Chinese Academy of Sciences and in a number
of top universities.[19]

Development of a quality monitoring system
This is a focus recently emphasized by policies. The law on agro-food quality
and safety was passed in April 2006 and implemented from November
2006.[20] An agency called 'Centre for Agro-food Quality and Safety' was
established in 2003 functioning under the jurisdiction of the Ministry of
Agriculture. The agency is responsible for standards development, assessment and certification of green products, and approval and evaluation of
the newly created 'Quality and Safety Testing Stations', with the aim of
effectively implementing laws and regulations on food safety and quality. A
nationwide network of Quality and Safety Testing Stations is being formed;
they are overseen by the national Agro-food Quality and Safety Centre of
the Agriculture Ministry. Far more than 100 units have been assigned as
branch stations, which have been reorganized or created within existing
central or local agents by assigning new objectives and functioning with
specifically established methods and procedures. A National Testing Centre
of Vegetable Quality and Safety has been created in the leading Institutes of
Vegetables and Flowers, Chinese Academy of Agriculture Sciences.

Difficulties and lessons
The experience, reported above illustrates that building a modern and
multidisciplinary knowledge base for the vegetable sector specifically, and
for the agro-food sector more generally, is indispensable and urgently

needed. One of the lessons is that this knowledge base building takes a long time: after two decades such a base is still not fully ready for service. In retrospect, the process might have proceeded faster if the decision had been made more quickly and with less delay in investment. As a matter of fact, investment in agricultural R&D had been declining since 1985, when the market-oriented reforms for S&T system started. The decline reached rock bottom in 1997 when it was 0.19 per cent, from a rather modest level of 0.31 per cent of agricultural GDP in 1985 (Xu, 2003; Zhang, 2004). A bias of S&T investment, which favoured high-tech too much, also contributed to the slow pace. An reversal of the trends was triggered by the long-term complete dominance of multinational companies in high value added seed provision (for a general introduction to the biotech development in China, see Yu, 2007). Similarly, investment in knowledge and capabilities for the safety and quality of agro-food had been delayed until the problems became a major obstacle. Even now, with a legal and institutional framework in place, effective provision of services is still having to wait for cumulative learning from practice, not to mention other missing elements such as the provision of testing instruments, which have to continuously rely on international suppliers, particularly Japan, to provide large quantities.

This reveals a general difficulty in the transformation of the knowledge base, which rests in weak complementary industries and capabilities, a characteristic shortcoming of less-developed systems. In order to be competitive in seed supply, a relatively good R&D and dissemination system is far from sufficient. Seed companies have to enter the arena. They work on seed propagation, breeding, production, processing, distribution and demonstration, interacting closely with the knowledge centres while being adept at commercialization. Domestic seed companies in China are mostly small, weak in management and technology, and suffer from institutional separation from R&D centres and from seed production as well.[21] They are inferior compared with multinational companies. The need for institutional and capability building for the seed industry has attracted policy-makers' attention, but how the industry will improve itself in the future remains to be seen.

6.4 THE COFFEE SECTOR IN COSTA RICA: MOVING TOWARDS INTERNATIONAL LEADERSHIP AND LESSONS

6.4.1 Introduction

Costa Rica is a small country in Central America, lying between Nicaragua to the north and Panama to the south. Costa Rica has a population of slightly over 4 million in a land area of 50 660 km^2, which slightly exceeds that of Vermont and New Hampshire combined.

Costa Rica became independent from the Spanish colony in 1821. During Spanish Colonial times, Costa Rica's distance from the then hub, Guatemala City, made it relatively isolated, more or less free from intervention by the crown. The whites have dominated the composition of the population as a result of the unfortunate fact that the indigenous Indians expired almost entirely as a result of diseases brought over by Europeans.[22] While many Spaniards in the other colonies had tribal members working on their land, most of the Costa Rican settlers had to work on their own land themselves. These circumstances have led to the many idiosyncrasies which Costa Rica has now. Costa Rica developed a more egalitarian society than the rest of its neighbours; it became a 'rural democracy' with no oppressed mestizo or indigenous class (see http://en.wikipedia.org/wiki/Costa_Rica#Demographics).[23]

Coffee production has played a key role in Costa Rica's history; it was the number one cash crop export for a long time until the end of the twentieth century. Coffee has ceded first place in recent decades, by 2006 becoming Costa Rica's number three export as a result of the efforts the Costa Rican government made to pursue the inclusion of industry and tourism in the economy. Now agriculture contributes to less than 10 per cent of GDP, while it employs a much higher percentage of labour, at around 20 per cent. Industry accounts for more that 30 per cent of GDP and commerce, tourism and services produce the lion's share of more than 60 per cent. However, coffee is still important, not only making up a major part of the agriculture, but also serving as an integrated factor contributing to the knowledge-based society and economy of Costa Rica as a whole.

More importantly, but rarely noted in the literature, the coffee sector in Costa Rica is moving towards the productivity and quality frontier; it is also engaging in high-value roasting, which the sector had never entered before. How did this happen? Is this an indication of some new trends opening up to developing countries regarding forging ahead in the agro-food sector in the context of globalization and rapid technological advances? The case study attempts to address the first question.

Section 6.4.2 of this chapter depicts the characteristics of and changes in the international coffee value chain. As one of the most traded commodities, the coffee sector has had its input–output and production–consumption relations internationally stretched from the very beginning. A depiction of the sequential value activities helps to locate the Costa Rican sector: Costa Rica has been operating in the 'upstream' cultivation and milling of coffee, but now it is faced with new opportunities. The supply–demand relations for coffee have been changing over the last two centuries since coffee started to be a cash crop; this indicates the circumstances in which the sector in Costa Rica evolved. In the nineteenth century a booming demand facilitated the growth of the sector and the formation of economic–social networks that underpinned the sectoral system in its early development. The recent trends in demand differentiation serve as external reasons for the ongoing transformation of the sector.

The development of the coffee sector has gone through different stages. Section 6.4.3 briefly discusses the sector from the first half of the nineteenth century to the end of the twentieth century. Following the framework of sectoral innovation systems, we examine the main dimensions of the system: the specific actors, institutions, organizations and networks, human capital, technological choice, and learning processes. Growers, millers and traders entered the business under the promotion of the young Republic; dense dynamic social-economic networks emerged, that, together with the relatively superior wet processing technology, laid the foundation for a high-quality trajectory in the Costa Rican coffee sector from its inception. In most of the decades in the twentieth century when external conditions turned out to be less favourable for the upstream producers of the value chain, inside Costa Rica there was continued evolution in institutional and technological aspects in line with the established paths. Among these changes, the most important was the creation of sector-specific institutions which were initially regulatory, and later on carried out public R&D and extension services.

Section 6.4.4 focuses on changes in the sector since the 1990s. The sector seems to be in a fundamental transition to be more knowledge-intensive, more actively penetrating the global value chain. It consolidated competitiveness in quality and productivity in the segment of green coffee, and began expanding into roasting. It has achieved impressive progress in the reduction of the use of water in coffee milling under a much more aggressive programme and in rather effective coordination and collaboration. These are soundly based on technological capability, managerial experiences and ability in policy-making and implementation, accumulated in the century-long evolution. Restraints and difficulties that the sector is facing are also briefly discussed.

6.4.2   The Global Coffee Value Chain and the Costa Rican Coffee Sector

The coffee plant is native to subtropical Africa and southern Asia, and was first discovered in the highlands of Ethiopia in the ninth century. From Ethiopia and the Muslim world, coffee spread to Italy, then to France. The Dutch were the first to grow the crop in Java and Ceylon, and exported Indonesian coffee to the Netherlands in the early eighteenth century. The

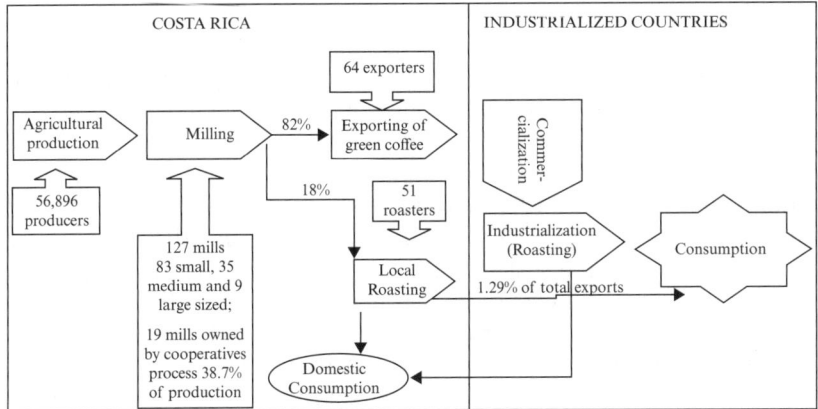

Source: Adapted from figure 5.1 (Díaz, 2003) with data by ICAFE, 2007

Figure 6.4 Costa Rican coffee chain (2007)

British East India Company made coffee popular in England. During the nineteenth century slave labour expanded first into Saint Domingo, a French colony, and then to other Caribbean areas in Central America and Brazil.

Today coffee is one of the most popular beverages worldwide, and one of the most traded commodities, ranking second only to petroleum.[24] Due to the limited areas suitable for coffee plantations which locate mainly in the South, and the high income elasticity of coffee consumption, which restricts coffee mainly to those in the North who can afford it, the coffee value chain is doomed to be international.

The coffee value chain

The value chain embraces cultivation, milling, roasting, distribution and consumption (see Figure 6.4). The two main cultivated species of the coffee plant are Arabica coffee and Robusta coffee. The former is considered more suitable for drinking than the latter. However, Robusta is less susceptible to disease and can be cultivated where Arabica will not thrive. Costa Rica cultivates Arabica; Central America, Eastern Africa and Arabia are Arabica cultivating areas; Western and Central Africa, throughout South-East Asia, and to some extent Brazil, cultivate Robusta. Harvesting of coffee fruits is made mostly by hand picking, a labour-intensive process. In some places like Brazil, where the landscape is relatively flat and the coffee fields immense, the harvesting has been mechanized.

Milling, or more generally, processing, can take the form of either wet or dry processes. In the wet process, the skin and pulp covering the bean is removed though processes in water. Coffees processed by the wet method, called wet processed or washed coffee, have a better quality. The wet method, however, requires the use of specific equipment and substantial quantities of water. In contrast, the dry process produces unwashed or natural coffees, in which the harvested coffee cherries are directly spread out in the sun to reduce the moisture to a certain level and then all the outer layers are removed in one step by the hulling machine. The dry method is widely used for most Arabica coffees and almost all Robustas.[25] Costa Rica has been using the wet process from the start of the coffee sector.

Roasting is the next step. It transforms 'green coffees', wet or dry processed, into roasted coffees; all coffees are roasted before they are consumed. During roasting, moisture is lost, coffee beans become less dense; intense heat breaks down starch to become caramel; aromatic oils, acids and caffeine weaken, and caffeol is created which is largely responsible for coffee's aroma and flavour.[25] Roasting requires fine skills, and uses increasingly advanced equipment and test techniques in order to produce fine and differentiated coffees such as light, medium-light, medium, medium-dark, dark, very dark, with various brands. Large food companies carry out roasting and sell roasted coffees in coffee shops or supermarkets; roasting is also part of the services of coffee houses where customers are provided with their own roasted coffees.

Other value-adding activities are included, such as packaging, storage, grading, transportation, distribution and retailing; and 'preparation' by grinding and brewing, which can be done by consumers themselves or in coffee houses.

Historically the input–output relations in the value chain were organized in such a way that colonies earlier and new republics later were in charge of providing raw (green) coffees, while imperial earlier and industrialized countries later ran the international commerce and roasting activities.

Governance of the international value chain

The governance of the international value chain changed over time. In terms of supply and demand relations, the nineteenth century saw an increase in demand, coming from increasingly widespread consumption in Europe. An excess of supply occurred between 1896 and 1908, which was associated with Brazil's massive entry into coffee production (Samper, 1994, p. 17). Afterwards, the state of supply-exceeded-demand was the norm. In the early decades of the twentieth century supply was increased through the expansion of cultivation; it continued increasing after the 1960s as a result of the intensification of cultivation caused by better technologies used in Kenya and Costa Rica and disseminated to Brazil and Colombia (Daviron, 1994, pp. 42–3). Supply became even more excessive after the 1990s when new participants, such as Vietnam, started coffee cultivation and exporting.

On the other hand, the governance of the value chain has always been dominated by the North, no matter what shortage or excess of supply there was. Throughout the twentieth century, commercial houses and later on big transnational companies (TNCs) from the industrialized North took control of high-value activities such as roasting and retailing, and took a large share of the profits. From the point of view of value chain governance, the power of TNCs is largely based on their strengths in technology (such as for roasting), information (close to consumers), and management of worldwide supply–demand chains; they earned so-called technological rents, organizational and 'relational' rents (Gereffi et al., 2005; Kaplinsky, 2006; UNIDO, 2002).

From time to time there were efforts aimed at the formation of rules or agreements in order to balance the unequal positions between producers and consumers, in which producer and consumer countries' governments were involved and some international organizations, such as the ICO (International Coffee Organization), acted as coordinators (Daviron, 1994; Samper, 1994; De Graaff, 1986). These efforts achieved limited success.

After the 1980s a new trend became apparent which was towards liberalization and privatization. Functions that producer governments had carried out in international negotiations were reduced, and relevant agents eliminated; examples include INMECAFE in Mexico, IBC in Brazil, FEDACAFE-Colombia, the coffee Marketing Board in Uganda, the Oficina Nacional de Comercialización de los Productos Básicos in Cameroon (Daviron, 1994). As a result, market power was freed from international coordination, and was further concentrated in the hands of a few roasting and soluble coffee firms. Financial capacity, which came from large banks that support TNCs and the soaring of the futures market, accelerated the concentration of power. For example five TNCs account for well over 60 per cent of sales across all major consuming markets (Talbot, 1995–6).

This was the background for a coffee price crisis in the late 1990s (Hallam, 2003; Osorio, 2002). Massive excess supply by the rapid expansion of production in Vietnam and Brazil triggered the crisis in an already poorly coordinated market. The price dropped dramatically, as shown in Figure 6.5. Osorio (2002, p. 1) commented on the crisis and the increasingly weakened position of producer countries in the following way:

'In the early 1990s earnings by coffee producing countries (exports f.o.b) were some US$10–12 billion and the value of retail sales of coffee, largely in

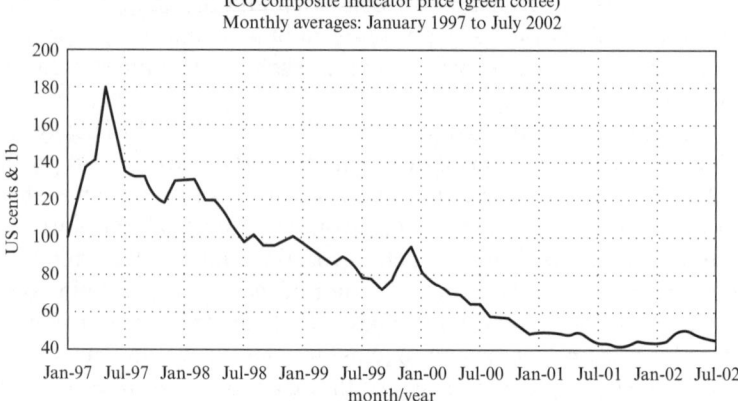

Source: Osorio (2002), p. 1.

Figure 6.5   ICO composite indicator price (green coffee)

industrialized countries, about US$30 billion. Now the value of retail sales exceeds US$70 billion but coffee producing countries only receive US$5.5 billion. Prices on world markets, which averaged around 120 US cents/lb in the 1980s, are now around 50 cents, the lowest in real terms for 100 years.

Alongside the concentration of control of TNCs based on the large quantity of 'industrial coffees' at lowest prices (fitting the emerging consumption in favour of soluble coffees and cappuccino), there are counter movements of consumption towards differentiation in quality and tastes (Lewin et al., 2004; Talbot, 1995–6). This change was reflected in the increasing concern about environmental effects by purchasing companies and final consumers, and in the rise of high-value niche markets such as speciality or gourmet coffees. Opportunities thereby opened for some of the coffee producers, especially those with better technological and institutional preparations like Costa Rica, to find alternative ways for sustaining or even upgrading the sector in the generally difficult circumstances. Besides, the increase in domestic consumption of producers, especially those with higher income levels like Brazil and Costa Rica, changed the demand structure as well, which offers additional opportunities for the coffee sector in producer countries.

Evolution of the Costa Rican coffee sector
The Costa Rican coffee sector has been evolving in the context of changing governance and input–output relations of the global value chain.

Costa Rica, like other Southern producers, has been engaged mainly in plantation and milling, in order to produce raw or green coffee for export throughout the nineteenth and twentieth century up to the 1990s (Díaz, 2003). Since then the Costa Rican coffee sector has been moving towards high-value activities. On the one hand, the Costa Rican sector started to roast its coffee, and then increased this activity; now about one fifth of green coffee produced is further roasted locally. Although the majority of roasted coffee is for domestic consumption, including that sold to coffee tourists, a small proportion is sold directly to international consumers, as shown in Figure 6.4. On the other hand, the quality and productivity of Costa Rican coffee is improving; the sector is now becoming a leader in these terms among international green coffee producers.

6.4.3 Early Development and the Formation of 'Thick' Social and Economic Networks

Coffee was introduced in Costa Rica in the late eighteenth century or very early nineteenth century, to the Meseta Central, an area with near perfect soil and climate conditions for its plantation.Coffee growing soon surpassed cacao, tobacco and sugar in importance, and since the 1830s has become the major source of foreign revenue. From 1844–45 Costa Rica has been a regular exporter of coffee to England. These developments were partly and importantly a result of the promotion of the independent Republic of Costa Rica (since 1821) by various instruments, with the main objective of establishing a stable connection to international markets.

Actors, social networks and the choice of technology
Coffee growers in Costa Rica are smallholders; they entered the business on a small scale and in great numbers. Authorities of the republic implemented a series of measures to promote entry; notable among these are: in 1821 the municipality of San José distributed free coffee plants among residents; in 1825 the government exempted coffee from tithe payments; in 1831 the National Assembly decreed that anyone who grew coffee for five years on idle land could claim the land as their own.[26] A brotherhood spirit among coffee farmers made Costa Rica the first Central American country to establish coffee as an industry.

Processors are another group of actors in the sector. The processors in Costa Rica chose wet processing from the very start. The social networks and the concentration of power in the coffee sector were closely associated with the main processing technologies. In contrast to the cheaper dry method, which was so extensively and economically used in Brazil, and used on a much smaller scale in certain more marginal parts of Costa Rica as well, Costa Rica's wet method led to central processing plants (*beneficios*). They were located either on large farms or in towns and cities, with increasingly technical procedures and attention to quality. Such processing had implications for the manner of harvesting (handpicking only ripe cherries rather than Brazil's more industrial and less discerning style), the development of transportation (first oxcarts, then railroads and trucking), and relations between coffee mill owners and their suppliers of fresh coffee fruit (Samper, 2001).

Traders entered the sector, some of them coming from main coffee growers who organized trade companies and invested in export processes. Owners of *beneficios* used to buy the coffee cherries and export parchment dry seed. In 1850 there were 76 exporters but 16 of them exported 85 per cent of the coffee. Local traders made their business jointly with European co-signatories and transporters, the latter managing the export outside the country. Private banks (in 1863, there were Banco Anglo Costarricense, Banco la Unión, Banco Internacional) helped small farmers to maintain and increase their cultivation until, and even afterwards, the nationalization of the banking system in 1949 (Samper, 2001).

The republican government, in addition to offering incentives for coffee growing, invested in infrastructure, mainly the construction of new roads, the rehabilitation of harbours, and later on the construction of rail routes, based on coffee revenues. Moreover, the regular link to international markets through coffee exports came to consolidate an agrarian capitalism in Costa Rica (Acuña and Molina, 1991, p. 90). It was during the coffee boom decades in the nineteenth century that the Federal Debt was paid; the postal service, the first government printing office, and the hospitals in San José and San Juan de Dios were founded; the first libraries and the Santo Tomás University were founded; and the National Theatre was erected. Politically, a coffee elite oligarchy emerged in the governance of the republic since its inception in 1849 up to the middle of the twentieth century.

In short, a high-quality trajectory was set up from the very start of the export-oriented coffee sector by a combination of many factors: the active growers and processors and other actors and their intense dynamic inter-linkages; the engagement in processing and chosen technologies; and the ideal land and climate – the volcanic rich soil, high altitude, afternoon sun, plentiful rain, and cool evenings – created perfect conditions for yielding beans that are rich and intense in flavour. All these factors were supported by, and support, the formation of social, cultural, economic and political reliability in the country. The coffee sector is an inherent part, in contrast to bananas, which was an enclave, of the socio-economic structure.

Technological and institutional consolidation

An important institutional innovation took place around the 1920s–1930s, which was the creation of a sectoral regulatory agency IDECAFE (1933, Institute for Costa Rican Coffee) (Acuña and Molina, 1991). One of the regulatory efforts IDECAFE made was in new mechanisms in order to resolve rising tensions between growers, processors and exporters. This resulted from the many conflicts that occurred in the 1920s and 1930s in which small farmers were struggling against powerful processing mills and large farmer exporters who joined together in price setting. The regulation of prices gave small farmers the opportunity to get better terms in the face of the processing factories, exporters, and local roasters. In 1948 IDECAFE was transformed into the Coffee Bureau as part of the Economy Ministry, and was organized in such a way that representatives of farmers, processing mills, roasters and exporters were all included. One of the main functions of the Bureau remained the regulation of prices. In addition, the National Bank was created in the same year, which further freed farmers from the restrictions posed by millers who had served as one of their creditors (Naranjo, 1999; Samper, 2001). Another initiative of IDECAFE involved regulations for the development of specialized private exporters. The presence of new actors specialized in negotiation gave the opportunity to get better prices, even in the futures market of New York for Arabica coffee and London for Robusta (Díaz, 2003).

An important change in terms of sectoral structure was that small farmers organized themselves into *cooperatives* from the 1960s. Some vertical integration appeared with the growth of cooperatives which developed processing mills and had technical advisors. A federation of cooperatives, FEDECOOP, became one of the main exporter firms later on. Cooperatives enabled farmers to earn better profits which otherwise went to processing mills, and processing mills had to compete with the new actor of cooperatives.

Technological changes were incremental in most of the years, based on a well-defined division of labour and beneficial relations among the actors of the system. Driven by the interest in cost reduction, processing mills were using more machines for some work; the number of *beneficios* were reduced and the scale increased because of better transport conditions and other changes. Coffee plantations employed chemical fertilizers, moving towards intensive use of the land, which is often called the 'green revolution'. Some new varieties were introduced, such as the tall variety of Arabic coffee. Planted areas increased significantly.

Institutional development for formal knowledge creation and dissemination evolved or was derived from the institutional basis already there for the sector, namely ICAFE (the Institute of Coffee, the successor of IDECAFE and the Coffee Bureau, established in 1985) and CICAFE (the Costa Rica Coffee Research Centre started in 1977, and was later part of ICAFE). These have been the most important knowledge centres specialized in coffee since the 1970s. The government has been the key promoter of the knowledge centres, which small farmers can not afford, nor do they have the ability to engage with them. CICAFE carried out research in variety breeding; among its achievements a short coffee tree variety has been widely adopted. One result from studies in agronomics in the centres was a standardization of technologies in plantations. It has a chemical laboratory and provides support for quality control. The Ministry of Agriculture, in coordination with CICAFE, developed an efficient system of extension of technologies (Orozco and Ruiz, 2002).

To sum up, in the twentieth century the Costa Rican coffee sector experienced institutional and technological development along with the high-quality trajectory that was created at the very beginning. As a producer in the South, the improvements were restricted to plantation and processing. The golden booming market of the nineteenth century no longer existed. In the less favourable international market the improvements meant that the Costa Rican sector was able to remain productive and competitive. In terms of the knowledge base transformation, one of the most important evolutions of this period was perhaps the formation of formal R&D centres and the extension/dissemination of the knowledge system: these were new key actors in an increasingly knowledge-intensive agro-food sector, which, together with the consolidation of the division of labour and links of the system, laid the very ground for the present time, when the sector is moving towards new opportunities.

6.4.4 Move Towards 'Gourmet Coffee' and Lessons

Opportunities for the ongoing movement, characteristically towards gourmet coffee, arose from a crisis – the price crisis of coffee in the 1990s.

In response to the crisis, international organizations like the ICO and FAO began promoting specialized (certified or speciality) coffees (FAO, 2003). The transition from conventional to specialized coffees is, however, difficult, and is only possible for those who are well prepared. Costa Rica is among those countries that are prepared, where the producers are opting for the production of high-quality coffees: gourmet coffee. Here 'gourmet coffee' or 'speciality coffee' are the expressions used to denote excellent coffee products produced in a more knowledge-intensive, higher value-adding and environmentally friendly coffee sector, in general.

Maintaining and improving productivity and quality

Good quality comes from careful management of every step throughout the value activities, plus favourable natural conditions. Good quality has traditionally been an asset of the coffee sector in Costa Rica, as discussed earlier. Since the 1990s better plantation management, particularly in organic farming, stricter quality control in milling – for example, the setting of the rule that berries should reach the mills within 24 hours of harvest – and the development of superior varieties, have all contributed to high productivity and quality. Best practices have been disseminated fairly quickly, thanks to the coordination by responsible government agencies and R&D centres, such as the Agriculture Ministry, ICAFE, and the Institute for Learning (INA) which is in charge of training. The cooperatives organize technological projects, which attribute to knowledge diffusion; farmers' active attitude towards the projects and technical advisors are also factors contributing to knowledge diffusion. Mills contribute their part; they, upon agreement, receive only ripe coffee berries to ensure good quality processed beans.

Most of the *beneficios* have introduced a coffee taster. This enables farmers to get a clear message as how to best manage harvesting (Díaz, 2003).

Costa Rica produced the highest coffee yield per hectare until the 1980s. Thereafter Vietnam overtook Costa Rica. Nevertheless, Costa Rica remains the highest in per hectare output in the group of Arabica coffee producers. For coffee quality, one of the key indicators is the differential obtained with respect to international prices. Costa Rican coffee has been getting a sustained *high differential*, and maintains a leading position in this measure, as shown in Table 6.9.

Environmentally-friendly milling

Environmentally-friendly milling is part of a broader effort aimed at a rational use of water and energy by means of introduction of cleaner technologies. The Inter-institutional Agreement for Cooperation (1992), made by coffee producers and authorities in Costa Rica, declared their goal to modernize coffee factories to improve the environmental performance of the coffee industry. International buyers' concern about the environmental impact of coffee production gave impetus to the initiative as well.

The coffee industry used to generate almost 60 per cent of the country's organic waste which was discharged into rivers. Besides, the coffee industry was responsible for 15 per cent of industry-originated CO_2 emission, 8 per cent of electricity consumption, and it produced hundreds of thousands tons of coffee flesh from 4 or 5 months' processing of coffee berries. This resulted in very negative environmental effects in spite of the positive economic and social benefits (Chacón, 1997).

Table 6.9   Differential in coffee prices obtained in selected ICO member countries (total exports all destinations; in US$/quintals), 1999–2006

Country	1999	2000	2001	2002	2003	2004	2005	2006
Kenya	29	−4.1	13.3	25.8	−29.4	36.11	11.4	7.5
Costa Rica	**10**	**11.9**	**10.3**	**14.1**	**11.6**	**9.6**	**4.7**	**12.8**
Mexico	−1.7	3.9	12	13.9	10.8	4.8	8.2	4.0
Colombia	5.2	10.3	12.4	11.8	5.7	3.7	5.4	9.4
Guatemala	−7.7	0.6	2.2	5.9	−2.3	−0.1	−3.1	−2.4
Nicaragua	6	6.9	4.3	10.8	8.5	−0.6	−2.6	4.7
El Salvador	−4.5	1.7	3.3	−0.9	−1.3	−6	−10.2	2.3
Peru	−19.5	−17.5	−2.9	−1.7	−6.4	−6.2	−9.6	−9.0
Honduras	−5.1	−0.4	−3.1	−1.4	−4	−6.8	−2.8	−3.1
Brazil	−22.4	−14.2	−8	−16.1	−16.1	−17.5	−23.7	−17.1

Source: International Coffee Organization (ICO) (http://www.ico.org/coffee_prices.asp), and New York Board Of Trade (NYBOT).

The Inter-institutional Agreement for Cooperation set forth a framework for allied action, in which new environmental regulations were stipulated based on research work at CICAFE with the participation of the milling factories. Implementation has been carried out under the coordination of a number of government agencies including the state agency in charge of water management, AYA (Instituto Costarricense de Acueductos y Alcantarillados), the state agency for regulation of public services, ARESEP (Autoridad Reguladora de los Servicios Públicos), and the Health Ministry, together with CICAFE as mentioned, and in close collaboration with the mills. It is worth mentioning that for necessary knowledge creation, international experts were invited to give advice to the works at ICAFE, and that research capacity at CATIE, an agricultural technology university, was involved, signalling a broad interplay of domestic and international scientific communities.

A four-stage action programme has been developed. The first step attempts to reduce water use to one quarter of the previous consumption in milling per kilogram of coffee fruit; the next steps have as their targets to largely eliminate small and even suspended solid waste, and finally a thorough anaerobic treatment of the water is planned so that water pollution is substantially reduced by 80 per cent (Orozco and Ruiz, 2002, p. 39). Apparently this aggressive action requires enormous inputs in terms of knowledge and investment. It is reported that the coffee sector had invested near 11 000 million colon (2000 exchange rate was approximately

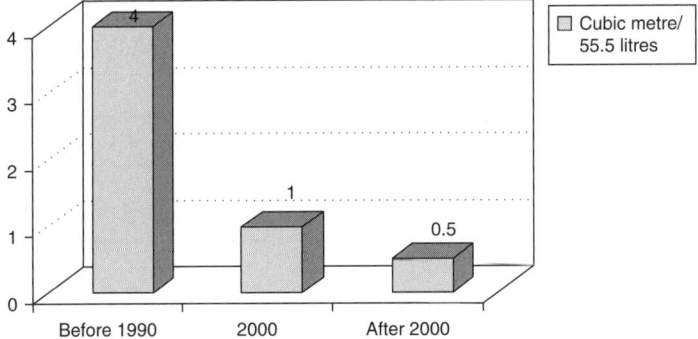

Source: Orozco and Ruiz (2002).

Figure 6.6 *Water consumption in the Costa Rican coffee mills*
(1990–2001)

300 colon to 1 USD) by around 2000 (CEPAL, 2001, p. 52). The results
have been very impressive thus far. Figure 6.6 shows water use reduction
by coffee mills in Costa Rica as part of the achievements from these efforts.

Entering into roasting and gourmet coffee, and restraints

Gourmet coffee, as a term for coffee strictly traded in the international
market, was very probably initially accredited by the Gourmet Coffee
Project that ICO, the International Trade Centre UNCTAD/WTO (ITC)
and the Common Fund for Commodities (CFC) jointly launched in 1997,
with the participation of 5 coffee-producing countries: Brazil, Burundi,
Ethiopia, Papua New Guinea and Uganda, and several organizations
and companies in the key markets of USA, Japan and Europe,[27] even
though the idea of high-quality or 'gourmet' coffee already existed in
those markets. Consumers' recognition of the value of gourmet coffee has
certainly been a driving force from the demand side; and coffee companies
such as Starbucks, the world's largest retailer and roaster of speciality
coffee, have had an impact on the popularity of gourmet coffees.[28] With
its high-quality coffee, Costa Rica is penetrating the higher-value niche
market which is expanding rapidly. Table 6.10 gives a picture in which a
large share of coffee from Costa Rica sold on the international market has
been in the category of gourmet coffee in recent years.

Entering into roasting is, however, more important in terms of profitability and learning opportunities, which implies a breakthrough in the
long-lasting international division of labour. Local roasters' participation in roasting has been taking small, while steady steps in recent years.

Table 6.10   Costa Rica participation in gourmet[a] coffee market(as a share in total exports of coffee, harvests 2003/04–2006/07, data for 46 kilo sacks)

Harvest	2003–04	2004–05	2005–06	2006–07 [b]
Amount	1 252 759.14	1 103 684.06	1 050 091.82	1 020 933.02
Participation	68.31%	71.51%	75.35%	71.20%

Notes:
a: Gourmet coffee includes: Strictly Hard Bean, Good Hard Bean and High Grown Atlantic
b: Preliminary data.

Source: Instituto del Café de Costa Rica (ICAFE).

Table 6.11   Composition of Costa Rica coffee exports (2000–2007 in percentages)

SAC Code	Export item	2000	2001	2002	2003	2004	2005	2006	2007
0901.1	Coffee without roasting	95.01	96.97	97.94	99.13	99.06	99.07	98.85	98.61
0901.2	**Roasted coffee**	**4.99**	**3.02**	**2.04**	**0.85**	**0.90**	**0.90**	**1.06**	**1.29**
0901.9	Other coffees	0.00	0.01	0.00	0.00	0.02	0.02	0.01	0.01
2101	Extracts, essences and concentrates of coffee	0.00	0.00	0.02	0.01	0.01	0.01	0.08	0.09
Total		100	100	100	100	100	100	100	100

Source: Authors' elaboration with data from Central Bank of Costa Rica.

Some one fifth of the green coffee produced in Costa Rica has been further roasted locally as shown in Figure 6.4. But the pace at which Costa Rica is exporting roasted coffee is almost at a standstill or is going backwards (Table 6.11).

Roasted coffee has been consumed mainly domestically. There is a link between the increasing domestic consumption of coffee and the rapid growth of tourism. It is reported that more than 1.9 million tourists arrived in 2007 in this small country with a population of only 4 million, which represents a 10.6 per cent growth relative to the previous year.[29] And tourists who come to the country make up an important proportion of coffee consumers in the 'domestic' market, which actually is a kind of export, albeit indirect.[30] In this connection, it is interesting to see that coffee farms actively use the Internet as a means of indirect marketing for coffee tourism.

Heavy restraints to fair competition in the international market remain a problem, as can be seen clearly in the case of roasted Costa Rican coffee exporting. The international roasters put pressure on the local exporters and roasters not to challenge their normal trading in which they buy only green coffee; and local roasters and exporters prefer not to risk damaging their relationship with the main buyers, as the authors learned from businessmen.

There are *other problems* from inside the system too. Businessmen feel that regulations, which used to focus on the protection of growers, are rigid. However, to produce roasted coffee economically needs relatively cheap raw coffee to be imported for mixing with expensive Costa Rican beans; otherwise this export is less competitive.

Overall, this is a rather new period for the coffee sector in Costa Rica. Some progress has been achieved of which the most impressive is probably in environmentally-friendly processing and the increase in roasting activities, even though thus far mainly for the internal market. On the other hand, the challenges and necessary efforts may not have yet fully unfolded. Management capabilities seem to be significantly improved, provided that the whole sector needs to operate in a much broader international and multinational arena so as to explore the newly opened opportunities. Knowledge centres face unprecedented requirements; however, they have contributed greatly. ICAFE, the key research centre for the coffee sector, underwent a transformation in 1997 to become decentralized and more market oriented. Criticisms have been made that ICAFE probably should not be involved in some works that business companies can do, and it should not leave, but rather stay in the dissemination functions which are part of public service. Besides, the capacity of universities in knowledge creation and human resource development is to be further incorporated into the efforts for a knowledge-intensive coffee sector.

6.5   THE SOYBEAN SECTOR IN BRAZIL: FROM CATCHING UP TO TECHNOLOGICAL FRONTIER[31]

6.5.1   Introduction

Brazil is the largest Latin America country, the fifth largest in the world. It covers 8.5 million km² and has a population of 170 million (2000 census), of whom only 18.8 per cent reside in rural areas.[32] Today the estimated population is 190 million and the estimated rural population is even less. Brazilian agribusiness is considered a leading industrial complex of the economy, being responsible for 30 per cent of GDP, 37 per cent of employment and around 40 per cent of the total exports (Rodrigues, 2005).

Since the middle of the 1990s the Brazilian agro-food system has been able to be characterized by enhanced capacity for increasing international competition.

This chapter intends to approach the progress of the soybean sector from catching up to technological leadership. Section 6.5.2 of this chapter describes the soybean complex and its relevance to the Brazilian economy. Section 6.5.3 presents a brief overview of the catching-up process and institutional driving factors that have led the soybean complex to a technological leadership position. Section 6.5.4 concludes by outlining the Brazilian perspectives towards opportunities and challenges of the new millennium.

6.5.2   The Soybean Complex and its Relevance to the Brazilian Economy

The relevance of the soybean agro-industrial complex to the Brazilian economy rests on the fact that this sector is related to many processed foods; it enjoys a number of markets. The most important market for soybeans has been the production and export of raw beans to the emerging international consumers in recent decades. Also important are the production of soybean oil (brut and refined) and its by-products, and the production of animal feed. All these relate to agro-industrial meat chains. To be able to complement the grain–bran–oil and grain–meal–meat sequences, soybeans have enabled the industry to provide more diverse and sophisticated foods, spreading along different food chains – and processed foods – which is helping the industry not only to become more competitive but also to attend to increasingly new consumer demands (for example, functional foods and organic food in contrast to traditional foods).

Many factors have contributed to the presence of so many different agro-industrial chains in the Brazilian soybean complex. From the demand side there are huge demands for the commercial provision of fat and oil, and protein, directly from soybeans and indirectly from meat, dairy products and eggs, in order to substitute for traditional sources such as vegetable sourced oil and animal sourced protein.

From the supply side, effective production has been key to Brazil's success. Brazil has achieved technical progress in the improvement in seed varieties with good protein and oil contents, the reduction of toxicity, high cost/profits in production, and the industrial utilization of vegetable oils. These achievements have been made with relevant economic policies and supported by science and technology infrastructure, transportation

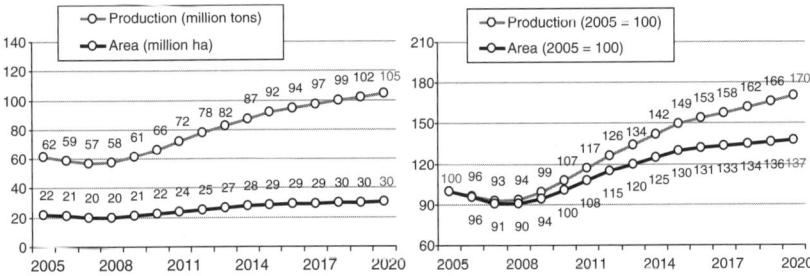

Note: In 2020, Brazil will produce around 105 million tons of soybeans, in 8 million ha. 70% of production growth will require only 37% of additional area, due to 1.5% per year growth in productivity.

Figure 6.7   Soybean production

and other physical infrastructure. The strategic vision and management of leading agro-business conglomerates have been very central. Many of them operate with great diversification. The fact that the biggest firms integrate both chains – oil and meat – might explain the synergy-like effect that they enjoy, multiplying added value by producing many intermediate and final products. Leading firms have also increasingly been the home of R&D and international marketing, a number of them becoming not only the leaders in Brazil, but also worldwide. They are also involved in the systemic influence in the reduction of production costs, and in the transportation, communication, and logistics efficiency.

In 2008 the Companhia Nacional de Abastecimento (CONAB, from the Ministry of Agriculture) forecasted a harvest of 142.4 million tons of grains, 8.1 per cent higher than the previous year.[33] The rapid growth of the sector has continued for thirty years and, as a result, the output of the sector has increased by approximately 170 per cent. Of the five principal grain crops (soybeans, corn, rice, beans and wheat), soybeans and corn are the major contributors in terms of performance, while rice and beans remained relatively stable during the period. In 2008 Brazil produced 117.3 million tons of soybeans and corn, or 82.4 per cent of the total national grain production. Soybeans and corn together have contributed 70.1 per cent of the growth in that year; not only have they been the major contributors over the past thirty years, but according to this forecast the two key grains will be very important in the coming years. Figure 6.7 shows soybean production in current years and the production forecasted for the coming ten years up to 2020.

The increase of planted area   2.1 per cent in 2008, which was higher than the previous year – was not the main reason for this increase. Brazil

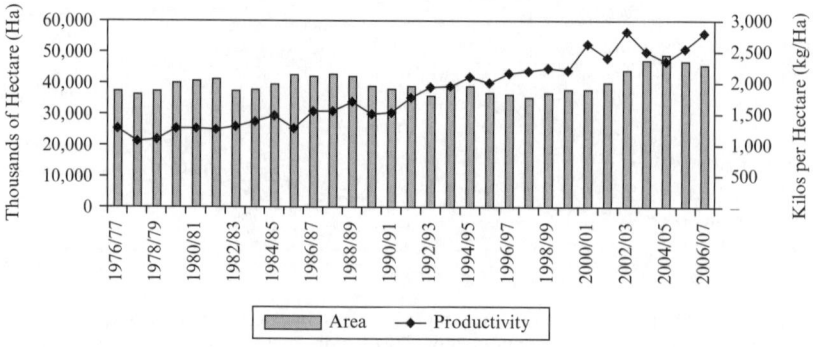

Source: FIBGE. Anuário Estatístico Brasileiro.

Figure 6.8   Area and land productivity (principal grains, 1976/77 to 2006/07)

had a grain cultivated area of 47.17 million ha in 2008 (almost 80 per cent is in the central-South of the country and only 3.5 per cent in the Northern region, which includes part of the Amazon region). Productivity growth has been the main reason for the remarkable performance, and this should be attributed to the investments in knowledge creation and diffusion, the development of infrastructure and institutional creation. Figure 6.8 shows the evolution of the principal grains cultivated in Brazil.

The growth in Brazil's agricultural exports is remarkable. Between 2000 and 2005, agro-food exports grew by 131 per cent. The soybean complex comprises 22 per cent of total exports in 2005, and meat comprises 19 per cent. Meat exports grew by 319 per cent from 2000–2005 (see Table 6.12). Considering that corn and soybeans are used as basic feedstock for chicken and pork, the increase in soybean production, as well as corn, also explains the competitiveness of Brazilian meat exports.

6.5.3   A Brief Overview of the Catching-up Process and Institutional Driving Factors

The Brazilian agro-food catch-up could be divided into two phases.

The first phase, from the late 1940s to the 1970s, could be characterized, on the one hand, by the institutional setting – research, technical assistance and extension services, credit system – and on the other by the introduction of the material base for agricultural modernization – transport and commercial infrastructure, seed companies, machine and tools sector, fertilizers and agrochemicals.[34]

Table 6.12   Agro-food exports (2000 to 2005, US$ billion)

	2000	Part. %	2005	Part. %	Var. %
Soybean complex	4.1	22.2	9.4	21.7	125.8
Meat	1.9	10.3	8.1	18.8	318.6
Forestry products	3.8	20.1	7.1	16.5	89.4
Sugar-Alcohol complex	1.2	6.6	4.7	10.8	277.6
Leather and sub-products	1.3	7.4	3.0	7.0	118.6
Coffee	1.7	9.4	2.9	6.7	64.1
Tobacco	0.8	4.4	1.7	3.9	102.8
Fibres and Textiles	0.8	4.6	1.5	3.6	83.6
Orange complex	1.0	5.6	1.1	2.7	10.4
Fruits and Nuts	0.3	1.7	0.7	1.7	128.5
Others	1.4	7.5	2.8	6.5	100.2
Total	18.9	100.0	43.6	100.0	130.7

Source: Secex/MDIC – DPI/SRI/MAPA.

The Brazil–United States Mixed Technical Commission (the Abbink Mission) played a role in catalysing the development in policy and institution setting, from the end of the 1940s to the mid-1950s. These developments include the creation of the BNDES (National Bank for Economic and Social Development) in 1952, and the Targets Plan (Plano de Metas) which was proposed in order to produce results in targeted areas, and, especially, the development of a transport and communication infrastructure during the government of President Juscelino Kubistchek (1956–61). Some key industrial sectors were developed in that period, for example, machinery, fertilizers and agro-chemicals, which are either necessary tools or basic inputs for the modernization of the agribusiness system.

The policies and institutions articulated or created at the beginning of the 1950s were made directly in response to the need of agricultural development at a time when the agro-food sector was still very backward, being a sector in which family farms' subsistence agriculture was predominant. These initiatives had a triple structure. The first part concerned public agronomical research within the DNPEA family (National Department of Agriculture and Livestock Research); some of the institutes were old, having been in existence since the nineteenth century, such as the Institute Agronômico de Campinas (coffee, corn, cotton) and the Instituto Biológico de Campinas, or the early twentieth century, such as the Instituto Agronômico do Paraná (mainly cotton) and the Instituto Agronômico de Pernambuco (sugar cane). The second

part was the ACAR system for technical assistance and rural extension system, created in the 1950s. And the third part was related to the
modernization of farmer credit services, provided by the Carteira Rural
do Banco do Brasil, which was established earlier, in the 1930s (Castro,
1984, 1985).

International exchange programmes, created at that time were also
important for academic and managerial capability-building. An early
result was the success in hybrid corn in Brazil.[35] The programmes established international networks for academic and entrepreneurial relationships. International exchanges have been continued well up to the present
time; the capability-building at the EMBRAPA (Brazilian Enterprise for
Agricultural Research) has been benefiting from the exchange and many
academic and corporate leaders had their training or studied abroad based
on these programmes.

The successful cases of agribusiness enterprises include the leading
hybrid corn producer Agroceres (founded in 1945), the well-known Sadia
enterprise, a leader in Brazil and the world in chilled and frozen meat, and
Aracruz Celulose (founded in the 1960s), the world's largest exporter of
short fibre cellulose (Castro, 1988; Gertner et al., 1997). The reasons for
their success are their own dynamic capabilities, or the capacity for search-
ing and selecting new profitable opportunities and new technologies,
both in Brazil and abroad, their corporate structure and their strategies
(Castro, 1997, 1999; Teece and Pisano, 1998).

The second phase of catching up took place after the 1970s. Soybeans
were representative of the agro-food sector, which boomed together with
the rapid growth and transformation of the Brazilian economy, and
which was supported by the strengthening of agricultural public research;
EMBRAPA as just mentioned (established in 1973), was the foundation.
The boom was linked to the economic conditions at the time and the policies made by the Brazilian government: the establishment of EMBRAPA,
and the emphasis on agriculture among other industries, was part of the
Second National Development Plan (II PND), as a strategic response to
the petroleum crisis. The formulation of a science and technology project
for the agro-food system within the National Economic Development
Plans, was backed by the creation of EMBRAPA on the eve of the II
PND. Furthermore, with the establishment of EMBRAPA, interaction began to intensify between public research institutes (EMBRAPA,
institutes, universities) and research institutions from the private sector,
both agricultural and agro-industrial, as well as the part played by
research funding institutions – namely, the FINEP (Research and Projects
Financing).[36]

Social relations, including the involvement of local people, were important in accompanying the acquisition and dissemination of technology together with the changes in the production structure in the period. In the case of soybeans, for instance, the introduction of soil correction technology, which uses calcium to adjust the soil to be suitable for soybeans, was initially tested and implemented in the state of Rio Grande do Sul, at the very south of the country at the beginning of the 1960s. The initial success led to the spread of soybeans in the Cerrados, centre-west of Brazil, in the following decade. The Federal University of Rio Grande do Sul and the University of Wisconsin worked together and made the soil analysis and its 'correction' viable. Rural credit offered by Banco do Brasil provided the needed resources for the initial implementation and afterwards the completion of the transfer towards new production territory.[37]

More than the changes in knowledge base and yield, the soybean boom in the 1970s caused an agrarian redistribution that led to the successful involvement of small and medium producers in the south of Brazil, mainly by allowing the production of both wheat and soybeans in the same agricultural year. The knowledge base was transformed by the introduction of a biannual crop system, with good results in terms of productivity and profitability. The consequences were not only in terms of the necessary introduction of the modernized production system, but mainly in that it made small farm agriculture viable in the south; it then moved further towards the centre-West (mainly in the 1980s), where cheap land and the vast terrain made large-scale production of soybeans, corn, cotton and cattle possible. This movement has redefined in depth the space configuration of the Brazilian agro-food system.

Together with approaching the level of the US and Argentina in terms of efficiency, the agricultural boundaries in Brazil shifted to the mid-West and the mid-North (Castro and Fonseca, 1994), which dramatically increased Brazilian production potential (Castro, 1995). This led to a search for solutions to the technological problems brought about by the expansion of these frontiers, which were needed to make production cheaper. This led to the development of an, as yet non-existent, transport network, based on different modes of transportation (roads, railroads and ferryboats), which did reduce costs further. Above all, research on soybeans in Brazil has since the beginning concentrated on technologies for biological nitrogen fixing in the soil. This technological trajectory requires less use of fertilizers, and has facilitated and sustained the expansion of soybean production.[38] Since the 1990s the Brazilian soybean complex has taken a leading role in international markets based on its ability to remain at the technological frontier.

6.5.4   Brazilian Perspectives Towards Opportunities and Challenges of the New Millennium

The Brazilian agro-food system is an example illustrating that catching up in the sector can be very successful. This is proved by its performance during the entire period in terms of growth rates, competitive position (measured by increased participation) in the global markets, labour productivity and land yield, prices, and product diversification. Brazil's extremely rich resources provide enormous potential for the coming years of the new millennium. The technological transformation of the Brazilian agro-food system in general and the soybean agribusiness in particular, have given the country a leading position both in biotech and information technologies. Together with its uniquely rich natural resources, this might enable the country to prosper in the new millennium.

What are the Brazilian perspectives in relation to the agro-food sector and to the opportunities and challenges opening at the beginning of the new millennium? A tentative answer points to the following considerations.

The resources available
In term of land availability, Brazil possesses 50 million ha of cultivated land; additionally it has the potential for 400 million ha, and 90 million ha of free land that could be used for the production of food and agricultural raw materials (Rodrigues, 2005). Brazil has qualified technical personnel trained at universities, who want to live in the countryside.[39] The labour supply is in decline, which is in favour of improved income for agricultural labour. Brazil has also developed a reasonably good credit and monetary system.

The demand for food from the international market
International demand is very strong for agricultural and livestock products. Demand is especially high from the emergent markets like China and India. China and India have been responsible for most of the increase in soybean sales in the past, and according to estimates the two countries will continue to be the main buyers of soybeans in the coming years. The worldwide growth in urbanization and aging of the population will also entail strong demand for agro-food, especially meat products (Contini et al., 2006). Consumers' increasing concern about organic and functional foods is creating new niche markets that will push technological frontiers further.

The demand for bio-fuels
This demand is strong, especially in the growing market of ethanol.

Competitive firms
Brazilian agribusiness enterprises are already well established in the global market.[40]

The required institutions
Institutions have been built in the two previous catching-up phases. The needed institutions are embedded in shared beliefs of well-established actors such as sustainability, export leadership and production cost reduction (including competitive use of land for different crops, such as sugar cane and bio-diesel raw materials). Other institutions include grade and standards regulation, and WTO rules.

The existence of a solid knowledge base
The high-performing EMBRAPA and other institutes, universities, and a network of research teams including the private sector foundations, such as the Fundação Mato Grosso in the state of Mato Grosso, and COPERSUCAR, Cooperativa dos Produtores de Açúcar, in São Paulo, and UNICA, form a solid knowledge base.[41] A huge number of networks in public agro-food research have been established, which can be shown in the number of research groups registered in CNPq, the data base of the National Research Council. The creativeness of the knowledge base is demonstrated in the achievements in the following areas: molecular male sterility; 'apomixia' for hybrid strength in traditional crops; biotic and abiotic resistances; high nutritional value (vitamins, amino acids, oils and iron); more efficient plants regarding their capacity for absorption of soil nutrients, which reduces the use of fertilizer; plants and animals as bio-reactors for the production of new biomolecules; transgenic animals with resistance to common diseases; vaccines and other genetic recombinant inputs for farming; and new trends in bio energy.

New institutions for IPR
Cultivars are under protection. The new cultivars represent a more open and diversified market, which explains the fastest growth of Brazilian soybean production and high land yield.[42]

The renewal of the Brazilian innovation system with a new set of policies
A number of policies and new actions have been developed recently aiming at the renewal of the Brazilian innovation system: the Industrial and Technology Policy; the Innovation Policy; the Biotechnology Programme; the innovation incentives and financial support at BNDES; the strengthening of the Fundos Setoriais (Sector Funds) at FINEP; the new incentives and policies at the INPI (Brazilian Patent Office) involving capacity

building in regulation for intellectual property rights with special concern for development and catching up.

6.6   FINDINGS AND DISCUSSION

6.6.1   The Richness of Evolutionary Paths

A first finding from the study is that the development processes of agro-food sectors differ greatly among the cases.

The different paths are largely shaped by the particular history and current status of the respective countries in their broad catching-up process
Consider the subject areas that the study covers: all are fast growing and the most representative sectors in the recent decades in the respective countries. Cassava, one of the most important staple crops in Nigeria, and vegetables, also basic foods only second to cereals in the food consumption of the Chinese, are as national subsistence agriculture. They are becoming important as a result of population pressure and with the changing structure of food consumption, either from the need for domestic production to secure food supply (in the Nigerian case), or by the increase in urban residents during rapid economic growth (in China). In contrast, coffee and soybeans in Costa Rica and Brazil are either historically worldwide commodities or a new presence in the international market, sold in massive quantities. Historical reasons, distinct natural endowments, and technological capability have determined the latter two countries as being net exporters of agricultural products.

Also consider institutional, infrastructural, and relative industry development, which are supportive to the sectors in study. Brazil and Costa Rica have both developed relatively mature systems in the sectors and supportive conditions. Both have developed a higher level of links for complementarities or 'synergies' among value activities in the systems. The interactions between coffee plantation and milling in Costa Rica, and the integration of the soy–oil and soy–meat value chains in Brazil are illustrations, which are backed up by distinctive social networks. Relatively less-developed systems are looser in interconnections and thinner in social networks, and in terms of supportive institutions, there remain many holes and weaknesses, such as the lack of fertilizers as input in the Nigerian cassava case and a weak seed sector in China. And consider physical infrastructure: among the cases, Nigeria is the one showing clearly that it is suffering from unreliable electricity and water supplies, and access to roads is also poor there. Consider the strengths of the knowledge base:

both Costa Rica and Brazil have developed relatively strong agricultural knowledge bases. In terms of public spending for agricultural R&D as a percentage of agricultural GDP, Brazil spent 1.81 per cent in 2000; in comparison, this figure for China was 0.4 per cent for 2000. China in particular, and Asia and the Pacific in general (the Asia and Pacific group as a whole had the figure of 0.41 per cent as an average in 2000), spent even less in this investment than the sub-Saharan Africa group, which was 0.72 per cent on average for 2000 (The World Bank, 2008, p. 167, Table 7.1).[43] To an extent, there are preferable regional modes concerning investment in agriculture. Policy makers in Asia (perhaps except in Japan and Taiwan) have often shown a tendency rather in favour of high-tech manufacturing, in comparison to agriculture and rural development.

The observations mentioned above fit well with the World Bank distinction (World Bank, 2008) between the 'agriculture based', the 'transforming' and the 'urbanized' worlds of agricultural development in developing countries. This distinction, by taking into account the factors in relation to the level of development, natural endowments, population density and regional characters combined, does indicate useful categories and policy implications. However, the richness and diversity of development paths go beyond this relatively broad distinction.

Choice and creation of technology, and co-evolution between technology and institutions

Characteristics of technological regime, chosen for or created in the sector, make a significant impact on the unique strengths or weaknesses of a certain sector, which is a result of the co-evolution between technology and institutions of the sector. Consider the cases of coffee in Costa Rica and soybeans in Brazil. Both have based their competitiveness on their capability in creating novelty and at the productivity frontier, in gourmet coffee in Costa Rica and in soybeans in Brazil.

In terms of choice and creation of technology, adopting wet processing at the beginning and then breeding new varieties have been important for the sector in Costa Rica. And for Brazil, the technological innovation regarding varieties – directed to biological nitrogen fixing; and the introduction and adaptation of plantation techniques – including the biannual crop system combining soybean and wheat; and soil correction technology – which employs calcium to alter the soil composition so as to be suitable for the varieties, have all been crucial.

In spite of this, the two sectors passed rather distinctive processes that were cast by their respectively unique systems' evolution which their technological strengths refined and materialized into economic value. In terms of actor structure of the systems, Brazil evolved a structure where large and integrated agribusiness enterprises were dominant. The big agribusiness enterprises are becoming the most important bases for exploring the synergy effect; they are also the major hubs for linking the business sector with the public R&D centres. In comparison, Costa Rica has smallholder farms dominating the coffee sector; meanwhile wet processing tends to prefer relatively concentrated processing plants (*beneficios*). Wet processing requires precise technical procedures and high-quality coffee cherries for processing, hence the manner of harvesting is to handpick only ripe cherries rather than that prevailing in many other coffee producers where harvesting is carried out in an industrial and less discerning style. 'Thick' social networks, with the spirit of agrarian democracy, support the close interaction of the system, and policies have to deal with the problem of power imbalances between concentrated processers and the small coffee planters. Policies in Costa Rica have also more actively involved R&D and extension services: the boundary between public and private goods is conditioned by, among other factors, the structure of a sector.

Furthermore, there are differences between the Brazilian and Costa Rican cases in terms of market structure. Brazil took part in the booming international bulk soybean market, changing from a relatively negligible player to become the second largest exporter in the world after the United States. In comparison, the way in which Costa Rica followed was to move into high-value niches of the coffee market. We should accept that there are many paths, market opportunities and institutional settings possible to lead a country moving towards improvement in productivity and competitiveness in the agro-food sector.

To sum up, the particular history and current status of the broad catching-up process of the respective countries, the intrinsic co-evolution between technology and institutions of a sector, together with the richness and diversity in geographical conditions, biological resources and consumption traditions are among the reasons for the much greater potential for the agro-food sector to evolve along its many characteristic paths. These factors even offer the potential in which a new 'technological trajectory' (Dosi, 1988) can be created in a developing country, which as a whole remains in catching up. The Brazilian biological nitrogen fixing technology may be understood as a new technological trajectory for soybeans. It is a non-GM (genetically modified) technological trajectory, produces high yields, and employs fewer fertilizers; it has advantages over the dominant technology which is used in another leader of the sector (the United States) and relies on a GM technological trajectory. With the advantages of a superior technological trajectory, Brazil has moved quickly to enter the emerging international market and has consolidated its competitive position in a short period of time.

6.6.2   Demand as a Powerful Driver and the Relation between Domestic and International Marketing

Opportunities for the development of the agro-food sector come from dynamic new demands, consumers' (and producers') concerns about food security and safety and environmental protection, the advances of technology, and from entrepreneurship and proactive government policies that push for technological and institutional changes. Agriculture shows great dynamics for development, so it should no longer be considered a passive sector.

The scenario in relative strength or competitiveness in the agro-food sector changes over time along with the dynamic evolution. One sees that Nigeria overtook Brazil to become the largest producer of cassava. Brazil reduced its cassava production while increasing soybean production almost to the same level as the USA. China, as the original cultivator and producer of soybeans, has been stagnant in this sector, but is growing fast in vegetables so that China is now becoming the largest and most competitive producer in vegetables. Costa Rica is enjoying the opportunity provided by the speciality coffee niche market.

Demand as a powerful driver
Demand has been one of the most powerful drivers; it can come mainly from domestic needs which is the case for cassava in Nigeria and vegetables in China. The population growth that increased the demand for foodstuffs is common to the two cases. Recently the Presidential Initiative on Cassava Production and Export (PICPE, 2004) of Nigeria has assigned more roles to cassava, encouraging its use as livestock feed and an industrial raw material and with significant exports as well. As an 'agriculture based' country, the initiative of Nigeria may have implied an important departure in development strategy, by the awareness of the importance of agriculture in sustainable social and economic development. And in the case of China, in addition to the population increase and urbanization, an increase in income has also contributed to the demand for vegetables which have higher income elasticity (compared with cereals), driving the vegetable sector to become the fastest-growing segment in the agro-food industry in terms of both quantity and quality.

Demand can come from the international market as well. The opening of new markets, like those in China and India, has been a major driver for soybean export from Brazil. Brazil increased its production from 24 million tons, accounting for 19 per cent of the world total in 1995/1996 to 61 million tons and 28 per cent of the world total in 2007/2008. The 25.4 million tons of exports of soybeans from Brazil in 2006/7 explains that most of the increase in production in Brazil was driven by external demand; this made Brazil become the second largest exporter of soybeans from being a minor player during a period of just ten years.[44]

External demand that serves as a trigger to the coffee sector in Costa Rica took a slightly different path. It resulted from the restructuring of the coffee value chain which has taken place since the late 1990s. International organizations, such as the International Coffee Organization (ICO) and the Food and Agriculture Organization of the United Nations, initiated or coordinated the restructuring of the sector, in response to the coffee price crisis of the 1990s, which reached its peak in 2002. Differentiation of production to cope with the change in consumption patterns, was among the means for the restructuring. To satisfy the tastes of the consumers at the high-price end, the niches for specialization-based coffees, such as certified, organic, or gourmet/speciality coffees, began being recognized in international trade deals. And Costa Rica, by seizing this opportunity, is moving up towards the higher value edge, based on its accumulated high-quality strengths.

Marketing orientation: domestic versus international, and their relation
Trading partnerships formed over many years have meant that the coffee sector in Costa Rica has remained oriented to the international market. More generally, as mentioned, natural endowments, the size of population, and the productivity of the agriculture sector together determine whether a certain country tends to be a net agriculture exporter or a net importer. Among the four countries the study covers, Brazil is the richest in natural endowment in terms of per capita arable land (cultivated and potential) and has high productivity in the agro-food sector. This explains why Brazil, as a latecomer, has had great momentum in its emergence and fast growth in the international soybean market when the opportunity has been given to it. The same factors also explain why the vegetable and cassava sectors in China and Nigeria are basically domestic demand-oriented.

The distinction of an agro-food sector as international market-oriented or domestic market-oriented is a rather vague one, according to the evidence presented in the study. The soybean sector in Brazil had long been domestic market-oriented until the 1990s, and now around 60 per cent of the output of the sector is consumed domestically, even though a large part of the domestic consumption was and is used for animal feed to produce meat and dairy products which have been the traditional agricultural exports from Brazil. The traditional exporting coffee sector in Costa Rica now has one fifth of the total product consumed domestically by local people who are enjoying a higher standard of living, but meanwhile part of the domestically consumed coffees are consumed or bought by coffee tourists, which is actually an indirect export in a sense. The vegetable sector of China has been increasing to meet the needs from the domestic market. However, it became competitive in the external market, especially over Japan, after the sector grew and consolidated in the process of satisfying domestic consumers. On the other hand, the tough standards that were set up by Japan when China started exporting, frustrated Chinese exporters. This in turn became a trigger for the improvement in quality control of the sector.

Altogether, the study demonstrates that catering for the external market and the domestic market is increasingly mixed now. Policies need to consider how to combine the two orientations so as to attain the complementary effects of deepening and expanding value activity and networking. Simply pursuing agricultural exports for the sake of exporting performance is misleading. And as the 2008 food price crisis has warned, food security has to be one of the highest priorities in development policies especially for populous developing countries, which is basically domestic needs-oriented.

6.6.3 The Importance of Institutions

Development of market institutions
Institutions involve rules, norms and routines with which a system's actors make decisions and operate in connection with the rest of the system. One of the most interesting observations in the study is the importance of the development of market institutions. Market development has been underpinning the rapid emergence of the vegetable sector in China in the context of a double transformation: the transformation of the economic regime by and large and the transformation of the agriculture sector in particular.

There were many participants involved in this development. Wholesalers and their networking have been central in the development of market institutions in the case of China. Local authorities contributed to the necessary physical investment and managerial capacity for the construction of key wholesale centres, given that wholesale markets require certain managerial capacity and physical conditions such as sheltered space, and transaction and storage facilities. Villagers collectively opened relatively smaller and nearby wholesale spots. The Ministry of Agriculture played a role in the field of regulatory and certification services, and by 1995 it began providing information services on prices and supply–demand status based upon data from key wholesale centres; the information is delivered electronically on a daily basis. This made the sector connected nationwide by the mid-1990s. Mediated by the market system, the vegetable sector in

China now embraces activities by dozens of millions of vegetable plant-ers, thousands of millions of vegetable consumers, and a large number of specialized venders and blockers.

In addition to the transaction and distribution functions, the market system can play a role in quality monitoring. Recently the wholesale centres in China have been assigned to work for quality control in response to the criticisms about unstable vegetable quality. For this reason, the wholesalers have to improve their information capabilities and cooperate with testing and standardization agencies.

Governance of the market

Markets never operate in a vacuum, nor do they stand as 'perfectly com-petitive'. The governance of the market concerns how the rules are devel-oped, the prices formulated and where incentives are directed; these are dependent on, among other factors, the power relation between the actors and regulatory efforts. Relevant to our study is the weakness of small-holder producers in the market place compared to their large and powerful partners in the value chain.

The experience in Costa Rica is informative in this regard. One mecha-nism for dealing with the smallholder problem was a regulatory way. The government agency, Institute for the Costa Rica Coffee (IDECAFE) was created in 1933, and one of its objectives was to regulate prices in order to balance the distribution of benefits between large mills and small coffee growers. This was a result of many social conflicts occurring in the 1920s and 1930s, in which small farmers were struggling against power-ful processing mills' joint action in price setting. A second mechanism is changing the power relation by encouraging the formation of small growers' cooperatives which started in the 1960s. With the cooperatives' enhanced capacity some vertical integration appeared, and their activi-ties expanded into milling and marketing from the previous activity of merely coffee plantation. Small farmers also enhanced their negotiation position, so that now the mills have to compete to get their input from the growers.

The development of market institutions entails enormous physical, reg-ulatory, managerial and knowledge input, takes time, and grows through learning and social interaction. The market institutions in China, though impressive in their speed of development, remain weak in many aspects. The distributional effect is still low, and, more profoundly, pricing is to an extent formed arbitrarily with small producers squeezed to the lowest margins of profit. For the agro-food sector, the governance issue of the market is crucial to balance the relationship among actors who often have different strengths, for the sake of sustaining its development.

Long or short value chains, thick or thin social networks

Interactions or links of a sectoral system depend on learning dynamics. Relatively well-developed sectors have links established more broadly and deeply, while emerging sectors are often characterized by restricted engagement in some areas of the value activity and thinner underlying social networks which are yet to be cultivated. The development of market institutions facilitates the participation of producers and consumers in an emerging sector, and has vast significance for forming and strengthening links so that the sector is given further impetus for growth, as illustrated in the case of vegetables in China. Emerging sectors, if they are to stay alive and grow successfully, require certain basic preconditions; transportation and electricity supply are among the conditions, as shown in the Nigerian cassava case.

Food processing has great capacity for stretching the chains longer and deeper, and so does the development of the economic use of by-products from processing. The coffee sector in Costa Rica is now moving into coffee roasting, and Brazil has been active in making use of by-products from soybean processing. In certain cases the nature of the product leads to the engagement in processing even in the emerging period of the sector, as is shown in the cassava case in Nigeria. The capacity for cassava processing is an indispensable part of the commercial development of the sector, because cassava roots are perishable, can deteriorate within two or three days after harvesting, and the roots contain a toxic ingredient which has to be reduced to a level for safe consumption. There is no choice but to sell cassava as a processed product for either foodstuffs or industrial materials if the consumption is to take place some distance away from the cropping field. The processing of cassava will become crucial in Nigeria if the ambitious 2004 Presidential Initiative on Cassava Production and Export is to become operational.

The characteristics of the technology impact on the evolution of social networks. The choice of wet processing technologies in the coffee sector in Costa Rica provides evidence of this. This choice lends impetus to quality care. Thereupon handpicking for harvesting, improvement in transportation, careful management of processing, exchange and agreement between grower and miller, have all been pushed ahead, and this has led to, and in turn has been backed up by, a coffee elite composed thick social network.

Linkages and learning dynamics can be strengthened further through diversification by means of complementing related but distinct value chains. Brazil's soybean sector integrated the chains of soy–oil and soy–animal feed, both with raw soybeans as input. This might explain the capacity of the sector in multiplying added value and in creating many potential intermediate and final products.

6.6.4   Knowledge Base undergoing Rapid Change

One of the most impressive findings from the study is that knowledge bases in the agro-food sector have been undergoing rapid change in recent decades, along with fast technological advances and increasingly intense interplay among scientific communities around the world. Biotechnology, that is the knowledge, tools and methods developed in it, has been broadly employed mainly in the creation of new varieties, facilitating the pace of agricultural 'product' innovation faster than ever before. Also used broadly are technologies for food processing, information technologies for marketing, and knowledge and technologies for quality monitoring and green and environmentally-friendly production.

Three modes in modernization and strengthening of the agro-food knowledge base

Three modes in the modernization and strengthening of the agro-food knowledge base are observed in the study; they match primarily with the 'three agricultural worlds'.

The first mode, which is observed in the cassava case of Nigeria, shows the leadership of international R&D. It can be called the *international R&D-led mode*. One of the most influential international institutions, the International Institute of Tropical Agriculture (IITA), located in Ibadan, Nigeria and belonging to the Consultative Group on International Agricultural Research (CGIAR) family, contributed to the development of a number of new cassava varieties including the famous TMS varieties, which have the advantages of higher root yield and tolerance of major pests. International extension programmes also played significant roles in the extension of new varieties, as did international financial support for the extensions.

The division of labour for domestic R&D has thus far been that domestic S&T personnel and R&D organizations have cooperated with their international counterparts in providing the capability for the extension of improved cassava varieties that international R&D created. Recently, with the strategic initiative for cassava, the institutional construction of domestic R&D is being facilitated, which includes R&D centres under the Federal Department of Agricultural Sciences and in federal and state universities. Some of the centres, such as the National Root Crops Research Institute (NRCRI) and Umudike, now pursue rather comprehensive R&D objectives. Institutions for the extension and financing of agricultural technology are also in development.

A second mode of transformation of the knowledge base is shown in the vegetable sector in China. China's experience is characterized by a reliance on externally introduced technologies, especially new varieties, on the one hand, and intensive local adaptation and R&D capability-building in parallel to the introduction, on the other. It is a *rapid introduction–adaptation mode*, along with rapid structural change of agricultural production. Multinational companies, either directly through sales of their subsidiaries opened in China, or indirectly through local seed agencies' importation and distribution, have thus far supplied the lion's share of new varieties of vegetables. Local agricultural R&D centres have played a role in selection of imported varieties regarding their suitability for local conditions. Meanwhile plantation skills that peasants had built up over generations laid the foundations for the successes in employing imported seeds in production.

The effort in China towards the establishment of a bio-agricultural R&D infrastructure for vegetables has led to the system now becoming operational, which has taken some two decades. The fact that China lagged behind international suppliers in seed breeding has been a trigger for the decision to improve the knowledge base, which (compared with cereals) was not a priority before the 1980s. A system of R&D institutions for vegetables and flowers is being developed embracing dozens of R&D centres at the central and provincial academies of agricultural science and some more centres or branches specialized in vegetables at the lower municipal/city levels. Furthermore, a number of vegetable and gardening departments established or strengthened in agricultural universities, and a number of research centres more generally on life sciences have been created or improved in the prestigious Chinese Academy of Sciences and in top comprehensive universities.

A third mode is demonstrated in the Costa Rica coffee case and the Brazil soybean case, where biotechnology-centred knowledge bases have entered a relatively mature stage, being able to create speciality varieties and services or develop new technological trajectories. This can be understood as the *competitive and creative mode*.

Both Costa Rica and Brazil have established rather modern bioscience and biotechnology infrastructures since the 1970s, and have developed institutions for financing and extension services. They also developed complementary industries and capabilities in processing, machinery, chemicals and so on. Now the Brazilian public agriculture R&D corporate EMBRAPA (Brazilian Enterprise for Agricultural Research, started in 1973) is becoming one of the world's top knowledge centres in agricultural biotechnology, contributing to the creation of non-GM varieties of soybean employed in Brazil, which have the advantages of high yields and low fertilizers use, and which are responsible for Brazil's distinct competitiveness in soybean. The Costa Rica Coffee Research Centre (CICAFE), created in 1977, has contributed to the coffee sector with new varieties, organic coffee-growing and environmentally-friendly coffee processing technologies.

Investment in agricultural R&D that has been maintained in Brazil and Costa Rica has been at a much higher level than the average for Asia and Africa, which has been a factor responsible for their strengths in their respective knowledge bases. International academic exchange has also played a role for the creative dynamics of Brazil and Costa Rica. The Brazilian and Costa Rican governments, continued for decades to subsidize advanced education and training abroad; some dozens of those who were trained in the United States thirty years ago are now leading scholars at EMBRAPA. Their strengths may also come from the tradition in agriculture exporting that brought about strong incentives to compete for opportunities opening in emerging markets or in differentiated niches.

The role of traditional knowledge
Traditional knowledge is the knowledge accumulated based on long-term experience. Farmers make up one of the richest pools of traditional knowledge. Everywhere farmers' knowledge about the soil, water, ecosystem of the particular locus of where they live, and their skills in planting, has been an important basis for the implementation of new varieties in the field.

Traditional knowledge-based innovation – that is, farmers' innovation – has contributed to a considerable extent to the vegetable sector in China. The example of this is a kind of simple, cheap and effective greenhouse that appeared in the late 1980s as a result of a determined effort of a group of farmers. This greenhouse has a thick soil wall on the north side to protect vegetables from the cold wind and a transparent roof that opens in daytime and is covered with a straw shade in the night. The greenhouse enables fresh vegetables to be grown in winter time without the use of fuel (coal) for heating. This innovation, rather than those more scientifically designed which were mainly imported, was soon widely adopted in the mid-China provinces.

Similarly, in Nigeria, it is observed that cassava grating machines were often made by semi-educated, determined young men and women who needed to make a living from this work. The processes they created were easy, convenient, cost effective and sustainable. Also, by and large, the processing technologies developed by government agencies in Nigeria have achieved limited adoption (Adegboye and Akinwumi, 1990).

To cope with the rapid transformation and strengthening of knowledge bases in the agro-food sector, the exploration and renovation of traditional knowledge will provide great potential. What can be seen from the observations in the study is that first, formal R&D needs to communicate with traditional knowledge where it provides not only valuable techniques and wisdom, but also rich information about the conditions and foundations for the applicability of scientifically developed technologies. Second, improvement of rural education will enable practising farmers to better perceive, create, summarize and employ both traditional and modern knowledge. Costa Rica is probably the best provider of universal compulsory education of the case countries, which explains the active role of coffee growers and their cooperatives as an important foundation for the good performance of the coffee sector.

6.6.5 The Role of Government Policies

Addressing the missing factors and institutions, and changing public–private partnership

Government policies play very important roles in the agro-food sector. According to the observations the study developed, catching up of the sectors is a very complicated process, in which the most important attributes have been the creation and renewal of institutions, factors and capabilities which were previously non-existent or weak and laggard. Development spaces could only be opened by continuous efforts in the creation and renovation of the factors, institutions and capabilities. Therefore it is useful to state that the role of policies should be to 'address missing factors, institutions and capabilities' rather than to follow the conventional divide between public goods and private goods in which policies are assigned to take care of public goods provision. With this understanding, we need not only policies in regulatory and infrastructure services of a typical public goods nature, but also policies for missing factor creation, which are often related to 'direct' involvement and in a rather ad hoc manner.

Policies that directly involve the creation of factors and capabilities appear in the Nigerian case where some state government grants are lending to a key processing company for the sustainable supply of cassava. The state government is also becoming a commercial partner of the company with an equity share for which it will make a capital investment in the company to renew its equipment. This seems unavoidable in the context of the case studied where the company lacks the most primary factors for its operation and the financial institutions might remain incapable or reluctant to give loans of this kind that would involve a high risk. Similar cases are seen in Costa Rica but appeared much earlier (some two hundred years ago) when the government gave land and coffee trees for the birth of the coffee sector in the first place. To a lesser extent, such grants or subsidies were made to the vegetable sector in addition to the local government-offered subsidies to farmers who agreed to turn to vegetable production.

Institutional development, a key area of public policy, is observed as costly not only in regulatory construction but also in terms of investment in physical facilities. The vegetable case in China shows enormous involvement by a mix of public and private partners into the set-up of wholesale centres of vegetables, which afterwards were mostly privatized as the wholesale centres accumulated wealth, and private sources became more readily available.

Scientific and technological infrastructure has conventionally been the realm of public policy, and it has remained so for developing countries, by and large. However, in Brazil, with the growth of agribusiness companies, the private sector has been comparable in the creation of new varieties of soybeans (Pardey et al., 2002). In contrast, in Costa Rica, public R&D remains the dominant contributor in the development of new varieties for the coffee sector. Once again, the difference can be seen in specific contexts. The presence of large agribusiness companies in Brazil explains the role of the private sector, while the coffee sector in Costa Rica has achieved a similar high performance although it has been based on small growers and is largely supported by public S&T services.

A public–private mixture in the provision of agricultural extension services has developed in Brazil and to a less extent in China, and perhaps in Costa Rica as well. The reason for this is partly the trend in which new seed varieties increasingly contain 'packaged' knowledge which is tradable in the market place, and partly that private companies, especially multi-national seed companies, adopt a strategy in which they provide extension services as part of their aggressive marketing.

To sum up, we have seen that the means and focuses of public policy are rather context- and subject-specific in addressing missing factors, capabilities and institutions. Also the public–private relations in handling various problems regarding weaknesses in factors, institutions and capabilities, including knowledge infrastructure and extension services, become rather intertwined in various ways. All these provide great challenges to the formation and implementation of policies for the sector.

Responsive versus proactive policies

Responsive policies are observed in the vegetable case in China. Policy is adjusted in response to bottlenecks and impediments revealed over time, hence there has been a stage-wise movement in the objectives and means of policies: the construction of production and consumption links for vegetables surrounding selected large cities; the expansion and networking of the segmented regions to become a nationwide system; and the pursuit of a safe and quality supply of vegetables, respectively in different stages. The merits of responsive policies are that concrete information can be directed to the problem areas; hence, policy objectives and means can be focused towards handling the problems.

The Presidential Initiative on Cassava Production and Export (PICPE) of Nigeria, officially announced in 2004, is an example of a proactive policy. The initiative has set the ambitious goal of raising the production level of cassava to 150 million tons by 2010 from around 40 million tons in 2004. It thereby intends to deepen the cassava cropping and processing system by assigning the roles for the sector as a springboard for the structural and capability upgrading of the Nigerian economy and for a diversification of the export structure. Even though Nigeria's sector has enjoyed fast growth for decades, the initiative nevertheless implies a departure (initiated for a 'discontinuous' development) from the previous path in terms of quantity (much faster in output increase), and quality (entering into processing and many industrial usages).

The Second National Development Plan (II PND) of Brazil (for the period of 1974 to 1980) might be seen as another example of a proactive policy. The plan was aimed at oil production and substitution (the alcohol-as-fuel programme), in response to the first oil crisis. The establishment of EMBRAPA – the most important R&D centre for bio-science and biotechnology now in Brazil – was part of the initiative as a scientific and technological back-up. As a result, Brazil enhanced its institutional basis for agricultural biotechnology research, not only on sugarcane, which is the biological raw material for fuel alcohol production as a substitute for fossil oil, but also on soybean and other agricultural products.

In contrast to responsive policies, proactive policies look forward to a long-term development with a strategic vision, and these initiatives entail higher risks at the same time. In the case of the Brazilian II PND, the strategic vision has been in the exploration of Brazil's rich biological resources to overcome the relative shortage of fossil oil in the country. The strategic vision of proactive policies helps the necessary long-term efforts even when there might be instant difficulties and interruptions. For example, it took the II PND several decades to achieve the important consequences; and among the consequences the agribusiness and the sugarcane-based fuel industry are now the industries that are 'ready to go'. The two angles, the responsive and the proactive, are both useful. Combining the merits of both would improve policy making.

6.7 CONCLUSIONS

- *The agro-food sector in developing countries has shown unprecedented dynamics in recent decades.*

Population increase, worldwide economic booms especially in emerging economies, demanding consumers with their considera- tion for food safety and the environment, advances in technologies, especially biotechnology, intensifying academic exchange, and liber- alization of agricultural markets, all contributed to the rapid growth and structural transformation of the agro-food sector.

- *The developments of the agro-food sector show great diversity in paths and patterns.*

The boom segments range from a staple crop (cassava), a non-staple while basic foodstuff for daily meals (vegetables), to commercial commodities massively traded in the international markets (soy- beans and coffee). The vastly diverse history and current status of development levels are important attributing factors; this indicates that the growth and modernization of the agro-food sector is to be analysed against the broad catching-up background of certain countries.

In spite of this, the characteristics of the technology that is employed and its co-evolution with institutions cast trajectories of development intrinsic and unique to each agro-food sector. The richness in geographical conditions, the biodiversity, and the involvement of consumers, who have so many preferences, together may expand even further the potential in many paths and patterns. With all these factors, the creation of a new technological trajec- tory is not impossible even in a catching-up country; the Brazilian non-GM nitrogen-fixing technology for soybeans exemplified this possibility.

- *Institutions matter, especially for developing countries that open space for actors to operate with each other and facilitate the formation of links.*

Of the cases studied, we observe that the development of market institutions for the vegetable sector in economic transition in China entailed comprehensive regulatory, managerial and technological efforts, and physical investment.

The value chain structure of a sector embodies, to a large extent, the quality and intensity of interaction and learning dynamics of a sectoral system. With the cases we are able to distinguish 'long' or 'short' value chains and thick or shallow social networks that charac- terize the nature of linkages. An engagement in food processing, and the extension of input–output, or complementary activities among and between value chains, are positively related to higher levels of interactive learning and dynamics in growth and effectiveness.

- *The knowledge base of the agro-food sectors is experiencing rapid change.*

Modern biotechnology, among other technologies, has been employed broadly in developing countries, mostly for the facilitation of breeding new varieties. The so-called 'old' and 'traditional' agro-food sector should no longer be considered as a traditional or low-technology sector even in least developed countries.

The ways in which the agro-food sectors modernize and strengthen their knowledge bases differ, according to the observations in the study. We distinguish between 'international R&D-led mode', 'rapid introduction and adaptation mode', and 'competitive and creative mode', as demonstrated in the respective cases. Traditional knowledge played an important role in all the cases. We suggest that agro-food policies should focus on to the exploration and renovation of traditional knowledge.

- *The role of government policy proved in the study is very important.*

We observe that the focus and means of policies for the agro-food sector have to be subject-specific and adjusted over time. In the context of developing countries, policies may have to be involved in the creation of missing factors and capabilities – functions that in mature sectors are assumed by private sectors. Meanwhile, evidence shows a recent tendency for some conventional public functions such as R&D and extension services to be provided by various public–private partnerships. These changes make up the challenges to policy capacity in developing countries.

We observe responsive policies and proactive policies for the agro-food sector, and we have explored the merits of the two lines of policies. We suggest that both these perspectives of policy making are employed. A strategic vision with regard to the agro-food sector that underpins proactive policies may have particular importance now, provided that the agro-food sector increasingly bears the impact for economic, societal and environmental sustainability. We are living at a time when human beings are facing the most critical problems such as population explosion, depletion of resources, and environment crisis. In all these problems the agriculture sector has a central role to play.

- *The analytical approach of sectoral innovation systems employed in the study has proved productive and informative.*

With a perspective of focusing on the specificities of a sector, the SIS approach is rewarding in the scrutiny of particular details. The analysis of the driving forces clearly indicated the type and feature of opportunities; they are unique to the agro-food sector. The analysis of the transformation of the knowledge base is very illuminating. It shows several modes for the transformation and strengthening of the knowledge base, and overall the analysis indicated that the conventional notion about the sector should be changed, that is the sector should no longer be considered as 'traditional'. The exploration of linkages and knowledge flows uncovered important information about the structure and dynamics of the sectors, which extend beyond national boundaries. All these findings have made our understanding of the agro-food sector much more precise, and they contain useful policy implications that are specifically relevant to the sector.

We chose some representative products – cassava for Nigeria, vegetables for China, coffee for Costa Rica and soybeans for Brazil – as the analytical unit for the study of the agro-food sector. This design has proved appropriate, given that the agro-food sector is composed of many different segments.

NOTES

1. Nigeria produces a third more than Brazil and almost double the production of Indonesia and Thailand. Cassava production in other African countries, such as the Democratic Republic of the Congo, Ghana, Madagascar, Mozambique, Tanzania and Uganda appears to be on a very minor scale (Phillips et al., 2004).
2. 'Processing of roots and tubers', available at the FAO website: http://www.fao.org/docrep/X5415E/x5415e05.htm#TopOfPage.
3. Nweke et al. (2001) identified four stages in the evolution of the cassava agro-industry in Africa: as famine reserve crop; as rural food staple; as cash crop for urban consumption; and as livestock feed and industrial raw material. In Nigeria cassava has never served as a famine reserve crop.
4. This census has usually been considered an undercount; it nevertheless has generally been seen as less problematic than any of its successors. Source: http://www.country-studies.com/nigeria/census-history.html.
5. The TMS (Tropical Manioc Selection) cassava is high yielding, early bulking and disease resistant. For example, Nweke (2004) reported that the TMS variety boosted the cassava yield by 40 per cent with no fertilizer application.
6. It has been estimated that a reduction in wheat flour imports of 15 per cent through substituting cassava flour could save Nigeria US$14.8 million per annum in foreign exchange. The net return to processors from this saving would be in the region of

US$12.7 million and cassava farmers could expect to receive a gross benefit of US$4.2 million (Nweke et al., 2001).

7. The Nigerian new democratic government launched an economic reform programme tagged NEEDS (National Economic Empowerment and Development Strategy) in March 2004. The implementation of NEEDS was known to have actually started in 2003 (Adeoti, 2006).

8. Cassava initiatives in Nigeria (2005). Source: http://www.nigeriafirst.org/article_4301.shtml.

9. Begun in the 1980s, this 'temporary' migrant labour force increased over the years. About 100 million of them came to urban areas by the first decade of the twenty-first century. Many of them kept their family members in their village homes and left the land for their family members or other contractual planters. We put them into the category of the population as requiring commercial provision of foodstuffs.

10. Data source: FAO: Statistical Yearbook 2005–2006, table B3.

11. Xinhua News Agency: 'vegetable basket' Project memorabilia, released 24 July 2002: see http://www.cctv.com.cn/news/china/20020724/132.html.

12. See http://www.agri.gov.cn/pfsc/.

13. See: (1) WEN Jiabao: Speech to the National Working Meeting on Vegetable Basket Project, 23 July 2002, Xinhua News Agent reports 18 August 2002 at http://news.xinhuanet.com/newscenter/2002-08/18/content_528865.htm and (2) State Council: Requisition on Advancing the Vegetable Basket Project, 19 August 2002, see: http://www.people.com.cn/GB/paper464/7025/681240.html.

14. Source: http://www.agri.gov.cn/dfxxlb/cqxxlb/t20070109_753495.htm.

15. See www.chinagate.com.cn.

16. The vegetable blocker population is the author's estimation based on scattered reports. Roughly one blocker deals with the vegetable output of 500 MU (slightly more than 30 Hectares).

17. Consumers are mainly domestic. Exports grew when the sector because stronger. Japan has been one of the major destinations for exports and ShanDong the biggest exporter of vegetables to Japan. The heightening food security standards, set out by Japan, the European Union and the United States, lifted the non-tariff barrier, which was an element pushed for quality and safety production of the sector too. Refer to *The Economic Observer* (in Chinese: jingji guancha), 19 June 2002.

18. The author's field survey revealed that about 80 per cent of seeds sold in ShouGuang were from foreign companies. A report confirms this estimation for ShouGuang (People's Daily of ShouGuang, 27 March 2007). At the national aggregate, the share of multinational companies in the vegetable seed market is reportedly above 50 per cent (Huang Gang 2006: Newsletter on Work in the Rural Areas, Issue No. 449, May 30 2006). Being vice-president of the Academy of Agriculture of SiChuan Province, Huang's estimation should have credibility. Multinational companies dominate the superior and high quality end of the seed market. By 2005, 70 foreign companies had entered China's vegetable seed market. The size of the overall seed market is estimated at 100 billion yuan or more; a not insignificant share of it is for vegetables (ibid.).

19. For the Research Institute of Vegetables and Flowers at the Chinese Academy of Agriculture Science, see http://www.ivfcaas.ac.cn/ENGLISH/index.asp.

20. See the Chinacourt website: http://www.chinacourt.org/flwk/show1.php?file_id=109820.

21. The Seed Industry Association of Shanghai provides a detailed analysis at http://www.snhx.org.cn/zhongzi/hydt/t20040720_105988.htm.

22. Costa Rica has a population of 4 133 884. The combined white and mestizo groups constitute 94 per cent of the population. In the official Costa Rican census the whites and mestizos are combined in one category; hence no exact breakdown is available. See http://en.wikipedia.org/wiki/Costa_Rica#Demographics.

23. See also the official web overview in: History of Costa Rica: http://www.infocostarica.com/history/history.html.

24. See 'coffee' at http://en.wikipedia.org/wiki/Coffee#cite_note-tap-0.

25. See http://en.wikipedia.org/wiki/Coffee_processing#Processing.
26. Source: see http://www.aboutcoffee.net/2008/10/history-of-gourmet-coffee-in-costa-rica.html, written by Mission Grounds Gourmet Coffee.
27. See the UNCTAD/WTO International trade centre website, at http://www.intracen.org/mds/coffee_gourmet_report.htm.
28. See Starbucks home page at http://www.starbucks.com/ where gourmet coffee produced in Costa Rica is in the list.
29. Refer to one of the official home pages of Costa Rica at http://www.costaricapages.com/blog/business/economy-in-a-nutshell/661.
30. The Doka Estate Coffee Plantation located in San Luis de Sabanilla de Alajuela has reportedly up to 100 visitors a day. Of the highest quality beans they produce, 70 per cent is exported to the United States, 15 per cent to Japan and 5 per cent to Europe. The majority of the exports to the United States are sold to Starbucks where they are toasted and sold under the company's name. The remaining 10 per cent is toasted locally and is sold in tourist destinations under the Doka 'Tres Generaciones' name. See the 'Costa Rica' page at http://www.costaricapages.com/blog/press-releases/doka-estate-coffee/600.
31. Ana Castro wishes to thank Dr Monica Desiderio (PPED/IE/UFRJ; INCT in Innovation in Neglected Diseases and INCT-PPED) for the inestimable help in the development of this Brazilian soybean sector case.
32. See FIBGE, www.ibge.gov.br.
33. CONAB – Companhia Nacional de Abastecimento, Serviço de Previsão de Safras, www.conab.gov.br.
34. The Green Revolution depends on the introduction of new seeds and plants, necessarily adapted to the environmental conditions of tropical and subtropical agriculture. The corn seeds coming from the USA could not be grown in Brazil because of the hotter climate, unless they were adapted to local conditions. In short, the pre-condition was the existence of a research background.
35. The introduction of hybrid corn in Brazil was possible after an exchange programme abroad, when Antonio Secundino de São José, at the time teaching at the University of Viçosa, Minas Gerais, went to Purdue University and brought back to Brazil some Mexican maize strains. These gave birth to the first commercial crops of the Sementes Agroceres SA, the enterprise founded in association with Rockefeller and a group of University geneticists, in 1945. See Castro (1988).
36. The foundation of EMBRAPA in 1973 gave an unprecedented impulse to the national agriculture and livestock research system, which had in that time already composed a number of research institutes including the Instituto Agronômico de Campinas (Campinas Institute of Agronomics) established at the end of the nineteenth century, the IAPAR (Paraná) in the 1930s, and the Agronômico de Pernambuco (Pernambuco Agronomic). There was also the IAA (Instituto do Açúcar e do Álcool (Sugar and Alcohol Institute) as part of the DNPEA (Departamento Nacional de Pesquisa Agropecuária (National Agriculture and Livestock Research Department).
37. The correction of the soil was a local government programme, known as Operação Tatu, with the participation of the University of Wisconsin through Professor John Murdock who had coordinated the mission. See De Christensen and Bindé (2004), *Soja: 80 Anos de Produção 1924–2004* [Soybeans: 80 Years of Production 1924–2004], commemorative edition of 80 years of soybean production in Santa Rosa, promoted by the 15th Fenasoja.
38. The biological nitrogen fixing in the soil is still an important area of the biotechnological research carried out by EMBRAPA.
39. In Brazil the number of undergraduate courses related to agribusiness increased from 3 in 2000, to 100 in 2005 (Gepai/UFScar) in 'Anuário Exame, Agronegócio 2006/2007'.
40. They are, for example, Cargill, Bunge, Sadia, ADM do Brasil (Archer Daniel Merchants), Louis Dreyfus Commodities, Aracruz Celulose, Klabin, Perdigão, several cooperatives, such as Itambé, Coama and Cocamar in the seed industry, Syngenta, Monsanto, Pfizer, Agroceres.

41. Good examples are the Institute for Technological Research (IPT), the Institute of Metrology (INMETRO), the National Institute for Technology (INT), besides other private foundations organized by large agribusiness companies (Zackiewicz et al., 2005).
42. Brazilian Law of Cultivars, 1997 (Lei de Proteção de Cultivares no. 9.456/97, Decreto no. 2366/97, Regimento Interno do SNPC, Portaria no. 503/97).
43. Although for the sub-Saharan Africa group international sources have been contributing a large part of the agriculture R&D expenditure.
44. See 'Oils and fats in the market place', at http://www.lipidlibrary.co.uk/market/soybean.htm, accessed on 10 August 2008.

BIBLIOGRAPHY

Sections 6.1 and 6.6

Adegboye, R.O. and J.A. Akinwumi (1990), 'Cassava processing innovations in Nigeria', Faculty of Agricultural Economics, University of Ibadan, Nigeria.

Chandra, V. (2006), *Technology, Adaptation and Exports, how some Developing Countries got it*, Washington, DC: The World Bank.

Cusmano, L., A. Morrison, and R. Rabellotti (2008), 'Catching-up and sectoral systems of innovation: a comparative study on the wine sector in Chile, Italy and South Africa', paper presented at the VI GLOBELICS Conference, Mexico City, 22–24 September.

Dosi, G. (1988), 'The nature of the innovation process' in G. Dosi, C. Freeman, R.R. Nelson, G. Silverberg and L. Soete (eds), *Technical Change and Economic Theory*, London: Pinter Publishers, pp. 221–38.

FAO (2003–4), 'The state of food and agriculture 2003–2004: agricultural biotechnology, meeting the needs of the poor?', FAO.

FAO (2007), 'The state of food and agriculture: paying farmers for environmental services', FAO.

FAO, 'Special Programme for Food Security', available at http://www.fao.org/spfs/national-programmes-spfs/nationalprogrammes-food-sec-npfs/en/.

Flyvbjerg, B. (2003), *Making Social Science Matter: Why Social Inquiry Fails and how it Can Succeed Again*, New York: Cambridge University Press.

Gereffi, G. (1999), 'International trade and industrial upgrading in the apparel commodity chain', *Journal of International Economics*, **48**(1), 37–70.

Hayami, Y. and V.W. Ruttan (1971), *Agricultural Development: An International Perspective*, Baltimore, MD: Johns Hopkins Press.

Kaplinsky, R. (2000), 'Spreading the gains from globalization: what can be learned from value chain analysis?', IDS Working Paper 110, University of Sussex.

Lewis, W.A. (1954), 'Economic development with unlimited supply of labour', *The Manchester School*, **22** (2), 139–91.

Lundvall, B.-Å. (ed.) (1992), *National Systems of Innovation: Towards a Theory of Innovation and Interactive Learning*, London: Pinter Publishers.

Malerba, F. (2004), *Sectoral Systems of Innovation: Concepts, Issues and Analyses of Six Major Sectors in Europe*, Cambridge: Cambridge University Press.

Malerba, F. (2006), 'Catch-up in different sectoral systems: some introductory remarks', paper presented at the IV GLOBELICS Conference, Trivandrum, Kerala, India, 4–7 October.

Mjøset, L. (2006a), 'A case study of a case study: strategies of generalization and specification in the study of Israel as a single case', *International Sociology,* **21**(5), 735–66.

Mjøset, L. (2006b), 'Three attitudes and six notions of theory in social science', lectures presented to CICALICS Academy held in Beijing, August.

Nelson, R.R. (1993), *National Innovation Systems: A Comparative Analysis*, New York: Oxford University Press.

Nelson, R.R. (2006), 'Economic development from the perspective of evolutionary economic theory', paper provided to the 2006 Milan meeting for the Catch-up Project.

Pardey, P.G., J.M. Alston, C. Chan-Kang, E.C. Magalhães and S.A. Vosti (2002), 'Assessing and attributing the benefits from varietal improvement research: evidence from Embrapa, Brazil', EPTD Discussion Paper, Environment and Production Technology Division, International Food Policy Research Institute, Washington, DC.

Pietrobelli, C. and A. Sverrisson (2004), *Linking Local and Global Economies: The Ties that Bind*, London: Routledge.

Prebisch, R. (1959), 'Commercial policy in the underdeveloped countries', *American Economic Review*, **49**(2), 251–7.

Sisler, D.G. and E.B. Oyer (2000), 'The past as prologue to the future: 50 years of change in international agricultural development', paper presented at the International Agriculture 602 Millenium Conference on Agricultural Development in the 21st Century Cornell University, San José, Costa Rica, March.

Stokes, B. (2008), 'Food is different', *National Journal*, 7 June, available at: http://www.nationaljournal.com/njmagazine/cs_20080607_6060.php.

UNIDO (2002), 'Industrial development report 2002/2003: competing through innovation and learning', UNIDO.

von Tunzelmann, N. and V. Acha (2005), 'Innovation in "Low-Tech" Industries' in J. Fagerberg, D. Mowery and R.R. Nelson (eds), *The Oxford Handbook of Innovation*, New York: Oxford University Press, pp. 407–32.

The World Bank (2006), *Technology, Adaptation, and Exports: How Some Developing Countries got it Right*, Vandana Chandra (ed.), Washington, DC: World Bank.

The World Bank (2008), *World Development Report 2008: Agriculture for Development,* Washington, DC: The World Bank.

Cassava in Nigeria

Adegboye, R.O. and J.A. Akinwumi (1990), 'Cassava processing innovations in Nigeria', Faculty of Agricultural Economics, University of Ibadan, Nigeria.

Adeniji, A.A. (2007), 'Cassava varieties for ethanol', paper presented at the I International Ethanol and Biofuels Conference, Abuja, Nigeria, 29–30 March.

Adeoti, J.O. (2006), 'Technology foresight and economic reforms in Nigeria', manuscript for NISER's book on Reform and Development in Nigeria, NISER, Ibadan, Nigeria.

Adjebeng-Asem, S. (1990) 'Technical entrepreneurship and socio-economic development: the Nigerian experience', *Technovation*, **10**(4), 213–34.

APMEU (1997), 'IFAD cassava multiplication programme (loan no. 177 NR): borrowers', final evaluation report, Agricultural Projects Monitoring and

Evaluation Unit, Federal Ministry of Agriculture and Natural Resources, Kaduna, Nigeria.

Asher, E.A. (1980), 'Nutritional requirements of cassava', Australian Institute of Agricultural Research, Canberra, Australia.

Berry, S.S. (1993), 'Socioeconomic aspects of cassava cultivation and use in Africa: implication for the development of appropriate technology', COSCA Working Paper No. 8, Collaborative Study of Cassava in Africa, IITA, Ibadan, Nigeria.

Central Bank of Nigeria (2007), *Annual Report and Statement of Accounts 2007*, Abuja: Central Bank of Nigeria.

Cock, J.H. (1985), *Cassava: New Potential for a Neglected Crop*, Boulder, CO: Westview Press.

Fresco, L. (1986), 'Cassava in shifting cultivation: a system approach to agricultural technology development in Africa', Royal Tropical Institute, Amsterdam, The Netherlands.

Moser, G., S. Rogers and R. van Til (1997), 'Nigeria: experience with structural adjustment', Washington, DC: IMF.

National Root Crops Research Institute (1992), *Annual Report*, Umudike, Umuahia, Nigeria.

NPC (2007), *Nigeria: Draft National Economic Empowerment and Development Strategy – NEEDS2*, Abuja, Nigeria: National Planning Commission.

Nweke, F.I. (1994), 'Processing potential for cassava production growth in sub-Saharan Africa', COSCA Working Paper No. 11, Collaborative Study of Cassava in Africa, IITA, Ibadan, Nigeria.

Nweke, F. (2004), 'New challenges in the cassava transformation in Nigeria and Ghana', EPTD Discussion Paper No. 118, IFPRI, Washington, DC.

Nweke, F.I., D.S. Spencer and J.K. Lynam (2001), *The Cassava Transformation: Africa's Best Kept Secret*, East Lansing, MI: Michigan State University Press.

Ogun, O. (1995), 'Country studies: Nigeria', in S.M. Wangwe (ed.), *Exporting Africa: Technology, Trade and Industrialization in Sub-Saharan Africa*, UNU/INTECH Studies in New Technology and Development, London: Routledge.

Phillips, T.P., D.S. Taylor, L. Sanni and M.O. Akoroda (2004), 'A cassava industrial revolution in Nigeria: the potential for a new industrial crop', The Global Cassava Development Strategy/IFAD-FAO, Rome.

Stoorvogel, J.J. and L.O. Fresco (1991), 'The identification of agro-ecological zones for cassava in Africa with particular emphasis on soils', COSCA Working Paper No. 5, Collaborative Study of Cassava in Africa, IITA, Ibadan, Nigeria.

Vegetables in China

Cheng, G. (2007), 'The development of agricultural distributional system: the status, problems and policy recommendations' [woguo nongcun liutong tixi jianshe de xianzhuang, wenti yu duice], in *Hongqi Rengao*, No.10, available at: http://www.drcnet.com.cn/new_product/drcexpert1/showdoc.asp?doc_id=199150.

Gu, S. (2004), 'The role of market in transition of agricultural production and innovation system', paper presented to the II GLOBELICS Conference, Beijing, China.

Metcalfe, J.S. (1997), 'Science policy and technology policy in a competitive economy', *International Journal of Social Economics*, **24**(7/8/9), 723–40.

Metcalfe, J.S., R. Ramlogan and E. Uyarra (2003), 'Economic development and the competitive process', paper presented to the I GLOBELICS Conference, Rio, Brazil.

Nelson, R.R. (2006), 'Economic development from the perspective of evolutionary economic theory', paper presented to the 2006 Milan meeting for the Catch-up Project.

Nelson, R.R. and S.G. Winter (1982), *An Evolutionary Theory of Economic Change*, Cambridge, MA: Harvard University Press.

Orozco, J. and R. Díaz (2007), 'Evolution of the sectoral system of innovation: Costa Rican coffee sector', manuscript paper for R.R. Nelson and F. Malerba: 'Sectoral innovation systems in catch-up'.

Verspagen, B. (2005), 'Innovation and Economic Growth' in J. Fagerberg, D. Mowery and R.R. Nelson (eds), *The Oxford Handbook of Innovation*, New York: Oxford University Press, pp. 487–513.

Xu, X. (2003), 'Science and technology resources in China: current situation and problems' [zhongguo keji ziyuan de xianzhuang ji kaifa liyongzhong cunzai de wenti], *Resources Science [ziyuan kexue]*, **25**(03), 83–9.

Yu, J. (2007), 'Biotechnology research in China' in L. Jakobson (ed.), *Innovation with Chinese Characteristics: High-tech Research in China*, Basingstoke: Palgrave Macmillan.

Zhang, Q. (2004), 'The status of agricultural R&D investment and optimization of resources allocation' [nongye keyan touru xianzhuang ji youhua peizhi shexiang], *China Venture Capital and High-tech [zhongguo chuangyetouzi yu gaokeji]*, **4**, 43–7.

Coffee in Costa Rica

Acuña, V. and I. Molina (1991),'Historia económica y Social de Costa Rica (1750–1950)', San Josè: Editorial Porvenir.

CEPAL (2001), 'Aplicación de instrumentos económicos en la gestión ambiental en América Latina y el Caribe: desafiós y factores condicionantes', Serie Medio Ambiente y Desarrollo, no. 31, Santiago de Chile: CEPAL.

Chacón, Luis Roberto (1997), Estudio de Evalución del Efecto e la Implementación de Technologías Limpias de Procesamiento Sobre el Consumo de Energía Eléctrica en al Beneficio Húmedo de Café (Estudios de Casos), San José: ICAFE.

Daviron, B. (1994),'La crisis del mercado cafetalero internacional en una perspectiva de largo plazo', in M. Samper (ed.), *Crisis y Perspectivas del Café Latinoamericano*, Heredia: Convenio ICAFE-UNA.

De Graaff, J. (1986), *The Economics of Coffee*, Wageningen: Pudoc.

Díaz, R. (2003), 'A developing country perspective on policies for sustainable agribusiness chains: the Case of Costa Rica', *NICCOS*, **43**.

FAO (2003) 'Commodity and trade division: *Commodity Market Review* 2003–2004', FAO.

Gereffi, G., J. Humphrey and T. Sturgeon (2005), 'The governance of global value chains', *Review of International Political Economy*, **12**(1), 78–104.

Hallam, D. (2003), 'Falling commodity prices and industry responses: some lessons from the international coffee crisis', FAO Commodity and Trade Division: Commodity Market Review 2003–2004.

ICAFE (2007), 'Censo cafetalero: turrialba y coto brus 2003, Valle Central y Valle Central Occidental 2004, y Pérez Zeledón, Tarrazú y Zona Norte 2006

Principales resultados', Instituto Nacional de Estadística y Censos. Instituto del Café de Costa Rica, 1st edn, San José: INEC.

Kaplinsky, R. (2000), 'Spreading the gains from globalization: what can be learned from value chain analysis?', IDS Working Paper 110, University of Sussex.

Kaplinsky, R. (2006), 'Revisiting the revisited terms of trade: will China make a difference?', *World Development*, **34**(6), 981–95.

Lewin, B., D. Giovannucci and P. Varangis (2004), 'Coffee markets, new paradigms in global supply and demand', The World Bank Agriculture and Rural Development Discussion Paper No. 3.

Naranjo, C. (1999), 'La modernización de la caficultura Costarricense 1890–1930', Thesis, University of Costa Rica.

Orozco, J. and K. Ruiz (2002), 'Uso de instrumentos económicos para la gestión Ambiental', Serie Medio Ambiente y Desarrollo No. 51, Chile: CEPAL.

Osorio, N. (2002), 'The global coffee crisis: a threat to sustainable development', Submission to the World Summit on Sustainable Development, Johannesburg.

Samper, M. (1994), *Crisis y Perspectivas del Café Latinoamericano*, San José: Convenio ICAFE-UNA.

Samper, M. (2001), *La Cadena de Producción y Comercializatión del Café: Perspectiva Histórica Comparada*, Costa Rica: Progreso Editorial.

Talbot, J. (1995–96), 'Regulating the coffee commodity chain: internationalization and the coffee cartel', *Berkeley Journal of Sociology*, **40**, 112–49.

UNIDO (2002), 'Industrial Development Report 2002–3', UNIDO.

Soybeans in Brazil

Castro, A.C. (1984), 'Ciência e tecnologia para a agricultura: uma alalise dos planos de desenvolvimento', *Cadernos de Difusão de Technologia*, **1**(3), 299–482.

Castro, A.C. (1985), 'A industrialização incompleta da agricultura brasileira: a questão da heterogeneidade tecnológica', *Pensamiento Iberoamericano*, **8**, 171–212.

Castro, A.C. (1988), 'Crescimento da firma e diversificação produtiva: o caso agroceres', doctoral thesis, IE/UNICAMP.

Castro, A.B. (1993), 'Renegade development: rise and demise of state-led development in Brazil', in W.C. Smith, C.H. Acuna, and E.A. Gamarra (eds), *Democracy, Markets, and Structural Reform in Latin America: Argentina, Bolivia, Brazil, Chile, and Mexico*, Miami: Transaction Publishers, pp. 183–213.

Castro, A.C. (1995), *Estudo da Competitividade da Indústria Brasileira: O Caso da Indústria de Óleos Vegetais*, Rio de Janeiro: Forense Universitária.

Castro, A.C. (1997), 'Agribusiness Brasileiro e o papel do sistema de transportes intermodal', in F.C. Teixeira da Silva, R. Santos and L.F.C. Costa (eds), *Mundo Rural e Política, Ensaios Interdisciplinares*, Rio de Janeiro: Campus/ Pronex, pp. 177–208.

Castro, A.C. (1999), 'O plano Brasil em ação e as oportunidades de investimento para as empresas agroalimentarcs', in L.F. Costa, R. J. Moreira and R. Bruno (eds), *Mundo Rural e Tempo Presente*', Rio de Janeiro: Editora Mauad.

Castro, A.B. (2003), 'El segundo catch-up Brasileño: características y limitaciones', *Revista de la Cepal*, **90**, Agosto.

Castro, A.C. (2005), 'The catching-up of Brazil's agro-food system: globalization, international relations and development', mimeo, presented in the Catch-up Workshop, The Earth Institute, Columbia University, 13–14 May.

Castro, A.C. and M.G.D. Fonseca (1994), 'O potencial do agribusiness na fronteira', *Revista de Economia Política*, **14**(1), 63–84.

Castro, A.B. and A. Proença (2001), 'Novas estratégias industriais; sobrevida ou inflexão?', in J.P.R. Velloso (ed.), *Como Vão o Desenvolvimento e Democracia no Brasil?*, Rio de Janeiro: José Olympio Editora.

Contini, E., J.G. Gasques, R.B.A. Leonardi and E.T. Bastos (2006), 'Projeções do agronegócio no Brasil e no mundo', Revista de Política Agricola, EMBRAPA, **XV**(1).

De Christensen, T.N. and C.J.R. Bindé (2004), *Soja: 80 Anos de Produção 1924– 2004*, Santa Rosa: Lucano.

Gertner, D., P. May, A.C. Castro, V. Vinha and C. Leme (1997), 'Case study of Aracruz Celulose Communication Plan', in S. Ward and L. Pratt (eds), *Sustainable Enterprise in Latin America: A Case Study*, Washington, DC: Management Institute for Business and Environment, MEB.

Nelson, R.R. and S.G. Winter (1982), *An Evolutionary Theory of Economic Change*, Cambridge, MA: Harvard University Press.

Rodrigues, R. (2005), 'Perspectivas do agronegocio', in J.P. Reis Velloso (ed.), 'O desafio da China e da Índia: a resposta do Brasil', Rio de Janeiro: José Olympio Editora.

Teece, D. and G. Pisano (1998), 'The dynamic capabilities of firms: an introduction', in G. Dosi, D. Teece and J. Chytry (eds), *Technology, Organization and Competitiveness*, New York: Oxford University Press.

Trigueirinho, F. (2006), 'Uma perspectiva para o crescimento do agronegócio no Brasil', ABIOVE (Associação das Indústrias de Óleo Vegetal).

Zackiewicz, M., M.B.M. Bonacelli and S.L.M. Salles-Filho (2005), 'Estudos prospectivos e a organização de sistemas de inovação no Brasil', *São Paulo em Perspectiva*, **19**(1), 115–121.

7. Conclusions

Franco Malerba and Richard R. Nelson

A central reason for doing the studies reported in this book was the conviction that, while there are important factors and relationships that are common across economic sectors, the requirements and mechanisms for successful catch-up differ significantly across economic sectors, and the concept of a sectoral innovation system provides a useful framework for illuminating these differences. We think the studies reported here support all of these premises. In all of the cases of successful catch-up one can observe certain things, regardless of the sector. Yet there are also important differences across economic sectors in the institutions and mechanisms that are behind successful catch-up experiences, and the sectoral innovation system framework is quite useful in putting a spotlight on these. In this concluding chapter, we first highlight the common elements coming from each chapter (section 7.1) and then the differences across the sectors (section 7.2). Section 7.3 discusses the role of national factors and systems, and section 7.4 draws some final lessons.

7.1 COMMON ELEMENTS AFFECTING CATCH-UP IN ALL SECTORS

We have stressed that a principal purpose of this book is to call attention to significant differences across economic sectors in the nature of the development processes involved. However, these differences must be viewed against a background of certain broad basic commonalities in successful catching up. In all of the cases of successful catch-up one can observe certain things, regardless of the sector.

7.1.1 Firms' Learning

The main factor behind catch-up is the learning and capabilities of domestic firms. This confirms what previous studies have found, and what has been mentioned before. Learning and the formation of capabilities by domestic firms has proven a necessary condition for catching up because they provide the catching-up country with the ability to absorb foreign knowledge and technology and to adapt and modify them to the features of local demand and local needs, generating new knowledge, creating new products and technologies and exporting.

7.1.2   Access to Foreign Knowledge

A second factor common to all cases of successful catch-up has been access to foreign knowledge. However, the channels through which this access has taken place have differed from country to country and from sector to sector. When access to foreign knowledge did not take place, as in telecommunications in India and Brazil, the catch-up process was seriously impaired (see Chapter 2 of this book by Lee et al.).

7.1.3   Skilled Human Capital

A third common factor has been the development of skilled human capital. This factor proved particularly relevant in sectors highly dependent on skilled labour, entrepreneurship and the creation of new firms. The cases of catching up in software (see Chapter 3 of this book by Niosi et al.) and of India in pharmaceuticals (see Chapter 5 by Ramani and Guennif) are very good examples. Related to that, the international mobility of skilled labour from advanced countries has been key for countries such as India, China and Taiwan in sectors such as software, semiconductors and pharmaceuticals.

7.1.4   Active Government Policy

In the five sectors, active government policy has indeed stimulated and fostered the learning processes and the capability formation of domestic firms. As we will see later, however, government intervened with a different intensity and used different tools according to the specificity of the sector and the characteristics of the national innovation system in which government policy occurred.

Most of the time all these factors worked together in a systemic and complementary way. Learning and capability formation by firms has been possible through an educational system that developed a skilled labour force and through a government that launched policies that favoured learning and the acquisition of foreign knowledge though alliances, opening to foreign direct investments or licences.

The overall dynamics of learning and capability building have been similar across the sectors and countries. The first stage of capability building is associated with the start of exports or sales on the domestic market or with both. At this early stage, the leading firms may be indigenous, or local branches of multinationals. For indigenous firms, access to foreign knowledge and links with multinationals are no substitutes for internal learning but they are complementary to it. Access and links are needed in order to feed the learning process of domestic firms with key knowledge, technologies and know-how. Often this initial stage is characterized by subcontracting and low-cost production in an international division of labour or by specialization in low-end products, which are then exported to international markets. In this early stage, for larger countries such as China, India or Brazil, production at a low price of low-end products for the domestic market has been quite common. In this book these early stages have characterized the cases of generic products in pharmaceuticals, business services and business process outsourcing in software, and back–end processes in semiconductors. With time, the process of learning and capability formation shows a change in the relationship between domestic firms and foreign firms, in the products offered, in the type of specialization, and in the extent of exporting. The relationship between domestic firms and multinational companies becomes more equal, and involves the creation of partnerships and joint-ventures. Production and specialization upgrade from subcontracting and low-end products to more innovative, higher-end products. Innovation here is not of the radical type. Rather, it is an adaptation or an incremental change of existing products. Exports increase.

7.2   DIFFERENCES ACROSS SECTORAL SYSTEMS

Given these features of almost all successful experiences of sectoral catch-up, as we have stressed there are also significant differences across the industries studied in this project.

7.2.1   Industry Structure

Differences in industry structure are evident in the sectors examined, and can be related to differences in technological regimes, in the scale and scope of production, and in demand features. These differences can also be related to the stage of the industry life that a sector is actually in. This is a confirmation of the key distinction between sectors resembling more a Schumpeter Mark I type (with small firms, high entry and high turbulence in the ranking of firms) or more similar to a Schumpeter Mark II type (with large firms, limited entry and high persistence in the ranking of firms) (Nelson and Winter, 1982; Malerba and Orsenigo, 1997). In those sectors in which scale and large R&D expenditures have been important for innovation, production and growth, and in which technological advance has been cumulative, large firms have been key drivers of the catch-up process. This is the case of automobiles and telecommunication equipment (see Chapter 2 of this book, by Lee et al.). Where the knowledge base is more varied, the technological entry barrier low, economies of scale and scope not high and division of labour possible, new firms and a large variety of actors play a major role in the catching-up process. This is the case for software and agro-food (see Chapters 3 and 6 of this book by Niosi et al. and Gu et al.).

Of course, industry structures are not necessarily constant over time, but can change as an industry develops. Thus, when catch-up starts, the new domestic firms are usually relatively small. In the process of catching up, they grow in size. So, in several sectors after the catch-up has started one can observe the coexistence of small, medium and large size domestic firms. This is the case for software in many countries, the Indian pharmaceutical industry and the Chinese and Taiwanese semiconductor industries: in these cases, an articulated industry structure was the result of the life cycle of the industry and of the process of catch-up that started some time before, fed by the continuous entry of new actors and the growth of the successful domestic producers (see Chapters 3, 4 and 5 of this book, by Niosi et al., Rasiah et al., Ramani and Guennif).

In some sectors, technological and market discontinuities favoured new countries or new (small) domestic players. This has been the case for software. In other sectors with either a highly cumulative knowledge base (telecommunications), or science as a driver of innovation (pharmaceuticals), the discontinuity (such as mobile phones or biotechnology) often favoured countries that were already faring well or that had established large domestic firms (rather than new countries or new actors with completely new competences). The reason is that in countries already doing well, large domestic actors had accumulated a broad set of competences able to lead the transition from the old to the new in terms of technology and market (see Chapters 2 and 5 of this book, by Lee et al. and Ramani and Guennif). In the case of the transition to mobile telecommunications, Korea and China, countries already successful in digital switches, continued to be successful in the new regime, while India and Brazil, which were not advanced in digital switches, did not (see Chapter 2 of this book, by Lee et al.). Also, in the case of the discontinuity represented by biotechnology, in India and Brazil the pharmaceutical firms that did not already have advanced capabilities were not able to catch up or even leapfrog compared to the established domestic pharmaceutical firms or the foreign multinationals (see Chapter 5 of this book by Ramani and Guennif).

The role of multinationals also differed across sectors. In some sectors multinationals globally govern the innovation process through global value chains, and outsource international production to emerging countries. In software (India, Ireland and Israel), semiconductors (China, Taiwan and Malaysia), agro-food (coffee in Costa Rica), textiles, clothing, footwear and furniture, specialization in different stages of the global value chain has been a way to get access to foreign knowledge and international markets and then, with the development of domestic capabilities, to a process of upgrading and moving up the learning ladder within the value chain (see Chapters 6, 4 and 3 of this book, by Gu et al., Rasiah et al. and Niosi et al.; Gereffi et al., 2005; Ernst, 2002; Lee, 2005; Morrison et al., 2006). In other sectors, such as automobiles, the use of licences from multinationals (or from foreign firms) or the establishment of joint ventures and alliances with multinationals have been a key tool for domestic firms to learn and accumulate capabilities. The cases of licences used by Korean automobile firms and of alliances and joint ventures established by Chinese automobile and semiconductor producers are examples of ways in which multinational corporations have shared their knowledge with domestic production. For the catching-up country licences and alliances had to be complemented with some level of capability by domestic firms in order to learn from the knowledge gained through foreign sources and to be able later on to develop new processes and products in an autonomous way. This is what the Korean and Chinese firms did. Finally, in some sectors, competent local branches of multinational corporations have been quite active in the development of new products and processes in the catching-up countries. This is the case for automobiles in Brazil. Here the presence of a large domestic market has led international car producers to open subsidiaries and to develop capabilities in production at their local branches, stimulating the growth of local suppliers of parts. However, this has not been the case in other industries. For example, in pharmaceuticals and software the local branches of multinationals have mainly produced for the global market or for their headquarters, within an international division of labour managed by the multinational company (see Chapter 5 of this book, by Ramani and Guennif). As a consequence, the generation and diffusion of new knowledge and new competences by the subsidiary to the rest of the host country has also often been quite limited.

Finally, in some sectors, such as semiconductors and software, strong links with advanced international suppliers have provided new inputs, complementary knowledge, and key information for production and innovation in the catching-up country and has led to learning and capability development by domestic firms. This is the case in Taiwan, China and Malaysia (see Chapters 3 and 4 of this book by Niosi et al. and Rasiah et al.).

7.2.2   Demand and Vertical Links

Sectors also differed in the type and role of demand. In some catching-up industries, standard demand coming from advanced or developing countries is predominant: this is the case for pharmaceuticals, semiconductors, automobiles and the package software industry. This had as a consequence that the catching up by China and Malaysia in semiconductors, by Korea in telecommunications, by India in pharmaceuticals, by India, Ireland and Israel in software and by Korea in automobiles have been driven by exports. Exports have fostered the learning processes and the accumulation of capabilities by domestic firms by exposing local producers to developed markets, advanced customers and intense competition.

In addition to standard demand, other sectors are characterized also by custom or segmented demand: this is the case for software, pharmaceuticals and agro-food. Particularly in large countries, such as China, India or Brazil, a large custom or segmented domestic demand has favoured specific solutions that have then been the basis of the learning process and the accumulation of capability by domestic firms (see Chapters 5 and 6 of this book by Ramani and Guennif and Gu et al.).

Finally, in sectors such as software, industrial demand coming from the local clusters has also triggered growth. This local cluster demand has been relevant for catching up in Indian software and in Taiwanese electronics: this type of demand has triggered intense formal and informal interaction, knowledge sharing and intense division of labour (see Chapters 3 and 4 of this book, by Niosi et al. and Rasiah et al.). However, local industrial demand has not always triggered the development of the capabilities of local suppliers. As mentioned in the previous pages, in those sectors that compete on a world scale, such as automobiles, local industrial demand has not favoured local learning by domestic suppliers if local suppliers are in a very backward position and industrial producers need advanced machinery and components to improve their capabilities and performance, therefore going abroad for those inputs and machinery. This phenomenon has been discussed for the Korean automobile and machine tool industries by Kim and Lee (2009). In Korea the highly competitive automobile producers looked for advanced machine tools abroad, purchasing their equipment from the world's best machine tool producers rather than from local firms. While this has increased the competitiveness and innovativeness of the automobile producers, it has blocked the development of capabilities by the domestic machine tool producers.

7.2.3 Other Sectoral System Elements

Universities and public research laboratories
In some sectors, such as agriculture, telecommunications and pharmaceuticals, universities and advanced research laboratories have conducted research in scientific and technological areas that proved quite relevant for domestic firms. However, the actors conducting research and the type of research have differed across sectors. In agriculture (as in China, Korea and Taiwan) research and experimental stations had a pragmatic orientation and a focus on user needs (Hayami and Ruttan, 1985; see Chapter 6 of this book by Gu et al.). In telecommunications (as in Korea and Taiwan), large public research laboratories carried out advanced research and collaboration with domestic firms (see the Korean KIET/ETRI and the Taiwanese III/ITRI/ERSO) (see Chapter 2 of this book by Lee et al.; Mazzoleni and Nelson, 2006). In pharmaceuticals (such as in India), universities have conducted significant research which proved useful for domestic firms (see Chapter 5 of this book by Ramani and Guennif).

Finance
A difference across sectors between internal finance and venture capital has emerged from the studies. In telecommunications (in Korea and India) and automobiles (in Korea and China), characterized by large corporations, internal finance has played a paramount role in the support of the development of capabilities by domestic firms (see Chapter 2 by Lee et al.). In contrast, in software and pharmaceuticals (in India, Ireland and Israel), characterized by many small, new domestic firms, new financial actors, such as venture capital companies, have been important for the development of the sector (see Chapters 3 and 5 by Niosi et al. and Ramani and Guennif).

Types of government policy
Active government policy has differed across sectors in the tools and measures used. In telecommunications, public policy used R&D support, R&D consortia and public research organizations. Those sets of policies were present in Korea and China, which were able to successfully support and coordinate firms' domestic efforts and to help domestic firms to move into new generations of telecom technologies and products. They were lacking in Brazil and India, characterized also by a less direct and coordinated intervention: these two countries were less successful in actively fostering innovation and change in the domestic industry (see Chapter 2 in this book, by Lee et al.). In software, governments have used different policies and tools: support for education, R&D funding to small

and medium enterprises, favourable company tax rates, and incentives to attract foreign direct investments (see Chapter 3 by Niosi et al.). In agro-food, the focus of policies has been on the technological and scientific infrastructure and on private–public partnerships in experimentation and technology diffusion (Brazil, China and Costa Rica) (see Chapter 6 in this book, by Gu et al.). In pharmaceuticals, policies of mild IPR protection, coupled with the support of human capital formation and university research, have been quite successful (India) (see Chapter 5 by Ramani and Guennif). Finally, in semiconductors, government policies for attracting foreign direct investments of multinational corporations early on and for building firms' domestic capabilities later, worked successfully (China and Taiwan) (see Chapter 4 by Rasiah et al.).

Standards, regulations and norms
The role and types of institutions have greatly differed across sectors, sometimes fostering and sometimes blocking catch-up. In pharmaceuticals, the type (or the lack) of the IPR system has affected innovation and development. India and Brazil, for example, enjoyed a period of lax intellectual property regulation that created a window of opportunity for the accumulation of domestic technological capabilities (see Chapter 5 of this book by Ramani and Guennif). In agro-food, the spreading of market institutions has been an essential element for the growth of the vegetable sector (in China) and effective regulation has played a role in the development of coffee (in Costa Rica) (see Chapter 6 by Gu et al.). Finally, in telecommunications, product standardization, according to an international setting, has accompanied the growth of the Korean and Chinese industries (see Chapter 2 by Lee et al.).

In sum, in the various sectoral systems, specific complementarities have triggered virtuous circles at the base of catching up. In software, catching up has been based on vibrant entrepreneurship, dynamic local clusters of small and medium size firms, and close links with advanced customers (see Chapter 3 by Niosi et al.). In telecommunications, major investment by large firms and active government policies have gone together (see Chapter 2 by Lee et al.). In semiconductors, a key role in catch-up has been played by government R&D support and export activity (see Chapter 4 of this book by Rasiah et al.). In pharmaceuticals, a relaxation of IPR regimes has been accompanied by advanced university research and entry of new domestic firms (see Chapter 5 by Ramani and Guennif). Finally, in agro-food, the development of market institutions, an advanced agricultural knowledge base, a good technological infrastructure, and major public R&D spending have proven key elements for local developments (see Chapter 6 by Gu et al.).

7.3 NATIONAL DIFFERENCES

We have so far examined the differences in sectoral systems. However, national differences in terms of institutions and government policy have also played a key role in catching up. This, in turn, has affected the type of sectors in which domestic firms accumulated capabilities and specialized. For example, since the 1970s, the Korean government has supported the growth and consolidation of large firms, and therefore a concentrated industrial structure and a pattern of innovation, resembling the Schumpeter Mark II model (large firms and concentrated industrial structure): this is the case for automobiles, semiconductors and telecommunications. Taiwan, on the contrary, has had since the 1970s a policy of supporting new, small firms, and, consequently, of high entry in the industry, resembling the Schumpeter Mark I model (new entrants and small and medium size firms, and high industrial turbulence): this is the case for several segments of ICT. In the last decades, Brazilian policy has been quite favourable to the presence and investment of multinational corporations: therefore, those types of actors have been present in many Brazilian sectors such as automobiles, pharmaceuticals and telecommunications.

Of course, an evolving two-way relationship has taken place over time between the national institutional setting and the sectors' dynamics. In fact, feedbacks and forces, going from the specific leading sectors of an economy to some key dimensions of the national innovation system, have also been present. For example, the Korean leading sectors have pushed for national policies in favour of large-scale firms and certain types of technologies, while the Taiwanese ICT industry has fostered national policies in favour of entrepreneurship.

National differences also played a key role in cases where within-sector specialization has been possible. In software, which is characterized by the possibility of several trajectories, due to the heterogeneity of the knowledge base and the variety of technologies and demand, different country specialization took place. India focused on software services, Israel on high-tech software products and Ireland on products for the European market. Cross-country differences also emerged due to the different role of the domestic and international markets. The large size of the domestic market in China and Brazil represented a clear target for the activities of domestic firms. On the other hand, smaller countries, such as Ireland and Israel, have focused on exports. Countries differed also in terms of evolution, with India representing the clearer example of a trajectory of scaling up and moving up the ladder and of maintaining links with foreign customers (see Chapter 3 of this book by Niosi et al.). Semiconductors is another example. In this industry, Korea specialized in large-scale integrated design and manufacturing (a typical Schumpeter Mark II activity). Other countries have benefited from the increasing modularity of semiconductor design and production and the emergence of fables and foundries: Taiwan followed a strategy of capability development with a major contribution from a local government laboratory, and of strong links to foreign firms; China pursued a more incremental strategy of capability development and Malaysia a strategy of chip fabrication and assembly by local firms (see Chapter 4 by Rasiah et al.). Finally, in agro-food, the variety of crops, related to different natural endowments, large domestic demand, or a global value chain, dominated by multinationals led to national differences in catching-up trajectories. In vegetables, the development trajectory of China was due to the presence of a large domestic demand, the specialization of Brazil in soybean was related to a large integrated international agro-businesses market, and Costa Rica's catching up in coffee was linked to small firms focusing on high-value product niches.

7.4   LESSONS

This book provides support for some of the basic conclusions drawn from other studies of the processes through which countries behind the economic frontier close the gap on the leaders. The development of capabilities of firms is key. Firm learning, in turn, requires access to knowledge about how things are done in the leading countries, and to a labour force that has the skills needed for productive operation. In general, catching up requires active government policies of a number of different kinds, to encourage and support the innovation that catching up requires. While not highlighted in our study, successful catching up is associated with high levels of both private and public investments in new productive capital, infrastructure and people.

   This book also brings sharply into focus an important feature of economic development that has tended to be neglected in earlier studies. Economic sectors are different. They differ both in how they develop, and in the kinds of conditions and policies that are needed to support catching up. In some sectors, firms need to be large in order to be competitive; in others, firm size is not of major importance. In some sectors, catching up requires a university system that is relatively strong both in performing its advanced training functions and in research; in others, universities play little role in catch-up. Intellectual property rights are important in some sectors, sometimes blocking catch-up and also acting as a vehicle for accessing foreign technologies; in other sectors, intellectual property hardly matters. Sectors of course differ in other factors as well.

We are convinced that this book will help to build greater recognition of sectoral differences and their implications for the development process and for effective policy, both among scholars and among policy makers. In this context, a sectoral system view of industries allows differences to be identified across sectors not just in terms of firms' competences and market structure, but also in terms of other actors relevant for innovation, production and catching up, and in terms of the institutions. Our belief that sectoral differences matter a great deal points also to the need to identify the sector-specific dynamic processes that are the basis of change and catching up. Often these processes imply the co-evolution of several variables and actors in a sector. This is a major analytic and policy challenge for future research.

REFERENCES

Ernst, D. (2002), 'Global production networks and the changing geography of innovation systems: implications for developing countries', *Economics of Innovation and New Technology*, **11**(6), 497–523.

Gereffi, G., J. Humphrey and T. Sturgeon (2005), 'The governance of global value chains', *Review of International Political Economy*, **12**(1), 78–100.

Hayami, Y. and V. Ruttan (1985), *Agricultural Development: an International Perspective*, Baltimore, MD: Johns Hopkins University Press.

Kim, Y.-Z. and K. Lee (2009), 'Making a technological catch-up in the capital goods industry: barriers and opportunities in the Korean case', in F. Malerba and S. Mani (eds), *Sectoral Systems of Innovation and Production in Developing Countries*, Cheltenham, UK and Northampton, MA, USA: Edward Elgar, pp. 259–86.

Lee, K. (2005), 'Making a technological catch-up: barriers and opportunities', *Asian Journal of Technology Innovation*, **13**(2), 97–131.

Malerba, F. and L. Orsenigo (1997), 'Technological regimes and sectoral patterns of innovation', *Industrial and Corporate Change*, **6**(1), 83–117.

Malerba, F. and L. Orsenigo (2000), 'Knowledge, innovative activities and industry evolution', *Industrial and Corporate Change*, **9**(2), 289–314.

Mazzoleni, R. and R. Nelson (2006), 'The roles of research at universities and public labs in economic catch-up', LEM Working Paper Series.

Morrison, A., C. Pietrobelli and R. Rabellotti (2006), 'Global value chains and technological capabilities: a framework to study industrial innovation in developing countries', working paper.

Nelson, R. and S. Winter (1982), *An Evolutionary Theory of Economic Change*, Cambridge, MA: The Belknap Press of Harvard University Press.

Index

1G wireless telecommunication 56, 59, 61

1st Silicon 118, 131, 136, 137, 143, 149

2G wireless telecommunication 56, 59, 61

2.5G wireless telecommunication 56, 59–60

3G wireless telecommunication *see* wireless telecommunication

absorptive capabilities 4, 6, 80, 99, 116, 125, 198, 282

Accent 148–9

access to drugs 161, 163, 164, 167, 170–71, 175, 177–8, 180–81

actors 5–8, 11–12, 13, 14, 33, 34–5, 37–8, 50–55, 66, 67, 284

ADPs (Agricultural Development Projects) (Nigeria) 213, 214

Africa 15, 159, 234, 235
  see also Nigeria

after-sales services 79, 83, 98
  see also call centres

agents, in evolutionary theory 5, 7

agricultural sector
  Brazil 247–52, 254–6, 260
  China 201–4, 207, 209–10, 218, 220, 221, 287
  Costa Rica 201–4, 233
  developing countries 194–5
  international 202, 203
  Nigeria 201–4, 205, 218
  'three agricultural worlds' 204, 257, 264

agro-food sector catch-up: Nigeria, China, Costa Rica and Brazil case studies
  catch-up strategy sectoral and national comparisons 284, 285, 286, 287, 288, 290
  conclusions 269–72

findings and discussion 256–69
  demand a driver and domestic and international markets 259–61
  evolutionary paths, richness of 256–8
  government policies 267–9
  institutions, importance of 261–3
  knowledge base undergoing rapid change 264–7
  introduction 194–204
  sectors *see* cassava sector in Nigeria; coffee sector in Costa Rica; soybean sector in Brazil; vegetable sector in China

AMD (Advanced Micro Devices) 81, 115, 117–18, 122, 124, 126, 127, 134, 135, 142, 144, 147

Amsden, A.H. 2, 6, 7, 113, 121, 125, 132, 136, 139

analogue standards for wireless telecommunication 55, 56

analogue telephone switches 25, 28, 37, 43

ANATEL (Brazil) 32, 48–9, 64

ANDA (Abbreviated New Drug Application) 165

animal feed 15, 208, 213, 248, 250, 259, 260, 263

API 10, 158, 167, 168, 169, 171, 172–3, 176, 177–8, 179, 183, 187

Arabica coffee 15, 235, 236, 241, 243

Argentina 89, 97, 98, 99, 253

Asia 15, 234–5, 236
  see also individual countries

ASICs 118, 123, 128, 129–30, 131, 132, 134, 137, 138, 142, 152

Athreye, S. 75–6, 85, 86, 87, 100, 163, 164

backward integration deficits 168, 169, 172, 173, 178, 179, 180, 187–8

Banco do Brasil 252, 253
bio-fuel 254, 255, 269
biotechnology
    agro-food sector catch-up: case
        studies 226, 229, 232, 254,
        255–6, 265, 269, 271
    pharmaceutical sector 10, 11, 157,
        158, 159, 167, 188, 284–5
BNDES (National Bank for Economic
    and Social Development, Brazil)
    32, 53, 54, 251, 255
bottlenecks, cassava sector in Nigeria
    210, 217
BPO (business process outsourcing) 80,
    81, 86, 87, 90, 93, 94, 97, 100–101,
    102, 103, 283
branded drugs 158, 160, 162, 163,
    167, 168, 174, 175, 176, 184,
    187
Brazil
    catch-up strategy sectoral and
        national comparisons 282,
        283, 284–5, 286, 287, 288, 289,
        290
    coffee sector 15, 235, 236, 237, 238,
        244, 245
    computer software and service sector
        78, 83, 87, 92, 95, 97–8, 99, 100,
        101, 104, 105, 106
    economic and agricultural
        characteristics 182, 200–204,
        247–52, 254, 260
    telecommunication equipment
        industry 21–2, 30–32, 38, 44–5,
        48–9, 52–4, 64, 66, 282, 284,
        289
    telecommunications services 31–2
    see also pharmaceutical sector catch-
        up in India and Brazil; soybean
        sector in Brazil
BTM (Bell Telephone Manufacturing
    Company) 25, 40, 43
Bulgaria 96–7
bulk drug production 10, 158, 159,
    160–61, 163, 164–5, 166–7, 175–6,
    177, 179

C-DOT (India) 23, 29, 30, 45, 49, 55,
    64
call centres 12, 72, 78, 80, 86, 94, 98

capabilities 3–4, 5–6, 7, 8, 9–10
    see also absorptive capabilities;
        human capital; innovation
        capabilities; knowledge;
        managerial capacity;
        manufacturing capabilities; re-
        engineering skills; regulation
        handling capabilities; skilled
        labour; technological and
        scientific capabilities
capital 126–8, 130, 174, 177, 217, 267
    see also FDI (foreign direct
        investment); finance;
        government funding; human
        capital; R&D funding; venture
        capital
Carsem 118, 127, 130–31, 143
cash crops 207, 209, 233, 234
cassava sector in Nigeria
    case selection 200
    described 14, 205–17
        crucial importance of cassava
            processing and bottlenecks
            216–17
        importance of cassava 206–8
        introduction 205–6
        knowledge sources 214–16
        transformation and driving forces
            208–14
    research findings and discussion 256,
        259, 260, 263, 264, 266, 267,
        268–9
Castro, A.C. 252, 253
catch-up
    concept 2–3
    economic development and
        innovation systems 3–4
    elements in all sectors 281–3
    lessons 290–91
    models *see* independent catch-up;
        interdependent catch-up;
        leapfrogging catch-up; path-
        creating catch-up; path-
        following catch-up; wave-like
        evolutionary trajectory
    sectoral and national differences
        283–90
    sectoral systems of innovation 4–10
CDMA (Code Division Multiple
    Access) 38, 56, 57–8, 59, 61, 62, 66

CEME (Central de Medicamentos) (Brazil) 171–2, 173
Central America 15, 235, 236
China
    catch-up strategy sectoral and national comparisons 282, 283, 284, 285, 286, 287, 288, 289, 290
    economic and agricultural characteristics 14, 200–204, 207, 209–10, 212, 218, 219–20, 256, 287
    pharmaceutical sector 177, 180, 182
    see also computer software and service sector; semiconductor industry catch-up strategies in China, Korea, Malaysia and Taiwan; telecommunication equipment industry in Brazil, China, India and Korea; vegetable sector in China
Chinese Academy of Sciences 140, 231, 265
Chinese Academy of Telecommunications and Technology (CATT) 61, 62
Chippac 116, 125, 126, 147
Cho, D.S. 121, 123, 131, 132, 139
Chu, W.W. 2, 6, 7, 113, 121, 132, 139
CICAFE (Costa Rica Coffee Research Centre) 242, 244, 265–6
CIT (Center for Information Technology) (China) 26, 40–41, 42
clusters
    computer software and service sector 86, 90, 95, 98, 106, 286, 288
    semiconductor industry in Korea, Malaysia and Taiwan 120, 121, 148, 286
CMOS (complementary metal oxide semiconductor) technology 115, 118, 129, 131, 133, 140, 150
co-evolution 149–50, 152, 257–8, 270
CODETEC (Brazil) 172–3
coffee sector 15, 234–5, 236–8, 244, 245
coffee sector in Costa Rica
    case selection 200
    catch-up strategy sectoral comparisons 285, 288

early developments and the formation of 'thick' social and economic networks 239–42
global coffee value chain and the Costa Rican coffee sector 14–15, 234–9
introduction 232–4
move towards 'gourmet coffee' and lessons 242–7
research findings and discussion 256–7, 258, 259, 260–61, 262, 263, 265–6, 267, 268
commercialization 158–9, 163, 164–5, 174, 183, 187
competition
    catch-up strategy sectoral comparisons 286
    coffee sector in Costa Rica 247, 262
    computer software and service sector 75, 84, 89
    internationalization theories 84
    pharmaceutical sector in Brazil and India 162, 166, 168, 170, 174, 175, 176, 183, 188
    semiconductor industry in China, Korea, Malaysia and Taiwan 148
    telecommunication equipment industry in Brazil, China, India and Korea 34–5, 50
competitive advantage
    computer software and service sector 86, 88, 89, 90–91, 94, 95, 96, 97, 98, 104, 105–8
    pharmaceutical sector in Brazil 176
    semiconductor industry in Korea 130
    telecommunication equipment industry 34, 35, 47–8, 50–51, 63–4
competitive and creative mode 265–6, 271
competitive disadvantage 89, 91, 95–6, 97–8, 104–5, 106
computer hardware manufacturing firms 13, 72, 73, 80, 99
computer software and service sector
    catch-up strategy sectoral and national comparisons 282, 283, 284, 285–6, 287–8, 289

conclusions: computer software as a
window of opportunity 103–8
described 12–13
internationalization *see*
internationalization of the
computer software and service
sector (1980–2007)
national models of catching up
99–101
overview (1950–2007) 30, 72–83
evolution 72–3
main characteristics 77–83
segmentation 73–7, 82
policy implications 102–3, 104
computer software development cycle
84, 85
contracts 163, 166, 168
cooperatives 95, 226, 235, 241, 243,
262, 267
coordinating conferences,
telecommunication equipment
industry in China 51
cost effectiveness 83, 126–7, 215, 266
Costa Rica 200–204, 232–3, 288, 290
see also coffee sector in Costa Rica
costs *see* fixed costs; labour costs; prices;
production costs; variable costs
CPqD (Brazil) 30, 31, 32, 44, 53, 64
credit 35, 50, 51, 52, 54, 241, 250, 252,
253, 254
see also loans; subsidized credit
cropping and cultivation technologies
212, 213, 214, 215, 221–2, 236–7,
245, 269
crossbar telephone switches 24, 25, 26,
28, 37
customized software 12–13, 72, 73–7,
82, 93, 100–101
Cwill Company 61

Daiichi-Sankyo 166–7
Datang 26, 38, 42, 51, 61, 62–3
Daviron, B. 237
de-licensing 164
de-verticalization 134, 135, 148, 149,
152–3
demand
agro-food sector catch-up 14, 209,
210, 219–20, 224, 236, 238, 248,
254–5, 259–61, 286

catch-up strategy sectoral and
national comparisons 286, 290
computer software and service sector
75–6, 77, 82–3, 99–100, 102,
106, 286
pharmaceutical sector 11 158, 159,
161, 162, 163, 170–72, 175,
177–8, 180–81, 286
sectoral innovation systems 6, 10, 33
semiconductor industry: case studies
114, 124, 126, 127, 136–9, 151,
286
telecommunication equipment
industry 11–12, 34, 35
telecommunication equipment
industry: case studies 27, 29, 30,
43, 46–50, 60, 63–5, 66
deregulation 12, 21, 22, 174
developed countries 21, 34–5, 36, 78,
82, 83–4
developing countries
agriculture 194–5, 204
computer software and service sector
78, 79–80, 83, 84
economic growth 1–2
internationalization theories 83–4
pharmaceutical sector 158–9, 185,
186–7
telecommunications equipment
industry 11, 12, 34, 35–6
telecommunications services 21
vertical integration 2
Díaz, R. 226, 235, 239, 241, 243
differentiation 5
see also product differentiation;
segmentation
digital standards for wireless
telecommunication 55–6
digital telephone switches 22–3, 25–6,
27, 28, 29, 30, 36, 37, 40–44, 45,
47–8, 50–51, 66, 284
diodes 115, 121, 122, 123, 131
distribution 223–6, 227–8, 232, 235,
236, 261–2
distribution technologies 198
division of labour
agro-food sector catch-up: case
studies 215, 241, 242, 245–6,
264, 284
capability building 283, 284, 285, 286

computer software and service sector 13, 284, 286
pharmaceutical sector in India 166, 187
semiconductor sector 8, 128, 286
domestic firms
 agro-food sector catch-up: case studies 216–17, 235, 236
 catch-up strategy sectoral comparisons 282, 283, 284–6, 287, 288
 computer software and service sector 78, 86, 88, 89, 91, 93, 96, 97, 98–9, 101, 104, 287
 pharmaceutical sector 287, 288
  Brazil 169–70, 171–4, 176–7, 179, 180–81, 182, 186
  India 161–2, 163, 164–5, 166–7, 179, 186, 188, 287
 sectoral innovation systems and catch-up 5–8
 semiconductor industry: case studies
  China 116, 125, 128–9, 130, 133, 134, 135–6, 140–41, 143, 147–8, 149, 150, 152–3
  Korea 122, 123, 125, 126, 129, 130, 133, 134–5, 139, 144, 146–7, 148, 149, 150, 151–2
  Malaysia 123, 127, 129, 130–31, 133, 134, 136, 143, 147–8, 149, 153, 290
  Taiwan 119–20, 122, 123, 127, 128, 129, 131–2, 133, 134–5, 139, 143–4, 147–9, 150–52
 telecommunication equipment industry: case studies 26, 28, 29, 30–31, 32, 39, 40–42, 43, 44–5, 46, 47–8, 50, 51, 52, 57, 58, 59–60, 62–4, 66, 67, 287
 see also domestic MNCs; indigenous technological and scientific capabilities
domestic markets
 agro-food sector catch-up: case studies
 agricultural sector in Brazil 248, 260
 cassava sector in Nigeria 200, 205, 206, 207, 209, 211, 212, 256, 259, 260

coffee sector in Costa Rica 235, 239, 246–7, 260–61
vegetable sector in China 200, 219–20, 223–4, 256, 259, 260, 261, 290
catch-up strategy sectoral and national comparisons 283, 285, 286, 289, 290
computer software and service sector 82, 83, 91, 98, 99, 101, 102, 104–7, 108
pharmaceutical sector in Brazil and India 162–3, 168, 170–72, 175, 176, 177, 179, 182
sectoral innovation systems and catch-up 6
semiconductor industry in China and Korea 114, 136, 137, 139, 151
telecommunication equipment industry: case studies 27, 29, 30, 40, 44, 63–4
domestic MNCs
 computer software and service sector 79, 87–8, 89, 92, 96, 98–9, 101, 104, 105, 107, 108
 pharmaceutical sector in India 166–7, 177, 180, 184
 semiconductor industry: case studies 114, 115, 116–17, 118, 119, 120, 126, 128–9, 130, 131–2, 133, 134, 135
 telecommunication equipment industry in China and Korea 22
DRAM chips 37, 114, 116–17, 122, 123, 128, 129, 130, 131, 132, 133, 134, 135, 137, 138, 140, 142, 146, 147, 149, 150
drug industry *see* pharmaceutical sector catch-up in India and Brazil
drug policies 175–6

economic crises 118, 144–5, 172, 175, 237–8
economic development, catch-up and innovation systems 3–4
economic growth 1–2, 14, 161, 218, 219–20, 256
economic liberalization 12, 21, 45, 52, 164, 168, 174, 237

economies of scale
    catch-up strategy sectoral
        comparisons 284
    computer software and service sector
        75, 79, 100–101
    pharmaceutical sector 169, 173, 188
    semiconductor manufacturing
        industry 14, 113, 141, 143
economies of scope 75, 284
Edquist, C. 7, 32, 116, 130, 134, 160
education 4, 145, 172, 230, 267, 282,
    287–8
    see also capabilities; higher/tertiary
        education; human capital;
        knowledge; skilled labour;
        training
electromechanical telephone switches
    28, 36, 37
electronic telephone switches 28, 36
embedded software 72, 75, 82, 89, 91,
    101
EMBRAPA (Brazilian Enterprise for
    Agricultural Research) 252, 255,
    265, 269
English language proficiency 47, 86,
    88, 91, 94, 95–6, 97–8, 106
entrepreneurship 26, 32, 103, 105, 252,
    259, 282, 288, 289
entry 10, 77–8, 79, 83–4, 283–4
environmental change, evolutionary
    theory 5
Ericsson 43–4, 59
ERSO (Taiwan) 119, 121, 132, 135,
    139, 143–4, 149, 151, 287
ETRI (Korea) 27, 43–4, 52, 57, 58, 287
EU (European Union) 96, 97, 105, 117
Europe
    computer software and services
        sector 77, 82, 83, 88, 99
    markets 236, 240, 245, 289
    pharmaceutical sector 164, 166, 169,
        170, 178, 180
    semiconductor industry 13, 118, 125,
        134, 139
    telecommunication industry 57, 58
    see also EU (European Union);
        Western Europe; *individual
        countries*
evolutionary theory 5–6, 7
exit 77, 83, 84, 170, 174

experiential and tacit knowledge
    agro-food sector catch-up: case
        studies 198, 199, 214, 219, 233
    semiconductor industry catch-up
        116, 127, 130, 131, 132, 134,
        139, 140, 143, 146, 147, 151
export processing zones (EPZs) 115,
    116, 119, 120, 134, 135
exports
    agro-food sector catch-up: case
        studies 285
    cassava sector in Nigeria 210, 211,
        213–14, 216–17, 259, 263
    coffee sector 234–5, 237–8, 245,
        246, 247, 258
    coffee sector in Costa Rica 200,
        235, 239, 240, 241, 256,
        260
    soybean sector in Brazil 15, 200,
        248, 250, 253, 254, 255, 256,
        258, 259–60, 290
    vegetable sector in China 224, 228,
        232, 261
    catch-up strategy sectoral and
        national comparisons 283, 285,
        286, 289
    computer software and service sector
        78, 83, 84, 86–7, 88, 90, 91–3,
        94–5, 96, 97, 98–9, 100, 101,
        103, 104, 105–7, 108, 285, 289
    pharmaceutical sector in India 161,
        163, 164–5, 168, 182
    sectoral innovation systems and
        catch-up 6
    semiconductor industry: case studies
        114, 115, 116, 119, 120, 125,
        132, 134, 135, 136, 137–9, 142,
        143–4, 151–2, 285, 288
    telecommunication equipment
        industry in China, India and
        Korea 22, 26, 45

FAO (United Nations Food and
    Agriculture Organization) 200,
    201, 202, 203, 242, 260
Far-Manguinhos (Brazil) 177–8,
    180–81
farmers
    cassava sector in Nigeria 207, 209,
        210, 211, 213, 215

coffee sector in Costa Rica 235, 239, 240, 241, 243, 247, 256, 258, 262
soybean sector in Brazil 252, 253
vegetable sector in China 219, 221, 229, 230–31, 266
FDI (foreign direct investment)
catch-up strategy sectoral comparisons 182
computer software and service sector 78, 85, 86, 87–8, 99, 103, 107
pharmaceutical sector in India and Brazil 170, 175, 182
semiconductor industry in China and Korea 116, 134, 140, 152
telecommunication equipment industry in Brazil, China and India 25–6, 29–30, 44, 288
FIIRO (Federal Institute of Industrial Research, Oshodi) (Nigeria) 214
finance 7, 32, 34, 35, 287, 288
see also capital; credit; government funding; government R&D funding; loans; private sector R&D funding; subsidized credit; tax incentives; venture capital
financial organizations 7
FINEP (Research and Projects Financing, Brazil) 32, 53, 252, 255–6
firms 5–7, 33, 34, 38
see also domestic firms; domestic MNCs; incubators; independent software vendors; joint ventures; large firms; medium-sized firms; mergers and acquisitions; MNCs; processors; small firms; spin-offs; start-ups; state-owned firms; strategic alliances; subsidiaries of MNCs
first mover advantage 34, 35
fixed costs 75, 76, 77, 173, 176
fixed telephones 11, 29, 30, 31, 36, 37, 48, 64, 65, 66
see also telephone switches
food import controls 209–11
food processing
cassava sector in Nigeria 207–8, 210, 212, 213, 214–15, 216–17, 263, 269

coffee sector in Costa Rica 235, 236, 237, 239–40, 241, 243–5, 258, 262, 263
food processing technologies 198, 209, 210, 212, 213, 214–15, 216–17, 237, 241, 243–5
food security 14, 205, 206, 207, 256, 261
foreign knowledge transfer
agro-food sector: case studies 252, 285
catch-up strategy sectoral comparisons 282, 283, 285–6
computer software and service sector 80, 86, 90–91, 94, 97, 98, 104, 105, 285–6
education, importance for catch-up 4
internationalization theories 84
sectoral innovation systems and catch-up 8
semiconductor industry in China, Korea, Malaysia and Taiwan 116, 125–6, 127, 130, 132, 134–6, 139–40, 146–7, 151, 152, 285–6, 288, 290
telecommunication equipment industry: case studies 24–6, 36, 37, 39–46, 61, 62, 63, 66
formulation of drugs 10, 158, 159, 160–61, 162, 163, 164, 168, 177, 183
France 72, 97, 157, 202, 203, 234
Freeman, C. 5, 8, 160
Freescale 116, 125, 128, 144, 147
FUNTTEL (Fund for Technological Development and Telecommunications) (Brazil) 32, 53–4
Furtado, J. 170, 171, 172, 173, 174, 176, 177

gari 207, 208, 210, 211, 212, 214
generic drugs 164–5, 166–7, 168, 175–6, 177, 180, 183–4, 186–7, 188, 283
Generics Act 1999 (Brazil) 175–6, 177, 183–4
Germany 25, 78, 88, 92, 97, 115, 123, 125, 144, 157
global computer software and service sector *see* computer software and service sector

global value chains 8, 14–15, 198–9,
      235–9, 285–6, 290
Globetronics 118, 127, 130, 131, 143
GoldStar 43, 44
gourmet coffee 238, 242, 245–7, 259,
      260
governance of markets 262
government funding
   agro-food sector catch-up: case
         studies 198, 204, 217, 223, 224,
         266, 267
   computer software and service sector
         89, 95, 100, 102
   pharmaceutical sector in India and
         Brazil 161, 172
   semiconductor industry in Korea,
         Malaysia and Taiwan 118, 121,
         139, 141, 142, 144
   telecommunication equipment
         industry in China and India 30,
         51, 61
government policies
   agro-food sector catch-up: case
         studies 267–9, 271, 272, 288
   cassava sector in Nigeria 209–14,
         267, 268–9
   coffee sector in Costa Rica 235,
         239, 240, 243, 266, 267, 268,
         288
   soybean sector in Brazil 251–2,
         268, 269, 288
   vegetable sector in China 223–5,
         229, 268–9, 288
   catch-up and sectoral innovation
         systems 7
   catch-up strategy sectoral and
         national comparisons 282–3,
         287–8, 289–90
   computer software and service
         sector 78, 86, 102–3, 104,
         287–8
   pharmaceutical sector in India and
         Brazil 161–2, 168, 169–76,
         177–8, 181–4, 288
   semiconductor industry in Korea,
         Malaysia and Taiwan 283, 288,
         289–90
   see also drug policies; government
         support; industrial policies;
         industrial policy deficits

government protection
   pharmaceutical sector in India and
         Brazil 161, 162, 168, 169–70,
         172, 179, 181–2
   telecommunication equipment
         industry 35, 50–51, 52, 54
government R&D funding
   catch-up strategy sectoral
         comparisons 287, 288
   computer software and service sector
         79, 101, 102, 287–8
   semiconductor industry in China,
         Korea and Taiwan 119, 126,
         128–9, 139, 141, 144, 152, 288
   telecommunication equipment
         industry 32, 35, 52, 53–4, 63,
         287
government R&D funding deficits 232
government research institutes (GRIs)
   agro-food sector catch-up: case
         studies
      agro-food sector in Brazil 251–2,
            255, 265, 266
      cassava sector in Nigeria 210, 213,
            214–16, 264
      coffee sector in Costa Rica 242,
            243, 244, 247, 268
      vegetable sector in China 229, 231,
            261
   catch-up and sectoral innovation
         systems 4, 6, 7, 8
   catch-up strategy sectoral
         comparisons 287, 288
   pharmaceutical sector in India and
         Brazil 163, 169, 177–8, 179,
         180–81, 183, 186, 188
   semiconductor industry in China,
         Korea and Taiwan 119–20,
         128–9, 139, 140, 142, 152, 290
   telecommunication equipment
         industry in Brazil, China, India
         and Korea 22, 23, 27, 29, 30,
         31, 38, 41, 43–4, 45–6, 57, 58,
         59–60, 66
   telecommunication equipment
         industry in developing countries
         34, 35
government support
   agro-food sector catch-up: case
         studies 198, 271, 288

cassava sector in Nigeria 210, 213, 217, 259, 263, 267, 269
coffee sector in Costa Rica 235, 239, 240, 243, 266, 267, 268
soybean sector in Brazil 252, 266, 269
vegetable sector in China 223–4, 268–9
catch-up strategy sectoral comparisons 282–3, 287–8
computer software and service sector 78, 79, 89, 90, 95, 100, 101, 102–3, 105, 287–8
pharmaceutical sector in India and Brazil 161, 170–71, 179, 288
sectoral innovation systems 7, 33
semiconductor industry: case studies 114, 115–16, 119, 120–21, 139–45, 148, 151, 152, 288
telecommunication equipment industry 22, 34–5, 37–8, 40, 50–54, 57–8, 61–2, 63, 66, 287, 288
see also government funding; government protection; government R&D funding; government research institutes (GRIs); public procurement
GPRS (General Packet Radio Services) 56
grains 200, 202, 207, 209–10, 212, 217, 218, 220, 221, 229, 248, 249–50, 256, 259
Great Dragon (Julong) 26, 42, 51
green coffee 236, 238, 239, 246, 247
'Green Passages' (China) 222, 228
green products 220, 221, 222, 228, 238, 243–5, 247, 266
greenhouses 221, 227, 229, 230 31, 266
GSM (Global System for Mobile Communications) 55–6, 59, 61, 62, 64
Gu, S. 226

Hatch–Waxman Act 1984 (US) 164, 168, 178, 184
HCI (Heavy and Chemical Industry) programmes (Korea) 116, 121, 139, 141
HCL Technology 87, 88

high-end markets 6, 35
high labour costs 86–7, 106
high prices
agro-food sector: case studies 210, 238, 241, 243, 244, 260
drugs in Brazil and India 161, 162, 168, 170, 175
high-tech infrastructure 119, 128, 140
high value added products and services
agro-food sector catch-up: case studies
coffee sector in Costa Rica 233, 236, 238, 239, 240, 242–3, 245–7, 258, 259, 260, 263, 290
soybean sector in Brazil 249, 263
catch-up strategy sectoral comparisons 283
computer software and service sector 72, 82, 87, 88, 101, 108
semiconductor industry in China and Korea 135–6, 140–41, 152, 153
telecommunication equipment industry in Brazil, China, India and Korea 39, 40
higher/tertiary education
catch-up 4, 6, 290
computer software and service sector 79, 88, 89, 90–91, 95, 98, 99, 100, 102, 103, 104
pharmaceutical sector in India and Brazil 163, 179, 181
semiconductor industry in Korea, Malaysia and Taiwan 130, 142, 146, 147
see also skilled labour; university-based R&D
Hindustan Antibiotics Limited 161
Hitachi 118, 126, 134, 142, 147
HJD-04 digital telephone switches 26, 40–42, 47
Hoch, D. 72, 75
HP (Hewlett-Packard) 73, 80, 81, 82, 89, 96, 97, 116, 118, 126, 134, 142, 147
Hsinchu Science Park 119, 139, 144, 146
Hua Hong 128–9, 149
Huawei 26, 38, 42, 47, 51, 59–60, 61, 62–3, 82

human capital
    computer software and service sector
        75, 78, 99, 100, 102
    semiconductor industry: case studies
        115, 121, 125, 127, 130, 140,
        141, 143, 145–7, 151, 152
    see also labour markets; skilled
        labour; skilled labour shortages
Hynix 126, 130, 144, 148
Hyundai 117, 130, 134, 146, 148

IBM 72, 73, 74, 79, 80, 81, 86, 89, 92,
    96, 97, 98, 116, 130, 136, 137
ICAFE (Institute of Coffee of Costa
    Rica) 235, 241–2, 243, 244, 246, 247
ICO (International Coffee
    Organization) 237, 238, 242, 244,
    245, 260
ICs 115–16, 121, 122, 123, 128–30, 133,
    136, 137, 138–9, 140–41, 142, 149,
    153
IDECAFE (Institute for Costa Rican
    Coffee) 241, 242, 262
IFAD (International Fund for
    Agricultural Development) 210,
    215
IITA (International Institute of
    Tropical Agriculture) 208, 210,
    212, 213, 215, 216, 264
IMF (International Monetary Fund)
    174, 209–12, 213
imitation 5–6, 163, 174, 177, 182, 183
immigration 89, 102, 107–8, 146, 152,
    208, 210, 282
IMP (Industrial Master Plan)
    (Malaysia) 119, 121, 142
import substitution 102, 104, 161, 162,
    168, 169–70, 179, 181–2
imports
    pharmaceutical sector in Brazil
        169–70, 172, 173–4, 177, 179,
        181–2, 183, 187–8
    pharmaceutical sector in developing
        countries 159
    pharmaceutical sector in India
        160–61, 162, 163, 164, 168, 179,
        181–2
    semiconductor industry: case studies
        116, 119, 126, 136, 138, 140,
        150, 151–2

telecommunication equipment
    industry 22, 25, 26–7, 28–9, 39,
    43, 46, 50–51, 52, 54, 55
IMT-2000 (International Mobile
    Telecommunications) standards
    56–7
income growth 2, 219–20, 231, 235,
    238, 259, 260–61
incremental innovation 4, 45, 125, 183,
    186–7, 188, 241, 283, 290
incubators 100, 103, 119, 132, 143–4
independent catch-up 39, 67
independent software vendors 72–3,
    78, 80
India
    catch-up strategy sectoral and
        national comparisons 282, 283,
        284–5, 286, 287, 288, 289
    semiconductor industry 65
    see also computer software and
        service sector; pharmaceutical
        sector catch-up in India and
        Brazil; telecommunication
        equipment industry in Brazil,
        China, India and Korea
Indian Drugs and Pharmaceuticals
    Limited 161
indigenous technological and scientific
    capabilities
    agro-food sector catch-up: case
        studies 215, 219, 222, 229, 265,
        266
    catch-up strategy sectoral
        comparisons 281–2, 283, 285–6
    computer software and service sector
        80, 84, 99, 285–6
    pharmaceutical sector in India and
        Brazil 157–8, 163, 166, 285, 288
    semiconductor industry in Korea,
        Malaysia and Taiwan 114, 125,
        285–6
    telecommunication equipment
        industry in Brazil, China, India
        and Korea 22–3, 25, 27, 28, 29,
        35, 36, 38, 40–42, 43–6, 49, 59,
        62–3, 66
industrial markets 207, 208, 209, 210,
    211, 216, 248, 263, 286
industrial policies 255–6
industrial policy deficits 52, 169–74

industrial structure 9–10, 283–6
industry life cycle (ILC) 83–4, 103, 284
Infineon 115, 118, 119, 131, 136, 144, 147
information 223–4, 225–6, 261, 262, 268–9
Infosys 79, 87, 92
innovation capabilities
  agro-food sector catch-up: case studies 215, 219, 221, 229
  evolutionary theory 5–6
  pharmaceutical sector 158, 159
  pharmaceutical sector in Brazil and India 167, 168, 169, 172–3, 179, 180, 181, 187
innovation systems 3–4
institutional deficits 232
institutions
  agro-food sector catch-up: case studies 198, 241–2, 250–52, 255, 256, 261–3, 268, 270–71, 288
  catch-up strategy sectoral and national comparisons 288, 289–90
  computer software and service sector 13, 100, 103, 104
  pharmaceutical sector 11
  pharmaceutical sector in India and Brazil 33, 288
  sectoral innovation systems 9–10, 33
  telecommunications equipment industry 12
  see also IPR (intellectual property rights); legislation; market institutions; regulations; standards
Intel 81, 87, 91, 96, 98, 115, 116, 118, 122, 124, 125, 126–7, 128, 130, 131, 133, 134, 135, 139, 142, 144, 145, 147, 149
Inter-institutional Agreement for Cooperation 243–5
interdependent catch-up 39, 67
international cooperation 158–9, 185, 186–7, 188
international exchange programmes 252, 266
international organizational policies 209–12

international R&D 210, 212, 215–16, 264, 271
internationalization 83–4, 164–8, 169, 174–5, 180
internationalization of the computer software and service sector (1980–2007)
  as a characteristic of computer software and service sector 78
  domestic versus foreign demand 82–3
  emerging third wave: Russia, Eastern Europe and Latin America 94, 95–9, 104–5
  first wave: India, Ireland and Israel 84–90, 91, 94–5, 104, 105
  product life cycle and industry life cycle theories 83
  second wave: China and Philippines 90–95, 104, 105
  theories 83–4, 103
Internet 11, 55, 73, 89, 99–100, 247
IPR (intellectual property rights)
  agro-food sector in Brazil 255–6
  computer software and service sector 80, 88, 92, 94, 98, 101
  pharmaceutical sector in Brazil 157, 175, 179, 182, 183–4, 188, 288
  pharmaceutical sector in developing countries 159, 160, 185, 186–7
  pharmaceutical sector in India 157, 162–3, 165–6, 167–8, 179, 182–3, 187, 188, 288
  sectoral innovation systems and catch-up 9
  semiconductor industry in China, Korea, Malaysia and Taiwan 122, 128, 149
Ireland
  catch-up strategy sectoral and national comparisons 285, 286, 287, 289
  computer software and service sector 78, 82, 84–5, 88–9, 91, 94, 95, 99, 100, 104, 105, 106
ISDN 28, 45, 52, 55, 56
Israel
  catch-up strategy sectoral and national comparisons 285, 286, 287, 289

computer software and service sector
78, 82, 84–5, 89–90, 91, 92, 94,
95, 99, 100, 101, 104, 105, 106,
108
ITRIs (Industrial Technical Research
Institutes) (Taiwan) 119, 121, 134,
139, 149, 152, 287

Jacobssen, S. 116, 130, 134
Japan
agro-food imports 228, 232, 245,
261
computer software and service
sector 72, 78, 82, 91, 94, 97,
101, 105
markets 228, 232, 245, 261
pharmaceutical sector 163, 166–7,
187, 188
semiconductor manufacturing
industry 7, 13, 117, 118, 123,
125–6, 128–9, 134, 144, 145,
148
telecommunication equipment
industry 25
JIT (just-in-time) practices 124, 125,
126, 127, 145
joint ventures
catch-up strategy sectoral
comparisons 283, 285
sectoral innovation systems and
catch-up 6
semiconductor industry in China
and Taiwan 132, 140
telecommunication equipment
industry: case studies 25–6,
39–40, 43, 47, 48, 50, 51, 61,
62–3, 65

kaizen practices 125, 127, 128, 145
Kim, L. 5, 7, 44, 48, 116, 121, 124, 125,
129, 130, 133, 139, 141, 142, 146,
148
Kim, Y. 134, 146, 147
knowledge 8–9, 10, 11, 12–14, 33, 34,
35–6, 128
see also capabilities; education;
experiential and tacit
knowledge; foreign knowledge
transfer; R&D; traditional
knowledge; training

Korea 284, 285, 286, 287, 289–90
see also semiconductor industry
catch-up strategies in China,
Korea, Malaysia and Taiwan;
telecommunication equipment
industry in Brazil, China, India
and Korea
Korea Telecom 43, 44, 48, 57

labour costs 75, 86–7, 89
see also high labour costs; low
labour costs
labour-intensity 78, 118, 119, 145, 188,
201, 229, 235
labour markets
agricultural sector in Brazil 254
computer software and service sector
75, 78, 79, 82, 86–7, 88, 98, 99,
100, 101, 102
semiconductor industry in China,
Korea, Malaysia and Taiwan
115, 140, 147, 152
see also human capital; labour
costs; labour-intensity; labour
productivity; skilled labour;
skilled labour shortages
labour productivity 128, 254
Lall, S. 162, 163
land
Brazil 201, 253, 254, 255, 260
China 201, 218, 219, 220, 221, 226,
228, 229
Costa Rica 201, 233, 239, 240, 241,
267
Nigeria 201, 207, 217
large agribusinesses 196, 216, 236, 240,
241, 252, 253, 257–8, 262, 268
large firms 9, 11, 87–8, 119–20, 284,
287, 289–90
see also domestic MNCs; large
agribusinesses; MNCs
Latin America 83, 88, 97, 104–5
see also individual countries
leapfrogging catch-up 6, 27, 37, 38, 57,
58, 66, 149, 188, 284–6
Lee, K. 6, 7, 8, 23, 27, 33–4, 36–7, 39,
50, 51, 57, 58, 60, 67, 285, 286
legislation
computer software and service sector
78

pharmaceutical sector in India and
Brazil 161, 162–3, 164, 166, 167,
168, 175–6, 177, 178, 183–4
telecommunication equipment
industry in Brazil and Korea 31,
32, 48–9, 52–3
Lenovo 62, 63, 73, 116, 130, 132, 136,
137
LG Electronics 38, 57, 117, 130, 135,
136, 139, 146–7, 148
licensing
catch-up strategy sectoral
comparisons 282, 285
pharmaceutical sector in India
161–2, 168
semiconductor industry: case studies
122, 129, 130, 134, 135, 139,
140, 151, 152, 285
telecommunication equipment
industry in India and Korea 28,
29, 43, 66
Lim, C. 6, 7, 23, 33–4, 36, 57, 58, 60
Lin, Y. 113, 119, 121, 123, 128, 131,
132, 134, 139, 145, 149
loans 210, 215, 227, 237, 240
see also credit; subsidized credit
local authorities
agro-food sector catch-up: case
studies 205, 206, 213, 217, 223,
224, 225, 227, 261, 267
semiconductor industry in Taiwan
290
low-end markets 6, 35, 46, 63, 99–100,
101
low labour costs
computer software and service sector
86, 88, 89, 90, 94, 95, 96, 97, 98,
102, 105, 106
semiconductor industry in China,
Korea, Malaysia and Taiwan 115
telecommunication equipment
industry in China 47
low prices 35, 163, 168, 176, 177, 182,
183, 211, 283
low value added products and services
100–101, 108, 119, 135, 141, 145,
152, 238, 283
see also BPO (business process
outsourcing); customized
software

LTEF (Luoyang Telephone Equipment
Factory) 26, 41, 42
Lundvall, B.-Å. 5, 7, 33, 160, 195
Luxoft 92, 96

Malaysia 285, 286, 290
see also semiconductor industry
catch-up strategies in China,
Korea, Malaysia and Taiwan
Malerba, F. 2, 5, 10, 23, 32, 33, 77,
113–14, 128, 135, 157, 160, 196,
284
managerial capacity 4, 223, 226, 228,
247, 252, 261, 262, 270
Mani, S. 2, 23, 28, 33–4
manual telephone switches 28, 36, 37
manufacturing capabilities
pharmaceutical sector 10, 158, 159
pharmaceutical sector in Brazil 169,
172–3, 177–8, 179, 180–81
pharmaceutical sector in India
160–61, 162–3, 164–5, 166, 168,
179, 180
market discontinuities 11, 284
market institutions 14, 222–6, 227–8,
261–2, 263, 270, 288
market segmentation 13, 35, 46, 47,
63–4, 75–6, 286
marketing
agro-food sector catch-up: case
studies 199, 207, 223, 237, 247,
249, 260–61, 262, 264, 268
computer software and service sector
75–6, 77, 88, 100
pharmaceutical sector in India and
Brazil 164, 167, 174, 175, 176,
180, 183
semiconductor industry: case studies
120, 123, 148
Mathews, J.A. 6, 7, 121, 123, 131, 132,
135, 139, 144–5
meat 202, 215, 248, 249, 250, 251, 252,
254, 256, 260
medium-sized firms 32, 53, 97, 149,
165, 235, 253, 284, 287–8, 289
memory chips/products 13, 113, 115,
120, 123, 129, 130, 133, 134, 142,
148
see also DRAM chips; SRAM
chips

mergers and acquisitions
  computer software and service sector
    79, 81, 101
  pharmaceutical sector in India and
    Brazil 166–7, 170, 180
  semiconductor industry: case studies
    115, 116, 118, 122, 123, 129,
    130–32, 134, 135, 136, 137, 143,
    146, 151, 152
Mexico 16, 97, 98–9, 105, 117, 237, 244
microprocessors 113, 115, 120, 121,
    122, 130, 149
Microsoft 73, 74, 79, 81, 86, 87, 89, 91,
    92, 94, 97
military 13, 105, 107–8, 113, 114, 121
milling, coffee sector in Costa Rica
    235, 236, 239, 256, 262
MIMOS (Malaysian Institute of
    Microelectronic Systems) 118,
    119, 131, 136, 142–3
Ministry of Agriculture (China) 221,
    223–4, 231, 261
Ministry of Communications (Brazil)
    32
Ministry of Electronics Industry
    (MEI) (China) 25, 42, 114, 115–16
Ministry of Information and
    Telecommunication (Korea) 57, 58
Ministry of Post and
    Telecommunication (MPT)
    (China) 24, 26, 40, 41, 42, 51, 61–2
MNCs
  agro-food sector catch-up: case
    studies 232, 237, 238, 265, 268,
    285, 290
  catch-up strategy sectoral and
    national comparisons 89, 283,
    285, 288, 290
  computer software and service sector
    73, 78, 79–80, 84–6, 87–8, 89,
    91, 92, 93, 94, 96, 97, 98, 99,
    104, 107, 285
  internationalization theories 83–4
  pharmaceutical sector in Brazil
    169–70, 171–2, 173, 174, 176–7,
    178, 179, 180, 182, 187–8, 285,
    289
  pharmaceutical sector in India
    160–62, 163, 166–8, 179, 180,
    182, 187, 285

sectoral innovation systems and
    catch-up 8
semiconductor industry 144
semiconductor industry in China,
    Korea, Malaysia and Taiwan
    114–15, 116, 117–18, 119–20,
    123, 124–5, 126–7, 130, 131,
    132, 134–6, 143, 144, 148, 151,
    152, 285, 290
telecommunication equipment
    industry 12, 21
telecommunication equipment
    industry in Brazil, China, India
    and Korea 22, 23, 25–6, 29–30,
    31–2, 39, 44, 46, 47, 50, 58, 59,
    60, 61, 62, 63–4, 67, 289
  see also domestic MNCs;
    subsidiaries of MNCs
mobile phones/technology 11, 12, 26,
    27, 38, 45, 55–65, 66, 284
modularity 11, 14, 60–61, 80, 290
Motorola 59, 96, 116, 118, 127, 139,
    142, 143, 146, 147
Mowery, D.C. 10, 72, 79, 95
MTDC (Malaysian Technology
    Development Corporation) 118,
    143
Mu, Q. 23, 28, 33–4, 36–7, 39, 42, 44,
    50, 51–2

NAND/NAND Flash chips 114, 117,
    120, 122, 129, 133, 149, 150
NASSCOM 80, 91, 100, 106
National Development Plan, Second
    (PNDII) (Brazil) 252, 269
National Semiconductor 116, 117, 124,
    125, 127, 134, 135, 142
national systems of innovation 5, 32–3,
    35, 160, 196, 255–6, 282, 289–90
NEC 94, 118, 128–9, 140, 144, 149
Nelson, R.R. 3, 4, 5, 6, 8, 9, 10, 33,
    114, 124, 160, 184, 195, 196, 222,
    225, 284, 287
networks *see* social network
    externalities; social networks
new drug discovery skills 158–9, 166,
    168, 187
niche markets
  coffee sector in Costa Rica 238, 245,
    258, 259, 260, 290

computer software and service sector
73–5, 77, 88, 89, 94, 97, 98–9,
100, 101, 102, 103, 105
pharmaceutical sector in India and
Brazil 165, 172, 181, 186
soybean sector in Brazil 254
Nigeria 200–204, 205
see also cassava sector in Nigeria
Niosi, J. 80, 84
NMOS (n-type metal oxide
semiconductor) 115, 133
North America 78, 86, 88, 89
NRCRI (National Root Crops
Research Institute) (Nigeria) 210,
213, 214, 215–16, 264
Nweke, F.I. 205, 206, 209, 211, 212

OBM 6, 128, 133
OEM (own equipment manufacturing)
6, 59, 125–6, 127–8, 132, 133, 138,
141–2, 149, 150
offshoring 80–82, 84, 85, 104, 132
Ondo State 217
online software service applications
73, 89
open source software (OSS) 13, 73,
79, 83
operating systems 73, 74, 76, 80, 83
Oracle 74, 79, 81, 86, 87, 89, 91, 92, 94,
97, 98
organic products 220, 221, 243, 248,
254, 260, 266
Orozco, J. 226, 242, 244, 245
Osorio, N. 237–8
Osram 115, 131, 136
outsourcing
catch-up strategy sectoral
comparisons 285
computer software and service sector
30, 75, 76, 80, 81, 84, 86, 91,
93–4, 96, 97, 98, 105
semiconductor industry in China,
Korea, Malaysia and Taiwan 115
see also BPO (business process
outsourcing)

packaged software products 12, 13, 72,
73, 75–7, 82, 89, 101, 105, 286
Patent Act 1970 (India) 162–3, 164,
166, 167, 168

patent expiration 165, 166, 188
patents
computer software and service sector
80, 89, 91, 92
pharmaceutical sector in Brazil 170,
171, 175, 179, 182
pharmaceutical sector in developing
countries 158, 159, 160, 186–7
pharmaceutical sector in India
162–3, 166, 167, 168, 179, 180,
182, 186, 187
sectoral innovation systems and
catch-up 9
semiconductor industry in Korea
and Malaysia 127, 130, 149
path-creating catch-up 6, 38, 57–8, 66
path-following catch-up 6, 99
pharmaceutical sector 10–11, 157,
158–60, 164–5, 169, 175, 180, 185,
186–7
pharmaceutical sector catch-up in
India and Brazil
Brazil 157–8, 168–78
catch-up strategy sectoral and
national comparisons 282, 283,
284–5, 286, 287, 288, 289
conclusions 184–8
discussion of results 178–84
India 157–8, 160–68, 177
introduction 157–60
Philippines 87, 94–5, 99–100, 101, 106
Philips 123, 131, 132, 134, 135, 144
physical infrastructure 223, 261
physical infrastructure deficits 217,
226, 256, 263
PICPE 210, 213–14, 216–17, 259, 263,
269
population growth 209, 219, 256, 259
poverty reduction 14, 205, 206, 207
Pradhan, J. 87–8
price controls 161, 164, 170
prices
agro-food sector catch-up: case
studies 211, 216, 226, 237–8,
242, 243, 244, 254, 260, 262
computer software and service sector
76
drugs in Brazil 170, 175, 176, 177
drugs in India 161, 162, 163, 168,
179, 182, 183

private oil companies 210, 212
private sector R&D 30, 31, 38, 44, 93,
     180–81, 188, 252, 255, 268
   see also private sector R&D funding;
     R&D consortia
private sector R&D funding 79, 139,
     144
privatization
   coffee sector in Costa Rica 237
   telecommunication equipment
     industry in Brazil, China, India
     and Korea 22, 29, 31, 32, 45, 48,
     53, 64
   telecommunications equipment
     industry 12
   telecommunications services 21,
     31–2, 45
   vegetable sector in China 268
process technology 124–8, 145–6, 198,
     209, 210, 212, 213, 214–15, 216–17
   see also food processing
     technologies; processors
processors 239–40, 241
product differentiation 34, 35, 174, 236,
     248, 249, 254
product life cycle (PLC) 83–4, 103
product technology 128–33, 145–6, 198
production costs 47, 115, 125, 127, 141,
     179, 248–9, 255
productivity
   agro-food sector catch-up: case
     studies
     cassava sector in Nigeria 210,
        213–14, 216–17, 259, 263, 269
     coffee sector in Costa Rica 233,
        239, 243, 257, 258, 260
     soybean sector in Brazil 249–50,
        253, 254, 257, 258, 260
   computer and software service sector
     in India 87
   semiconductor industry in Malaysia
     126–7
   telecommunication equipment
     industry in India 39
profits
   agro-food sector catch-up: case
     studies 199, 226, 237, 241, 245,
     248–9, 252, 253, 262
   computer software and service sector
     75, 77, 83

pharmaceutical sector in India and
     Brazil 162, 167, 173, 175, 182,
     183, 187
semiconductor industry 115, 124,
     141
telecommunication equipment
     industry in Korea 52, 58
Project 909 (China) 128–9
PTIC (Posts and Telecommunications
     Industrial Corporation) 26, 40–41,
     42, 62–3
public–private cooperation 172–3,
     177–8, 180–81, 188, 252, 255, 268,
     271, 287
public procurement
   computer software and service sector
     79, 91, 100, 101
   pharmaceutical sector in Brazil
     171–2, 173, 175
   telecommunication equipment
     industry in Brazil, China, India
     and Korea 22, 29, 30–31, 48,
     49–50, 55
public telephone and telegraph (PTT)
     providers 21

Qualcomm 58, 144
quality control and safety
   agro-food sector catch-up: case
     studies 213, 223–4, 225, 226,
     231, 242, 243, 261, 262, 263, 269
   pharmaceutical sector in Brazil and
     India 165, 168, 174, 175, 176
   see also high value added products
     and services; quality control
     deficits; quality control
     technologies
quality control deficits 161, 168, 232
quality control technologies 198, 226,
     231, 232, 242, 243
Queiroz, S.R.R. 169, 170, 171, 172, 173
quotas 52, 136

R&D
   agro-food sector catch-up: case
     studies 198, 264–7, 271
     agro-food sector in Brazil 251–2,
        255, 265, 266
     cassava sector in Nigeria 210, 212,
        213, 214–16, 264

coffee sector in Costa Rica 242,
258, 265–6
vegetable sector in China 224,
229–31, 232, 264–5
computer software and service sector
78, 84, 89, 91, 93, 94, 96, 97, 98,
102, 107
pharmaceutical sector 10, 11, 157,
158
pharmaceutical sector in Brazil and
India 163, 166, 169, 172–3,
177–8, 180–81, 186, 187
sectoral innovation systems and
catch-up 6, 7, 8
semiconductor industry in China,
Korea and Taiwan 115–16,
119–20, 121, 126, 128–9, 130,
131, 132, 134, 136, 138, 139,
141, 144, 146–7, 148, 149, 150,
151, 152
Taiwan 290
telecommunication equipment
industry in Brazil, China, India
and Korea 31, 60, 66
R&D consortia
agro-food sector catch-up: case
studies 253, 255, 288
catch-up strategy sectoral
comparisons 287, 288
pharmaceutical sector in India and
Brazil 172–3, 177–8, 180–81,
188
sectoral innovation systems and
catch-up 6
semiconductor industry in China,
Korea, Malaysia and Taiwan
132, 136, 140, 142, 148, 152
telecommunication equipment
industry in China, India and
Korea 26, 27, 40–42, 45–6, 58,
62, 287
R&D expenditure 35, 76, 187, 257, 284
R&D funding 32, 53, 252, 255–6
see also government R&D funding;
private sector R&D funding;
R&D expenditure
Ramani, S.V. 161, 166
Ranbaxy 164, 165, 166–7
rapid introduction–adaptation 264–5,
271

Rasiah, R. 113, 115, 119, 121, 123, 124,
126, 127, 128, 131, 132, 134, 135,
136, 139, 145, 149
RCA 123, 131, 132, 134, 135, 143
re-engineering skills
pharmaceutical sector 158, 159, 162
pharmaceutical sector in Brazil 170,
171, 177, 179, 182, 188
pharmaceutical sector in India
162–3, 166, 168, 179, 180, 182,
183, 188
regulation handling capabilities 164–5,
168, 180, 186
regulations
agro-food sector catch-up: case
studies 223, 231, 241, 243–5,
247, 261, 288
catch-up strategy sectoral
comparisons 288
pharmaceutical sector 158–9, 160,
164–5, 168, 175
pharmaceutical sector in India and
Brazil 161–3, 164, 165–6, 167–8,
170, 174–6, 181, 184, 186
rents 199, 237
replication 3, 5, 213
retailing 74, 76, 176–7, 205, 236, 237–8,
245
see also vegetable vendors and
blockers
roasting, coffee sector in Costa Rica
235, 236, 237, 239, 245–7, 263
Robusta coffee 15, 235, 236, 241
Romania 96, 97
Ruiz, K. 242, 244, 245
rural markets
cassava sector in Nigeria 207, 211,
212
telecommunication equipment
industry case: studies 26, 35, 44,
45, 46, 47, 48, 51, 62
Russia's computer software and
services sector 78, 83, 87, 88, 92,
94, 95–6, 99, 100, 104, 105, 106

Samper, M. 236, 237, 240, 241
Samsung 38, 43, 44, 52, 57, 58, 82, 114,
115, 116–17, 118, 120, 126, 129,
130, 133, 134, 136, 139, 141, 142,
144, 146, 147, 148, 152

SAP 74, 79, 86, 89, 92, 96, 97, 100
SAP (Structural Adjustment
    Programme) 209–12, 213
Schumpeterian Mark I (creative
    destruction) 3, 128, 135, 143, 183,
    283–4, 289
Schumpeterian Mark II (creative
    accumulation) 135, 283–4, 289–90
sectoral innovation systems
    agro-food sector catch-up: case
        studies 196–8, 272
    catch-up 4–10
    described 23, 32–3, 195–6
    national systems of innovation 32–3,
        35, 160, 196
    telecommunication equipment
        industry in Brazil, China, India
        and Korea 23, 33–6
sectors 1–3, 33, 196
segmentation 73–7, 82
    see also market segmentation;
        product differentiation
semiconductor industry 13–14, 65, 117,
    123, 144
semiconductor industry catch-up
    strategies in China, Korea,
    Malaysia and Taiwan
    building blocks 133–50
        access to foreign knowledge 134–6
        co-evolution: driver and driven
            149–50, 152
        demand conditions 136–9
        human capital 145–7
        networks, alliances and consortia
            147–9
        role of government 139–45
    catch-up strategy sectoral and
        national comparisons 282, 283,
        284, 285–6, 287, 288, 289–90
    catch-up trajectories 120–33
        process technology 124–8
        product technology 128–33
    conclusions and implications 150–53
    historical backdrop 114–20
    introduction 113–14
ShanDong Province (China) vegetable
    production 220–22, 226, 227–8,
    229, 230–31
Shanghai Bell 25, 26, 39–40, 41–2, 47
Shen, X. 26, 40, 41, 42

Shenzhen Agricultural Products Co.
    Ltd. 227
ShouGuang (China) vegetable
    production 222, 226, 227–8, 229,
    230–31
ShouGuang Vegetable Wholesale
    Market Co. Ltd. 226, 227–8
Siemens 25, 61, 62, 118
Silterra 118, 127, 129, 131, 133, 136,
    137, 139, 141, 143, 147, 149
'similar' drugs 176, 184
skilled labour
    agro-food sector catch-up: case
        studies 247, 254
    catch-up 4, 6
    catch-up strategy sectoral
        comparisons 282, 288
    computer software and service sector
        13, 78, 79, 82, 86–7, 88, 89, 90,
        94, 95, 96, 97, 98, 99, 100, 101,
        105–7, 282
    pharmaceutical sector in India and
        Brazil 157, 163, 181, 186, 282,
        288
    semiconductor industry: case studies
        116, 126, 140, 143, 145, 146–7,
        282
    telecommunication equipment
        industry in China 41, 42, 62, 63
skilled labour shortages
    computer software and service sector
        89, 98, 99, 101
    pharmaceutical sector in Brazil 172
    semiconductor industry in Malaysia
        131, 145, 147, 153
    vegetable sector in China 226
small farms 211, 218, 240, 241, 242,
    253, 262
small firms
    catch-up strategy sectoral and
        national comparisons 283–4,
        287–8, 289, 290
    coffee sector in Costa Rica 290
    computer software and service sector
        97, 102, 284, 287–8, 289
    pharmaceutical sector 11, 165, 173,
        284, 287
    semiconductor industry 14, 119, 284
    telecommunication equipment
        industry in Brazil 32, 53

social network externalities 79
social networks
  agro-food sector catch-up: case
    studies 223–4, 239–40, 252, 255,
    256, 258, 261, 263, 270–71
  computer software and service sector
    13
  sectoral innovation systems 7–8, 33
  telecommunication equipment
    industry 11–12
social relations, soybean sector in
  Brazil 252–3
software and service sector *see*
  computer software and service
  sector
soybean sector in Brazil
  Brazilian perspectives towards
    opportunities and challenges of
    the new millennium 254–6
  case selection 200
  catch-up strategy sectoral and
    national comparisons 288,
    290
  introduction 247–8
  overview of the catching-up process
    and institutional driving factors
    250–53
  research findings and discussion
    256–7, 259–60, 263, 265, 266,
    268, 269
  soybean complex and its relevance
    to the Brazilian economy 15,
    248–50
SPC telephone switches 25, 26, 36
spin-offs 78, 177, 181
SRAM chips 122, 129, 131, 134
stage-skipping catch-up 6, 27, 37, 38,
  57, 58, 66, 149, 188, 284–6
standards 12, 13, 55–7, 288
  see also legislation; quality control
    and safety; quality control
    technologies; regulations
start-ups 6, 137, 149, 181
state-owned firms 22, 28, 29–30, 31, 44,
  45–6, 48, 98, 161
step-by-step telephone switches 24, 25,
  27, 28, 37
strategic alliances
  catch-up strategy sectoral
    comparisons 182, 285

pharmaceutical sector in India 166,
    168
  sectoral innovation systems and
    catch-up 6
  semiconductor industry case studies
    128–9, 131, 134–5, 147–9, 151,
    152, 285
subcontracting 8, 75, 85, 86, 93–4, 97,
  98, 283
subsidiaries of MNCs
  catch-up strategy sectoral
    comparisons 283, 285
  computer software and service sector
    86, 87–8, 89, 98, 285
  internationalization theories 83–4
  semiconductor industry in China,
    Korea, Malaysia and Taiwan
    134
  telecommunication equipment
    industry in Brazil, China and
    India 22, 25–6, 29–30, 31–2, 44
subsidized credit 136, 139, 141–2,
  151
Sun Microsystems 73, 74, 80, 95
suppliers/supply
  agro-food sector catch-up: case
    studies 216, 217, 229, 233–4,
    236–7, 248–9, 265, 332, 340
  sectoral innovation systems and
    catch-up 6, 7
  semiconductor industry: case studies
    123, 125, 126, 127 132, 136, 149,
    285–6
  telecommunication equipment
    industry in Brazil, China and
    India 25, 26–7, 51, 55, 60
sustainable development 194–5, 259,
  262, 271
Sweet, C. 174, 175, 176, 177, 179

tacit knowledge *see* experiential and
  tacit knowledge
Taiwan 282, 284, 285, 286, 287, 288,
  289, 290
  see also semiconductor industry
    catch-up strategies in China,
    Korea, Malaysia and Taiwan
tariffs 51, 54, 161, 162, 172, 182
Tata Consultancy Services 79, 87, 88,
  92, 97, 98

tax incentives 78, 90, 100, 102, 103,
    119, 177, 288
TD-SCDMA (Time Division
    Synchronous CDMA) 38, 57,
    61–4, 66
TDMA (time division multiple access)
    56, 57
TDX (time division exchange) 27, 28,
    43, 44, 48, 51–2
technological and scientific capabilities
    agro-food sector catch-up: case
        studies 198, 265–7, 270, 271,
        272
    agro-food sector in Brazil 248–9,
        252, 253, 254, 255, 256–7,
        258, 268
    cassava sector in Nigeria 210, 211,
        212, 213, 214–16, 264
    coffee sector in Costa Rica 236,
        237, 238, 241–2, 243, 244,
        247, 256–7, 268
    vegetable sector in China 14, 224,
        226, 228–32, 268
    catch-up and economic development
        3–4
    catch-up strategy sectoral
        comparisons 281–3, 284
    pharmaceutical sector 11, 157, 158,
        169
    pharmaceutical sector in Brazil
        157–8, 172–3, 176, 177–8, 179,
        180–81, 184, 185, 186, 187
    pharmaceutical sector in India
        157–8, 163, 164, 168, 179, 180,
        181, 182, 183, 184, 185, 186,
        187
    sectoral innovation systems 5–6, 7,
        8–9, 33
    telecommunications equipment
        industry 11
technological discontinuities
    agro-food sector catch-up: case
        studies 14, 218, 241
    catch-up 9–10
    computer software and service sector
        80
    pharmaceuticals sector 184, 284–5
    telecommunication equipment
        industry in Brazil, China, India
        and Korea 11, 21, 38, 66–7

technological infrastructure 198, 204,
    217, 251, 267, 287, 288
technology 33, 34, 35–6, 39–46, 66,
    197–8
    see also biotechnology; cropping
        and cultivation technologies;
        food processing technologies;
        process technology; product
        technology; quality control
        technologies; technological
        and scientific capabilities;
        technological discontinuities;
        technological infrastructure;
        technology/science parks
technology/science parks 90, 95, 100,
    103, 119, 121, 128, 140, 146
    see also Hsinchu Science Park
telecommunication equipment industry
    11–12, 287
telecommunication equipment
        industry in Brazil, China, India
        and Korea
    catch-up strategy sectoral and
        national comparisons 282, 286,
        287, 288, 289
    evolution 21–3, 24–32, 82
    introduction 21–4
    SSI building block 1: technologies
        and access to foreign knowledge
        39–46
    SSI building block 2: demand
        conditions 46–50
    SSI building block 3: actors
        50–55
    summary and concluding remarks
        66–7
    theoretical framework and
        hypotheses 23, 32–9
    transition to wireless communication
        55–65
telecommunications infrastructure
    computer software and service sector
        78, 79, 88, 89, 90, 94, 95, 96, 99,
        100, 102, 103, 104
    semiconductor industry in China,
        Korea, Malaysia and Taiwan
        115
    wireless telecommunications 56
telecommunications services 21, 31–2,
    45

telephone switches 27, 28, 36–9
  see also analogue telephone switches;
    crossbar telephone switches;
    digital telephone switches; SPC
    telephone switches; step-by-step
    telephone switches
Texas Instruments 82, 86, 118, 124,
  125, 126, 132, 135, 142, 144, 147
trademarks 80, 88, 101
traditional knowledge 187, 214, 216,
  266–7, 271
training
  agro-food sector catch-up: case
    studies 213, 216, 243, 266
  computer software and service sector
    82
  pharmaceutical sector in India 181
  semiconductor industry: case studies
    125, 126, 127, 131, 134, 142,
    146, 147, 148
'transforming' world of agriculture
  204, 257
transistors 113, 115, 118, 121, 122,
  123
transportation infrastructure
  agro-food in Brazil 249, 250, 251,
    253
  cassava sector in Nigeria 214, 217,
    263
  coffee sector in Costa Rica 236, 240,
    263
  vegetable sector in China 222, 224,
    226
TRIPS 122, 160, 165–6, 167–8, 175,
  178, 185, 186–7, 188
Tropico telephone switches 30, 31,
  44–5, 49
TSMC 114, 119–20, 122, 123, 128, 129,
  131, 132, 133, 134, 135, 141, 144,
  147, 148–9, 151

UMC (United Microelectronics
  Corporation) 115, 119, 123, 128,
  131, 132, 134, 135, 143, 144, 151
Unisem 118, 127, 130, 131, 143
United Kingdom 82, 86, 87, 88, 97, 157
United States
  computer software and service sector
    72, 77, 78, 79, 80, 82, 83, 84, 87,
    88, 91, 92, 97, 98, 101

pharmaceutical sector 157, 164, 165,
  168, 170, 175, 178, 184
semiconductor manufacturing
  industry 13, 113, 114, 123, 125,
  134, 136, 143, 144, 146–7
university-based R&D
  agro-food sector catch-up: case
    studies 231, 247, 253, 255, 265
  catch-up strategy sectoral
    comparisons 287, 288
  pharmaceutical sector in India and
    Brazil 172–3, 177, 179, 186, 287,
    288
  sectoral innovation systems and
    catch-up 6, 7, 8
  semiconductor industry in Korea
    and Taiwan 119–20, 121, 130,
    132, 136, 140, 147
  telecommunication equipment
    industry in Brazil, China and
    Korea 31, 41, 44
urban markets
  agro-food sector catch-up: case
    studies 207, 209, 211, 212, 219,
    224, 256, 268
  telecommunication equipment
    industry in China, India and
    Korea 26, 44, 45, 46–7, 48, 51,
    63
urbanization 204, 219, 254, 257, 259
Urias, E. 170, 171, 172, 173, 174, 176,
  177

value chains
  agro-food sector catch-up: case
    studies 270–71
  semiconductor industry in China,
    Korea, Malaysia and Taiwan
    120, 122, 123, 140–41, 152, 153
  soybean sector in Brazil 248–50, 256,
    263
  see also global value chains; high
    value added products and
    services; low value added
    products and services
variable costs 75, 77
Vegetable Basket Programme (China)
  223, 225, 229
vegetable oils 15, 220, 221, 248–9, 254,
  256, 269

vegetable sector in China
  case selection 200
  catch-up strategy sectoral and
    national comparisons 288, 290
  description 14
    driving forces 219–22
    introduction 218–19
    policy-steered development of
      market institutions and
      evolution of the sector 222–6,
      227–8
    technology acquisition and
      knowledge regime
      transformation 226, 228–32
  research findings and discussion 256,
    259, 260, 261–2, 263, 264–5,
    266
vegetable vendors and blockers 224,
  226, 262
venture capital
  catch-up strategy sectoral
    comparisons 287
  computer software and service sector
    82, 88, 89, 99, 100, 101, 102,
    103, 104, 105, 287
  sectoral innovation systems and
    catch-up 7
  semiconductor industry in Malaysia
    118
vertical integration
  agro-food sector catch-up: case
    studies 217, 241, 262
  catch-up 4, 7
  catch-up strategy sectoral
    comparisons 286

developing countries 2
semiconductor industry 13, 14, 113
semiconductor industry in Korea
  and Taiwan 134, 138, 139, 148,
  150–51, 152

wafer fabrication 115, 118–20, 121,
  123, 127–8, 129, 131, 132, 133,
  136, 137, 138, 141, 143–4, 145,
  147, 149, 150–52
Wang, L. 229, 230–31
wave-like evolutionary trajectory 225
Western Europe 72, 78, 80, 83, 86, 98
WHO (World Health Organization)
  164, 165
wholesale markets 223–4, 226, 227–8,
  261, 268
Winter, S.G. 5, 8, 225, 284
Wipro 79, 87, 92
wireless telecommunication 21, 22, 23,
  26, 27, 29, 30, 36–7, 38, 45, 55–65,
  66
World Bank 14, 145, 194–5, 204,
  209–12, 213, 257
WTO (World Trade Organization) 54,
  117, 122, 138, 139, 160, 165–6,
  197, 245, 255
  see also TRIPS
Wu, J. 25, 26, 41, 42

Xin-Xin, K. 116, 125, 140

Zhang, X.P. 24, 26, 40, 41, 42
ZTE (Zhongxing) 26, 38, 42, 47, 51,
  59, 60, 61, 62–3